Wreck Ashore

The United States Life-Saving Service on the Great Lakes

Frederick Stonehouse

*Endorsed and Registered by
the Association for Great Lakes Maritime History
as Publication B4*

Lake Superior Port Cities Inc.

5 4 3 2 1

LAKE SUPERIOR PORT CITIES INC.
P.O. Box 16417
Duluth, Minnesota 55816-0417
USA   800-635-0544
Publishers of *Lake Superior Magazine* and *Lake Superior Travel Guide*

Library of Congress Cataloging-In-Publication Data

Stonehouse, Frederick
   Wreck Ashore: The United States Life-Saving Service on the Great Lakes
   Bibliography, p. 209
   1. United States Life-Saving Service – History. 2. Shipwrecks – Great Lakes– History. 3. U.S. Coast Guard.– History. 4. Navigation – United States – History. 5. Navigation – Great Lakes – History. 6. Life-Saving – United States – History. I. Title.
   VK1323   363.12/381/0973   94-76420
ISBN 0-942235-22-3

Printed in the United States of America

   Editor: Paul L. Hayden
Designer: Stacy L. Winter
   Printer: BookCrafters, Chelsea, Michigan

Front Cover Photo: Life savers from Holland, Michigan, make a breeches-buoy rescue of a passenger from the ill-fated *Argo* during the great November 1913 storm.
Back Cover Photo: At the ready, an old life saver stands prepared to heave a line.

This book is dedicated to the

memory of the men of the old

Life-Saving Service on the Great Lakes

long gone but not forgotten

In Remembrance of my father

FREDERICK STONEHOUSE JR.

My special thanks is extended to the following institutions:

Grand Haven Library
Great Lakes Coast Guard Museum, Two Rivers, Wisconsin
Great Lakes Historical Society
Great Lakes Shipwreck Historical Society
Holland Historical Trust
Huron City Museum
Institute for Great Lakes Research
Iosco County Museum
Jesse Besser Museum
Lake Superior Maritime Museum
Manistee County Museum
Manitowoc Maritime Museum
Mariners Museum
Marquette County Historical Society
Marquette Maritime Museum
Mason County Historical Society
Michigan Historical Museum
Michigan Maritime Museum
Michigan State Archives and Museum
Milwaukee Public Library
Mystic Seaport Museum
National Archives and Records Administration
Northwestern University Archives
Presque Isle Lighthouse Museum
Sleeping Bear Dunes National Lakeshore
Sturgeon Point Lighthouse Museum
U.S. Coast Guard Academy Library

Very Special Thanks To Ted Richardson
For So Graciously Sharing His Enthusiasm and Knowledge.

Contents

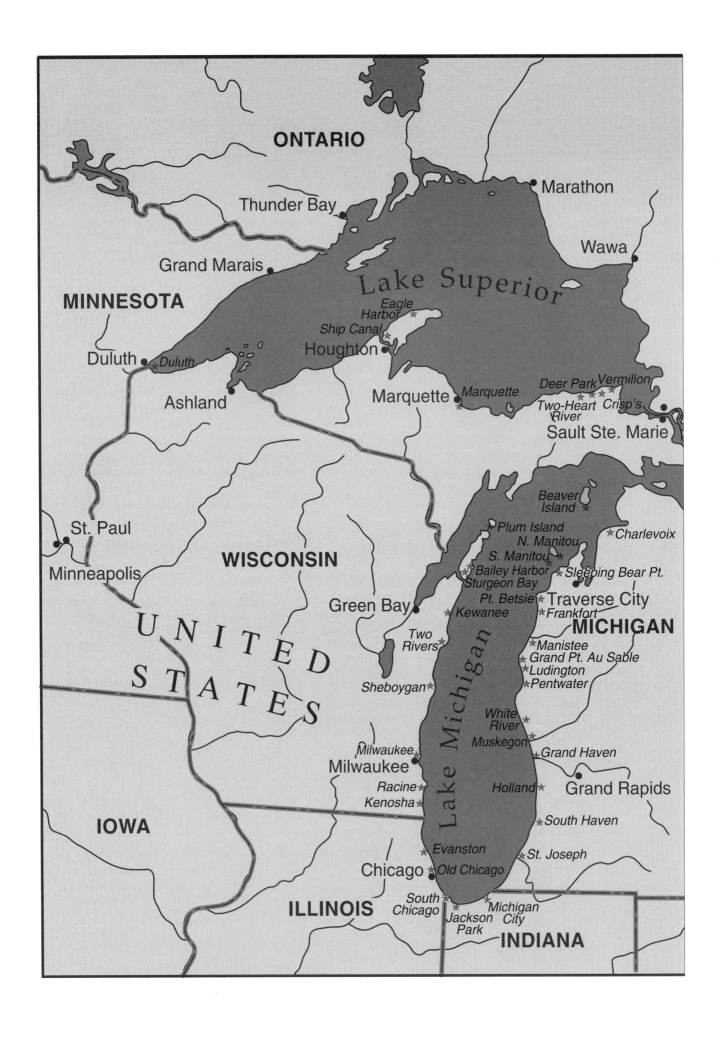

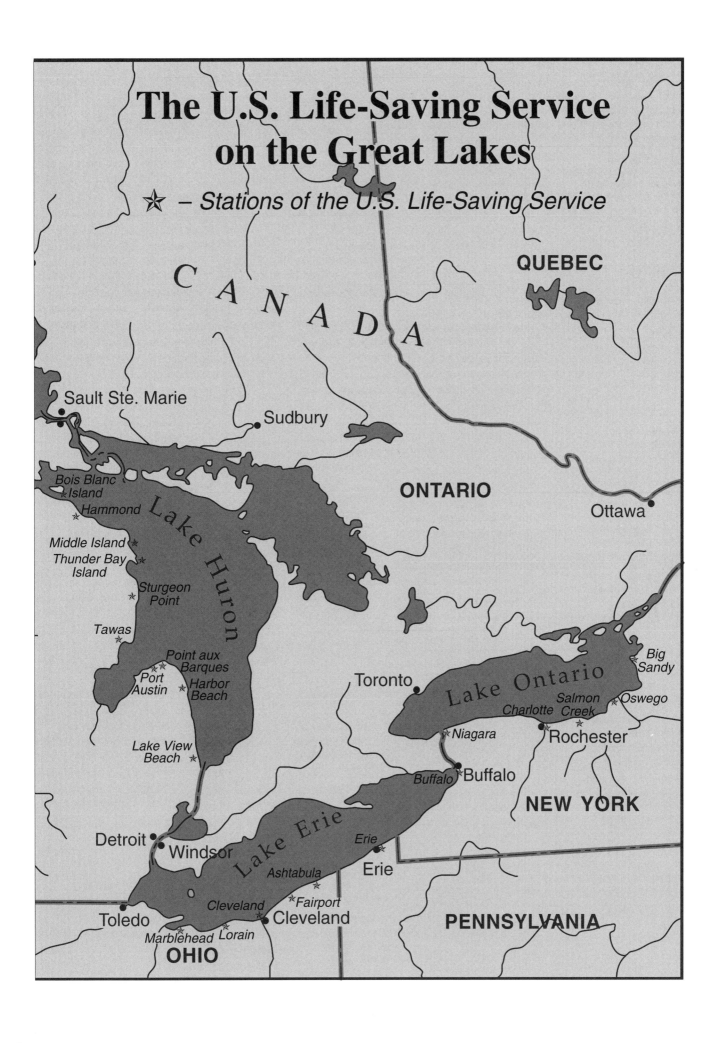

The U.S. Life-Saving Service on the Great Lakes

☆ – *Stations of the U.S. Life-Saving Service*

QUEBEC

CANADA

Sault Ste. Marie

Sudbury

ONTARIO

Ottawa

Bois Blanc Island

Hammond

Middle Island

Thunder Bay Island

Sturgeon Point

Lake Huron

Tawas

Point aux Barques

Port Austin

Harbor Beach

Lake View Beach

Toronto

Lake Ontario

Big Sandy

Salmon Creek

Oswego

Charlotte

Rochester

Niagara

Buffalo

Buffalo

NEW YORK

Detroit

Windsor

Lake Erie

Erie

Erie

Ashtabula

Fairport

Cleveland

Cleveland

Toledo

Marblehead

Lorain

PENNSYLVANIA

OHIO

Unique in the Annals
of American Maritime History

This book started with a very simple purpose, to chronicle the history of the United States Life-Saving Service on the Great Lakes. Specifically to explain:

1. Reasons for the Life-Saving Service.

2. Organization of the Service from the general superintendent to surfman.

3. How stations and crews trained, operated and lived.

4. How and where stations were constructed.

5. Development and employment of the various items of life saving equipment.

Finally to provide descriptions of life saving operations illustrative of how the organization, training and equipment came together to perform a rescue.

It is my belief that unless we understand something of the minutiae of the Service, the details of how the equipment was developed and used, how the crews trained, operated and organized and the difficulties encountered, we cannot fully appreciate their tremendous accomplishments.

I feel this book is also necessary because the few available existing texts are all inclusive, treating the Service as a whole without giving the Great Lakes the individual attention they deserve. They also do not treat the Service realistically and are lacking in detail.

One frustration is that I am dealing with a "moving target." The Life-Saving Service was dynamic, always in a state of improving. As the Service matured, all aspects of it changed. Pay and personnel policies, station design and construction, boat types and equipment, all evolved to meet increasing operational requirements. In some respects parts of the book are a "snap shot" in time, showing how the Service functioned at a particular point. In other ways it is a composite of the various changes in an attempt to tell the broad story of the life savers on the Lakes.

Throughout my research on Great Lakes shipwrecks, every time I investigated a wreck that involved the old life savers, I always came away tremendously impressed with their exploits. It seemed despite the danger or difficulty, the life savers invariably accomplished the rescue.

The deeds of the life savers became the stuff of legends. In the contemporary press they were "storm warriors" and "heroes of the surf."[1] In the eyes of the public they could do no wrong. It was an image the Service worked hard to cultivate and to present to the community at every opportunity. Although the image was a myth, it did have a basis in fact. Time and again they accomplished incredible feats of rescue against impossible odds. But they were not saints in surfboats or monks of the lake shore. They were humans with all of the foibles of the species. There were instances where surfmen were drunk on duty, belligerent, failed to perform patrols, disobeyed orders, showed cowardice in the face of danger or deserted. During times of economic boom, they departed in droves for the higher wages offered by the shipping industry or civilian community. At the stations they left short handed, crews were often made up of inexperienced men, all that could be mustered. To the great credit of the Service, it dealt with each problem head-on. The difficulties may have been hidden from public view, but they were not ignored. The Service tried its best to solve each with direct action. Failure to perform to the standard required meant dismissal. Incompetence was not tolerated for any reason. The Service always struggled to maintain the lofty standards it set for itself. Time and again, in record after record, the Service took every possible step to live up to the ideals of the "storm warriors." Their unofficial motto only added to the legend: "Regulations say we have to go out, but they don't say anything about coming back."[2]

After I completed my research, the Life-Saving Service that remained was different than the one I started with. The new organization was all the more remarkable because of the problems it overcame. By force of the Service leadership and organization, the disparate groups of men were forged into the highly efficient crews that accomplished the remarkable rescues.

It is my conclusion that the men of the Life-Saving Service were unique in the annals of American maritime history. A fully manned and functioning crew was a sight to behold. Honed to a razor's edge of sharpness with the boats, beach apparatus and other skills, they were capable of performing extraordinary feats.

It is my belief that to write effectively about the Life-Saving Service, you really have had to have been one of them. You must have experienced the same crashing surf, howling wind and lonely stretches of beach patrol. At this date, such first-hand knowledge is, of course, impossible, but I have had several experiences that did help me focus on the type of men they were.

Several years ago I rode with a Coast Guard crew in a 44-foot motor lifeboat on the back end of a lake gale. The wind was a steady 40 miles per hour with gusts in the 50-mile-per-hour range. Waves ran 12 feet with an occasional 15-footer. Rain squalls danced across the lake accompanied by periods of hail and sleet. Although safely belted in, it was all I could do to hold on for dear life. The boat moved like a thing possessed. I remembered an old story about the violent motion of a surfboat in a heavy sea. After an especially monstrous wave passed beneath, the boat dropped suddenly from under the crew leaving them frozen in mid-air. One surfman came down so hard he broke through the thwart!

Looking across the cold, gray lake, I could imagine a life saving crew of a century ago battling its way through the waves in its trusty lifeboat, heading bravely for a vessel in distress. It would have been a hell of a trip for them, but one they would have made without complaint. It was simply their job. Although my run in the 44 boat wasn't easy, it could not be compared with the difficulty faced by the old life savers.

While doing some field work along Lake Superior's old shipwreck coast from Whitefish Point west to Deer Park, I watched a storm roll in from the lake with amazing speed. Standing on the site of the long gone Deer Park Station, I saw the black clouds literally boil along the coast. From nearly dead calm to black squall took only minutes! The watch in the tower would have seen the same phenomenon often, but knew the storm potentially would have meant distress for an unwary vessel, requiring the alarm to sound calling the crew to action. With just a little imagination, I could see it all in my mind's eye.

In another instance, during mid-October, I was hiking the old life saver's trail from Vermilion west to the halfway house. The wind was blowing a gale from the northwest, and waves on Lake Superior were rolling high, making progress against the wind difficult

without trying to keep sharp watch for vessels in distress. The wind-whipped sand stung both eyes and exposed skin. Other than my companion, there likely wasn't another soul on the beach for 20 miles in either direction. But this was the environment of the life savers. Should a storm-damaged schooner have required it, the Vermilion crew would have dragged its gear down the same stretch of beach and either launched the surfboat into the billowing waves or set up and fired the Lyle gun for a breeches buoy rescue. In the prevailing weather conditions either action would have been extremely difficult, but they would have done it because it was their job.

In these small ways, I have tried to reach back through time to feel the pulse of the old life savers. It is important to remember that history is not about facts and dates; it is about men and what they did.

FIGURE 1
After the rescue, the storm warriors head back from the stricken vessel.
Edward Pusick

1. The term "storm warrior" is a British one, taken from a book by the title *Storm Warriors* by Reverend John Gilmore detailing the achievements of English lifeboatmen. Copies of the book were distributed to many of the early American stations.

2. Evidence of the high public regard manifested itself in different ways. During the early 1900s the Milton Bradley Company marketed a board game called "Life-Saver."

Part I

Early Life Saving

Chapter 1

From the Beginning

FIGURE 3
Death in the surf.
Author's Collection

Since man began to sail the world's seas, death from shipwreck has been commonplace. An early writer stated that since "men began to go down to the sea in ships," they sometimes went "under the sea, ships and all, and stayed there."[1] When a wreck occurred it was literally every man for himself, both afloat and ashore. If a sailor or passenger survived the ordeal of the wreck itself, arriving alive on the beach was no guarantee of survival. In some instances, although not on the Great Lakes, local inhabitants would kill those that made it ashore for the value of their personal belongings and to speed salvage of cargo washed ashore.

As time passed, civilizations developed laws to protect abandoned cargo or vessels that washed ashore. To recover them, owners generally needed to claim such goods within specified periods. Government officials were expected to protect them when possible. Of course the

law was only as effective as far as the control of the government extended. Along desolate coasts where wrecks were more commonplace, effective control was often non-existent.

For example, in England during the reign of Henry III (1216), a law was promulgated that if a man, cat or dog escaped alive from a vessel, the ship was not considered abandoned. The vessel and goods had to be protected by a king's officer. Should anyone sue for the property within a year and a day and prove ownership, it would be returned to them. In contrast, if no living thing survived, then everything belonged to the crown. The coastal lords, however, periodically disputed it.[2]

Causing a wreck by showing false signals or plundering a stranded vessel, which included killing the crew, was a crime, and the perpetrators received heavy penalties. It was treated as nothing less than piracy. The practitioners of this murderous enterprise were among other names often known as wreckers, land pirates and mooncussers. Eleventh century English law was severe. Those who murdered shipwreck victims were to be thrown into the sea until half dead then stoned to death. Coast pilots who set false lights were excommunicated and punished as robbers. The lords on whose property the pilots set the false lights were to be "tied to a post in the middle of their own houses, which shall be set on fire at all corners and burned with all therein....The site of the house shall be converted into places for the sale of hogs and swine."[3]

Popular legend claims that "Nag's Head," North Carolina, was named for the practice of hanging a lantern from the neck of a horse and then leading it at night over the sand dunes. Observed from sea, the light looked like another vessel. Misled by the false light, a vessel would strike an offshore bar, thus becoming plunder for the wreckers. The same accusations were made of people in the Barnegat, New Jersey, area. No hard evidence, however, has ever been presented proving such vile actions. City newspapers ran sensational stories about shipwrecks, often claiming that shore residents robbed bodies and plundered cargo. Old tales about false lights were repeated.

On the East Coast, the worst stretch of beach for plunderers was Long Island. Reportedly, "...stevedores and riggermen...regular New York toughs" often robbed survivors, including cutting fingers off the living to remove rings. By contrast, the residents along the New Jersey coast claimed that they never touched the body until it was dead.[4] However, an 1846 New Jersey commission did investigate charges of refusing to give aid to shipwreck victims, stealing from the dead and demanding money for delivery of the bodies.[5] The commission reported the charges untrue.

The bounty of goods a wreck could deliver to the poor inhabitants of a lonely shore was considerable. There is an old story telling of a New England preacher who, during the Sunday sermon, called on God to protect the sailors on the sea, but begged that in the event of a disaster, the wreck would come ashore on his parish coast!

Life saving as a government sponsored activity appears to have started with the Chinese in 1737. Taxes paid for the service, although volunteer crews manned the boats.[6] The Netherlands was apparently the first European nation to start a life saving organization, establishing one in 1767. In 1774, the English founded the Royal Humane Society. The efforts of both groups were initially directed toward the recovery and resuscitation of drowning victims. It wasn't until 1824 and the formation of the Royal National Institution for the Preservation of Life from Shipwreck (later the Royal National Lifeboat Institution) that a society was dedicated to rescue from shipwreck.[7] The same year also saw the organization of two lifeboat societies in The Netherlands, the North and South Holland Lifeboat Institution and the South Holland Institution for Saving the Shipwrecked. Coastal responsibilities were divided between them.[8] The impetus for both the British and Dutch, as with other nations, was to take the business of life saving away from an ad hoc arrangement of local communities forced to react to a wreck with the personnel and equipment at hand and give the responsibility to organized and properly equipped crews. The spark for the Dutch was the 1824 foundering of the frigate *De Vreede*. Although brave local fishermen were successful in removing many of those aboard, during the second run back from the wreck their boat capsized and all but one of the rescuers drowned. The loss of life for those aboard the frigate was heavy. The public outrage that followed led to the formation of the previously mentioned groups.[9]

1. Rev. T.J.A. Freeman, S.J., "The Life-Saving Service of the United States," *American Catholic Quarterly Review*, Vol. 18, (July 1893), p. 650.

2. Freeman, " The Life-Saving Service," p. 651.

3. Bise Shepard, *Lore of the Wreckers* (Boston: Beacon Press, 1961), pp. 28-30.

4. Rebecca Harding Davis, "Life-Saving Service," *Lippencotts Magazine*, Vol. XVII, (March 1876), p. 305.

5. Peter J. Guthorn, *The Sea Bright Skiff and Other Jersey Shore Boats* (New Brunswick, NJ: Rutgers University Press, 1971), p. 81.

6. Bernard C. Nalty, Dennis L. Noble, Truman R. Strobridge, ed. *Wrecks Rescues & Investigations., Selected Documents of the United States Coast Guard and Its Predecessors* (Wilmington, Delaware: Scholarly Resources Inc., 1978), p. xviii.

7. Nalty, *Wrecks*. p. xviii.

8. E.W. Middleton. *Lifeboats of the World* (New York: Arco Publishing, 1978), p. 144.

9. Nalty, *Wrecks*. p. 145.

Chapter 2

Early United States Efforts

The Humane Society of the Commonwealth of Massachusetts, formed in Boston in 1786, was the first life saving group established in the United States. The society's purpose as stated in the charter was "for the recovery of persons who meet with such accidents as to produce in them the appearance of death and for promoting the cause of humanity, by pursuing such means, from time to time, as shall have for their object the preservation of human life and the alleviation of its miseries." Among the society's acts was the building of huts for the "shelter and comfort of persons escaping from wrecked vessels upon exposed and desolate positions of the coast of Massachusetts." The first hut was built on Lovell's Island near Boston in 1789. The hut cost $40 and was equipped with food, blankets and fire making material. Unmanned, the huts were often the victim of vandals.[1]

As circumstances dictated, huts were erected in various locations on the Massachusetts coast. In 1807 a lifeboat station was built at Cohasset. Other stations followed. All were equipped with boats, lines, mortars and other equipment. Although a full-time keeper was appointed for each, the crews were volunteer. They were given a small cash payment only when a rescue was made or drill performed. In some instances medals were awarded to signify a rescue of special difficulty. These benevolent activities did result in attracting some minimal government aid, both state and Federal. In addition, that same year the Congress appropriated $5,000 to equip selected Atlantic coast lighthouses with the "means of rendering assistance to shipwrecked mariners."[2] But for two years the money remained unspent. In 1848 it was finally permitted to be expended by the Massachusetts Humane Society.[3] Other than the Massachusetts Humane Society, there were several other benevolent organizations that sought to work to save lives put at risk due to shipwreck. Such societies were organized in major port cities by well-to-do citizens, usually representing merchant and shipping interests. They also worked to improve lighthouses, license bar pilots and provide medals for heroism in life saving.[4]

Despite a decidedly hazardous coast, the Federal government was not too active in either providing lighthouses or surveying dangerous areas. By 1820, only 55 lighthouses were operating and no efforts had been made to mark navigation hazards. Most coastal charts were those made by foreign governments dating from colonial times. They were also unreliable. A government coastal survey was not initiated until 1832. No provision was made by the government to provide relief for shipwreck victims.[5]

As in The Netherlands, the best rescue efforts were made by local fishermen and wreckers.[6] Although such efforts were often valiant, they were usually wholly inadequate. Gradually, as the result of increasingly frequent disasters, the government became more involved in the general issues of maritime safety.

As had been the practice in England, the American colonies, and later the states, had established the right of the government to levy part of the cargo recovered from a wreck within its borders. To enforce such laws, the states appointed local officers to assure administration and compliance. There were many names for such individuals, among them "commissioners of wrecks" and "wreck masters." Crews of local surfmen were employed to provide a pool of competent salvagers to protect the interests of the state, owner and underwriter. While politics often played a role, thus insuring a degree of corruption, the ability of the local surfmen was unquestioned. Their aid rendered to wrecked vessels was invaluable, but was still far less than needed.[7]

The system was very simple and well suited to the times. The first man who sighted a vessel on the bar immediately contacted the local wreck-master. He assumed control of both the men ashore and, on behalf of the insurance companies, the ship's cargo.

There was no official signalling system to summon a crew. In the words of an old wrecker, "...every man warned his neighbor. There weren't but a few scattered folks along the coast then, but in time of a wrack you'd see them in the dead of night ready and waiting along the beach. No need of your signal-flags for them, I reckon. They knew there'd be dead men and plenty of wrack coming ashore before morning."[8]

The men that went out in the boats were special. The old wrecker continued. "There was regular wracking-boats, built for the surf and crews for each you see: best man in the starn. The man in the starn, he generally owned the boat and chose his crew. Picked men. He kept them year after year. Then the wrecking-masters hired him, his boat and his crew. Best crew chosen first of course. Two dollars a day each day was reckoned good pay."[9]

There were never very many wrecking boats. An 1846 New Jersey legislative report stated that there were only about 10 along the Jersey shore. To quickly reach the scene of the wreck, each boat was hauled by horse and wagon.[10]

Although the boat crews did their best to save life, their primary purpose was to save cargo. Often, the government life savers and wrecking crews worked side by side. The government concentrated on crew and passengers and the wrecking crew on cargo and the vessel itself, but in the words of another wrecker, "Its not likely any man's a-goin to bring trade out of a wrack's long's there a live critter aboard."[11]

The wreckers had to work fast to try to save the vessel, if it was still in one piece. If the ship struck bow first, the basic technique was to run a kedge anchor as far off the stern as possible. At the flood tide all hands heaved on a windlass in an attempt to haul her free. If she was too badly holed or would not come free, then it became a desperate race to salvage the cargo before the sea beat her to kindling. The wreckers' fee was determined by their success and the degree of difficulty and danger. It was larger if the vessel was saved, smaller if only the cargo was recovered.

In 1832 the U.S. Coast Survey came into being and immediately started the daunting task of surveying the Atlantic coast and publishing up-to-date charts.[12] The U.S. Lake Survey began in 1841. As stated in an early report, "The lakes present peculiar and distinctive characteristics. They are a cluster of seas, enormous in their extent, containing about 80,000 square miles, and frequented by an immense commerce. Their American coastline is nearly 2,500 miles in length. Excepting for certain periods at the opening and close of navigation, during the spring and fall, their waters are generally tranquil, though at times swept by sudden and violent storms. Their natural harbors are few, and these are mostly narrow and lie at the mouths of small rivers, from which piers and breakwaters have been built and jut out for a considerable distance. Unlike our other coasts, they are closed to navigation by ice for five or six months of the year.

"The special differences in the lakes are not numerous nor marked. Lake Superior, the largest body of fresh water in the world, has few harbors, and its coast has several projecting points upon which shipping is liable to be driven in seasons of tempest; but disasters are mostly confined to the lower portion between Marquette and Sault Ste. Marie. Lake Michigan has generally regular shores; no islands except in its northern portion; few harbors and bays, and is subject to severe storm at certain times of the year. Lake Huron has a deep and good harbor at Mackinaw; and Saginaw Bay, which sets back 60 miles from the lake, offers excellent shelter to shipping under its islands and shores; but besides these, its harbors on the American shore are few. Lake Erie has the peculiarity of being much shallower than the other lakes; and being thus more readily convulsed by gales, it is the most dangerous of any to navigation, being, besides, subject to violent storms, and swept from its one extremity to the other by winds which heap up the water at its lower end, and cause great disaster. Its natural harbors are, moreover, few in number and are generally at the mouths or rivers, and increased in amplitude by the customary device of long, projecting piers. Lake Ontario has great depth, is less visited by storms than Erie, and is generally favorable to navigation; but, like the other lakes, has few harbors."[13]

As the result of government action, by 1837 the number of lighthouses had increased to 208 with 26 floating lights. With the inception of the Lighthouse Board in 1852, both growth in the number of lights and the efficiency of their operation and administration accelerated. In 1852 there were 320 lights; 1860, 486; 1876, 637 with 30 lightships.[14]

To provide direct aid to shipwrecked mariners, in 1837 an act of Congress authorized the President to "cause any suitable number of public vessels adapted to the purpose to cruise upon the coast in the severe portion of the season to afford such aid to distressed navigators as their circumstances and necessities may require."[15] Although naval vessels were originally assigned to this duty, it was later given to the Revenue-Marine.[16] Naval vessels had proved too large and cumbersome for this exacting job. By contrast the smaller Revenue-Cutters were more capable. The Revenue-Marine was founded on August 4, 1790, to collect customs duties and preventing smuggling. While the use of the Revenue-Marine as ad-hoc life savers was not by any means the entire answer to the problem, they did make a significant contribution. Between the period 1860 and June 30, 1876, a total of 2,386 vessels in distress were assisted, an average of over 140 per year.[17]

It is difficult today to imagine the terrible toll of wrecks that the Atlantic coast claimed. As America grew, so did its dependence on maritime transportation. The nation's thirst for trade increased yearly. The new world especially beckoned immigrants. The destination for most of them was New York, which, considering the hazards of the coasts of Long Island and New Jersey, was an especially dangerous one. It was said that these coasts "were so terribly calamitous as to be held in the utmost dread by ship owners and mariners, and the names of Fire Island, Barnegat and other localities were synonyms of horror."[18] Caught in a roaring nor'easter, great sailing packets regularly were forced into the breakers, either on the beach or on an offshore bar. As the ships broke apart in the pounding waves, their crews and passengers perished in the cold surf. The only hope for those aboard was the local wreckers and their crews. In truly high surf, however, no boat could survive and their fate was sealed.

An example was the February 15, 1846, wreck of the *John Minturn* on the treacherous New Jersey shore. As described by a local wrecker: "The current was a-settin' south. Sech a tide hadn't been known since the oldest men could remember: the sea broke over all the marshes clear up to the farm houses. I was but a lad, but I couldn't sleep: seemed as ef I ought to be a doin' something, I didn't rightly know what. About three o'clock in the morning I heerd a gun, and in a minute another. Mother, I says, there's a vessel on the bar. So, as I gets on my clothes, she makes me a mug of coffee. You must drink this, Jacob, an' eat some'at, she says, before you go out. So to quiet her I takes the mug, but I hadn't half drunk it when I hears shouting outside. It was one of the Shattucks: he says, there's a ship come ashore up by Barnegat. I says, No. I says, The guns are from off the inlet. So I runs one way and Shadduck the other. The night was black as pitch and the storm was drivin' like hell. And we was both right, for there was two vessels – a coast schooner down by Squan and this big ship the *John Minturn* (on the bar)."

To the question of the number of lives lost the wrecker replied, " Over three hundred – all but 14. They come ashore tied on to the boards or hencoops or the like – seven of the crew and seven of the passengers. We tried to launch the surfboat, but the boat was never built that could live on that sea. She was bound from New Orleans to New York, and most of her passengers were wealthy people, going to the north for the winter.

"At least, so we jedged from her papers and the bodies and clothes of them that come ashore – some pretty little children, I mind, babies and their black nurses, and their mothers – delicate women with valooable rings on their hands. Some of them's buried in the graveyard in the village and their friends took some away."

The wrecker related, "There was the *Minerva,* too. I forgit how many emigrants went down on that ship, (but there were)...hundreds of human lives lost. And there was the *New Era* – went down near Deal: three hundred immigrants drowned. The captain had nailed down the hatches on them. Oh, that's generally done. In a storm the steerage can't be managed otherwise."[19]

The fear of shipwreck was also reflected in popular culture.

Not only did the press carry the lurid details of death in the breakers, but several Protestant hymns were also written on the theme. "Jesus, Savior Pilot Me" by Edward Hopper was one. Another based on a Great Lakes wreck was "Keep the Lower Lamps Burning" by P.P. Bliss.[20]

1. U.S. Life-Saving Service, *Annual Report of the Operations of the United States Life-Saving Service For the Fiscal Year Ending June 30, 1876,* p. 834.

2. *Annual Report, U.S. Life-Saving Service, 1876,* p. 840.

3. *History of the Great Lakes, Volume I* (Chicago: 1899), p. 377.

4. Robert F. Bennett, USCG, "The Life-Savers: For Those in Peril on the Sea," *Proceedings., United States Naval Institute,* (March 1976), p. 56.

5. *Annual Report, U.S. Life-Saving Service, 1876,* pp. 834-835.

6. The term "wreckers" can have a double meaning. Often it refers to those who cause wrecks through showing false lights (Nags Head). It can also mean those individuals who earned a living as the result of shipwrecks, in effect salvagers. Sometimes the two were the same.

7. Bennett, "The Life-Savers," p. 57.

8. Davis, "Life-Saving Stations," p. 302.

9. Davis, "Life-Saving Stations," p. 302.

10. Guthorn, *Sea Bright Skiff,* pp. 80-81.

11. Davis, "Life-Saving Stations," p. 303.

12. Arthur M. Woolford, *Charting the Inland Seas: A History of the U.S. Lake Survey* (Detroit: U.S. Army Corps of Engineers, 1991).

13. *Annual Report, U.S. Life-Saving Service, 1876,* pp. 836-837.

14. *Annual Report, U.S. Life-Saving Service, 1876,* p. 839.

15. *Annual Report, U.S. Life-Saving Service, 1876,* pp. 839-840.

16. Revenue-Marine and Revenue-Cutter Service were synonymous terms. Revenue-Marine was used prior to the 1890s and Revenue-Cutter Service afterwards.

17. *Annual Report, U.S. Life-Saving Service, 1876,* p. 840.

18. *Annual Report, U.S. Life-Saving Service, 1876,* p. 857.

19. Davis, "Life-Saving Stations," p. 304.

20. *Newsletter,* Association of Great Lakes Maritime History, May 1993; Some versions credit the wreck off Cleveland, others off Avon or Buffalo.

Chapter 3

The First Stations

The Federal government's active involvement in life saving stations began as the result of the efforts of New Jersey Representative William A. Newell. His district included an especially dangerous stretch of New Jersey coast that had been the scene of particularly devastating shipwrecks. Newell had been witness to at least one of the wrecks. As the result of his efforts on August 14, 1848, Congress appropriated $10,000 for "providing surf-boats, rockets, carronades and necessary apparatus for the better preservation of life and property from shipwrecks on the coast of New Jersey lying between Sandy Hook and Little Egg Harbor, the same to be expended under the supervision of such officer of the Revenue-Marine Corps as may be detached for this duty by Secretary of the Treasury."[1]

Revenue-Marine Captain Douglas Ottinger was charged with the responsibility of executing Congress's will. Working with a committee of New York marine underwriters and with the advice of local wreck-masters and surfmen, he located and constructed eight stations between the specified points. Each was roughly 28 x 16 feet and equipped with "one metal surf-boat, with air-chambers and cork fenders, seven oars and two India-rubber bailing-buckets; one met-

al life-car, with cork or India-rubber floats and fenders, and rings and chains for each end; 310 fathoms; two rocket-lines, nine-tenths ounce per yard, 300 yards each; one coiling-frame for rocket-line and box; one crotch and range for throwing rockets; one sand-anchor, strap and bull's-eye; one tackle, with twenty-fathoms fall, 2½-inch manila; one heaver and strap; one mortar of iron, and ten shots fitted with spiral wire; one copper powder canister, and four pounds of powder for same; twelve blue-lights, and box containing fifty quick-matches; five rockets and rocket-box of tin; eight pieces of match-rope, and twelve pieces of port-fire; two lanterns and oil-can, and oil for same; one lamp-feeder and wick; one stove and pipe; one cord of wood; ten shovels; one firing-wire."[2]

Each station was little more than a boathouse built on cedar pilings. Large barn doors allowed quick access to the surfboat. The metal surfboat was unique for its time. Based on the cedar surfboats common on the New Jersey coast, it was 26½ feet long, 6½ feet in beam, had galvanized iron sides and a wooden bottom. While in theory its integral air tanks made it nearly unsinkable, it weighed almost twice as much as the cedar boat, 1,500 versus 900 pounds. Joseph Francis of the Novelty Iron

Works of Brooklyn was the builder. Early versions had a reputation of sinking from under the crews. After a design change, which involved replacing the wood bottom with an iron one, the boat was more seaworthy and remained in use for many years. Metal surfboats had the great advantage of being able to be stored for long periods of time without deteriorating. If not frequently used, a wood boat would dry out. When quickly pulled out of the boat house for a rescue, it would be unseaworthy.[3] Some Francis boats sent to the Great Lakes during the 1854-55 period were still in use as late as 1899 although only as work boats.

The following year Congress appropriated additional funds to construct and equip stations along the coasts of Long Island and New Jersey. Six stations were added to the south Jersey coast and eight on Long Island. As in the original appropriation, a Revenue-Marine officer superintended the New Jersey construction while a civil engineer employed by the Treasury Department handled those on Long Island.[4] Although the stations were constructed and given keepers, there was no provision for providing crews or facility maintenance. They relied strictly on volunteers from the community to man the boats.

The overall scheme of the location of the stations was very important. Spread as they were on the Cape Cod, Long Island and New Jersey coasts, they effectively guarded the approaches to the nation's principal ports of Boston, New York and Philadelphia.

The coasts these original stations protected were remarkably similar. An early article described it as "...a strip of sand beach varying from a quarter of a mile to five miles in width...separated from the main land at some places by rather narrow stretches of water, at others by veritable bays."[5] Harbors were few. The sand beach itself presented little particular danger for a ship. Driven on the shore during a storm, wave action would tend to force the vessel further ashore, causing comparatively slight damage. But the same forces of nature that formed the sandy beaches also built up sand bars. The bars varied from one to four hundred yards offshore and frequently shifted due to storm and current. During heavy gales, monstrous walls of surf broke over them. When a vessel was storm driven on a bar she literally was beat to pieces. Waves alternatively picked her up and dropped her down, each time pounding her to death on the back of the bar. The

grasping seas swept her decks clean of houses, boats, masts, passengers and crew. It was a horrible scene of destruction that repeated itself time and again. The beaches were strewn with the remains of once proud vessels, and the graveyards of coastal towns all held the bodies of the human carnage. The situation was not dissimilar to many areas on the Great Lakes also plagued by offshore bars.

According to Representative Newell, during the period 1841-1848 an estimated 158 vessels wrecked on the New Jersey coast. Another 180 wrecked on Long Island.[6] The need for an organized life saving crew was clear.

The stations quickly proved their value during the 1849-50 shipwreck season. Using the lifecar, New Jersey volunteers rescued 201 of 202 persons from the stranded ship *Ayrshire* in January 1850. Many of those saved were women and children. The surf was reportedly so high that no boat could have lived in it. During the same season 264 persons were saved from Long Island wrecks and another 90 from New Jersey disasters.

Based on the clear proof of their effectiveness, Congress continued to appropriate funds for the construction of additional stations. By 1854, the government had funded 137 of them according to the 1876 *Annual Report.* They were located in Maine, New Hampshire, Massachusetts, Rhode Island, New York, New Jersey, North Carolina, South Carolina, Georgia, Florida, Texas and also on Lakes Michigan, Ontario, Erie and Superior.[7] However, evidence indicates that stations as such were never provided for the Lakes.

But because the stations were strictly volunteer manned, they did not approach the high standard of capability that was necessary to be a true life saving asset. The volunteers often lived at locations distant from the station, and it took time to assemble and reach the wreck site. Often the alarm bell was not heard. The time for adequate drill training was not always available. Equipment maintenance also suffered.

The problem of maintenance was very serious. In those instances where the facility was built near a lighthouse and placed under the supervision of the light keeper, it was well cared for. However when placed under the control of towns, private citizens or short lived benevolent societies, it usually deteriorated and became unfit for use. Since the stations were unmanned, vital equipment was stolen or vandalized. Sometimes, shipwreck loss of life occurred because the surfboats and gear had become unfit for use. Disasters happened directly off stations, but when the volunteer crews pulled the equipment out to make a rescue, it was discovered to be decayed and useless. Brave volunteer crews stood by helplessly watching men, women and children drown in the surf, unable to aid them.[8] When the *Powhatten* wrecked in May 1854 on New Jersey, between 300 and 400 people were lost. The vessel was a bare 200 feet offshore![9]

The attendant high loss of life and property caused by a station inefficiency, as well as public outcry, prompted Congress in the Act of December 14, 1854, to authorize the Secretary of the Treasury to establish additional stations, move existing ones as necessary, make required repairs to facilities and equipment, appoint a superintendent for the coasts of Long Island and New Jersey with the powers of inspectors of customs and appoint a keeper for each station. The superintendents were to be paid $1,500 per year and the keepers $200. The Congress also prohibited the placement of facilities in the care of any neighborhood individuals without proper bond. Efforts were made to assure that the boats would only be used for the intended purpose and not for private gain.

equipment were brought to more serviceable conditions and a degree of responsibility was established. A marked improvement in life saving efficiency resulted.

But at best the Congressional action was only a small part of the complete answer. No regulations were promulgated, nor standards developed. The superintendents and keepers were not held responsible for the proper discharge of their duties or accountable for the property in their charge. There was no requirement to record shipwrecks in their areas or report them to the government. The Secretary of the Treasury exercised little actual control over the stations.

The central problem was that the legislation failed to provide for the employment of full-time life saving crews. In some locations volunteers were plentiful, but in more desolate areas of the coast, inhabitants of any kind were sparse, let alone skilled surfmen. What was desperately needed were crews of full-time life savers who could be drilled to a razor's edge of proficiency. Only long days of practice could develop the close teamwork necessary to field truly competent professional life saving crews.

The Service was firmly in the hands of the

FIGURE 6
Launching the surfboat.
Author's Collection

Wooden boats were provided to stations in addition to the metallic ones.[10]

In 1870 the pay for keepers was increased to $400. Volunteer crewmen received $3 for each day of drill and $10 for duty during an actual wreck. Keepers were appointed as inspectors of customs to enable them to protect revenue interests as well as the interests of the owners of stranded property.[11]

As the result of these actions, the stations and

politicians. Where the old wrecking master selected his men for their muscle and skill, politicians chose crews based on party affiliation. Often the lifeboatmen were considered tavern loafers, utterly incompetent to manage a rescue. These important positions became the reward for small village political hacks. Professional wreckers refused to have anything to do with the government crews. The consequence was tax dollars wasted and hundreds of human beings left to perish within sight of land.[12]

The Great Lakes did not receive life saving stations as such. Instead of the full stations and equipment provided to East Coast stations, the Lakes received only Francis metallic surfboats. Starting in the spring of 1854 and continuing into 1855, a total of 51 boats were sent to the Lakes. No beach wagons or other equipment were provided.[13]

Where possible, the boats were assigned to government officials, lighthouse keepers or collectors of customs, with the understanding that they would provide for their protection and ensure proper use. To protect other locations, boats were stationed in ports if "suitable persons at the places where they are to be located will signify to the department their willingness to enter into bond for their safe keeping and proper use."[14] Normally the bond had to be posted by two or more people and a certificate forwarded to the Treasury Department with the request for the boat. In addition, an assurance was required that there were sufficient people in the area ready and able to man the boat when required. When these conditions were met, the Treasury ordered a boat from Francis, which on completion was shipped to the designated local individual.[15] The bonded man was charged that "...it is expected every effort will be made by you to preserve the public property committed to your charge and that you will use the boat on every occasion that may offer for the saving of life and property from shipwreck."[16]

Despite the government's best intentions to prevent illegal use of the boats, abuses evidently occurred. The Great Lakes were a long way from Washington, and with no system of inspections or management, misuse was only to be expected.[17]

The Francis boats cost the Treasury Department $450 each. Shipping was another $25, although sometimes additional charges for transportation to the western Lakes were paid.[18] Not all the boats arrived at their intended destinations. In the spring of 1854 some Lake Michigan boats were lost en route. Records are not clear concerning the circumstances, but they were apparently replaced in 1855.[19]

Special buildings for the surfboats were generally not provided. The Treasury Department initially felt it did not have the authority under the legislation to construct them. Protecting them was the responsibility of the local bonded citizens. Later, storage sheds were built at New Buffalo and Saugatuck, Michigan, and Racine, Wisconsin.[20] Since records are sparse, it is not unlikely that sheds were built for other loca-

tions, either by government funding or local subscription.

The use these early boats were put to, the rescues they assisted in and their eventual fate has largely disappeared into oblivion. Since there was no requirement for operational use reports or system of inspection or maintenance, their long-term effectiveness was severely limited. The Treasury Department did not feel obligated to provide any funds other than for the purchase and transportation of the boats. There was not a single dollar for repair. This was the responsibility of the bond holder.[21] Based on the appearance of the Francis surfboats on the equipment lists of many of the early Great Lakes Life-Saving stations, we can surmise that some original 1854 boats were still available for use. What happened to the others is largely unknown. One of the Great Lakes Francis boats was restored by the Great Lakes Historical Society and was later given to the Kelly Island Historical Society. It is believed that it is the old Marblehead or Kelly Island boat. Another Francis boat is in private hands.

The period between the arrival of the boats in 1854 and the establishment of the Life-Saving Service on the Lakes in 1876 is a black hole. Records are nearly nonexistent. Those meager

FIGURE 7
The Francis metallic surfboat shown in this very early photo is probably one of the original boats shipped to the Lakes in the 1854 period. Note the unusual uniforms.
Ted Richardson Collection

references that can be found offer at best only tantalizing glimpses of this forgotten period.

The 1876 *Annual Report* states that of 82 boats purchased during 1854, 47 were shipped to the Great Lakes: 14 for Lake Erie, nine for Lake Ontario, 23 for Lake Michigan and one for Lake Superior. Lake Huron received none.[22] Research into the Service records shows a different count: 16 to Lake Erie, nine to Lake Ontario, 25 to Lake Michigan and one to Lake Superior. The following data is the result of that research.

FRANCIS METALLIC SURFBOAT LOCATIONS[23]

Lake Ontario

LOCATION	BONDED	LIGHTHOUSE OR CUSTOMS
Oswego, NY	James D. Colver (2 Boats)	
Big Sandy Creek, NY	Roswell Kinney	
Tibbits Point, NY	Robert Moon	
Sodus Point, NY	Thomas Wickham	
Salmon River, NY	Reuben G. Wellington	
Rochester, NY	Malty Strong (2 Boats)	
Youngstown, NY	A.G. Skinner	

Lake Erie

LOCATION	BONDED	LIGHTHOUSE OR CUSTOMS
Vermilion, OH	C.L. Burton	
Huron, OH	John Sprague	
Sandusky, OH	John Boult	
Fairport, OH	Matthew L. Root	
Avon Point, OH	Charles H. Livingston	
Conneaut, OH	John B. Lyon	
Erie, OH	G.D. Addison, W.D. Kelly	
Put-in-Bay, OH	A. Jones	
Marblehead, OH	J.B. Keyes	
Cleveland, OH	Benjamin Stannard	
Cunningham's Island, OH	A.S. Kelly	
Barcelona, OH		
Arrowpoint, OH		
Buffalo, NY	D.P. Dobbins	
Sturgeon Point, NY	Ira Joy	
Dunkirk, NY	David Goodwin	

Lake Superior

LOCATION	BONDED	LIGHTHOUSE OR CUSTOMS
Marquette, MI		Harvey Moore

Lake Michigan

LOCATION	BONDED	LIGHTHOUSE OR CUSTOMS
Michigan City, IN		John M. Clarkson
New Buffalo, MI		Reuben W. Smith
St. Joseph River, MI		Thomas Fitzgerald
Muskegon, MI		Alexander Wilson
Kalamazoo Light, MI (Saugatuck)		Timothy S. Coats
Grand River, MI		Peter Vanderberg
S. Manitou Island, MI		Alonzo Styfield
Manistee, MI		Roswell Canfield
White River, MI		
South Black River, MI		
N. Manitou Island, MI	N. Pickard	
Chicago, IL (2)		Henry M. Fuller
Calumet, IL		Hiram Squires
Milwaukee, WI		Andrew Sullivan
Sheboygan, WI		Godfrey Stanmer
Twin Rivers, WI		David Ward
Manitowoc, WI		Abraham W. Preston
Port Washington, WI		David Tuttle
Waukegan, IL		Thomas McCaul (customs)
Racine, WI		Issac I. Ulliman (customs)
Kenosha, WI		Nelson Pitkin (customs)
Washington Harbor, WI	I.M. Crane	
Death's Door, WI		unidentified
Bailey's Harbor, WI	Newton Bacon	

---

1. *Annual Report, U.S. Life-Saving Service, 1876*, p. 840.

2. *Annual Report, U.S. Life-Saving Service, 1876*, p. 841.

3. Bennett, "The Life-Savers," p. 57: Robert F. Bennett, *Surfboats, Rockets and Carronades* (Washington, D.C.: U.S. Government Printing Office) pp. 39-40.

4. *Annual Report, U.S. Life Saving-Service, 1876*, p. 841.

5. Freeman, "The Life-Saving Service," pp. 654-655.

6. Guthorn, *Sea Bright Skiff*, p. 82.

7. *Annual Report, U.S. Life-Saving Service, 1876*, p. 843.

8. *Annual Report, U.S. Life-Saving Service, 1876*, p. 844.

9. Horace L. Piper, "The Life-Saving Service," *The Technical World*, Vol. 11, No. 1, (September 1904), p. 2.

10. Bennett, "The Life-Savers," p. 58; Bennett, *Surfboats*. pp. 31 32.

11. *History of the Great Lakes*, p. 378.

12. Davis, "Life-Saving Stations," pp. 305-306.

13. Letter Book 1854-55, RG 26, NARA.

14. Letter, James Gutherie, Secretary of the Treasury, to John Wentworth, House of Representatives, July 11, 1854, RG 26, NARA.

15. Letter, James Gutherie, to M.O. Lyman, September 16, 1854, RG 26, NARA.

16. Letter, James Gutherie to Almond Hallet, January 28, 1854, RG 26, NARA.

17. Letter, James Gutherie to Secretary of the Light House Board, February 19, 1855, RG 26, NARA.

18. Letters, James Gutherie to Joseph Francis, May 23, 26, October 9, 1854, RG 26, NARA.

19. Letter, James Gutherie to John Otto, March 26, 1855, RG 26, NARA.

20. Letters, James Gutherie, January 23, May 27, 1854; February 26, October 23, 1855. RG 26, NARA,

21. Letter, James Gutherie to Addison and Kelly, July 1854, RG 26, NARA.

22. *Annual Report, U.S. Life-Saving Service, 1876*, p. 843.

23. Letter Book, RG 26, NARA.; although actually surfboat in design and use, some official correspondence refers to the Francis boats as lifeboats.

The U.S. Life-Saving Service Is Born

Chapter 4

FIGURE 8
Launching a surfboat.
Author's Collection

No substantive changes to station manning occurred until 1870 when, on an experimental basis, full-time surfmen were employed for the three winter months at alternate stations on the New Jersey coast. The winter of 1870-71 was especially devastating for East Coast shipping. Many wrecks occurred, some in areas beyond the reach of stations, others right on their doorsteps. There was great loss of life with much of it blamed on the life saving crews and the poor condition of their equipment.

The Great Lakes were also hard hit. During the same period there were 1,167 disasters with 214 lives lost.[1] The large number of deaths were laid directly at the doorstep of the life savers. The *Annual Report* for 1876 stated: "The loss of life was largely due to the lack of proper attention to duty on the part of the employees of the Service and the inefficient conditions of the boats and apparatus."[2]

Part of the trouble with the alternate manning plan was that the odd numbered stations located near towns were manned, while the even numbered stations, located in desolate areas, were not. Thus when the unmanned stations required volunteers to work a wreck, there were few men locally available, contributing to the overall poor performance.[3]

The alternative manning scheme was a compromise. In 1869 Representative Haight tried to provide for permanent manning of the stations, but his motion was defeated. Representative S.S. Cox then offered the alternative station plan. It wasn't the answer, but did open the door for future legislation.[4]

Driven by the appalling loss of life and clear evidence that seasonal surfmen at alternate stations was a wholly inadequate solution, on April 20, 1871, Congress authorized $200,000 for the Secretary of the Treasury to "employ crews of experienced surfmen at such stations and for such periods as he might deem necessary and proper."[5] This action effectively, but not yet officially, marked the birth of the United States Life-Saving Service as an agency of the Revenue-Marine.

The old volunteer stations were now a relic

of the past. However in their time they did contribute to the saving of lives put at peril due to shipwreck. The Secretary of the Treasury

FRANK LESLIE'S

POPULAR MONTHLY.

Vol. XIII.— No. 4.   APRIL, 1882. $3.00 Per Annum.

FIGURE 9
The "storm warrior" tradition caught the public fancy. Stories of the life savers in action were common place in the popular press.
Author's Collection

reported that while 512 lives were lost within their area of operations, 4,163 were saved at a cost of $280,000 or $67.25 per life.[6]

To organize and execute the Department's new responsibility, the Secretary of the Treasury, George S. Boutwell, appointed the Chief Clerk of the Treasury Department, 37-year-old Sumner I. Kimball, as the chief of the Revenue-Marine. His responsibilities included not only the new life saving stations, but also the Steamboat Inspection Service and Marine Hospitals.[7] At the time, the Revenue-Marine as well as the Life-Saving Service was rife with politics and deeply in need of reform. A clean sweep was needed, and Kimball would wield the broom.

Kimball in turn decided that before any of the appropriation was spent, his first job was to determine the true state of what he had inherited. Under his direction, Revenue-Marine Cap-

tain John Faunce made a thorough tour of inspection. Kimball accompanied him on some visits. Faunce's report found "...that most of the stations were too remote from each other, and that the houses were much dilapidated, many being so far gone as to be worthless, and the reminder in need of extensive repairs and enlargement. With but few exceptions, that they were in a filthy condition, and gave every evidence of neglect and misuse.

"The apparatus was rusty for want of care, and some of it ruined by the depredations of vermin and malicious persons. Many of the most necessary articles were wanting, and at no station was the outfit complete. At some of the stations where crews were employed in the winter months, such indispensable articles as powder, rockets, shot-lines, shovels, &c., were not to be found. At other stations not a portable article was left. Some of the keepers were too old for active service, others lived too far from the stations, and few of them were really competent for their positions. Politics had more influence in their appointment than qualification for the duties required of them. Even in the selection of crews for the stations where they were employed, fitness was a secondary consideration. The employment of paid crews at alternate stations had provided crews where they comparatively little needed, while it had left others, where regular crews were most necessary, to rely upon such aid as might be volunteered. It had also excited discontent among those who had habitually volunteered their services at the intervening stations, and a feeling that an unjust discrimination was made against them."[8]

Fired up by Faunce's dismal report, Kimball set out to completely reorganize the life savers. He did his best to remove incompetent men and political hacks, replacing them with qualified men despite political affiliation. He promulgated detailed regulations and instructions to assure efficient operations. Additional stations were established where necessary. Old facilities were torn down or rebuilt as required. Quarters for crews were added, as well as a mess room and equipment room. All stations were supplied with appropriate gear. To find the best equipment available, he established a Board of Life Saving Appliances to test it before acceptance for Service use.

Full-time six-man crews were hired from the best local surfmen available. In the service's early years crews were only employed for the winter storm season. Gradually this expanded to a 12-month season for many stations. A seventh and eighth crewmen were later added as required.

To improve efficiency, Kimball organized the coast into three districts, with the duties of superintendents, keepers and inspecting officers of the Revenue-Marine clearly defined. Thorough inspections of the stations were required by the inspecting officers at specified periods. An examination of drill proficiency was a critical part of the inspections. Keepers were to compile careful reports of wrecks and rescues. Station logbooks were required to be maintained and submitted to Washington.

To signal between stations, a simple but effective system of flags for day and rockets or hand lights for night was devised. This allowed night patrolling surfmen to notify their own station of a wreck and provide a method of calling for help from nearby stations.

As part of the act of 1873 many East Coast stations were connected to the storm signal system of the Signal Service. The signal stations at Oswego, Buffalo, Erie, Cleveland, Grand Haven, Chicago and Milwaukee were also available to the Great Lakes districts. This co-operation provided a two-fold advantage. It gave an immediate means of communications between the stations, district superintendents and Washington. In addition, the stations were able to display the appropriate storm signals thus improving general maritime safety.[9]

Kimball's organizational reforms were an immediate success, and Congress provided appropriations for additional East Coast sta-

tions. Based on the requirement for greater capability, the new stations were designed to a larger standard.

A special Treasury commission consisting of the Chief of the Revenue-Marine Division of the Department, Superintendent of Construction of the Life-Saving Service and Revenue-Marine Captains John Faunce and J. H. Merryman, studied the general situation and recommended the establishment of three classes of station. A First Class life saving station was intended for remote locations and was fully crewed and equipped. Second Class or lifeboat stations were authorized at more populous areas where volunteer crews were available. The lowest class of station was a House of Refuge to be built only in Florida. Kimball's recommendation concerning the new classes was accepted by Congress and became law on June 20, 1874. Included in the authorization was the authority to establish additional stations on the East Coast and on the Great Lakes. The first of the new East Coast stations were built in Virginia and Maryland. By the winter of 1875-76 they were operational.[10]

The effectiveness of the new life saving organization could be measured in cold impersonal numbers. From November 1, 1871, until June 30, 1876, 273 vessels wrecked. Including their cargos, they were valued at $7,840,074. Of this amount, $5,354,300 in property was saved; of 3,230 lives imperiled, only 41 were lost. It was an outstanding record of achievement when compared with the earlier carnage.[11]

The life savers remained as part of the Revenue-Marine until 1878 when, through an act of Congress, they became a separate agency of the Treasury Department as the United States Life-Saving Service.[12] President Rutherford B. Hayes appointed Kimball as the General Superintendent of the new Service. It was at this point that the legend of the "storm warriors" was born.

1. *History of the Great Lakes*, p. 723.

2. *Annual Report, U.S. Life-Saving Service, 1876*, p. 48.

3. Bennett, "The Life-Savers," p. 58.

4. Piper, "The Life-Saving Service," p.2.

5. *Annual Report, U.S. Life-Saving Service, 1876*, p. 846.

6. Bennett, "The Life-Savers," p. 58.

7. Bennett, "The Life-Savers," p. 58; Sumner I. Kimball ran the Life-Saving Service as General Superintendent for 44 years, finally retiring at age 81 when the United States Coast Guard was created from the merging of the Service and the Revenue-Marine. By all accounts he ran an honest, efficient and non-corrupt organization.

8. *Annual Report, U.S. Life-Saving Service, 1876*, p. 846.

9. *Annual Report, U.S. Life-Saving Service, 1876*, p. 831; "The Life-Saving Service," Republic, p. 84.

10. *Annual Report, U.S. Life-Saving Service, 1876*, pp. 852-853.

11. *Annual Report, U.S. Life-Saving Service, 1876*, p. 861.

12. Bennett, "The Life-Savers," p. 59.

Part II

Life Savers on the Great Lakes

A Great Lakes Beginning

As the result of the June 20, 1874, Congressional action, the Life-Saving Service was organized into 12 districts, three of which were on the Great Lakes. The Eighth District consisted of lakes Erie and Ontario. The Ninth was lakes Huron and Superior and the Tenth, Lake Michigan.[1] Congress authorized the construction of 30 stations on the Great Lakes. They consisted of two complete life saving stations and two lifeboat stations on Lake Ontario, one complete life saving station and four lifeboat stations on Lake Erie, four complete life saving stations and one lifeboat station on Lake Huron, four complete life saving stations on Lake Superior, three complete life saving stations and nine lifeboat stations on Lake Michigan.[2]

A superintendent was assigned to each Great Lakes district at a salary of $1,000 per year. This was in contrast to the $1,500 for the superintendent of the New Jersey stations.[3] Keepers were appointed at a salary of $200. Full-time surfmen were paid $40 per month during the season. The 1874 act set volunteer wages at $10 for every occasion in which they actually

saved life during a wreck and $3 for every drill attended.[4] This was amended in the 1878 act to a maximum of $10 for each time of assistance without regard to actually saving of life, thus closing an irritating loophole. In addition, volunteers were to attend drills not more than twice monthly at the discretion of the general superintendent. Volunteer crews were required to be enrolled at the station and a list maintained in the office of the Secretary of the Treasury. They were also subject to all of the rules and regulations of the Service and were eligible to receive all applicable medals. The crews were not simply assembled from the public at large from whoever showed up at the station when the alarm rang.[5] Despite good intentions, securing volunteer crews was often a problem, even in a heavily populated area like Chicago. After trying for two years, in 1878 the Service admitted defeat and converted the Chicago lifeboat station to a life saving station complete with a full-time crew.[6]

Although authorized by the 1874 act, the stations varied as to when they were placed into operation.[7]

Eighth District

Station	Type	In Operation
Lake Ontario		
Oswego	Lifeboat	1876
Charlotte	Lifeboat	1876
Lake Erie		
Fairport	Lifeboat	1876
Cleveland	Lifeboat	1876
Marblehead	Lifeboat	1876
Presque Isle	Life Saving	1876
Lake Ontario		
Big Sandy Creek	Life Saving	1877
Salmon Creek (Mexico Bay)	Life Saving	1877
Lake Erie		
Buffalo	Life Saving	1877

Ninth District

Station	Type	In Operation
Lake Huron		
Point aux Barques	Life Saving	1876
Ottawa Point	Life Saving	1876
Sturgeon Point	Life Saving	1876
Forty-Mile Point	Life Saving	1876
Thunder Bay Island	Lifeboat	1876
Lake Superior		
Vermilion Point	Life Saving	1877
Crisp's Point	Life Saving	1877
Two-Heart River	Life Saving	1877
Sucker River	Life Saving	1877

Tenth District

Station	Type	In Operation
Lake Michigan		
Point aux Bec Scies	Life Saving	1876
Grande Pt. Au Sable	Life Saving	1876
Grand Haven	Lifeboat	1876
St. Joseph	Lifeboat	1876
Chicago	Lifeboat	1876
Racine	Lifeboat	1876
Milwaukee	Lifeboat	1876
Sheboygan	Lifeboat	1876
Two Rivers	Lifeboat	1876
Beaver Island	Lifeboat	1877
North Manitou Island	Lifeboat	1877
Grosse Point	Lifeboat	1877

As the Life-Saving Service grew in stature and experience and shipping expanded, the number of Great Lakes stations also increased. The 1878 act added two Lake Michigan life saving stations, one at Sleeping Bear Point and one at Bailey's Harbor and four lifeboat stations, at Manistee, Ludington, Muskegon and Kenosha. Lake Superior received a complete life saving station near the west end of the mouth of the Portage Lake and Lake Superior Ship Canal. Lake Huron received a complete life saving station at Port Austin, another at

FIGURE 12
One of the Lake Superior "shipwreck coast" stations.
Author's Collection

Middle Island and a lifeboat station at Sand Beach Harbor.[8] In 1882 Congress authorized a complete life saving station at Grand Marais, Michigan, on Lake Superior and complete Lake Michigan stations at Frankfort, Pentwater, the mouth of the White River, Holland and South Haven, Michigan, Michigan City, Indiana, and Sturgeon Bay Canal, Wisconsin.[9] By 1893 there were 47 stations on the Lakes and by 1900, 60.[10] When the Life-Saving Service end-

ed in 1915, 63 Great Lakes stations were in operation.[11]

By any standard there was a valid requirement for life savers on the Great Lakes. For example, in 1869, 97 vessels were destroyed by a single four-day system. During the storm season of 1870-1871, 214 people died as the result

FIGURE 13
Keeper's residence and life saving station at Cleveland, circa 1885.
Great Lakes Historical Society

of shipwreck. As on the East Coast, in great measure the large loss of life could be traced to poor crew training and equipment deficiencies.[12] No government life saving capability was on the Great Lakes until 1854 when an appropriation provided for $12,500 for that purpose. At the direction of the Secretary of the Treasury, nine lifeboats were placed on Lake Ontario, 14 on Lake Erie, 23 on Lake Michigan and one on Lake Superior. All were volunteer manned and maintained.[13]

In 1880 the commerce on the northern Great Lakes alone was considerable.[14]

1,459 sailing vessels of	304,932.32 tons burden
931 steam vessels of	212,045.30 tons burden
572 canal boats of	47,159.25 tons burden
165 barges of	40,965.26 tons burden
3,127 vessels of	695,162.13 tons burden

To put this amount of shipping into perspective, there were 552 wrecks on the Great Lakes during the 1879-80 season. This broke down into 25 in July, 47 in August, 72 in September, 72 in October, 119 in November, 12 in December, one in February, four in March, 118 in

April, 40 in May and 42 in June. A total of 35 lives and $1,168,675 in vessels and cargo were lost. The 552 disasters separated into eight founderings, 160 strandings, 182 collisions and 202 miscellaneous accidents such as explosions and fire.[15] This was all in just one shipping season. In the 20 years between 1878-1898, nearly 6,000 vessels wrecked on the Lakes.[16] The life savers clearly had their work cut out.

Great Lakes sailing is considerably different from the salt water variety. That difference is explained by the comments in the following 1882 article from *Frank Leslie's Popular Monthly.*

"No feeling is more deeply rooted in the heart of an old salt than is his profound scorn and contempt for the fresh-water sailor. To his thinking his brother tar of the Great Lakes is a wretched make believe, whom he mentally catalogues with river steamboat men and canal boat hands. He has small belief in the stories he hears of great storms and shipwreck on these landlocked waters, or if he accepts the fact of frequent and terrible disaster, he ascribes it to the poor seamanship of lubbers. He has always longed to try his hand at this apparently comfortable and very condensed navigation, and show them how a seaman does it.

"When in his wanderings finally gets afloat upon the great fresh water seas, there are surprises, there is disillusion in store for him. Looking about him, he finds the shipping of the Great Lakes of proportions amazing to his briny mind. Upon the waterways of the great Northwest he sees a marine of noble dimensions, handled by a navy of practical navigators, whom he finds as sailorly a lot as he could ask to see.

"Sailing north into Lake Huron he meets ship after ship; big steam barges running under screw and sail, with one, two, three or more consorts in tow, these latter under half-canvas, bare poles, or full sail, indifferently, as wind and weather permit, this tow making six, eight, and 10 miles an hour out of Chicago, Milwaukee and the Michigan ports, with grain, lumber, everything, or ore-laden from Escanaba or Marquette. Against the sky the sails stand thick. Smoke wraiths lie curling along the horizon.

"Steam makes lubbers, thinks he. And steam is king on the inland seas. Funnels belching everywhere. The great steamers of the Lake Superior Transit, the Northwest Transportation, the Anchor Line, flying their private colors at the peak; barges and two little tugs with long log-rafts trailing astern, make a lively scene of it. The skies are blue and the waters still. There is no suggestion of danger, no suspicion of ferocity. In the calm of the ocean there is an undertone of power. The mighty heave of its breast, the muttering of the surf upon the shore, are echoes of the terrible grandeur of the storm. On the lakes there are weeks, in the summertime, when these great bodies of water sleep like placid woodland ponds.

"In the early fall the treacherous calm is broken. Later on, storm after storm roars over the

lakes. Squalls, terrible in their sudden fury, launch themselves and rage along the waterways. The light, fresh water flies before the wind. Immense seas are made in an incredibly short space of time. The water is torn up in sheets and hurled through the air. The seas run short and quick, thundering against a vessel's sides with rapid, heavy blows. There is no time for recovery between them. The lee shore is even alarmingly near. After the first September gale, the "lame ducks" are numerous. All the old rotten hulks from everywhere have poked out during the fair weather, and the first real blow cripples them often fatally. It must be said for the hardiness of lake sailors that they will go to sea in craft of amazing craziness. In the colder months there is ice to fight. Spray

FIGURE 16
A crude sketch of an early breeches buoy rescue on the Great Lakes.

Great Lakes Historical Society

FIGURE 17
Shipwreck on the Lakes.
Author's Collection

freezes flying. Ice incases masts, and ropes, and sails, the decks and clinging men. The suffering from such exposure is intense. Endurance is put to a frightful test in this fight with the gale and the ice. The wind has a death-cold touch; the flying water wraps the ship in icy shrouds; the rocks or the sands are thundering at hand.

"From about the middle of December until the first of April, the ice blockade is almost unbroken. With the first sign of clear water there is a stir among the shipping. The steamers cut their way out. Risks and profits both are great on these first spring trips. In the towns on the upper lakes supplies are running short, and a boat-load of provisions is snapped up at fabulous prices."[17]

1. The designations would later change into the Ninth (Lakes Erie and Ontario), Tenth (Lakes Superior and Huron) and Eleventh (Lake Michigan) and again into the Tenth (Lakes Erie and Ontario), Eleventh (Lakes Huron and Superior) and Twelfth (Lake Michigan).

2. U.S. Life-Saving Service, *Annual Report of the Operations of the United States Life-Saving Service For the Fiscal Year Ending June 30, 1876*, p. 807.

3. By the 1882 act, district superintendents' salaries for the Great Lakes were increased to $1,800, equal to that of the New Jersey district superintendent and $300 more than the salary of the district superintendents for the smaller East Coast districts.

4. *Annual Report, U.S. Life-Saving Service, 1876*, pp. 807-808.

5. *Revised Regulations*, p. 13, 20; *Annual Report, U.S. Life-Saving Service, 1878*, pp. 55-56.

6. *Annual Report, U.S. Life-Saving Service, 1878*, pp. 27-28.

7. *Annual Report, U.S. Life-Saving Service, 1876*, p. 817. *1877*, p. 30.

8. *Revised Regulations*, p. 17.

9. *Revised Regulations*, p. 23; *Annual Report, U.S. Life-Saving Service, 1883*, p. 37.

10. T. Michael O'Brien, *Guardians of the Eighth Sea, A History of the U.S. Coast Guard on the Great Lakes* (Washington D.C.: U.S. Government Printing Office, 1976), pp. 41-42.

11. *Annual Report, U.S. Life Saving Service, 1914*, p. 6.

12. O'Brien, *Guardians of the Eighth Sea*, p. 34; Myron H. Vent, *South Manitou Island, From Pioneer Community to National Park*, 1973, p. 59.

13. O'Brien, *Guardians of the Eighth Sea*, p. 33.

14. A.B. Bibb, "The Life-Saving Service on the Great Lakes," *Frank Leslie's Popular Monthly*, Volume XIII, Number 4, (April 1882), p. 386.

15. Bibb, "Life-Saving Service on the Great Lakes," pp. 386-387.

16. Vent, *South Manitou*, p. 59.

17. Bibb, "Life-Saving Service on the Great Lakes," p. 386.

Chapter 6

Organization

FIGURE 18
For 44 years Sumner
Increase Kimball was the
General Superintendent of
the U.S. Life-Saving Serv-
ice.

Author's Collection

As the organization of the Life-Saving Service matured, the duties and responsibilities of its personnel became more clearly defined. Although some changes, especially in terms of pay, were made periodically, the general scheme of organization remained constant.

The General Superintendent

With the title of General Superintendent, Sumner I. Kimball performed the duties of the chief officer of the Service under the immediate direction of the Secretary of the Treasury. Appointed by the President, the position also required confirmation by the Senate. Serving at the pleasure of the President, there was no limit on the term of office. In 1889 his pay was at $4,000 per year. Responsibilities included being in charge of the Service including all of its administrative matters. An assistant general superintendent appointed by the Secretary of the Treasury, helped the general superintendent, as needed. He was paid $2,500 per year. The office of the general superintendent was located in Washington and employed numerous clerks as well as a civil engineer, topographer, hydrographer and draftsman. The Board of Life-Saving Appliances reported directly to the general superintendent.[1]

The position of general superintendent and S.I. Kimball were one and the same. Kimball was not only the first general superintendent, he was the only one. He shaped it in his own image. The great success achieved by the Service was directly due to his efforts.

FIGURE 19
Life savers at Sleeping Bear Point perform the resuscitation drill. The inspector is timing it with a stop watch while the keeper looks on.
Sleeping Bear Dunes National Lakeshore

Kimball was born in 1854 in Lebanon, Maine. He spent his early years in the nearby town of Sanford. In 1855 he graduated from Bowdoin College. Aside from a short period teaching school at Orleans on Cape Cod, he had little contact with the sea. However, like all New Englanders of the time, during the stormy nights the old admonition "God pity the poor sailors tonight" was a familiar plea. After studying law for three years in his father's law office (I.S. Kimball), in 1858 he was admitted to the bar. In 1859 he was elected to the state legislature. By 1860 he had moved to Boston. The Civil War greatly expanded the opportunities in government, and in 1861 he accepted a clerkship in the office of the second auditor of the Treasury. By 1870 he had by successive promotions become the chief clerk of the Treasury. In 1871 Secretary of the Treasury George Boutwell appointed Kimball chief of the Revenue-Cutter Service. When the Life-Saving Service was formally organized under the 1878 act he became the first general superintendent.[2]

Kimball was extremely well regarded. In speaking of the success of the Revenue-Cutter Service, Congressman O.D. Conger of Michigan stated, "...The little black-eyed man...won for himself...distinction." Congressman Samuel

S. Cox of New York spoke eloquently of Kimball. "He did what nobody else thought worth doing. He organized what he had. The officers who preceded him for 20 years might have done the same thing. This man...seized the unused opportunities. He has contrived to set barriers against the sea." Politically Kimball was well protected, Cox stating, "I do not believe that any administration would be courageous enough to remove him for any cause. Besides, there is no party politics in it in the slightest degree." Kimball later served in several important temporary positions during the absence of the incumbents. Appointments included acting first comptroller of the Treasury and acting register of the Treasury.[3]

The general superintendent was also required to submit to Congress through the Secretary of the Treasury an annual report. Included in it was an explanation of the expenditure of funds appropriated for the Service and a summary of operations.[4] These annual reports became remarkable achievements in themselves, not only for telling the accomplishments of the Service to Congress, but also providing an invaluable research tool for future historians. The original reports were resplendent in the statistical detail they provided. Included were the numbers of rescues, by station and district, lives and property saved and lost and other recapitulations of services rendered. The richness of the narratives of rescues accomplished was an extra bonus. The reports were professionally written with a careful eye to assure that they would tell the Service's story well. The *Annual Reports* were widely distributed. Copies were given not only to members of Congress, the executive branch and foreign life saving agencies, but also to selected libraries including some in high schools.

The reports served a variety of purposes beyond being a required submission to Congress. Publishing the details of station operations ensured a high degree of truthfulness in the incident reports forwarded from the keepers. The *Annual Reports* were closely read by local mariners, especially those incidents concerned with shipwrecks and casualties. Any dubious claims or self-serving reports would quickly be recognized as such. As a result, any semblance of exaggeration was strictly avoided. Reports tended to understate the difficulty of operations. This calm matter-of-fact approach to often truly heroic rescues only increased the life savers' reputation. Since the annuals were read by crews throughout the Service, they also worked to familiarize men from one area with the operations in another. This helped to avoid repeating errors and inspired them to achieve success under extraordinary conditions and fostered a healthy rivalry. Because the Service was essentially composed of crews located in widely distant and isolated stations, the annuals also provided the common communication that knit them together into a smoothly operating organization. They promoted the esprit de corps that became a Service hallmark. The Service found that the annuals promoted the spirit of invention in terms of new life saving methods and equipment. In addition, the reports were studied by life saving organizations in other countries. They were an important method of promulgating new ideas and technologies.

From the 1876 report until that of 1890, they not only contained a plethora of statistics but also very detailed narratives of rescues and other operations. Starting with the 1891 report, until the 1914 report, the detailed narratives were reduced to concise summaries. Although the benefits of the narratives were widely recognized, because of the growth in Service operations and the increase in the number of stations, the very limited Washington staff could not physically produce the old narrative report. In addition, the Service was under considerable pressure to economize, and reducing the report size was one method used.[5]

The man most directly responsible for the reports was William D. O'Connor, the assistant general superintendent. The production of the reports consumed the majority of his time and effort. Born in Boston in 1832, he spent his early life as a writer, working as a newspaperman as well as producing both fiction and nonfiction books. In 1861 he started government service as a corresponding clerk for the Lighthouse Board, advancing to chief clerk in 1873. He was librarian of the Treasury Department from 1873-1875 and from 1875-1878 was a clerk in the Revenue-Marine. In 1878 he was appointed to the Life-Saving Service post.

His selection was a wise one. O'Connor was widely experienced in the Treasury Department and able to operate effectively within the labyrinth of Washington. Although technically

appointed by the Secretary of the Treasury, it is likely that Kimball made the actual choice. Both were old friends from the Treasury Department.

From 1878 until his death in 1889, O'Connor personally wrote all of the accounts of shipwreck involving loss of life. This talented man was able to take the bare facts of the incidents as forwarded by the districts and, using his descriptive power and imagination, weave them into stories powerful enough to grab the reader's attention. After O'Connor's death, Kimball wrote, "The most romantic sea tales of fiction are no more absorbing; and yet there is not in them a word of exaggeration, and participants in the scenes described have often and invariably pronounced them absolutely correct."[6] It was a fine memorial to an old friend.

Kimball believed that it was O'Connor's carefully crafted narratives that attracted so much interest in the reports, in turn requiring larger printings.[7]

The general superintendent exercised very detailed financial supervision over the Service's operations. For example, the 1878 act organizing the Service required him to "examine, before authorization, all requisitions of the district superintendents for outfits and supplies, and in supervising the expenditure of the appropriations made for the maintenance and support of the Service will have regard to the strictest economy consistent with its proper management. No expenditure from such appropriations by any officer or employee of the Service will be permitted without authority previously obtained of him, except in the emergencies specified...."[8]

He was also charged to "exercise constant vigilance over the official conduct of all the officers and employees of the Service, and will cause all complaints and alleged derelictions of duty which appear worthy of notice to be thoroughly and impartially investigated, and such further action to be taken in the premises as the interests of the Service may require."[9]

The Inspector

Next in authority to the general superintendent was the inspector, an officer in the grade of captain provided by the Revenue-Cutter Service under detail to the Service. He was stationed in New York City instead of Washington. New York City was desirable because most the Service's apparatus including the self-righting and self-bailing lifeboats, surfboats and related equipment was built there, and he had the responsibility of inspecting them during and after construction. Under the prevailing system, the government also purchased large amounts of other goods intended for the station use, which also required examination and management. In short, he was required to inspect all aspects of the Service including the men, stations, construction, operations, supplies, etc. An assistant inspector was detailed to help in completing his duties. The inspector was also required to make periodic inspections of stations and perform other duties as directed by the general superintendent.[10]

Under the supervision of the inspector, the Service operated supply depots at New York City, San Francisco and Grand Haven, Michigan. The Grand Haven depot was located in the old Plate Glass Company building. The depots served as central points for the reception, storage, care, assembling and shipment for a variety of supplies and equipment. Examples include: white lead, linseed oil, various manila lines, lanterns, Coston signals, anchors, soap, linen towels, tin cases and kerosene. Major items such as beach carts, surfboats, lifeboats and associated gear were also included. Supplies not available at Grand Haven were purchased locally, but only after assuring that the Service received the best possible price. The supplies were often shipped to the stations on the revenue cutters such as the *Andrew Johnson* during the course of its normal cruising. Sometimes, railroads were used.[11]

Inspections of stations were to be made quarterly, with the bulk of the actual inspections normally accomplished by the assistants. The Great Lakes stations were omitted from this requirement during the first quarter of the year due to the suspension of navigation. The inspections were made without warning and were very much of a "white glove affair." At every inspection the inspector was charged "to minutely examine each station." He was to inspect and closely compare with the inventory every article to assure what was on hand or accounted for and to make a note as to its condition. He was also to check that all equipment was clean and in proper repair, especially that "deck hatches in the self-righting and self-bailing lifeboats when housed are kept open, in order to ventilate the interior spaces below their decks which insures their durability and that the rollers of the carriages and skids are kept oiled and free from rust, which is necessary to facilitate the launching and hauling up of the boats." He was to check that each piece of apparatus

was in working order. In addition, he was to muster the keeper and crew to "satisfy himself that each member is qualified for the discharge of his duties." As part of the inspection the crew was required to demonstrate their proficiency in launching and recovering the surfboat through the surf and the use of the beach apparatus, lifecar and breeches buoy. He made certain that all drills were performed to the standard prescribed. Any lapses of discipline, wasteful use of stores or "unnecessary consumption of fuel" was checked.[12]

Inspections could be very frustrating for both keepers and crews. The Manistee station had six 17½-foot oars but since there were no 17½-foot oars in the Service, the inspector would list them as 18-footers. The next inspector, unable to find any 18-foot oars as listed on the previous inspection inventory, would measure them and discovering them to be 17½ feet, would list them as 17 feet and "gave the old man hell" for not being able to produce the 18-foot oars. The next man, unable to find any 17-foot oars as listed, measured, found them to be 17½ feet. After he again "gave the old man hell" he would list them as 18 feet thus starting the cycle again.[13]

During the crew muster he asked each member if he had any complaints and listened carefully to any made. If necessary, he investigated to learn the facts. Serious problems were submitted with recommendations to the general superintendent. Trivial ones he settled on the spot by the "exercise of good judgement and kindly treatment."

The inspector also received from the district superintendents all requisitions for repairs and supplies and forwarded them to the general superintendent with his recommendations. Quarterly reports, wreck reports and property inventories also flowed through him from the district superintendents to the general superintendent.[14]

The first inspector was the legendary Captain James H. Merryman who held the position from 1878-1890. Captain Charles H. McLellan of lifeboat fame was the inspector from 1904-1907.

The Assistant Inspector

The Revenue-Cutter Service also provided an assistant inspector in the grade of lieutenant for each district. He was to perform the duties of the inspector within his assigned district as directed by the inspector. During the active season, he visited each station monthly checking not only routine administrative affairs, but also evaluating the crew in their performance of duty. On the opening visit of each season he checked both keeper and crew for the necessary qualifications and dismissed any found not up to standard. On subsequent visits he evaluated any men newly hired. Any wreck involving loss of life required the assistant inspector to visit the station and investigate the disaster. He was to determine its cause and especially whether any of the life saving crew could be held at fault. The results of the investigation were published in the *Annual Reports*.[15] In practice, the assistant inspectors assumed the inspection duties of the inspector, especially as the number of stations increased.

District Superintendents

A superintendent was in immediate charge of each district.

"These officers must be men of good character and correct habits, not less than 25 nor more than 55 years of age when appointed, able to read and write English readily and have sufficient knowledge of accounts to properly transact the district business.

"They must be residents of the respective districts for which they are chosen, familiar with the line of coast embraced within them, and conversant with the management of lifeboats and other life-saving appliances. They are rigidly examined as to these qualifications by the General Superintendent and the Inspector. They are disbursing officers and paymasters for their respective districts. They are also ex officio inspectors of customs. They conduct the general business of the districts, look after the needs of the stations, make requisition on the General Superintendent for station supplies, repairs, etc., and upon receipt of authority see that these are furnished. They visit the stations at least once a quarter to acquaint themselves with their condition. On these occasions they pay off the crews and make such other disbursements as are authorized."[16]

District superintendents were poorly paid, in 1880 receiving a mere $1,000 yearly, equal to that of the lowest clerk in government service. Yet their duties required not only the mundane features of account keeping, but also judging the real value of men and facing great physical danger. Their responsibilities were of the highest order. By 1880, of eleven districts presided over by superintendents, two had already been killed in the line of duty and a third only narrowly escaped the same fate.[17] By 1889 pay for Great Lakes superintendents was increased to $1,800 per year. By any judgement, it was far too little. By 1912 the district superintendent vacancies were filled by competitive examination with all keepers in the district under 55 eligible to compete.[18]

As the Service grew, so did the job of district superintendent, not in scope but certainly in volume. As new stations were added, more equipment had to be accounted for, more men paid and business conducted. To keep up with the overwhelming administrative demands, many district superintendents hired clerks at their own expense, further reducing the effect of their salary. It must be realized that while they administered their districts, their real job was the supervision of keepers and crews, which meant constant travel thus compounding the problems of paperwork.[19]

During the inspections they were tasked specifically to inspect the facility including all equipment. When he felt it necessary, or unless he was specifically directed by the general superintendent, he inspected the crews and exercised them in the required drills. This was especially important if the assistant inspector did not live in the district. He also attempted to find if the crews were properly discharging their duties. Fixing the exact limits of the beach patrol was also his responsibility.[20]

Kimball had effectively created a dual sys-

FIGURE 20
Old Lake Michigan district superintendents are honored by a series of plaques on the stairs at Grand Haven's Escanaba Park. Life-Saving Service district superintendents included: Captains William R. Loutit 1877-1881, Nathaniel Robbins 1882-1898, Charles Morton 1898-1913 and Lt. Commander G.B. Lofberg 1913-1920.

Author's Collection

FIGURE 21
The Plum Island crew, circa
1914. The No. 1 surfman is
to the keeper's right, the
No. 2 on his left.
Robert Steffes Collection

tem of supervision by using both district superintendents and assistant inspectors. The district superintendents reported directly to him. The assistant inspectors reported to him through the inspector. The assistant inspectors focused on operational concerns such as drills and investigations while the district superintendents looked after the more administrative concerns of the stations. In some measure, especially in terms of the stations and the crew drills, the duties of the assistant inspector and the district supervisor were nearly the same. While this represented a duplication of effort, the result was that Kimball was able to cross check virtually every aspect of station functioning.

Keepers

Each station was in direct charge of a keeper. This job was without a doubt the most important one in the Service. His selection was critical not only to the efficient operation of the station but also to the lives of his crew and those to be rescued. Today the casual student of Great Lakes maritime history may think of a keeper only in terms of his position of being the "captain" of the lifeboat. In reality his duties were complex and demanding and his personal qualifications exacting.

In a 1912 publication, Kimball stated: "The

indispensable qualifications for appointment are that he shall be of good character and habits, not less than 21 nor more than 45 years of age; have sufficient education to be able to transact the station business; be able bodied, physically sound and a master of boat craft and surfing. He is usually nominated by the district superintendent, the initial step being left to that officer because of the extensive acquaintance he is supposed to have with the class of men from which the choice must be made, by reason of long residence among them, and because of the degree of responsibility resting upon him for the condition and conduct of his district. So much depends, however, upon the selection that an effort is made to eliminate, as far as possible, the chance that any political, social or personal interest shall intentionally or unintentionally enter in to it. In the vicinity of nearly all the stations there are numbers of fishermen and wreckers who have followed their callings from boyhood and become expert in the handling of boats in broken water, and among them there is usually someone who, by common consent, is recognized as a leader par excellence. He is the man it is desirable to obtain for keeper unless there be some fault of character which should exclude him. The nomination is accompanied by a statement of the reasons which guided the district superintendent in his choice, and a certificate of the candidate's physical soundness, made by a surgeon of the Marine Hospital Service, after a careful examination. Before granting approval, the General Superintendent submits the nomination to the district inspector for his views, and if after a thorough inquiry he concurs, the General Superintendent approves and the appointment made. If he does not concur, and his stated reasons seem to justify his conclusion, the General Superintendent takes such action as he deems best, either calling upon the district superintendent to submit another nomination, or visiting the locality himself and seeking the proper person."[21] As the Service matured, vacancies were filled from within, either by the No. 1 surfman of the station or from a nearby station.

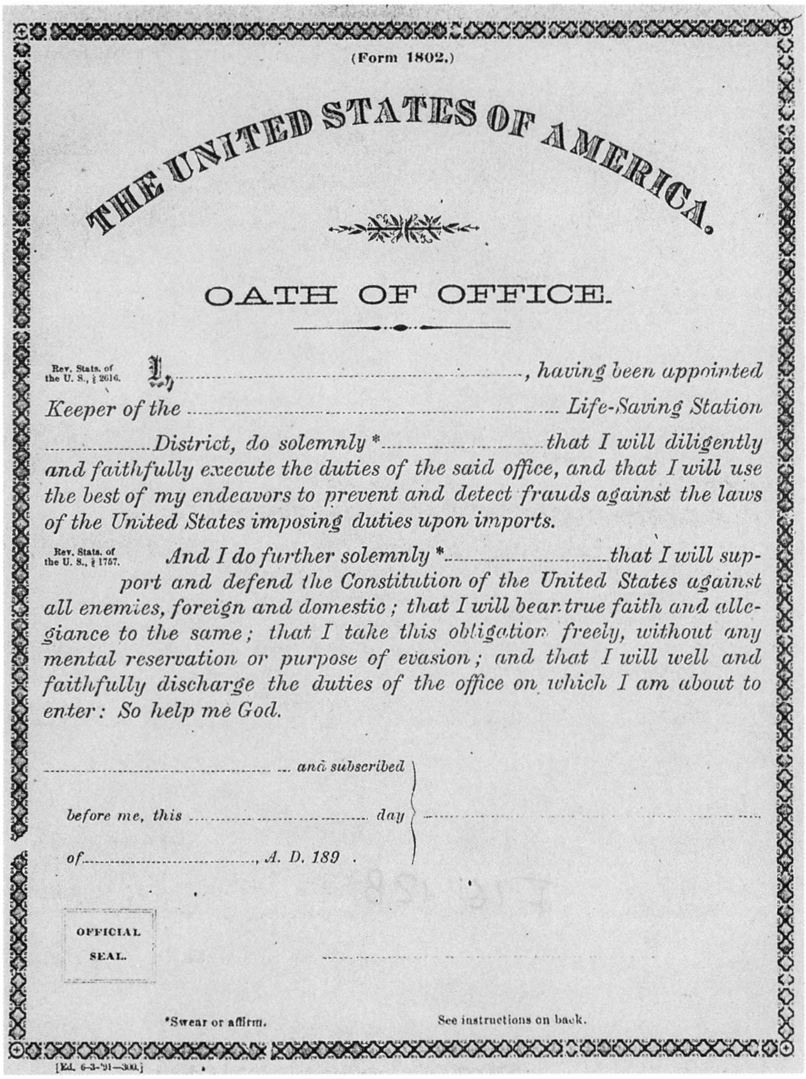

(Form 1802.)

THE UNITED STATES OF AMERICA.

OATH OF OFFICE.

Rev. Stats. of the U. S., § 2616. I, ..., having been appointed Keeper of the .... Life-Saving Station .... District, do solemnly * .... that I will diligently and faithfully execute the duties of the said office, and that I will use the best of my endeavors to prevent and detect frauds against the laws of the United States imposing duties upon imports.

Rev. Stats. of the U. S., § 1757. And I do further solemnly * .... that I will support and defend the Constitution of the United States against all enemies, foreign and domestic; that I will bear true faith and allegiance to the same; that I take this obligation freely, without any mental reservation or purpose of evasion; and that I will well and faithfully discharge the duties of the office on which I am about to enter: So help me God.

.... and subscribed before me, this .... day of ...., A. D. 189 .

OFFICIAL SEAL.

*Swear or affirm. See instructions on back.

[Ed. 6-3-'91—300.]

FIGURE 22
Keeper's oath of office.
Author's Collection

The Service was greatly concerned about the physical prowess of its keepers. Those over 55 years of age were required to have an annual examination by a medical officer of the Marine Hospital Service. The officer was to issue a certificate stating that the keeper was physically capable of performing all of the arduous duties of his position.[22]

By virtue of the conditions of their employment, keepers were sufficiently literate to be able to write the required reports and journal entries and maintain accounts, but they were not usually educated men. They were experts in rescue operations and handling crews in situations of extreme danger but not the sort of men that wrote extensively of their experiences. The author knows of no genuine keeper accounts of any rescue beyond those in official reports.

Keepers were required to live at the station and were held responsible for it and its property. Their biggest concern was their crews. "They are captains of their crews; exercise absolute control over them (subject only to the restriction of the regulations of the service and the orders of superior officers); lead them and share their perils on all occasion of rescue, always taking the steering oar when the boats are used, and directing all operations with the apparatus."[23] They also served as inspectors of customs and were responsible to take charge of all wrecked property until relieved by the owners or other authority.

The Life-Saving Service held the keeper strictly accountable for "proper care, preservation and good order of the apparatus, boats and their appurtenances and for the economical use of all supplies of every kind placed in their charge. They were to be careful to prevent waste, theft and misappropriation of all public property entrusted to their care and management, and the value of all articles not satisfactorily accounted for will be deducted from their pay."[24] The total equipment list for a station included 437 distinct types of articles "to be accounted for by the piece, or by the dozen, or by the thousand, or by the pound, ton, gallon or yard."[25] Even an item as mundane as paint was to be carefully rationed. It was not to be used on any station boats or apparatus without the approval of the district superintendent or the assistant inspector.[26] Keepers were especially charged to prevent the use of station property for private gain, a problem dating from the old East Coast volunteer days.

Regulations forbade the keepers from allowing intoxicating liquors to be kept or sold on the station premises or from having any person

FIGURE 23
This authentic Life-Saving Service library box is on display at the Huron City (Michigan) Museum.
Author's Collection

whatever from a person for a position in...the crew."[28]

Keepers were also held responsible for the security and contents of the station medicine chests. They were admonished not to open them unless required. The station library as provided by benevolent associations was another keeper responsibility. Most of the libraries were donated and maintained by the Seaman's Friend Society. Books were never to be removed from the station and had to be properly checked out by any crewmen or shipwreck survivor. The libraries were contained in portable wooden cases and could be exchanged between stations within the same district, but only after obtaining written approval from the general superintendent. Immediately after the exchange, the action had to be noted in the station journals to include a list of the books and the condition of each.[29]

The distribution of any clothing or supplies provided by the benevolent association to shipwreck victims was to be strictly controlled by the keepers. The items issued were to be entered in the journal and wreck report and also reported in the station expenditure book. The Women's National Relief Association was the principal supplier. If shipwreck victims were fed from the station mess, they were required to pay for the meals provided. If the victims were destitute, the vessel captain, owner or agent was to be billed at the rate of 25 cents for each meal. If the captain, owner or agent refused to pay, the bill was to be forwarded to the district superintendent.[30]

under the influence of liquor at the station. They were directed to be courteous and polite to visitors but not to allow them to either handle the equipment or deface the property by "writing or scratching."[27]

The keeper also maintained daily journals in which he dutifully recorded all station activities, both daily routine and shipwreck assistance. Forwarded through the district superintendent to the general superintendent, the journals provided a thorough written record of every aspect of station operations. Included were such items as the number of vessels passing, condition of the surf, surfmen on duty and drills conducted. If the station was involved in a wreck, or assistance of any kind, the keeper forwarded a complete report of every detail of the incident. The report, a Form 1806, was to be completed immediately after the incident and included the equipment used as well as a full narrative of the action. It was to be sent to Washington whenever help was provided, regardless of how little the actual assistance was. A false statement in any journal or report meant immediate dismissal. A keeper also would be instantly dismissed for accepting a "bonus, reward or compensation in any manner

Keepers were grossly under paid. Based on a surfman's pay of $40 per month in 1880 and a keeper's $400 per year ($33 per month), he received less per month than the men in his crew! He also paid the same 40 cents per day mess fee. The Service was particularly galled by the higher pay given a light keeper, an average of $600 per year. Keepers of important lights received between $800 and $1,000. When the duties of the two men were contrasted, the light keeper sat safe and warm in his light during a howling gale with only the responsibility of keeping the light burning, while the life saving keeper guided his surfboat through miles of raging waves threatening enough to make the boldest crew turn white, facing death at every moment, all for a paltry $400 a year![31]

By 1884 the pay for Great Lakes keepers increased to $700 per year and by 1912 to $1,000. The pay was determined by the length of the "season," or how long the station was open. On the Atlantic it was generally from September 1 to May 1. On the Great Lakes it ran from the opening of navigation, usually from April 15 to December 15. Kimball continued to plead for more money for the keepers, but judging by the miserly amounts of the increases, was never able to pay the men anything close to their true value.[32]

While the keepers were normally prohibited from hiring family members into their crews, "keeping" was often a family affair. There are several instances of brothers who were both captains of crews. For example: Henry Cleary at Marquette and George C. at Bois Blanc; Daniel L. Griesser at Marblehead and Winslow G. at Buffalo; Peter Olsen at Baileys Harbor and Ingar O. at Plum Island; and Albert Ocha at Portage and Frank O. at Tawas.[33]

Surfmen

The number of surfmen at each station was determined by the number of oars needed to pull the largest boat at the facility. Most commonly East Coast stations had only six men. Because the Great Lakes stations usually had the self-righting and self-bailing boats requiring eight oars, the crew was normally set at seven to eight men. For the 1899 season, 20 stations were crewed at eight men, 30 at seven, one at one and Cleveland at 10.[34]

Keepers were supposed to select the crews from the best of the able-bodied and experienced surfmen living in the local area. Since the quality of the crew not only reflected the reputation of his station, but also placed the lives of others and his own at risk, it was felt his selections would be good ones. The Life-Saving Service discovered however that sometimes "political, social and family influences were strong enough to so control the selection as to materially affect the efficiency of a crew."[35] Kimball considered this form of political corruption to be the "most insidious and potent evil that has ever threatened the welfare of the Service." To prevent such interference, regulations were implemented to require keeper and crew selection based solely on merit without regard to political affiliation. In 1882 the regulation was mandated by Congress and extended to the selection of district superintendents and inspectors. Another regulation prevented the keeper from having as crewmen, "his brother, father or son, except where adherence would be detrimental to the Service."[36]

Under these provisions, Kimball said that the stations were manned with the "...very pick and flower of the hardy race of surfmen which inhabit our shores. No better evidence of the virtue of the plan (Civil Service sic) can be desired than the fact that during the 18 years it has governed the selection of the men not one has shown the white feather. While the pages of

the annual reports of the Service are crowded with the records of gallant deeds that have made them famous throughout the land."[37]

The qualifications for becoming a surfman were stringent. As stated by Kimball in a 1912 Publication: "Upon original entry into the service a surfman must not be over 45 years of age, and sound in body, being subjected to a rigid physical examination by a surgeon of the Marine Hospital Service. Any surfman over 55 years of age could not be reenlisted without a certificate from a medical officer specifically stating that he was qualified physically for his duties. He is afterwards examined as to expertness in the management of boats and matters of that character by the inspector of the district. The regulations setting forth his duties being read to him, he is enlisted by signing articles by which he agrees to reside at the station continuously during the 'active season,' to perform

FIGURE 24
Captain John D. Persons of Thunder Bay Island in his punt, circa 1910. Keepers often built small boats in their spare time.
Jesse Besser Museum

such duties as may be required of him by the regulations and by his superior officers, and to hold himself in readiness for service during the inactive season, if called upon. Desertion entails a forfeiture of his wages, to be exacted in the discretion of the General Superintendent. His compensation is $50 per month during the 'active season' and $3 for each occasion of service at other times. Beyond the wages mentioned, the surfmen receive no allowances or emoluments of any kind, except the quarters and fuel provided at the stations. Their food and clothing they themselves supply."[38] Full-time crewmen were required to live at the station.

FIGURE 25
Surfmen in the cart harness. The North Manitou Island crew is ready to start the breeches buoy drill.
Sleeping Bear Dunes National Lakeshore

Rules prohibited a life saver from holding an interest in a salvage or wrecking company or from being entitled to any salvage resulting from his official actions. The regulation did however allow a surfman to claim compensation if any of his personally owned boats, wagons or other apparatus were used during an incident. He also could receive a reward for "labor performed, or risk incurred at wrecks, as owners or masters of vessels or other persons may see fit to voluntarily bestow upon them," but were forbidden to solicit any rewards.[39] Surfmen also could not be discharged without good reason. However, the keeper could dismiss him instantly for well proven "neglect of patrol duty or disobedience or insubordination at a wreck." Being absent without a satisfactory explanation or drunk at any time also meant instant dismissal.[40] Other cases required referral

to the general superintendent.[41] Regulations stated that drunkenness, profanity or any scandalous conduct showing lack of good morals was strictly forbidden. The punishment was dismissal.[42]

Once dismissed, it was possible for a surfman to be reinstated. For example, on June 13, 1898, a Thunder Bay Island surfman was discharged for failure to follow the station rules. Six months later, on the recommendation of the keeper and district superintendent and the admission of error and strong promise to be a model surfman, Kimball allowed him to be reinstated.[43]

Should a crewman become disabled by injury or disease in the line of duty, he was entitled to full pay for up to a year. The general superintendent could extend this entitlement for another year with the approval of the Secretary of the Treasury. Upon death in the line of duty the life saver's widow or children under 16 years were eligible to receive his pay for two years. The pay ceased when or if the widow remarried or the children reached age 16. In both examples any remaining pay would be divided among remaining beneficiaries.[44]

The surfmen in each crew were ranked by the keeper in terms of experience and ability. The most competent was the No. 1 and the least experienced or newest, No. 8. In the absence of the keeper, the No. 1 took over his duties unless two crews were working together and another keeper was present. Whenever two or more crews worked in tandem, the most experienced keeper took charge and coordinated the effort.[45] Once the Service was fully established, new keepers were usually selected from the ranks of the available No. 1 surfmen.

Normally keepers would rehire the past season's crew whenever possible. On the last day of the season, the keeper was required by regulation to inform the surfmen that if they have "given satisfaction, that they (he) will expect to engage them for next season." However, if any of the men were not satisfactory, he would inform them then. After making a report on the matter to the district superintendent, the keeper would request permission to hire others.[46]

Although at first consideration the only qualification for the job of surfman might be that of boat handling, the Life-Saving Service placed heavy emphasis on reading and writing. The regulations stated, "If others equally as good in point of character and professional skill can be obtained, men unable to read or write will not be engaged."[47] Surprisingly, there was no requirement for a surfman to be able to swim.[48]

Surfmen frequently transferred between stations and districts. Not only was approval necessary from the district superintendents involved, but Kimball's agreement was also necessary.[49]

Besides life saving, the stations performed a variety of missions relating to the saving of property. Included were assisting getting stranded vessels afloat, retrieving them from dangerous situations, pumping them out, running lines between wrecked vessels and salvage tugs as well as warning off vessels heading for danger. By using the station telephone lines, messages could be sent to vessel owners and underwriters, and tugs and salvage outfits could be called. When the owner's representatives arrived on the scene, the life savers often ferried them back and forth between the shore and the wreck.[50]

Pay

The low pay for the surfmen, as with the keepers, was a continuous problem. For example, in 1880 the Ninth District (lakes Erie and Ontario) was authorized 52 full-time life savers. But between the opening of navigation and June 30, there were 56 changes of personnel due to discharge or desertion. Each change affected crew efficiency. During this period, lake sailors were paid $2 a day for the spring and summer sailing seasons and up to $4 for the fall. By comparison, the surfman received a mere $1.33 a day; with 40 cents deducted for messing, that left him a only 93 cents! The Service found that "heroes on 93 cents a day" were difficult to find and keep, especially if they had families. Although Kimball repeatedly pleaded with Congress for more money for his beleaguered men, his requests normally were ignored. As with the keepers, although he did achieve some periodic success, the men were never paid what they were worth.[51] Crews were paid quarterly. Should a man be dismissed during the quarter, he normally lost all pay due for the quarter.[52]

In 1882 the basic rate of pay for a surfman increased from $40 per month to $50, but still included no allowance for food or uniforms. The period of service was still only eight

FIGURE 26
At the ready, an old life saver stands prepared to heave a line.
Author's Collection

months. When it was realized that common unskilled day laborers received $1.25 per day as opposed to the life savers' $1.66 and that street car drivers were paid considerably more than the surfman, the situation was especially galling. A surfman's pay was roughly equal to that of a soldier or sailor, both of whom were fed and clothed by the government and received free medical care and pensions. As the number of life saving stations increased and lake commerce grew, the dangers faced by life saving crews and the discipline and training required made their work more hazardous and demanding. The poor pay continued to result in retention problems. In the spring of 1888 alone 31 percent of the Great Lakes surfman left to take other employment.[53] In 1890, 30 percent of the lakes' crews left. Great difficulty was experienced in replacing them.[54] In the spring of 1894 there continued to be a 30 percent rate. With the pay for lake sailors running at $4 to $5 a day, temptation was too much![55] Pleas for a salary increase where a common part of every *Annual Report.*

Congress finally responded to the appeals for better pay with the Act of July 22, 1892, increasing compensation from $50 to $65 monthly. While the act went a long way toward helping retain good men, it also created problems. It stipulated that the $65 rate applied only to surfman serving eight months or less. Working a single day more than eight months resulted in a rate of $60. Since crews on the lakes were employed from the opening to close of navigation, the exact period was unknown. Those on Lake Superior, with a shorter navigation season, usually served less than eight months thus receiving the $65 rate; those on the lower lakes usually worked more, receiving only $60 for the same work. Since the exact

early years from the problems associated with low pay and the resulting high turnover of skilled personnel. Resignations were common place. The men who stayed and suffered the long hours, poor pay and great danger did so both out of a dedication to the ideals of the Service and the pure exhilaration of their chosen work. They were life savers!

An examination of employment records shows that most Great Lakes surfman listed their previous occupations as either fisherman or sailor. The exceptions included raftsman, longshoreman, laborer, woodsman, farmer and quarryman. In the northern stations, many were Canadian immigrants.[59]

Until the arrival of the Civil Service system in 1896, the old spoils system was very much the order of business. Whatever political party was in power held the authority to fire vast numbers of government workers and replace them with loyal party members without regard to qualifications. While doubtless many appointees were fully capable, many were not. It was this system that Kimball worked hard to negate, especially at the crew level. No one knew better than he that the ability to pilot a surfboat through a raging gale and make a rescue was not the least dependent on party affiliation.

The spoils system however often tended to cast all government workers as incompetent political appointees, despite their

FIGURE 27
A Great Lakes keeper and crew, circa 1910. The sleeve numbers designate the surfman's ranking.
Institute for Great Lakes Research

period of employment was unknown until the end of the season, the new pay rate created havoc with both crews and the district superintendents who acted as disbursing officers.[56]

Despite the pay increase, surfmen were still unemployed approximately four months a year. This period of enforced vacation moved one surfman to observe, "Guess Uncle Sam thinks we can save enough in eight months to go into the banking business the other four."[57]

The Act of March 26, 1908, provided some relief, increasing the keepers pay from $800 to $1,000 and the No. 1's from $65 to $70. In addition, it allowed both keepers and crewmen one ration a day or at the "discretion of the Secretary of the Treasury, commutation thereof at the rate of 30 cents a ration."[58]

The Service continued to suffer during the

ability. As public dissatisfaction with the spoils system increased, their suspicions also increased. Whatever their past performance, the Life-Saving Service was not above reproach. This was especially true when muckraking newspaper reporters hungry for material of any kind, without regard to its accuracy, became involved.

The depression of 1893, not only hit the country hard but also affected the Life-Saving Service. Surfmen were paid only $60 a month and then only during the active season. For the other four months, they needed to find whatever odd jobs were available to tide them over until the next season. This dissatisfaction with pay resulted in fewer men willing to take the dangerous jobs offered by the Service. In 1893 more than 30 percent of the Great Lakes keepers and surfmen resigned, the result of the perceived lack of public confidence as much as the result of being tainted with the spoils system and low pay.[60]

High crew turnover was also driven by reasons other than low pay, poor working conditions and a lack of retirement. When individual station records are examined, the overall situation becomes much clearer. Between June 24, 1882, and April 20, 1892, a total of 52 men were employed at the Buffalo Station. Twenty-four resigned voluntarily, many because of the poor pay, but one left because the station was infected with fleas. Two deserted, one was rejected by the surgeon and eight transferred to other stations. Twelve were discharged for various reasons, including drunkenness, neglect of patrol and being "cowardly and untrustworthy." The Sheybogan Station had 41 men employed between July 1, 1880, and April 1, 1890. Three deserted, one died, seven transferred and 15 voluntarily resigned. Thirteen were discharged for reasons including insubordination and "running away with another man's wife." Between April 15, 1882, and August 18, 1891, 25 men were employed at the Vermilion Station. Four were transferred, 11 voluntarily resigned and six discharged. The reasons for discharges included failing to discover and report a signal of distress, circulating scandalous stories and drunkenness. No. 4 Surfman Louis Fisher deserted after Keeper James Carpenter shot his dog.[61] At Muskallonge Lake, men left for diverse reasons. One resigned because the "rules of the Service (were) too rigid." Another was discharged for "taking and selling copper pipe belonging to the *Pacific.*" No. 2 Surfman Warren Williams was discharged by Keeper John Frahm for being "timid."[62]

The examples cited are typical of the period. While the life savers were the "very pick and flower of the men that inhabit our shores," the reality was that the Service hired the best men available. The stress of the job, of living closely with others and working under very tight rules culled out those unable to perform to standard. The men that remained were the best. Those that left were mere humans.

As indicated by the personnel turnover and discharges, crews were not always well-functioning organizations. The Oswego Station in 1885 was a good example of the type of problems that could develop. Keeper Blackburn had been having earlier difficulties with his crew. They had met secretly to plot on how to defeat his efforts to work them into a team and gener-

ally did not respond to his orders. Blackburn complained to District Superintendent David Dobbins that he had "the worst crew I have ever had," and that he didn't think "there is a man in the Oswego Station that you can rely on." When the keeper accidentally opened a surfman's letter, the man had him arrested. It took a special visit by Dobbins to stabilize the situation.

A crew's relationship with a keeper was not always harmonious. The diary of a surfman at the Manistee station for 1904 reveals numerous complaints.

As might be expected, food was a major source of irritation. In exchange for $16 a month from each man, the keeper's wife was to provide all the food and prepare it. While the resulting meals may have been wholesome, they were also monotonous. Veal or fish were near constant entrees, and an unidentifiable product known as "pink cookies" was served at every dinner. It seems that the first thing a surfman did on his day off was to go to town and get a "damn fine supper." Only after a man saw the keeper's books did he realize how rewarding the deal was for the keeper. Food costs ran $65 a month, but with seven surfmen contributing $16 each, gross income was $112, resulting in a handsome monthly profit of $47. To get even, the crew occasionally raided the food locker at night or liberated a cake or two when the wife was not looking.

Signal drill was a particularly trying experience. The keeper was a Swede named John Hanson. Although he was a master mariner with years of ocean experience, his command of English was at times less than fluent. The crew kept complaining they would do better at the drill if they knew Swedish! After one scrape with the "old man" on missed signals, the diarist was put to work "scrubbing the boatroom with a brick." Problems with the next day's gun drill resulted in three men being put to work with bricks in the boatroom. When the keeper was in town on business and the No. 1 man ran the drills, all ran like clock work.

Hanson worked hard to maintain good order and discipline, but from the diary it's plain that he had a hard crew. On July 23, the keeper bawled out the entire crew, calling them a "pack of thieves" and the "poorest crew he'd seen in 17 years." It seems that the tongue lashing was caused when one of the men broke into the keeper's "likker" locker.

Despite their obvious disagreements, the crew continued to do its duties, although rarely to the

FIGURE 28
The Grand Marais station and crew, circa 1910. The men constantly suffered from low pay.

Michigan State Archives

standards of the "old man." Regular lifesaving drills and patrols were conducted, as well as housekeeping chores such as applying "Irish paint" or whitewash to the station fences and tending to the flower beds. During the course of the season, three surfmen quit, all as the result of disagreements with the keeper.[63] It was tough working for a hard keeper like Hanson.

On rare occasions crews were charged with neglect of duty. For example, in 1885 the newspaper *Inland Marine* claimed negligence by the Racine Station for failing to go to the aid of the Canadian schooner *Elgin.* When the inspector investigated, he found that the vessel went ashore five miles above Racine Point, which is four miles above the station. The vessel was so tight against a high bank that even when a tug went to haul her off, the tug's captain couldn't find her with "good glasses" until he was three-quarters of a mile away. It was impossible for the patrol to have sighted her. The inspector wrote the charges off as sensationalism by the paper in an attempt to build circulation.[64]

Civil Service Rules

The Life-Saving Service came under the auspices of the civil service rules by order of the President on May 6, 1896. The Service experienced problems in trying to decide how to apply the principle of competitive examination to decide the relative qualifications of their applicants. What the Service essentially wanted was a method of evaluating practical, hands-on experience. But under the new rules this was difficult to address.

Change always caused anxieties and the application of the civil service rules to the Service was no different. Frictions and delays occurred. Initially when keepers had a sudden vacancy in their crew they complained about the length of time it took to fill it under the new rules, or that the resulting man was unfit. Once they realized that they had the authority to hire a temporary man pending a permanent hire, or that they could dismiss a regular surfman for any reason within the first six months, the complaints stopped.[65]

The most serious trouble with the new system was encountered near the beginning and was caused by well publicized misrepresentations concerning the effect of the new rules on men already in the Service. As the 1898 report stated: "In one instance a person in the guise of an evangelist, styling himself 'Volunteer Chaplain for Life-Saving Stations,' who traveled from station to station in one of the largest districts upon the seacoast for the professed purpose of preaching the gospel and administering to the spiritual wants of the crews, and who largely lived upon their bounty, declared over his signature in a newspaper to which he was a contributor that all the men then in the Service were to be put to the test of a competitive examination in arithmetic, grammar, algebra, etc., and all who could not successfully pass were to be dismissed; and that the examination for admission to the Service embraced the same tests of educational attainments. Not withstanding the absurdity of the statement, many newspapers repeated the tale, some adding comments indicating that they believed it, and severely criticizing and condemning both the Life-Saving Service and the Civil Service Commission for insisting upon such preposterous requirements. The uproar created upon the coast can easily be imagined. Considerable effort was necessary to quiet the excitement among the surfmen and to allay their apprehensions and alarm."[66]

The problem came to the Great Lakes when a later report published by the press claimed that the lake districts were in "deplorable condition" as the result of the new rules. "Sometime ago the employees of the Service were put under the civil service, and it is claimed that it is impossible to get the proper kind of employees through any examination the commission may require. The men who are able to pass the mental examination, it is said, are not capable of sustaining the endurance and physical labors required of those who go to sea in times of storm to save human life. The men who for years have done this work, and are hardy and accustomed to the danger of wind and water, and have been seasoned by constant contact with the elements, are unable to pass the examination required.

"It has been brought to the attention of Congressmen that the whole service has become disorganized and is unfit for the duties required of it. It is claimed that when it becomes necessary to go out to save vessels or remove sailors from ships in distress, the lighthouse tenders are required to tie up, and the crews from those tenders are substituted for the crews of the Life-Saving Service secured through the examination of the Civil Service Commission."[67]

Kimball reacted to the statements by asking each Great Lakes superintendent to reply as to the status of the Service in his district.

The Ninth District Superintendent (lakes Ontario and Erie) replied, "As yet I have no reason or cause to feel that the application of the new rules has been in any way detrimental to the efficiency of the Service, the class of men so far selected under the new rules being fully up to the standard of those previously selected. The statements contained...so far as relates to this district, are utterly false and without foundation of any kind. There is no disorganization here; on the contrary, I claim that the discipline, efficiency and personnel of the station crews are far superior to what they were a few years since, and I have yet to hear the first word of criticism against them from the local public...there are no facts within my knowledge upon which any of the statements contained in the article referred to can be based, and my experience with the new rules is as a whole satisfactory....That article is an insult to the life savers of the Great Lakes; when they fail, there will be no use of calling upon the crew of any lighthouse tender. You can rest assured that there is nothing in this district giving any foundation for such a false statement. The efficiency of this district will stand the searchlight of the most rigid examination possible. There is no disorganization here; that fact can be stated in the most emphatic language."[68]

The Tenth District Superintendent, (lakes Huron and Superior) answered, "I believe the crews are fully as capable of doing good work as they ever had been. I cannot imagine where a basis for the statement contained in the second paragraph was obtained, as nothing has occurred in this district that will bear out any such statement. My experience in connection with the application of the civil-service rules has been satisfactory, and I have every reason to believe the keepers of the stations are equally satisfied with them. So far as this district is concerned, I do not believe one of the statements contained in the clipping is borne out by the facts."[69]

The Superintendent of the Eleventh District (Lake Michigan) replied, "The Service in this district has not been affected unfavorably so far by the application of the civil-service rules, and so far the surfmen that have been selected have

FIGURE 29
The Ludington station, circa 1890. The Service was under constant pressure to hire the politically connected rather than the best.
*Rose Hawly Museum
Mason County
Historical Society*

in every case but one proved to be satisfactory. The statement referring to lighthouse tenders furnishing men to take the place of crews in case of emergency did not occur in this district, and there is no statement in the...clipping that is borne out by the facts so far as this district is concerned. There were 24 selections made under the civil-service rules in this district during the last active season, and as I have before said, they all proved to be satisfactory but one, and this one might have pleased some other keeper."[70]

The yellow journalism did impact negatively on the Service. Until the effects of the new rules were understood, many sailors and fishermen were deterred from seeking employment with the life savers resulting in more limited eligibility lists than desired. Some stations needed to use temporary men to maintain their full complement until permanent men could be hired. Within a year the situation had generally rectified itself.

On balance, the new selection methods may well have been better than the old. Between April 1, 1897, the date of the first admission under the new rules, and December 1, 1898, a period of 20 months, 398 surfmen were appointed, 17 of which proved unsatisfactory. During the preceding 20 months, August 1, 1895, through April 1, 1897, 459 men were appointed under the old rules, of whom 46 proved to be unsatisfactory. A comparison shows that under the old method, one in 10 was unsatisfactory while the rate for the new method was one in 23.[71]

Despite the difficulties of operating under the new rules, the Service on the whole welcomed them. The object of the civil service rules was to eliminate the politics of appointment to Federal jobs; to secure for the government the *best qualified* men available without regard to party affiliation or personal influence. This had long been the objective of the Life-Saving Service since its organization in 1871. The *best qualified* objective was reaffirmed in the act of May 4, 1882, providing that "the appointment of district superintendents, inspectors and keepers and crews of life saving stations shall be made solely with reference to their fitness and without reference to their party affiliations."[72] It is believed this is the first Federal act ever made specifically excluding political influence in government appointments. The Service had lobbied long and hard for this protection, but it wasn't always enough to keep scheming politicians at bay.

This simple idea, that only the best would be selected without regard to politics, was the most important credo of the Service. The men of the Service thought the rationale behind its logic was irrefutable. Surely even politicians could understand that in the midst of a howling gale and crashing seas, nobody gave a damn whether the man next to you was a Republican or Democrat, or who he was related to, only that he was the *best qualified* to man the oar.

However, as surely as politician and crook are synonymous, the leadership of the Service, from general superintendent to keeper, was constantly under pressure to make appointments and decisions based on the appeals of politicians, local and national. The life savers reported that "praise, flattery, promises, abuse, falsehood, ridicule, cunning, deception, diplomacy and the whole catalog of shrewd devices for controlling the action of men were resorted to."[73]

Although the 1882 act provided some protection, it wasn't iron clad. "...Frequent endeavors were made, sometimes springing from more reputable sources than could be expected, to induce the officers of the Service to circumvent the law or to treat it as a dead letter. Efforts to distort its meaning, specious arguments to show how appointments and employment could be confined to the ranks of the dominant party without its violation, and various devices were tried to render it abortive. It is gratifying to say that these attempts were always ineffectual, but it took time and effort to combat them and make them so."[74]

When administrations changed, unfounded charges were often made that the Service had violated the law on behalf of the party just voted out. This required the Service to devote critical time, effort and resources to prove the charges false, all of which made the principal duty of the Service only more difficult. This nearly constant political warfare continued for a quarter of a century, until the arrival of the Civil Service rules. Thus, while the new rules were difficult to adapt to, they provided an umbrella under which the Service could flourish.

Pensions

Similar to the problem of low salary was that of an adequate pension. However, there was a critical difference; there was a salary but there was no pension. Life savers no longer able to work due to age or illness, or their widows or orphans upon their death on duty, received no

payment beyond the temporary two year provision previously discussed. Old or disabled life savers no longer able to pass the annual physical sank into poverty. If killed in action, their families often became destitute.

Repeatedly, Kimball tried to maneuver an authorizing bill through Congress, only to meet with continuous failure. His efforts focussed strictly on those who faced the greatest danger, the crews, keepers and district superintendents. There was no attempt to include the Washington bureaucracy. Despite the hazards and dangers faced, and heroics performed, a parsimonious Congress refused to grant these deserving men even the pittance of a pension. The monies sought were not large. A district superintendent was considered equivalent to a captain in the Navy at $30 per month, a keeper equal to an ensign at $15 and a surfman a seaman at $8. The pensions would be paid only on discharge from the Service due to injury or disease incurred in the line of duty or to the widow in death. Congress had set an earlier precedent when it granted a pension of $30 per month to the widow of District Superintendent J.J. Gutherie, killed while assisting the rescue of survivors from the USS *Huron* on November 25, 1877. Similar legislation also was intro-

FIGURE 30
Working the boats was the most dangerous part of a life saver's job. The Grand Marais crew stands ready with the surfboat. A young Benjamin Trudell is at the stern.
Ted Richardson Collection

duced for District Superintendent Joseph Sawyer, lost off Rogers City, Lake Huron on October 20, 1880.[75]

The numbers of men lost in the line of duty were significant. Between May 1, 1876, and November 18, 1901, 177 life savers perished in the line of duty or died as the result of service-incurred disease and exposure. Forty (22.5 percent) of the losses were to the Great Lakes

FIGURE 31
Attracting and holding good men was always a problem. The Michigan City crew works its way through the rollers.
Grand Haven Library

crews. Of the 40 men, half died directly as the result of operations and the remainder of disease. The largest operational cause of death was the capsizing of boats, but other instances included drowning while practicing swimming, boat drill and being hit by a railroad train while on patrol duty. Six of the Great Lakes deaths came in the loss of the Point aux Barques crew in the ill-fated April 23, 1880, rescue attempt of the schooner *J.H. Magruder*. Included in the Great Lakes figures were three superintendents, nine keepers and 28 surfman.[76]

Life saving was considered so dangerous an occupation that until roughly 1890 it was virtually impossible for a surfman to purchase life insurance. It was largely through the efforts of H.M. Knowles, district superintendent of the Third District, that insurance companies were convinced of the acceptability of risk.[77]

Although often treated separately, pay and pensions were interrelated. While many men left the Service because of the poor pay, the leadership felt that the lack of pensions was the bigger problem. Those men that did remain usually did so only in the hope that Congress would eventually pass a pension bill. Although

on many instances pension bills were reported out of various committees, none were acted on by both houses. There was a widespread belief among many members of Congress that in granting a pension bill to the life savers, the precedent would be set for providing a pension generally to civil employees of the government. It was a principle Congress could not accept.[78] Since Congress did grant pensions to members of the armed services, the life savers attempted to argue that the similarities of dangerous duty also required an adequate pension for them.

The situation on the lakes was expressed by Mr. William Livingston, the president of the Lake Carriers Association. In a letter dated March 1, 1904, to the Committee on Interstate and Foreign Commerce of the House of Representatives, he advocated strong support for a pension bill. In part, he stated, "At the present time the Life-Saving Service upon the lakes...is in a seriously crippled condition on account of the lack of competent surfmen in the stations. When the lake stations closed last December, a large number of them were without full crews of regular surfmen, the vacancies being filled with untrained and undisciplined men. As the number of men constituting a crew generally corresponds to the number of oars to be pulled in the principal boat of the station – each man to an oar – and as a single poor oarsman always impedes the boat and is liable to jeopardize the safety of all on board, the inefficiency of an incomplete crew of regulars is obvious. I understand that the case will be worse at the opening of navigation in the spring, as many whose terms of enlistment then expire will have determined not to reenlist. In fact the crews are being depleted by the gradual separation from the Service of its best men, and only men inferior to these, and even then in insufficient numbers are obtainable for recruiting. This state of affairs, if continued, must soon result in disaster and shame."

He recommended two solutions: to increase the pay and, most critical, provide a pension. Livingston's letter went on to argue that in the long term it was far more cost effective to provide a pension and retain the best men than suffer the inefficiency of the high turnover rates.

Even a salary increase would not be as effective as a pension. His eloquent reasoning went unheeded.[79]

The employment records for the Great Lakes supported Mr. Livingston's concerns. During the 1904 season some stations were short as many as four regular surfmen. In their place temporary men or volunteers were used. The situation worsened in 1905 when some Tenth District (lakes Erie and Ontario) stations were short six men! During the same year the Eleventh District (lakes Huron and Superior) was in comparatively good shape with the stations being fully staffed or short no more than two. 1906 was a good year with minimal shortages. In contrast, 1907 was terrible. In the 10th District, Niagara, Fairport and Cleveland all averaged five men short. Others were missing two to four men. The 11th District was better off, but still the Two-Heart Station was short five men throughout the critical fall season. The Twelfth District (Lake Michigan) had severe problems at Michigan City, South Chicago, Old Chicago, Milwaukee and Sheboygan. 1908 was just as bad. The situation stabilized in the years 1909 through 1912, but spot shortages were a problem. Life saving was a job that increasingly failed to attract and hold the best men.[80]

The argument was made that the Service retained their high reputation in the face of a steady deterioration of the quality of personnel because of the continuous improvement in their equipment. In effect, better life saving boats and apparatus offset the lowered physical standards and morale of the corps.[81]

That the Service used men up at a rapid rate cannot be denied. The constant exposure to cold winds and water, long hours, physical exertion and danger simply burned men out. Using up their youth, it cast them aside like driftwood.

At first young men from the coast often looked to the Service as a good way to earn a living. It offered a career well suited to their unique skills. As cities grew and the cost of living increased, better opportunities presented themselves. Instead of joining the Service, the men took up such mundane professions as street car conductors, police officers and factory workers as well as a host of other "civilized" employment. The new jobs paid better. The work was easier and hours far less. Opportunities for advancement were increased as was the standard of living they could provide their families. Pensions were also more commonplace. When contrasted with what the Service offered, it was no wonder that problems manning stations with qualified men were encountered.

In the end, the Life-Saving Service's efforts at obtaining a pension were futile. It wasn't until the Service finally merged with the Revenue-Cutter Service to form the new Coast Guard that retirement benefits became a reality.

1. Sumner I. Kimball, *Organization and Methods of the United States Life-Saving Service* (Washington, D.C.: Government Printing Office, 1912), p. 11; There were only four assistant general superintendents during the Service's history: William O'Connor 1878-1889, Frank Baker 1889-1890, Horace L. Piper 1890-1905 and Oliver M. Maxam 1905-1915.
2. Edwin Emery, *History of Sanford, Maine* (Fall River, MA : privately printed, 1901), pp. 473-474.
3. Emery, *History of Sanford,* pp. 477-479.
4. *Revised Regulation for the Government of the Life-Saving Service of the United States and the Laws Upon Which They Are Based,* (Washington, D.C.: Government Printing Office, 1884), p. 19.
5. *Annual Report, U.S. Life-Saving Service, 1891,* pp. 83-85.
6. William D. O'Connor, *Heroes of the Storm* (New York: Houghton Mifflin and Co., 1904), p. xii.
7. O'Connor, *Heroes of the Storm,* pp. ix-xii.
8. *Revised Regulations,* pp. 38-39.
9. *Revised Regulations,* p. 39.
10. Kimball, *Organization and Methods,* p. 11.
11. Receipt, Muskallonge Lake Station, August 23, 1885; Receipt, Ship Canal Station, August 27, 1885; Letter, S.I. Kimball to Superintendent, 11th District, May 2, 1899; Letter, S.I. Kimball to Inspector, April 8, 1894, RG 26, NARA.
12. *Revised Regulations,* p. 40.
13. Surfman's Diary, Manistee County Historical Museum.
14. *Revised Regulations,* pp. 41-43.
15. Kimball, *Organization and Methods,* pp. 11-12.
16. By 1912 crews were paid monthly.
17. *Annual Report, U.S. Life-Saving Service, 1880,* pp. 44-45.
18. Kimball, *Organization and Methods,* p. 12.

19. *Annual Report, U.S. Life-Saving Service, 1900,* pp. 59-60.
20. *Revised Regulations,* pp. 43-44.
21. Kimball, *Organization and Methods,* pp. 13-14; By 1912 Keepers were appointed by joint recommendation of the district superintendent and assistant inspector.
22. *Annual Report, U.S. Life-Saving Service, 1882,* p. 38.
23. Kimball, *Organization and Methods,* p. 14.
24. *Revised Regulations,* p. 54.
25. Freeman, "The Life-Saving Service," p. 661.
26. *Revised Regulations,* p. 56.
27. *Revised Regulations,* p. 54.
28. *Revised Regulations,* pp. 49-50.
29. *Revised Regulations,* pp. 53-54.
30. *Revised Regulations,* p. 55.
31. *Annual Report, U.S. Life-Saving Service, 1881,* pp. 90-92.
32. Kimball, *Organization and Methods,* p. 14.
33. *Register of Life-Saving Stations,* 1901-1914.
34. Letter, Horace L. Piper, Acting General Superintendent to Superintendents 9th, 10th, 11th Districts, March 11, 1899, RG 26, NARA.
35. Kimball, *Organization and Methods,* p. 15.
36. Kimball, *Organization and Methods,* p. 15. *Annual Report, U.S. Life-Saving Service, 1884,* p. 63.
37. Kimball, *Organization and Methods,* p. 16.
38. Kimball, *Organization and Methods,* p. 16. *Annual Report, U.S. Life-Saving Service, 1882,* p. 38.
39. *Revised Regulations,* p. 58.
40. *Circular 175,* U.S. Life-Saving Service, December 8, 1884, RG 26, NARA; *Revised Regulations,* p. 58.
41. Kimball, *Organization and Methods,* p. 16.
42. *Revised Regulations,* p. 65.
43. Letter, S.I. Kimball to Secretary of the Treasury, January 6, 1899, RG 26, NARA.
44. *Circular 109,* July 12, 1900, U.S. Life-Saving Service, RG 26, NARA; Kimball, *Organization and Methods,* pp. 16-17; *Revised Regulations,* pp. 22-23.
45. *Revised Regulations,* p. 55.
46. *Revised Regulations,* pp. 44-49.
47. *Revised Regulations,* p. 48.
48. Letter, S.I. Kimball, to Muskegon Station, March 3, 1899, RG 26, NARA.
49. Letter, Horace L. Piper, Acting Superintendent to Superintendent 10th District, April 6, 1890, RG 26, NARA.
50. Kimball, *Organization and Methods,* pp. 31-32.
51. *Annual Report, U.S. Life-Saving Service, 1880,* pp. 44-45.
52. Francis Albert Doughty, "Life at a Life-Saving Station," *Catholic World,* Vol. 65, (July 1897), p. 516.
53. *Annual Report, U.S. Life-Saving Service, 1888,* pp. 49-50.
54. *Annual Report, U.S. Life-Saving Service, 1890,* p. 66.
55. *Annual Report, U.S. Life-Saving Service, 1891,* p. 85.
56. *Annual Report, U.S.Life-Saving Service, 1894,* pp. 11-12; *Circular 126,* September 1, 1894, U.S. Life-Saving Service, RG 26, NARA: *Circular 149,* August 26, 1892, U.S Life-Saving Service, RG 26, NARA.
57. *Detroit Free Press,* August 16, 1908.
58. *Annual Report, U.S. Life-Saving Service, 1908,* p. 24.
59. Permanent Record of Employment, U.S. Life-Saving Service, RG 26, NARA.
60. O'Brien, *Guardians of the Eighth Sea,* p. 41.
61. Record of Employment, U.S. Life-Saving Service, RG 26, NARA.
62. Record of Employment, U.S. Life-Saving Service, RG 26, NARA.
63. Surfman's Diary, Manistee County Historical Museum.
64. Letter, Inspector 10th District to S.I. Kimball, August 31, 1885, RG 26, NARA.
65. *Annual Report, U.S. Life-Saving Service, 1898,* p. 60.
66. *Annual Report, U.S. Life-Saving Service, 1898,* p. 51.
67. *Annual Report, U.S. Life-Saving Service, 1898,* pp. 51-52.
68. *Annual Report, U.S. Life-Saving Service, 1898,* p. 52.
69. *Annual Report, U.S. Life-Saving Service, 1898,* pp. 52-53.
70. *Annual Report, U.S. Life-Saving Service, 1898,* p. 53.
71. *Annual Report, U.S. Life-Saving Service, 1898,* pp. 53-54.
72. *Annual Report, U.S. Life-Saving Service, 1898,* p. 54.
73. *Annual Report, U.S. Life-Saving Service, 1898,* p. 55.
74. *Annual Report, U.S. Life-Saving Service, 1898,* p. 55.
75. *Annual Report, U.S. Life-Saving Service, 1881,* pp. 59-64, *1888,* pp. 55, 61-62.
76. *Annual Report, U.S. Life-Saving Service, 1888,* pp. 59-60; *List of Persons Who Have Died,* RG 26, NARA.
77. Valentine Scrap Book, Ted Richardson Collection.
78. *Annual Report, U.S. Life-Saving Service, 1910.*
79. *Annual Report, U.S. Life-Saving Service, 1904,* pp. 47-48.
80. Vacancies of Crews, 1904-1912, RG 26, NARA.
81. *Annual Report, U.S. Life-Saving Service, 1913,* p. 23.

Station Construction

Chapter 7

FIGURE 32
The old Point aux Barques station house is now at the Huron City (Michigan) Museum grounds. It is an important example of the original Great Lakes stations and distinctive of the "stick style" of architecture.
Author's Collection

The Act of 1874 provided for three classes of station. First class or life saving stations were intended for remote, uninhabited locations where volunteers could not be easily assembled for a rescue and where no shelter for shipwreck victims was nearby. These stations were equipped with surfboats, beach apparatus and other appliances designed to save lives from stranded vessels. Typically, these vessels stranded on offshore sandbars. The stations were built to be able to provide accommodations for victims as well as the life saving crews. A complete life saving station, including equipment, cost $5,302.15.[1]

As was common with stations throughout the Service, Great Lakes stations, both life saving and lifeboat, were not of one design. The designs and construction changes reflected both the added requirements for room for the crew and equipment and the architectural styles of the period. In addition, Wick York, in his paper *The Architecture of the U.S. Life-Saving Stations,* noted, "although many similar stations of a particular type were constructed from a single plan, no two were exactly alike."[2]

During this period in American history the "stick" architectural form was in great vogue.[3] The first stations built on the Great Lakes were known as a "stick style" or "1874" type. Build of wood, they were characterized by "decorative wood bracketing in the roof gable and under the eaves...overhanging eaves, steeply pitched gabled roofs, towers and pointed dormers...."[4]

A contemporary source described the early stations as two-story buildings "built of tongued and grooved pine, with gable roofs, covered with cypress or cedar shingles, and strong shutters to the windows, and are securely bolted to a foundation of cedar or locust posts, sunk in trenches....Their architecture is of the pointed order, somewhat in the chalet style, with heavy projecting eaves and a small open observatory or lookout deck, on the peak of the

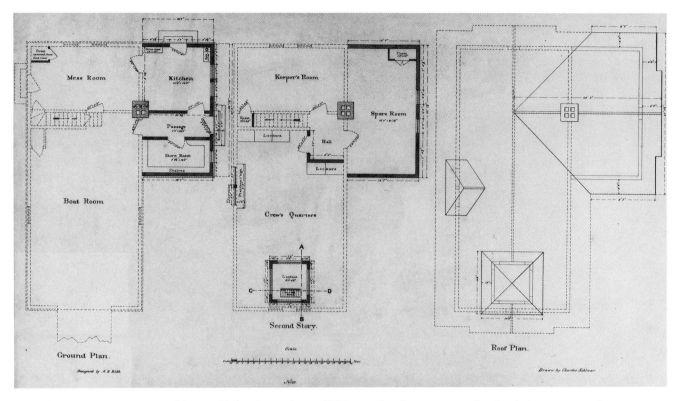

Ground Plan.   Second Story.   Roof Plan.

roof from which spires a flagstaff. The walls of the houses are painted drab, with darker color for the door and window trimmings, and the roofs dark red. Over the door is a tablet with the inscription 'U.S. Life-Saving Station.' The appearance of the houses is tasty and picturesque."[5]

In size, many early stations ranged from 18 to 20 feet in width by 40 to 45 feet in length. There were two rooms on the ground floor. The boat room was about 10 feet high and occupied

quarters for both keepers and crew were equipped with simple iron cots. Additional ones were available for shipwreck victims. In the better stations, interior walls were lath and plaster; otherwise bare wood was used.[8]

The architect for these original stations was Mr. J.L. Parkinson, the Service's assistant superintendent for construction. Among other accomplishments, a Parkinson-designed station was built as exhibit at the Philadelphia Centennial Exposition in 1876. Later it was disassembled and erected at Cape May, New Jersey.[9]

Second class or lifeboat stations were built near the entrances to ports or harbors. Because of the higher populations in the areas, they were strictly volunteer manned. Typically, vessels stranded near the harbor piers after failing to make the passage, or wrecked as the result of collision in the congested waters. Since the stations were constructed in protected areas

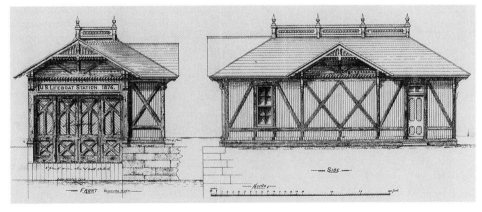

more than two-thirds of the space. A large double door opened to the outside. The boat, lifecar, mortar and other equipment were stored ready for use. The other room was about 12 x 16 feet and was the general living area of the crew.[6] The second story contained the keeper's room, crew's quarters and a storeroom.[7] The

behind the shelter of the piers, a marine railway ran from the boathouse directly into the water. This allowed the heavy lifeboats kept on cars, to be launched into calm water. Once afloat, they could easily run out into the open lake to the distressed vessel. The railway launch avoided the danger and difficulty of beach launch.

Typically, especially in later years, a double tramway was used. A windlass in the boathouse provided for the recovery of the boats. Lifeboat stations with all equipment cost $4,790.[10]

The lifeboat buildings were only large enough to shelter the station's equipment. No room was needed for either crew quarters or shelter for shipwreck victims. It was expected the victims would be taken in by local towns people. Keepers and their volunteer crews lived in the community. A story and a half, the buildings were 22 feet wide and 42 feet in length. The first floor was one large room for storage of the boat and related apparatus. A small loft was above.[11] The stations were built of matched and grooved pine with gable roofs and cedar shingles and were painted in the same scheme as the life saving stations. Over the door was the sign "U.S. Life-Boat Station."[12]

To put a selected few of the Great Lakes lifeboat stations into earlier operation, they were built only with the absolute necessities. Only later did the stations at Oswego, Fairport, Cleveland and Marblehead receive sheds for the storage of boat wagons and additional supplies.[13] In the case of the Marblehead, Ohio, station, the sheds were added to the rear of the building.

Third class stations, or houses of refuge, were designed only for the Florida coast. They were intended to provide adequate shelter, food and water for up to 25 victims. A light surfboat

was also provided. The cost for the house of refuge was $2,995.[14]

A good perspective of the differing capabilities of the early stations can be made by examining the equipment provided to each. The lists on the following pages reflect the original issues as noted in the 1876 *Annual Report.*

Despite the apparent completeness of the lists, modifications were made based on particular situations and circumstances. Also, as the Service grew, requirements were identified for additional specialized equipment which became part of the standard issue lists.

Styles

Stations were usually built with the front to the leeward of the prevailing storm winds. This simple act made the opening of the boathouse

FIGURE 35
The Marblehead station after a watch tower was added to the roof of the boathouse and an equipment shed to the rear. Stations usually grew incrementally as requirements increased.
*Institute for
Great Lake Research*

FIGURES 36 & 37
These two photos of an unknown station show the general layout and wide range of equipment.
*Sleeping Bear
National Lakeshore*

FIGURE 38
A life saver's cottage at Point aux Barques. Married surfmen often occupied small cottages on or near the station grounds.
Ted Richardson Collection

FIGURE 39
This picturesque life saver's home was at Bois Blanc. The surfman in the photo is Gardner E. Johnson. Families provided an important element of stability to the crews.
Ted Richardson Collection

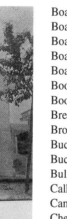

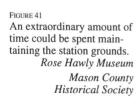

FIGURE 40
The intriguing sign leads one to believe that this Point Betsy building was a bunkhouse for unmarried surfmen.
Ted Richardson Collection

FIGURE 41
An extraordinary amount of time could be spent maintaining the station grounds.
Rose Hawly Museum
Mason County
Historical Society

EQUIPMENT
Life Saving Station

Anchor, boat	1	Chisel	1
Anchor, sand	1	Coal hod and shovel	1
Auger	1	Coffee can	1
Ax	1	Coffee pot	1
Bags for coal	80	Comforters	10
Beach-light	1	Cots	10
Blankets	20	Crotch	1
Blocks, double and single	2	Cups, tin	12
Blocks, double, 12-in.	2	Falls, manila, 2 3/4 in.	1
Boat, cedar	1	Falls, manila, 2 1/4 in.	1
Boat, metallic	1	Files, hand-saw	1
		Forks	12
		Forks, carving	1
		Fuel	q.s.
		Gimlet	1
		Gridiron	1
		Grindstone, 14 x 16	1
		Halyards, signal set	1
		Hammer, claw	1
		Hand-cart	1
		Hand-grapnel & cart	1
		Hand-mallet	1
		Hand-saw	1
		Hatchet	1
		Hauling-line, 2 1/2 in., 300 fathoms	1
		Haversack, rubber	1
		Hawser, 4-in.	1
		Ink stand	1
Boat-carriage	1	Jack-plane	1
Boat-drag	1	Journal	1
Boat-grapnel	1	Kettle, tea	1
Boat-hatchet	1	Knife, carving	1
Boat-hooks	4	Knives	12
Book, receipt & expenditure	1	Ladder, 24-ft.	1
Books, blank set	1	Lamp-feeder	1
Breeches buoy	1	Lamp-wick, balls	4
Brooms, corn	3	Lanterns, dark, brass	2
Buckets, water	6	Lanterns, globe	2
Buckets, rubber	2	Lanterns, signal	3
Bull's-eye and strap	1	Life-car	1
Calking irons, boat	1	Life-preservers	10
Camp stools or chairs	10	Life-raft	1
Chest	1	Line-boxes	2

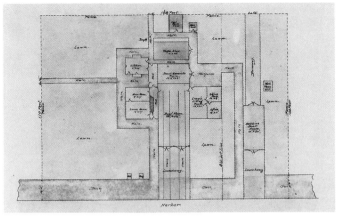

FIGURE 42
Plot plan of the Fairport Life-Saving station drawn in 1907. Note the number and type of additional buildings beyond the original boathouse.
National Archives

FIGURE 43
Second floor bunkroom at the Sleeping Bear Point station. Each man was allocated a separate locker for personal gear.
Author's Collection

Mallet	1
Marine glass	1
Marline-spike	1
Match-safe with rope	1
Match-safes	3
Mattresses	10
Medicine-chest	1
Monkey-wrench	1
Mortar and bed	1
Nails, boat	q.s.
Needles, sail	6
Oakum, pounds of	10
Oars, assorted, spare set	1
Oil, signal, gals. in cans	5
Oil, lamp, gals. in cans	5
Oil, linseed, gals. in cans	3
Paint-brushes	4
Palm, sailors	1
Pans, tin	12
Pans, dish	3
Paper	q.s.
Pen-holders	q.s.
Pens, steel	q.s.
Pickaxe	1
Pillows	10
Plates, tin	12
Powder, pounds of	10
Powder-flask	1
Powder-magazine	1
Quick-matches, box	1

Reel for shot line	1
Rocket-range	1
Rockets, line, 300 ftm	2
Rockets, signal set	1
Rubber suits	7
Sand-paper, sheets	6
Saucepans, 1 gal.	2
Shot	12
Shot-hooks	1
Shot-lines, 720 yds.	2
Shot-wires	12

FIGURE 44
The South Haven station, circa 1900. Comparing this photo with the following Charlevoix photo shows that although the stations were built of the same design, they were not identical.
Michigan Maritime Museum

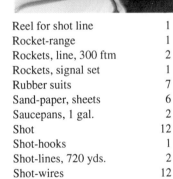

FIGURE 45
The Charlevoix station, circa 1900. The style was significantly different from earlier stations. Also note the strange paddle craft in the foreground.
Ted Richardson Collection

FIGURE 46
The original Jackson Park station built for the 1893 Columbian Exposition was a George Toleman design.
Ted Richardson Collection

FIGURE 47
The Duluth station was another Toleman design.
Ted Richardson Collection

FIGURE 48
Grand Marais station, circa 1910. Note the out structures including wreck pole, water tank, launch-ways and flag pole.
Lake Superior Marine Museum

Shovels	2	Spoons, iron, small	12
Signal lights, Coston, set	1	Spoons, iron, large	1
Signal-flags, set	1	Stove and fixtures	1
Skids	2	Twine, hemp, lbs.	1
Speaking-trumpet	1	White-lead, lbs.	25
Sponges	2	Wrench, boat-carriage	1

Lifeboat Station

Anchor, boat	1	Chest	1
Anchor, sand	1	Chisel	1
Auger	1	Crotch	1
Axe	1	Falls, manila, 2 3/4 in.	1
Blocks, double and single, 8-in.	2	Falls, manila, 2 1/4 in.	1
Blocks, double, 12 in.	2	Halyards, signal set	1
Boat-drag	1	Hammer, claw	1
Boat-grapnel	1	Hand-cart	1
Boat-hatchet	1	Hand-grapnel and warp	1
Boat-hooks	3	Hand-saw	1
Boat-trucks, set	1	Hatchet	1
Book, receipt and expenditure	1	Hauling-line, 2 1/4 in., 300 ftm.	1
Books, blank, set	1	Haversack, rubber	1
Brooms, corn	2	Hawser, 2 1/4 in., 300 ftm.	1
Buckets, water	2	Ink stand	1
Buckets, rubber	2	Jack-plane	1
Bull's-eye & strap	1	Journal	1
		Lamp-feeder	1
		Lamp-wick, ball	2
		Lanterns, globe	2
		Lanterns, dark, brass	1
		Life-boat, self-righting	1
		Life-car	1
		Life-preservers	10
		Life-raft	1
		Line-boxes	2
		Marine glass	1
		Marline-spike	1
		Match-safe	1
		Match-stave with rope	1
		Medicine-chest	1
		Monkey-wrench	1
		Mortar and bed	1
		Needles, sail	6
		Oakum, lbs.	5
		Oars, assorted, spare set	1

Oil, signal, gal.	5
Paint-brushes	4
Palm, sailors	1
Paper	q.s.
Pen-holders	q.s.
Pens, steel	q.s.
Powder-magazine	1
powder, lbs. of	10
Quick-matches, box	1
Reel for shot-line	1
Rocket-range	1
Rockets, line	1
Rockets, signal, set	1
Sand-paper, sheets	6
Shot	12
Shot-hook	1
Shot-line, 720 yds.	1
Shot-wires	12
Shovels	2
Signal-flags, set	1
Signal-lights, Coston's, set	1
Speaking-trumpet	1
Sponges	2
Tarpaulin	1

Twine, hemp, lbs.	1
Water-pails, galvanized	2
White-lead, lbs.	25

FIGURE 49
At the ready, the Charlevoix crew in full storm gear. Note the child fully outfitted with storm suit and life jacket. Comparing this photo with the previous Grand Marais one shows subtle differences in the two stations built from the same design.
Michigan Maritime Museum

FIGURE 50
The Two Rivers station was built in the Port Huron style. Even though a formal photo was obviously being taken, a surfman still remained at his post in the tower.

*Great Lakes Marine
Historical Collection
Milwaukee Public Library*

Houses of Refugee

Axe	1
Block, double, 8 in. with strapped hooks "U.S.L.S.S."	1
Block, single, 8 in. with strapped hooks with covers	1
Boat hook, Tiebout's No. 3, with staff, 8 ft. and 1/2 gal.)	1
Boat hook, Tiebout's No. 2, with staff, 8 ft.	1
Boat, galvanized iron, with sculls	1
Boat-grapnel (25 lbs.)	1
Brooms, corn	6
Brushes, scrubbing	6
Buckets, rubber	2
Buckets, galvanized iron	2
Chairs	18
Cots	15
Cups, tin	2
Gimlets, nail	2
Gridiron	1
Hammer, claw	1
Handsaw	1
Hatchet	2
Lanterns	2
Lead, white, lbs.	50
Marking-iron	1
Marline, coil, 15th d	1
Marline-spike	1
Mattresses, pillows	15
Nails, lbs., assorted galvanized	20
Oars	q.s.
Oil, boiled (in cans)	5
Oil, signal	5
Pans, sauce (1 gal.)	2

Pans, frying	3
Plates, tin	4
Plates, tin, dozen	3
Plates, tin, dozen	2
Pots, 4 gal., iron for cooking purposes	2
Pots, 2 gal., iron for cooking purposes	2
Sculls, 8 ft.	4
Shovel, steel	1
Signals, set	1
Twine, cotton, lb.	1

doors possible without having to fight the full force of the winds.

At the early life saving stations, it was not uncommon for married surfmen to build small cottages or houses for their families in close proximity to the station. This was especially true for isolated stations like those along Lake Superior's shipwreck coast. Construction material was often provided by the lake itself in the form of lumber and timber washed up on the beach from wrecked vessels. Since their homes and families were nearby, the men often stayed in the area during the periods of unemployment. They just caught whatever odd work they could to hold ends together until the next season. Working in the lumber camps appears to have been a common temporary job.

More was involved in the station's physical facilities than just buildings. Crews were expected to do considerable improvements to the station on their own initiative. An 1877 inspection trip to Ninth District (lakes Superior and Huron) revealed the great amount of general work done by the crews. At the Ottawa Point, Sturgeon Point and Forty Mile Point stations (Lake Huron) the crews had constructed piers in front of the stations to facilitate launching and landing boats. The Forty Mile Point station also saw the crew clear several acres of land of all vegetation to improve the lookout's view of the coast. The crew also cleared a 300 x 50-yard mortar range through the woods and built a log house for the boat carriage and beach cart. All of the stations cut roads from the station grounds to the nearest county or state road. As a matter of course, the work was completed without cost to the Service beyond that of normal wages.[15]

As time passed and additional room was needed, the original stations were enlarged and modified. Much of the early work was done with the authority of architect A.B. Bibb, working under the direction of the general superintendent. Typically storage sheds were added to the side of the original station building. When additional boats were provided, special unattached boathouses were often constructed. Other decorative structure changes were also made.[16] Minor modifications were performed, either by local contractors or the station crew.[17]

A good example of minor construction was done at the North Manitou Island Station in 1885. When the crew received a new supply boat, the district superintendent requested $91.78 for the purchase of materials to build a boathouse for it. Leaving the boat exposed to the harsh winters would unnecessarily damage it. Although the crew would do the bulk of the work, an extra $10 was added to pay for a week's work by a professional joiner to help with the windows and doors.[18]

When the roof at the Buffalo Station needed repair, the crew did the job. Similarly, when the floor of the lookout tower in Marquette required replacement in 1899, the Service purchased 256 feet of flooring for $4 and the crew did the work. The projects could be complex. In 1894 the crew at Muskegon repaired their

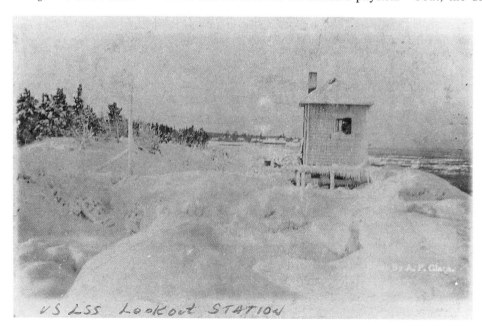

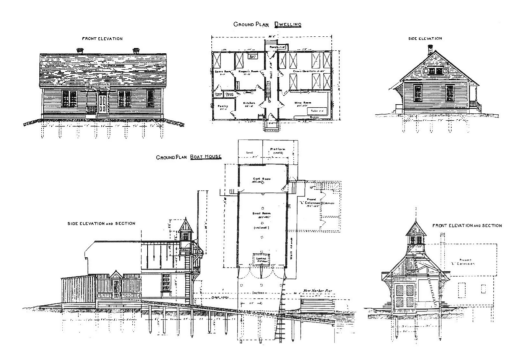

FIGURE 53
The plans for the St. Joseph Life-Saving Station clearly show how the facility grew from the original simple boathouse.
National Archives

entire water system, including the installation of a windmill pump designed by the keeper, tank, valves, pipe and clamps. The total cost was $27.[19]

Bibb also designed a new station known as a "Bibb Number 2," 15 of which were eventually built between 1886 and 1891. These stations resembled a private home more than a station. Relatively simple in style, a lookout tower was incorporated in the design.[20] The station at Marquette appears to be of this style, less the tower.

The South Haven Station, built in 1886, was of a different design. The main building was 25 feet by 52 feet. The front was intended for boat storage, and a launching ramp allowed quick access to the water. The beach cart and other equipment was stored in the rear. A 20 x 28-foot wing was built on the west side of the main building. The bottom floor included a mess room while a sleeping area for the crew was on the second. A shingled lookout tower rose through the second story. Several 12 x 8-foot outbuildings to the rear of the main structure were provided for wood and coal storage. In 1903 a new lookout tower was built on the north pier to provide a better view of the lake. To help solve the problem of always seeming to be on the wrong side of the river, a classic problem for many old lifeboat stations, in 1904

FIGURE 54
Vermilion station, circa 1906. As times passed, the facilities enlarged to become small communities. The building on the right is still standing. Note the watch tower in the foreground. The small houses on the left were the homes of married surfmen.
Michigan State Archives

FIGURE 55
Thunder Bay Island station,
circa 1900. Note the expan-
sion of buildings from the
original boathouse.
        Jesse Besser Museum

the South Haven Station had a separate 11 x 36-foot boathouse built on the south shore of the Black River almost directly opposite the station. The boathouse contained a surfboat and a second beach cart.[21]

The station built for the 1893 Chicago World's Columbian Exposition was designed by architect George R. Toleman. Similar to the 1886 Bibb stations, the 1½-story shingled building was considered very picturesque. A covered porch ran completely around one side and half of two adjacent sides, and a gabled dormer decorated the roof. A large ramp ran

from the boathouse to the water. The station cost $7, 878.[22]

Another Toleman design was known as the "Duluth" style. One and one-half stories, it was larger than previous stations. A two-bay boatroom was incorporated as part of the building as was a four-story roof lookout tower. Between 1894 and 1904, 15 of this design were constructed. The first was at Duluth.[23]

The Great Lakes was also the site of the construction of the next major style of station. Called the "Port Huron" type, it was named for the first city in which it was built. Two stories, it had a three-story, eight-sided tower projecting through the facade. The Port Huron station was constructed in 1897. A major design feature was the deliberate separation of the station and the boathouse. Previously they were usually in the same structure. Separating them allowed the station proper containing the office, messroom, kitchen and quarters to be located in the best site for seeing vessels in distress. The boat-

FIGURE 56
First operational in 1885,
the crew from the Portage
station launches directly
into the Portage Lake Ship
Canal. Note the shed-like
structure added to the left
of the building and the
roller system on the ways.
   *Michigan Technological
     University Archives*

house could be set at the water's edge to allow a quick launch.[24]

The last significantly different station built on the Great Lakes was at Eagle Harbor, constructed between 1910 and 1912. It was a combination of the Port Huron and Duluth designs.[25]

The only Great Lakes station destroyed by fire was at Salmon Creek, Lake Ontario on March 27, 1886. Although local citizens petitioned for its rebuilding, citing several wrecks in the area as proof of need, the facility was never reconstructed. Intervention by political channels was tried but without success.[26]

Local citizens also petitioned for a station at Forester in Sanilac County, Michigan, on Lake Huron. Despite public support, Kimball believed it was not sufficiently justified and it was not built.[27]

The lifeboat stations were eventually modified into full life saving stations. In the case of the St. Joseph Station, a story-and-a-half addition was made off the original building in 1881. It contained a mess room, crew quarters, kitchen, pantry and keepers room. The upper story was used for light storage. The old building remained for boat and equipment storage.[28]

To improve general facilities, many stations received 12 x 18-foot outbuildings combining the functions of coal bin, wood shed, oil room and two-hole latrine.[29]

Life saving stations were enlarged as additional equipment was provided and the role of the Service expanded. By 1905 the Crisp's Point Station had a separate lookout tower, crew building, oil house, beach wagon storage building and boathouse.[30] In 1888 the Fairport Lifeboat Station was modified to include a 16-foot-square kitchen complete with root cellar. It was connected to the main structure by a covered breezeway. Earlier, the original boathouse was enlarged to include quarters for a keeper and crew.[31] The stations slowly developed into small complexes, each unique.

By statute, all life saving station construction was under the supervision of two Revenue-Cutter Service senior captains, designated by the Secretary of the Treasury and under his direction. Augmented by a staff of several assistant superintendents, the officers selected sites for new stations, prepared plans and specifications

LIFE SAVEING STATION TAWAS POINT, TAWAS MICH.

including construction estimates, obtained proposals, supervised the work, made final inspections, submitted bills for payment, assembled equipment outfits and forwarded them to the stations. The office also handled all additions and alterations in the same manner. Quarters were shared with the Inspector in New York City. To a degree, Kimball's Washington office duplicated the architectural design functions of the superintendents of construction since he also employed a civil engineer and a topographer and hydrographer.[32]

Station specifications were closely written, even to where the flag pole was to be placed. All workmanship and materials were to be first class in every respect. During construction, the

FIGURE 57
Tawas station, circa 1900. Although the main building represents the normal style of the early stations, the copula lookout on the roof is distinctive.
Ted Richardson Collection

FIGURE 58
The outline of the original Tawas station can still be seen, although the building has since been covered in aluminum siding. The building is presently abandoned.
Author's Collection

FIGURE 59
The new Jackson Park station was the biggest and most elaborate on the Lakes.

Ted Richardson Collection

Valentine. Each house was a single story and consisted of a living room, dining room, kitchen and three bedrooms. A shed provided shelter for fire wood and other supplies. The communal root cellar located in a small hill served as a cold pantry in summer and kept vegetables in winter. A smokehouse provided cured hams, bacon and fish. To the greatest extent possible such communities were self-sufficient. Family gardens yielded a variety of vegetables including carrots, onions, potatoes, green beans and peas. Ice cut in the winter was packed in sawdust and stored in a shed. Foraging for wild berries was a job usually assigned to children. Huckleberries, raspberries, strawberries, blueberries and blackberries were all eagerly sought. Canning the surplus provided for good eating during the cold winters.[33]

work was carefully inspected, leaving little room for a contractor to provide less than the agreed on results.

Small communities often developed around stations, especially the isolated ones. At Hammond Bay in 1908 the homes used by the married men were rented from keeper Joseph

1. *Annual Report, U.S. Life-Saving Service, 1876,* pp. 851-852.
2. Wick York, "The Architecture of the U.S. Life-Saving Stations," (research paper, Boston University, 1981), p. preface.
3. Vincent J. Scully Jr., *The Shingle Style and the Stick Style* (New Haven: Yale University Press, 1971), p. 2.
4. York, "Architecture," p. 7.
5. W.D. O'Connor, "The United States Life-Saving Service," *Appleton's Annual Cyclopedia of the Year 1878,* p. 749.
6. O'Connor, p. 182.
7. York, "Architecture," p. 10.
8. O'Connor, pp. 182-183.
9. *Annual Report, U.S. Life-Saving Station, 1877,* p. 69.
10. *Annual Report, U.S. Life-Saving Service, 1876,* p. 851.
11. York, "Architecture," p. 11.
12. O'Connor, p. 183.
13. *Annual Report, U.S. Life-Saving Service, 1879,* p. 41.
14. *Annual Report, U.S. Life-Saving Service, 1876,* p. 851.
15. *Annual Report, U.S. Life-Saving Service, 1877,* p. 63.
16. York, "Architecture," pp. 15-16.
17. Letter, Superintendent Twelfth District to Keeper, Point Betsy Station, November 21, 1900, IGLR.
18. Letter, Superintendent, 11th District to S.I. Kimball, September 8, 1885; Letter, Assistant Inspector, 11th District to S.I. Kimball, RG Z6, NARA.
19. Letter, S.I. Kimball to Superintendent, 10th District, October 26, 1901; Letter Horace L. Piper to Superintendent, 10th District, April 26, 1899; Letter, S.I. Kimball to Superintendent, 11th District, RG 26, NARA.
20. York, "Architecture," pp. 17-18.
21. *South Haven Messenger,* January 1, February 26, 1886; July 24, 1903; July 15, 1904.
22. York, "Architecture," p. 20.
23. York, "Architecture," pp. 20-21.
24. York, "Architecture," pp. 21-22.
25. York, "Architecture," p. 25.
26. Petition, to S.I. Kimball, March 26, RG 26, NARA.
27. Petition, to S.I. Kimball, nd, RG 26, NARA.
28. Plans, St. Joseph Station, 1881, RG 26, NARA.
29. Plans, Holland Station, Marquette Station, Michigan State Archives.
30. Plans, Crisp's Point Station, 1905, RG 26, NARA.
31. Plans, Fairport Life-Saving Station, 1888, Michigan State Archives.
32. *The President's Inquiry in Re Economy and Efficiency,* November 12, 25, 1900, RG 26, NARA.
33. Rilla M. (Whitten) King, "The Years At Hammond Bay," Presque Isle Lighthouse Museum.

Locations of Stations

Chapter 8

Life Saving Station, Oswego, N.Y.

FIGURE 60
The railroad tracks in front of the Oswego station eventually caused the station to be relocated.
Ted Richardson Collection

The locations indicated in this chapter's tables reflect the sites as listed in the *Register of the United States Life-Saving Service With Post Office Addresses, July 1, 1914.* In many instances they may not be the site of original construction. For various reasons, including erosion of the shoreline, better land becoming available and difficulty of water access, stations were periodically moved. For example, in 1877 it was necessary to move the lifeboat stations at Oswego, Charlotte and Fairport. The Oswego station was too remote from the town to easily obtain volunteer crews and was relocated closer to the inner harbor. The original site for the Charlotte station was literally "on the wrong side of the tracks." A railroad line ran between it and the lake. Since long lines of box cars frequently blocked the station from the water, the building was moved to the shore side. Although on government land and thus inexpensive land, the Fairport site did not have a good means of efficiently launching the heavy

lifeboat directly into the water. The solution was to move it across the river where acceptable launching ways could be constructed.[1]

Apparently the following year the Oswego Station was moved again after the foundation for the original station washed away during a storm. At Marblehead the station was relocated forward 15 feet and an 80-foot pier constructed to facilitate launching the lifeboat. The St. Joseph Station was moved to a better site at the mouth of the harbor and the Racine Station also shifted.[2]

In 1883, the stations at Muskegon, Ludington and Manistee were moved to better sites as well and were also enlarged.[3] In 1884 the station at Grand Haven was shifted due to erosion of the lakeshore. At the new site it was also enlarged to accommodate additional crew and equipment. The St. Joseph station was relocated as the result of changes to the harbor plan.[4]

The isolated stations often suffered the most storm damage. A turn-of-the-century north-

FIGURE 61
St. Joseph Life-Saving Station. The large building in the background is the lighthouse depot for Lake Michigan.

Michigan State Archives

Station was in a precarious position. In 1885 the increased river flow due to spring run-off eroded the bank behind the station about ten feet, endangering the building. To stabilize the area, the Service had 75 piles driven by lumberman James Reid of St. Ignace. Since Reid was working in the area and had his steam pile driver available, the cost was much less than normal.[6]

The station at Racine was replaced by a new facility in 1904. Extensive repairs were also made at Charlotte and Evanston.[7] The next year saw the stations at Muskegon and Grand Pointe Au Sable rebuilt as well as continued repairs to Niagara, Charlotte, Evanston and Old Chicago.[8]

Because of the vast size of the lake commerce in and around Chicago, in 1906 two spe-

wester at Crisp's Point destroyed the station's quarter-mile-long breakwater. Made of immense timbers fastened with cross-timbers and steel drift bolts and filled with brush and gravel, the three-day blow destroyed it completely. Reportedly not a trace of it was left. The same storm swept away a hundred feet of sand beach in front of the station and wrecked

FIGURE 62
Other than some cement foundations, little remains of the old Two-Heart station.

Author's Collection

several lifesavers' homes. The station had already been moved three times and stood a full 200 feet back from the original site.[5]

Located on a spit of land between the Two-Heart River and Lake Superior, the Two-Heart

cial boathouses were constructed. Each was equipped with a surfboat and other lifesaving apparatus and was under the supervision of the keeper of the Evanston station. The first was placed at Evanston and would be used by his

FIGURE 63
The original Chicago lifeboat station was right in the middle of the harbor. Later it was converted into a boathouse.
   Ted Richardson Collection

crew as necessary. The second was built at Rogers Park, about three miles south of Evanston. It was to be manned by a volunteer crew from the Rogers Park Boat Club. A third boat was placed in the Farragut Yacht Club boathouse in Chicago. Under the control of the Chicago station, it would be manned by a volunteer crew from the club.[9]

In 1908 the Jackson Park station was rebuilt closer to the entrance to the new harbor.[10] During 1910 extensive repairs were made to the stations at Erie, Cleveland, Kenosha and Manistee.[11] 1912 saw significant work repairing the stations at Michigan City and Kewaunee. The

Eagle Harbor station was also completed and placed in service.[12]

Station construction was sometimes driven by other than pure life saving requirements. For example, the station built on the grounds of the 1893 Chicago Exposition continued as a permanent facility. In fact, while functioning as an exhibit, it performed several rescues from actual shipwrecks. The old station built at the mouth of the Chicago River, although considered too small to be economically enlarged, was maintained as a lookout point both during the exposition and afterwards.[13]

In 1908 the South Haven Station was load-

FIGURE 64
This 1993 photo shows the old Frankfort station in the same relative position as the 1905 photo. Since the original photo, the station was moved to the east slightly and turned 180 degrees. To improve the car ferry terminal, the station was eventually abandoned and operations shifted to the Coast Guard station on the north side of the harbor.
   Author's Collection

FIGURE 65
This unique postcard shows the Frankfort station, circa 1905 on the south side of the harbor. The 250-room Royal Frontenac hotel is in the background. The hotel, which burned to the ground in 1912, was larger than Mackinac Island's famed Grand Hotel. Doubtless the various drills thrilled the hotel guests.
Author's Collection

FIGURE 65
This unique postcard shows the Frankfort station, circa 1905 on the south side of the harbor. The 250-room Royal Frontenac hotel is in the background. The hotel, which burned to the ground in 1912, was larger than Mackinac Island's famed Grand Hotel. Doubtless the various drills thrilled the hotel guests.
Author's Collection

ed on a barge and moved across the Black River to the south side. A winch literally pulled the station from its old foundation and onto the barge. A new cutaway in the pier allowed direct access to the river via a launchway.[14]

Stations were always subject to storm damage that required repair, but that suffered during the infamous November 8-11, 1913, blow was particularly severe. The Cleveland station had the foundations and bulkhead washed away; Port Austin lost its boathouse and pier; Harbor Beach's boathouse and breakwater were destroyed; Lake View lost its boathouse and launchway and Pointe aux Barques had its boathouse wrecked, the lifeboat blown off the carriage, launchway torn out and breakwater swept away.[15]

Despite having to repair their lifeboat, the Port Austin crew was able to rise to the occasion and remove 25 crewmen from the wreck of the steamer *Howard M. Hanna* fast on Pointe aux Barques Reef. The repairs were

indeed rudimentary. The crew had to bail all the way!

The damage suffered by the life savers was mild compared to the carnage inflicted on the lakes fleet. The storm totally wrecked 20 vessels and severely damaged 51 others with a resulting loss of $4,157,400. A total of 248 sailors perished. Although only 28 of the 71 vessels involved were lost or damaged within the scope of the Service's operational area, not a man aboard the 28 was lost. Considering that the life savers were essentially a "coast guard," acting only on behalf of vessels wrecked close inshore and that most of those lost or damaged were offshore beyond their reach, the life savers had responded very well.[16]

In terms of overall density of stations, the Great Lakes was poorly served. In 1914 the Service-wide average distance between stations was 30.8 miles; 279 stations covered 8,594 miles of coast. In particular areas stations were much closer. For example, on the New Jersey coast there was a station roughly every $3\frac{1}{6}$ miles. On the coast between Cape Henry, Virginia, to Cape Fear, North Carolina, a station averaged every $8\frac{3}{4}$ miles. Howev-

FIGURE 66
Thunder Bay Island station. Note the alarm bell at the left.
Van Ingren Collection
Michigan Maritime
Museum

er on the Lakes, 3,000 miles of shore was protected by 62 stations giving a density of one every 48$^{1}/_3$ miles.[17]

While the stations were obviously established where the need was the greatest, nonetheless the density on the Lakes was far less than any other area of the Service other than the coast from Cape Fear, North Carolina, to the Florida Keys. In the author's opinion this relative remoteness fostered a greater sense of self reliance and ingenuity than elsewhere.

Station Tables

Instead of compiling the tables by district number, I have arranged them by lake with side notations whenever the official designations changed. Station numbers are also not included because of the speed and confusion of change. The practice of using station numbers was abandoned on April 12, 1883.[18]

Operational Dates

It is very difficult to determine an accurate operational date for each station. In some instances, stations appeared on the official station lists when they were in fact only authorized or still under construction. Some sources use the authorized dates, implying that they are the dates the stations were operational. To minimize the confusion, I have used the dates as they appeared in the *Annual Reports* and clearly stated as operational dates, or the dates of the first full-time manning. The source for each date is cited.

FIGURE 67
Sturgeon Bay Ship Canal station. Note the distinctive lookout tower on the right.
Grand Haven Library

LAKES ONTARIO AND ERIE

Eighth District: 1876-June 30, 1877
Ninth District: July 1, 1877-June 30, 1900
Tenth District: July 1, 1900-January 28, 1915

STATION	LAKE	STATE	LOCATION	YR/OPERATIONAL
Big Sandy	Ontario	NY	North side, mouth of Big Sandy Creek	Apr. 16,1877[a]
Oswego	Ontario	NY	East entrance, Oswego harbor	Sep. 28,1877[b]
Charlotte	Ontario	NY	East side entrance, Charlotte harbor	Oct. 2,1876[c]
Niagara	Ontario	NY	East side entrance, Niagara River	Nov. 1, 1893[d]
Buffalo	Erie	NY	South side entrance, Buffalo harbor	Sep. 19, 1877[e]
Erie[19]	Erie	PA	South side entrance, Erie harbor	Oct. 6, 1876[f]
Ashtabula	Erie	OH	West side of Ashtabula harbor	Sep. 15, 1894[g]
Fairport	Erie	OH	West side entrance, Fairport harbor	Oct. 10, 1876[h]
Cleveland	Erie	OH	West side entrance, Cleveland harbor	Sep. 20, 1876[i]
Lorain	Erie	OH	East side entrance of Black River	Jul. 1, 1911[j]
Marblehead	Erie	OH	Point Marblehead, near Quarry Docks	Sep. 20,1871[k]
Louisville[20]	Ohio River	KY	Falls of the Ohio River, Louisville	Nov. 3, 1881[l]
Salmon Creek[21]	Ontario	NY	East side of mouth of Salmon Creek	Apr. 1, 1877[m]

a. *Annual Report, U.S. Life-Saving Service, 1877*, pp. 35-36.
b. *Annual Report, U.S. Life-Saving Service, 1877*, p. 9.
c. *Annual Report, U.S. Life-Saving Service, 1877*, p. 9.
d. *Annual Report, U.S. Life-Saving Service, 1894*, p. 13. (first manning)
e. *Annual Report, U.S. Life-Saving Service, 1877*, p. 9.
f. *Annual Report, U.S. Life-Saving Service, 1877*, p. 9.
g. *Annual Report, U.S. Life-Saving Service, 1895*, p. 12. (first manning)

h. *Annual Report, U.S. Life-Saving Service, 1877*, p. 9.
i. *Annual Report, U.S. Life-Saving Service, 1877*, p. 9.
j. *Annual Report, U.S. Life-Saving Service, 1912*, p. 108. (first manning)
k. *Annual Report, U.S. Life-Saving Service, 1877*, p. 9.
l. *Annual Report, U.S. Life-Saving Service, 1882*, p. 12. (first manning)
m. *Annual Report, U.S. Life-Saving Service, 1877*, p. 9.

LAKES HURON AND SUPERIOR

Ninth District: 1876-June 30, 1877
Tenth District: July 1, 1877-June 30, 1900
Eleventh District: July 1. 1900-January 28, 1915

STATION	LAKE	STATE	LOCATION	YR/OPERATIONAL
Lake View Beach	Huron	MI	5 miles north of Fort Gratiot Light	Jul. 1, 1898[a]
Harbor Beach[22]	Huron	MI	Inside Harbor Beach harbor	Oct. 29, 1881[b]
Pointe aux Barques	Huron	MI	Near Light	Sep. 15, 1876[c]
Port Austin[23]	Huron	MI	About 2 miles northeast of Port Austin and about 2 miles southeast of Port Austin Reef light	Nov. 29, 1881[d]
Tawas[24]	Huron	MI	Near light	Oct. 6, 1876[e]
Sturgeon Point	Huron	MI	Near light	Sep. 15, 1876[f]
Thunder Bay Island	Huron	MI	West side of island	Sep. 25, 1876[g]
Middle Island	Huron	MI	North end of Middle Island	Nov. 23, 1881[h]
Hammond[25]	Huron	MI	Hammonds Bay	Sep. 30, 1876[i]
Bois Blanc[26]	Huron	MI	About midway east side of island	May 7, 1891[j]
Vermilion	Superior	MI	10 miles west of Whitefish Point	May 15,1877[k]
Crisp's[27]	Superior	MI	18 miles west of Whitefish Point	May 15,1877[l]
Deer Park[28]	Superior	MI	Near mouth of Sucker River	May 15,1877[m]
Two-Heart River	Superior	MI	Near mouth of Two-Heart River	May 15,1877[n]
Grand Marais	Superior	MI	West of harbor entrance	Sep. 16,1900[o]
Marquette	Superior	MI	Near light	May 9, 1891[p]
Eagle Harbor	Superior	MI	Near Eagle Harbor light	Oct. 2, 1912[q]
Portage[29]	Superior	MI	Old Portage Lake Ship Canal, 3/4 mile from north end, on east bank	May 14,1885[r]
Duluth	Superior	MN	On Minnesota Point, Upper Duluth	Jun. 1, 1895[s]

a. *Annual Report, U.S. Life-Saving Service, 1899*, p. 12. (first manning)
b. *Annual Report, U.S. Life-Saving Service, 1882*, p. 12. (first manning)
c. *Annual Report, U.S. Life-Saving Service, 1877*, p. 9.
d. *Annual Report, U.S. Life-Saving Service, 1882*, p. 12. (first manning)
e. *Annual Report, U.S. Life-Saving Service, 1877*, p. 9.
f. *Annual Report, U.S. Life-Saving Service, 1877*, p. 9.
g. *Annual Report, U.S. Life-Saving Service, 1877*, p. 9.
h. *Annual Report, U.S. Life-Saving Service, 1882*, p. 12. (first manning)
i. *Annual Report, U.S. Life-Saving Service, 1877*, p. 9.
j. *Annual Report, U.S. Life-Saving Service, 1891*, p. 13. (first manning)

k. *Annual Report, U.S. Life-Saving Service, 1877*, p. 9.
l. *Annual Report, U.S. Life-Saving Service, 1877*, p. 9.
m. *Annual Report, U.S. Life-Saving Service, 1877*, p. 9.
n. *Annual Report, U.S. Life-Saving Service, 1877*, p. 9.
o. *Annual Report, U.S. Life-Saving Service, 1901*, p. 13. (first manning)
p. *Annual Report, U.S. Life-Saving Service, 1891*, p. 13. (first manning)
q. *Annual Report, U.S. Life-Saving Service, 1913*, p. 136. (first manning)
r. *Annual Report, U.S. Life-Saving Service, 1885*, p. 13. (first manning)
s. *Annual Report, U.S. Life-Saving Service, 1895*, p. 13. (first manning)

LAKE MICHIGAN

Tenth District: 1876-June 30, 1877
Eleventh District: July 1, 1877-June 30, 1900
Twelfth District: July 1, 1900-January 28, 1915

STATION	LAKE	STATE	LOCATION	YR/OPERATIONAL
Beaver Island	Michigan	MI	Near light	1875[a]
Charlevoix	Michigan	MI	South side of harbor entrance	Jul. 1, 1901[b]
North Manitou Island	Michigan	MI	Near Pickands wharf	Jun. 23, 1877[c]
S. Manitou Island	Michigan	MI	Near light	Aug. 20, 1902[d]
Sleeping Bear Point	Michigan	MI	Near Glenhaven	Aug. 20, 1902[e]
Point Betsie[30]	Michigan	MI	Near light	Apr. 23, 1877[f]
Frankfort	Michigan	MI	South side of entrance to harbor	Apr. 1, 1887[g]
Manistee	Michigan	MI	North side of entrance to harbor	Apr. 1, 1880[h]
Grande Pt. Au Sable	Michigan	MI	One mile south of light	May 15, 1877[i]
Ludington	Michigan	MI	North side of entrance to harbor	Apr. 1, 1880[j]
Pentwater	Michigan	MI	North side of entrance to harbor	Apr. 1, 1887[k]
White River	Michigan	MI	North side of entrance to White Lake	Apr. 1, 1887[l]
Muskegon	Michigan	MI	South side of entrance, Port Sherman	Apr. 1, 1880[m]
Grand Haven	Michigan	MI	North of entrance to harbor	May 1, 1877[n]
Holland	Michigan	MI	In harbor, south side	Jul. 30, 1886[o]
South Haven	Michigan	MI	North side of of entrance to harbor	Apr. 1, 1887[p]
St. Joseph	Michigan	MI	In harbor, north side	May 1, 1877[q]
Michigan City	Michigan	IN	East side of entrance to harbor	Aug. 1, 1889[r]
South Chicago	Michigan	IL	North side of entrance to Calumet Harbor	May 3, 1890[s]
Jackson Park[31]	Michigan	IL	Seven miles south by east from Chicago River light	Jul. 1, 1892[t]
Old Chicago	Michigan	IL	In the harbor	May 25, 1877[u]
Evanston[32]	Michigan	IL	On Northwestern University grounds	Jul. 1, 1878[v]
Kenosha	Michigan	WI	In the harbor, on Washington Island	Apr. 1, 1880[w]
Racine	Michigan	WI	In the harbor, adjoining light	Jun. 2, 1877[x]
Milwaukee	Michigan	WI	Near entrance to the harbor, south side	May 7, 1877[y]
Sheboygan	Michigan	WI	Entrance to the harbor, north side	May 4, 1877[z]
Two Rivers	Michigan	WI	North side entrance to harbor	May 1, 1877[aa]
Kewaunee	Michigan	WI	North side of entrance	Jul. 1, 1894[bb]
Sturgeon Bay Canal	Michigan	WI	Eastern entrance of canal, north side	Jul. 28, 1886[cc]
Baileys Harbor	Michigan	WI	On easterly side of harbor	Apr. 1, 1896[dd]
Plum Island	Michigan	WI	Near northeast point of island, two miles northwest of Pilot Island light	Apr. 1, 1896[ee]

a. Noble, *Legacy*, p. 24. The *Annual Reports* do not list a full-time crew for this station. It is therefore likely that it was a volunteer lifeboat station only. A more likely start date is 1876 at the earliest.

b. *Annual Report, U.S. Life-Saving Service, 1901*, p. 13. (first manning)

c. *Annual Report, U.S. Life-Saving Service, 1877*, p. 9.

d. *Annual Report, U.S. Life-Saving Service, 1903*, p. 13. (first manning)

e. *Annual Report, U.S. Life-Saving Service, 1903*, p. 13. (first manning)

f. *Annual Report, U.S. Life-Saving Service, 1877*, p. 9.

g. *Annual Report, U.S. Life-Saving Service, 1887*, p. 13. (first manning)

h. *Annual Report, U.S. Life-Saving Service, 1880*, p. 12. (first manning)

i. *Annual Report, U.S. Life-Saving Service, 1877*, p. 9.

j. *Annual Report, U.S. Life-Saving Service, 1880*, p. 12. (first manning)

k. *Annual Report, U.S. Life-Saving Service, 1887*, p. 13. (first manning)

l. *Annual Report, U.S. Life-Saving Service, 1887*, p. 13. (first manning)

m. *Annual Report, U.S. Life-Saving Service, 1880*, p. 12. (first manning)

n. *Annual Report, U.S. Life-Saving Station, 1877*, p. 9.

o. *Annual Report, U.S. Life-Saving Service, 1887*, p. 13. (first manning)

p. *Annual Report, U.S. Life-Saving Service, 1887*, p. 13. (first manning)

q. *Annual Report, U.S. Life-Saving Service, 1877*, p. 9.

r. *Annual Report, U.S. Life-Saving Service, 1890*, p. 13. (first manning); Keeper assumed command April 28, 1889 (Dennis L. Noble, "Old Life-Saving Station at Michigan City, Indiana, 1889-1914," *Indiana Historical Bulletin*, October 1974) p. 136.

s. *Annual Report, U.S. Life-Saving Service, 1890*, p. 13. (first manning)

t. *Annual Report, U.S. Life-Saving Service, 1893*, p. 13. (first manning)

u. *Annual Report, U.S. Life-Saving Service, 1877*, p. 9.

v. *Annual Report, U.S. Life-Saving Service, 1879*, p. 12. (first manning); Northwestern University records claim April 1, 1877.

w. *Annual Report, U.S. Life-Saving Service, 1880*, p. 12. (first manning)

x. *Annual Report, U.S. Life-Saving Service, 1877*, p. 9.

y. *Annual Report, U.S. Life-Saving Service, 1877*, p. 9.

z. *Annual Report, U.S. Life-Saving Service, 1877*, p. 9.

aa. *Annual Report, U.S. Life-Saving Service, 1877*, p. 9.

bb. *Annual Report, U.S. Life-Saving Service, 1894*, p. 12. (first manning)

cc. *Annual Report, U.S. Life-Saving Service, 1887*, p. 13. (first manning)

dd. *Annual Report, U.S. Life-Saving Service, 1896*, p. 13. (first manning)

ee. *Annual Report, U.S. Life-Saving Service, 1896*, p. 13. (first manning)

FIGURE 69
The Louisville station was
considered part of the Great
Lakes districts by the Service. The station was a floating one that was constructed
on a barge.
   Ted Richardson Collection

1. *Annual Report, U.S. Life-Saving Service, 1878.*
2. *Annual Report, U.S. Life-Saving Service, 1878,* p. 41.
3. *Annual Report, U.S. Life-Saving Service,* p. 58; Plans, Ludington, Manistee, Muskegon Stations, 1883, Michigan State Achieves.
4. *Annual Report, U.S. Life-Saving Service, 1885,* p.31.
5. Rev. W.H. Law, *Heroes of the Great Lakes* (Detroit, 1906), pp. 42 43.
6. Letter, Jerome Kiah to S.I. Kimball, September 3, 1885, RG 26, NARA.
7. *Annual Report, U.S. Life-Saving Service, 1904,* p.45.
8. *Annual Report, U.S. Life-Saving Service, 1905,* p.55.
9. *Annual Report, U.S. Life-Saving Service, 1906,* p.17.
10. *Annual Report, U.S. Life-Saving Service, 1908,* p.23.
11. *Annual Report, U.S. Life-Saving Service, 1910,* p.26.
12. *Annual Report, U.S. Life-Saving Service, 1912,* p.20.
13. *Annual Report, U.S. Life-Saving Service, 1893,* p. 61.
14. *South Haven Daily Tribune,* April 27, June 26, 27, 1908.
15. *Annual Report, U.S. Life-Saving Service, 1914,* p.21.
16. *Annual Report, U.S. Life-Saving Service, 1914,* pp. 25-26.
17. Freeman, "The Life-Saving Service, " pp. 653-654; *Register,* pp. 6-25.
18. *Circular 42,* April 12, 1883, U.S. Life-Saving Service.
19. Originally was known as Presque Isle station. The name was changed to Erie in the *Annual Report* of 1883.
20. This was not a Great Lakes station but always appears within the Great Lakes district.
21. The Salmon Creek station was destroyed by fire on March 27, 1886. It was not rebuilt. Each successive *Annual Report* simply carried it as "destroyed by fire" until that of 1905, which stated it was discontinued as of January 21, 1899.
22. Also known as Sand Beach Harbor.
23. Prior to 1903 was known as Grindstone City.
24. Prior to 1903 was called Ottawa Point.
25. Prior to 1883 was called Forty-Mile Point.
26. Also locally called, "Walkers Point."
27. Prior to 1883 was simply referred to as "7 miles west of Vermilion Point." Later also called Crisp's Point.
28. Originally known as Sucker River, in 1884 was changed to Muskallonge Lake and in 1903 changed again to Deer Park.
29. Prior to 1904 was known as Ship Canal.
30. Prior to 1882 was known as Point aux Bec Scies. Later was often refered to as Point Betsy and Point Betsey.
31. Prior to 1903 was known as Chicago.
32. Previously known as Grosse Point.

Station Operations

Chapter 9

FIGURE 70
The lonely night patrol.
Author's Collection

Under the very exacting regulations of the Life-Saving Service, stations were carefully organized to provide the most efficient operation. Everything was subordinated to this concept.

As previously stated, crews at Great Lakes stations usually consisted of a keeper and eight surfmen. The surfmen were ranked No. 1 through 8, based on their experience and ability. The No. 1 was the most senior and replaced the keeper in his absence. The No. 8 was the most junior.

At the beginning of the active season, the crew returned to the station and after signing the articles for another year of service, set about establishing the facility for the season. The crew usually established a common mess, taking turns as the cook. Sometimes, the keeper ate at the mess at a cost rate established by the general superintendent.[1]

Beach Patrol

The keeper prepared station bills for the required day watch, night patrol, boat and apparatus drills and other duties. Patrol duty was considered to be one of the most important responsibilities in the Service. A crewman failing to perform it adequately could be instantly dismissed and barred from future employment. Each station had a set patrol line run as far as practical along the coast in each direction from the station. In the best case, the patrol lines met with that of an adjacent station. When this was not possible, a patrol distance of four miles was normally the extreme limit, with $2\frac{1}{2}$ miles being more common.

The collapsed remains of
the old halfway house can
still be found on the patrol
trail between Vermilion and
Crisp's Point.
Author's Collection

The night patrol was divided into four watches: sunset to 8 p.m., 8 p.m. to midnight, midnight to 4 a.m. and 4 a.m. to sunrise. Two surfmen were assigned to each watch. At the start of the watch they set out from the station heading in opposite directions. As much as the terrain allowed, the patrolmen kept close to the beach.[2] Later the procedure was modified. While two surfmen were assigned to each watch, one went on beach patrol while the other remained on watch in the tower. As far as possible, the patrolmen all departed simultaneously, in the same direction from all stations in the district. When the patrolman returned, he traded places with the other man who then patrolled in the opposite direction.[3]

If the patrol limits allowed it, at the end of the outbound leg, he would meet a patrolmen from the adjacent station and exchange metallic checks. Each check was marked with the station and crew number. Later the keeper would record them into the journal and return them to the originating station for reuse.[4] Of course this procedure was only followed at stations with interlocking patrols. It is the author's conclusion that this only occurred at the four Lake Superior "shipwreck coast" stations: Vermilion, Crisp's, Deer Park and Two-Heart River. Traditionally a "halfway" house was erected to provide shelter for the first surfman to reach the exchange point. Eventually special telephones were added to allow reports back to the station.

Should a patrol fail to meet the patrol from the opposite station at the designated location, the patrol reaching the location would wait for a short period then continue for the other station. There he would determine the nature of the problem and return to his assigned station

and report the incident to the keeper. If a patrol failed to return to the station on time, the next patrol departed as usual without delay.[5]

At isolated stations, those without other stations close enough that their patrols would meet, the patrol carried a time clock. A key was kept at a post at the end of the patrol limit. When he reached the limit post, the key was used to set the clock, recording the time and proving that the patrol was accomplished. This control method was instituted in 1885, but only after a period of testing.[6] To prevent possible tampering, the clocks were to be kept in the keeper's room when not in use. The keeper was also to retain the keys when not in actual use. Six keys were provided for each clock. Keys at the posts were to be changed at least once each week and more often if the keeper thought necessary to assure the integrity of the patrol. At the end of the week, all of the paper dials were sent to the district superintendent for his examination.[7] Failing to mark the dial of the patrol clock was a serious offense. In one instance, Kimball, after reading of an incident in the station journal, personally directed the dismissal of a Point Betsy crewman.[8]

Patrols also carried a beach lantern and two

A "bull's-eye" lantern as
used by the beach patrol.
Author's Collection

or three red Coston signals. If he discovered a wreck or a vessel running in too close to shore, he burned a Coston signal to both assure the victims that help was on the way and at the same time alert the station, or to warn the vessel offshore.[9] Regulations held the keeper responsible to "ascertain by personal inspection, that the patrolmen, before leaving the station, have provided themselves with the necessary signals."[10] Should the patrol discover a wreck, when he returned to the station he was still required to take his place with the crew no matter how tired he was. There were not any "spare" surfmen. Every man was needed.

After the patrol completed both the outbound and return legs and returned to the station, if there was any time left in their watch their duty was not yet finished. They were still expected to delay in the station building only long enough to warm up and trim the lantern before returning to the beach and spending the remainder of the watch on patrol.[11]

The beach patrols went out in every kind of weather. Surfmen slogged through blizzards, driving rain and sleet, hurricane-like winds, flashing electrical storms and violent squalls. Fair or foul, the patrol was made without fail.

The patrols could be brutally difficult. Rev. W.H. Law in his book *The Life-Savers on the Great Lakes* reported, "A surfman at Vermilion Station was taken sick while on night patrol a few years ago. He had been wading through the snow, and becoming exhausted, severe cramps set in and he could not reach the four-mile post, but was compelled to lie down on the beach and remain there until the next patrol came along and found him and ran back to the station for assistance. The men turned out and by means of a hand sleigh got him home, and under proper treatment saved his life." In another instance when it was "...very cold, a patrolmen was making his four-mile patrol at Vermilion Station, when the heavy seas were running up on the beach one hundred feet, and before another one would come up ice would form, and he would slip and fall, and then crawl on his hands and knees...."[12]

A constant day (and later night) watch was also kept from the station tower. To assure that the lookout didn't fall asleep during his long watch, no seats or benches were allowed. If the lookout was unable to have the entire patrol area within his view, at least three times a day

he was required to go far enough along the patrol route to cover any dead areas. He was also required to keep a record of the number and type of passing vessels.[13] Should the lookout have to leave the tower to help in a rescue, it was not uncommon on the Lakes for his wife to replace him. The requirement to man the tower was absolute. Even during the November 1912 funeral of Keeper Albert Ocha at Eagle Harbor, one of the surfman remained on duty in the lookout while the rest acted as pall bearers.[14]

Family members sometimes provided company for the watchmen during the long lonely hours. At Hammond Bay some of the younger children learned to tell time by standing watch with their fathers.[15]

Despite the Service's best efforts to assure the tower lookout kept a proper watch, the inevitable sometimes occurred. The journal for the South Manitou Island Station on November 14, 1906, noted that on checking the lookout, Keeper Jacob van Weldon caught a surfman lying on the floor asleep. After watching him for 13 minutes, the keeper woke him and suspended him for neglect of duty.[16]

Regulations promulgated in 1899 required

FIGURE 73
A life saver looks for signs of shipwreck during a beach patrol.
Author's Collection

the watch to be kept by each member of the crew in turn. A man could not be exempted by the keeper from standing his watch. This issue came to light when the keeper of a Chicago station regularly excused the best cook from patrol duty.[17]

was destroyed and the surfman on watch killed.[19]

During stormy or thick weather, a patrol similar to the night patrol was instituted. During such periods of foul weather keepers were expected to devote their strictest attention to

By 1903 the lookout had a number of tools available, including a telescope, marine glasses, megaphone, fog horn, a bell for striking "bells" and a time detector. Towers remote from stations also had signal flags. Later electric bells and telephones were added.[18]

Lookout could be dangerous duty. During a

discovering vessels in distress, using both the beach patrols and a sharp lookout from the tower. Crewmen, both full time and volunteer, were expected always to be on the lookout for bad weather whenever they were not at the station and to be prepared to return quickly when the recall signal was given.[20]

Mutual Support

The Service worked hard to establish procedures to allow notice of a wreck to be communicated quickly between patrols and stations and station-to-station. During the night when a keeper received word of a wreck, he immediately fired a red rocket thus alerting beach patrols, adjacent stations and the community at large. When the crew left for a wreck, either by boat or by shore, the keeper brought with him six red rockets. At intervals of five or six minutes he fired one until he was answered either by a

1903 electrical storm, the tower at Sleeping Bear Point was struck by lighting. The tower

rocket from an adjacent station or a red Coston signal from a beach patrol. Because of the dis-

FIGURE 76
The Thunder Bay Island crew demonstrates the breeches buoy drill. Note the wreck pole in the background and the woman riding the buoy.

Jesse Besser Museum

tance between stations, it was common for rockets fired from one to be unobserved by the other. A patrol seeing the red rocket was to answer with the red Coston signal and return as quickly was possible to the station. There, after alerting the keeper, a white rocket was fired in answer. The keeper then assembled his crew and headed in the direction of the rocket. In theory, the station on the left was to bring a No. 4 shot line and the one on the right a No. 7 or 9 line.[21]

operation, the Monday beach apparatus drill could be deleted. If a wreck interfered with a scheduled practice, it was entered in the journal and rescheduled for the earliest opportunity.[22] The drills were conducted almost despite the weather. Proficiency was gained not only as the

FIGURE 77
The Marblehead crew ready to conduct the breeches buoy drill, circa 1914. Left to right: Gilbert Clemons, John Gallagher, Jim Gordon, Ernest Hass, keeper Dan Griesser, Dan Mulcahy, Paul Farmer, Ray Morton and Jerry Tracy. The keeper is carrying the drill book in his right hand.

Institute for Great Lakes Research

Daily Routine

The daily schedule and activities were the same for every station throughout the Service: Monday, drill and practice with the beach apparatus and examination and maintenance of boats and other equipment; Tuesday, practice with the boats; Wednesday, practice with the International Code of Signals; Thursday, beach apparatus drill; Friday, practice of method for restoring the apparently drowned; Saturday, housekeeping of station and grounds. After the first month of

result of rote repetition under ideal conditions, but also during practice in the rain and cold typical of the conditions faced during an actual Great Lakes wreck.

FIGURE 78
High and away, the breeches buoy drill was also a great way for lonely surfmen to meet women.
Sleeping Bear Dunes National Lakeshore

At stations located in tourist areas, such as Michigan's Sleeping Bear Point, the drills provided a popular diversion for summer visitors.[23] Everyone went down to the station to watch the boys in action.

The keeper was responsible for the proficiency of his crew. It was his job to train, then to turn raw surfmen into expert life savers, both as individuals and as a crew.[24] Often, their own lives would depend on their competence.

Beach Apparatus Drill

A special drill ground was prepared near each station for the crew to practice with the beach apparatus. To provide the realism of the mast of a stranded ship, a spar known as a wreck pole was erected. The normal drill distance was 75 yards from the beach apparatus to the wreck pole. It was preferable that the interval be over water, if possible. In actual rescues the gun had a range of up to 600 yards. The drill was a very formal affair beginning with the crew mustering in the boathouse. As the keeper called out each surfman's number, he saluted the keeper and recited in sequence every action he was to perform as stated in the official manual. On the keeper's command, the crew placed themselves into the cart's drag lines and hauled it to the drill ground. Odd numbered crewmen were on the left of the cart and even numbered on the right. Throughout the exercise, whenever two men worked together, the odd numbered man was on the left. On the keeper's command "action," the full drill was executed.[25] Powder was to be used during every drill. The use of powder would only stop when the supply was reduced to three pounds at which point the district superintendent was to be notified.[26]

The speed with which the crews could execute the very complicated beach apparatus drill was amazing. General Superintendent Kimball considered that if after "one month after opening of the active season, a crew cannot accomplish the rescue within five minutes, it is considered that they have been remiss in drilling or that there are some stupid men among them. They are cautioned that if upon the next visit of the inspector a material improvement is not shown, some decisive action will be taken to secure it. This usually has the desired effect."

It was common for a rivalry to develop

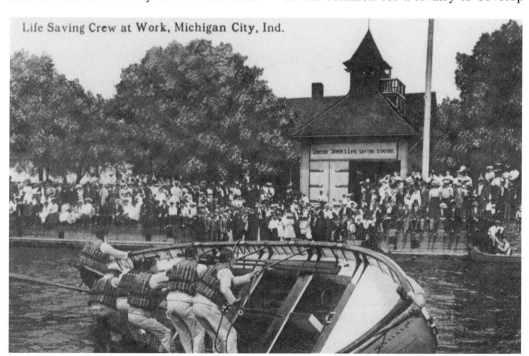

FIGURE 79
Over she goes! A crowd watches as the Michigan City crew rolls the surfboat.
Michigan Maritime Museum

FIGURES 80 & 81
When the weather and water turned warm, capsize drill was often performed in bathing suits as shown by the Ludington crew.
Ted Richardson Collection

between stations concerning the speed that the drill could be completed. Each station worked to be the fastest in the district. The daylight record was a remarkable two minutes 30 seconds. The night time record, with no light other than that provided by the stars and moon, was an amazing three minutes.[27] The drill was always a great crowd pleaser and often drew large numbers of the public to witness its excitement.

Despite the speed achieved during drill, the Service knew well that in the midst of a roaring gale the speed would be slower. The pitching of the vessel, tearing wind and strong currents would all combine to vastly increase the difficulty. The Service also knew that the only way the crews could be truly proficient, fully able to complete the complicated evolution under the stress of an actual wreck, was to practice it repeatedly until every man knew his job cold. Once a man achieved total proficiency in his assigned jobs during the drill, he changed with another man until every member of the crew became competent in every position. A full description of the drills is contained in Chapter 10, "Equipment."

Boat Drill

The boat practice was another great crowd pleaser and consisted of exercising both the light surfboat and heavier lifeboat. The surfboat was to be launched and landed through the surf, and the men exercised at the oars for a minimum of at least a half hour.[28] Part of the drill

required the crew to deliberately capsize the boats, then right them and continue. This deliberate capsizing simulated the type of accident that could occur during an actual rescue. The drill was done with both lifeboat and surfboat.

In calm water a well-trained crew could roll the boat and nimbly keep it rolling much as a log roller does while barely getting their feet wet. This drill was often performed during local celebrations such as July 4th, to the great delight of all.

Sometimes crews from nearby stations held competitions to provide entertainment during July 4th celebrations. Events included capsizing boats, breeches buoy drills and a surfboat race.[29]

The crew was also taught a few "tricks of the

FIGURE 82
General Superintendent Samuel I. Kimball, center with mustache, poses with one of the Service exposition crews. It is likely that the occasion was the 1893 Chicago World's Fair. Keeper Henry Cleary is to Kimball's left and Third District Superintendent H.M. Knowles to his right.
Grand Haven Library

trade." When working the boats they learned never to jump feet first into deep water. Unless they hit bottom they could force the early cork life jackets off right over their heads. Although fitting like a vest, there were no draw strings to hold them on.[30] For winter operations a little

FIGURE 83
The Point Betsy crew in their surfboat. Note the keeper is rowing and presumably the No. 1 is at the steering oar. Training each man to do another's job was considered very important.

Sleeping Bear Dunes National Lakeshore

known technique was the oiling of the bottom of a boat to make it slide easier over ice and slush.[31]

National Expositions

The Service participated in national expositions, most notably:
1893 Chicago World's Fair (Columbian Exposition)

1898 Trans-Mississippi Exposition (Omaha)
1901 Pan-American Exposition (Buffalo)
1904 Louisiana Purchase Exposition (St. Louis)
1907 Jamestown Exposition (Hampton Roads)
1909 Alaska-Yukon-Pacific Exposition (Seattle)

Typically the Service erected a model station on the shores of a natural or manmade body of water. The stations were completely equipped with all apparatus and furniture. At scheduled times the various drills were demonstrated, including breeches buoy, rescue from drowning and capsize of the surfboat or lifeboat. At the 1907 Jamestown Exposition, the crew performed the breeches buoy drill 146 times, the rescue from drowning drill 130 times and the capsize drill (both surfboat and lifeboat) 562 times. The speed achieved were nearly unbelievable. For example, the quickest time for capsizing and righting the surfboat was 13 seconds from the command "go" with the crew sitting in the boat until they were back in position. While the activities demonstrated were generally the same as those practiced at the stations, it was also showmanship of the highest order. They were meant to impress the public with the Service's expertise and indeed they did! The public exposure was often tremendous. During the Alaska-Yukon-Pacific Exposition an estimated more than 500,000 visitors toured the station grounds!

facts from actual rescues. Before the 1904 Louisiana Purchase Exposition in St. Louis, stations were directed to forward any Lyle gun

FIGURE 84
The Life-Saving Service crew at the 1898 Trans-Mississippi Exposition. The famous Indian chief Geronimo is visible in the stern.
Institute for Great Lakes Research

The facilities and operations were also closely examined by representatives of foreign life saving organizations. Occasionally, most notably during the 1893 Chicago Exposition, actual rescues were made for shipwrecks within the local area.

Crew members were selected from different stations and districts, both lake and ocean, to form the demonstration crews. It was good duty and a high honor to be chosen. Special care was taken in selecting the keeper. Captain Henry Cleary of Marquette, considered one of the best in the Service, was invariably designated to drill the "scratch" crews into the highest degree of sharpness possible.[32]

The best known life saver at an exposition was the "man on the mast," the surfman selected to play the role of a sailor aboard the stricken vessel during the breeches buoy. He also was the "victim" who contrived to capsize a small boat in the lagoon daily to allow the life savers to quickly row to his "rescue" and, by using their famous resuscitation drill, revive him.

The Service used the expositions to display arti-

projectiles used in operations resulting in the saving of life. Each projectile was to be painted with the name of the vessel on which it was used and would be displayed as examples of the Services' success.[33] From the author's research, it appears such marking was commonplace.

To bring the role of the life savers to an even wider audience, one New Jersey crew traveled for the 1901 season with Buffalo Bill's Wild West Show. They appeared on the same bill as Annie Oakley, Cossacks, rampaging Indians,

FIGURE 85
This photo shows Captain Cleary (third from left, front) and Geronimo (fourth from left, front) at the Trans-Mississippi Exposition in Omaha. Other Great Lakes crew members include Van Weelden, Grand Haven (second from left, back) and Johnson, South Haven (fifth from right, back). Contemporary sources indicate that Geronimo was a frequent visitor to the life saving exhibit.
Michigan State Archives

FIGURE 86
Captain Cleary and his crew welcome the steamer *Northland* to the 1901 Pan American Exposition at Buffalo.

Great Lakes Historical Society

FIGURE 87
This painted projectile commemorates the rescue of the crew of the schooner *George W. Prescott* by the Sleeping Bear Point life savers on November 11, 1911. In all, four sailors were brought ashore.

Author's Collection

pony express riders and a buffalo hunt. In between the Cossacks and sharpshooters, the life savers demonstrated the breeches buoy drill.[34]

Kimball was careful to cultivate public support in other ways. A special exhibit room of life saving equipment was established in the Treasury Building in Washington. Free to the public, it was reportedly visited daily by crowds.[35]

Signal Drill

Signal practice was conducted by the keeper, questioning each surfman in turn on the meaning of the various flags and the definition of one-, two-, three- and four-flag hoists and the use of the code book. Using a small set of flags provided for the purpose, crewmen would rehearse sending messages to each other.[36] The surfmen often became so adept at signaling that many transferred to the Army Signal Corps during the Spanish-American War.[37]

The life savers practiced both the Navy code (international code of signals) and the wig wag system. The Navy code consisted of 26 different colored flags, one for each letter of the alphabet and a code pennant to indicate that a signal was understood. Each flag was four feet by four feet and the code pennant four feet by six feet. When hoisted in predetermined combinations, the flags had different meanings as well as the ability to spell words. The wig wag system was a method of using the alphabet to spell out messages. As shown in the table below, all letters consisted of combinations of 1s and 2s. One flag wave to the left was a 2; two waves meant 22. A wave to the right was a 1. Thus two waves to the left and one to the right was 221 or the letter "L." Using this simple method, life savers could spell out messages quickly and communicate effectively over a long distance. A set of flags wasn't necessary. In a pinch, a cap or even bare arms worked just as well. The official wig wag flag set consisted of one red flag and one white flag, each mounted on a six-foot wood staff.[38] Ever cost conscious, the Service recommend that the staffs be made from crooked or condemned oars.

At those stations where families were present, the children proved remarkably adept at learning the various signals. Mimicking the life savers, they often passed various messages to each other up and down the beach.[39]

Special signals were used in the event of shipwreck. On discovery of a wreck at night, the patrol was to burn a red Coston or fire a red

rocket, signifying to those aboard that "you are seen, assistance will be given as soon as possible." Waving a red flag by day or a red Coston, rocket or Roman candle at night meant to "haul away." White signals meant "slack away." A combination of red and white signals or a blue Coston instructed "not to attempt to land in your own boats; it is impossible." A man on shore beckoning by day, or two torches burning together, meant "this is the best place to land." The flags were to be carried under the right side of the beach cart where they were protected from the weather but available for quick use. The torches were carried at the head board of the cart. At all times the pots were to be

filled with petroleum and matches at the ready in the handles. A torch burned for 20 minutes. Red and white lanterns were also carried on the cart, one secured to each upright.[40]

The Wig Wag System

A	22	N	11
B	2112	O	21
C	121	P	1212
D	222	Q	1211
E	12	R	211
F	2221	S	212
G	2211	T	2
H	122	U	112
I	1	V	1222
J	1122	W	1121
K	2121	X	2122
L	221	Y	111
M	1221	Z	2222

Restoring The Apparently Drowned

Crewmen were required to memorize the four rules of the Life-Saving Service procedure for restoring the apparently drowned. Pairing off with other members of the crew, each man would show his proficiency in this critical skill. The system the Service used was known as the direct method. As of 1894, it had been in use for 12 years during which time it had been applied service-wide to 118 victims, 60 of which recovered. During the same training session the station medicine chest was opened and the crew tested on the contents. Contained in

FIGURE 88
The lookout uses glasses to search to the northwest in this early photo of the Marquette Station tower. Note the alarm bell on the right and the halyard on the left. The halyard was used to hoist storm signals as well as international code signals.
Don Nelson Collection

FIGURE 89
The crew at the Muskegon station pose with their signal flags.
Michigan State Archives

the kit was a book of directions, also quantities of well known remedies and restoratives.[41] Included were wine and brandy, "mustard plasters, volatile salts, probangs and a few other simple remedies and appliances for reviving

Rescuing a drowning Man by the Life Savers, U.S. Life Saving Service.

FIGURE 90
Post cards depicting the life savers in action were common at the turn of the century. Virtually every station on the Lakes appeared on at least one post card. This one shows the rescue of a drowning victim.
Author's Collection

exhausted persons or aiding to restore those apparently drown."[42]

The life savers' resuscitation efforts not only saved strangers, but sometimes their own people. A case in point occurred on August 16, 1912, at Lake Superior's Little Two-Heart River Station. The two-year-old son of a surfman fell into the river while playing on two moored boats. Reacting to the cry from another child, two crew members ran over and found the child lying on the bottom of the river a hundred feet from the boats. By the time they hauled him from the water, an estimated four minutes had elapsed. He was not breathing and apparently lifeless. After 10 minutes of resuscitation, he began breathing on his own. Carried home by his overjoyed father, he was put to bed and the following day was fully recovered. In comparison with the general scheme of life, it was indeed a very small rescue. But in the eyes of one life saver on the lonely shores of Lake Superior, it was the best one ever![43] In another instance the South Manitou Island crew worked on a child for 20 minutes before he recovered. After an hour and 20 minutes of effort on the father, they gave up when a physician pronounced him dead.[44]

The life savers believed that their method of artificial resuscitation meant there was "always

a chance" of saving the victim. Some news accounts claim that the life savers applied manipulation for as long as four hours with eventual success. In the words of one captain, "no man's ever drowned till he's dead. If the city folks only knew that, there's many a poor cuss now in a grave who'd still be 'live and kickin'."[45]

The inspector kept a record in his drill book of the proficiency of keepers and crews in the various drills. Grades were given on a scale of one to 10. The ratings were sent to the general superintendent, thus giving him another method to monitor the effectiveness of the Service.[46]

After The Rescue

After the life savers removed the victims from the wreck, they were usually taken to the station and given every comfort possible. As a minimum they were provided with hot coffee, dry clothing, blankets and cots for those needing rest. For the sick and injured, the station medicine chest was available. For serious conditions, medical aid was sent for, if practical. The clothing provided came from a stock donated by the Women's National Relief Association. This organization was high-powered. In 1882 the wife of the President of the U.S. was the chief executive and the wife of the Chief Justice of the Supreme Court the vice president. In 1909 the name was changed to the Blue Anchor Society, Aid For the Shipwrecked, Women's National Association. The station library, often provided by the American Seaman Friend Society, and newspapers, donated by various publishers, were available to help pass the time for any victims forced to remain at the station.[47]

For the life savers, however, it was an immediate return to duty. In one instance, safely landing after a seven hour battle in a lifeboat, the keeper turned to his utterly spent crew and pleasantly said, "Now boys, straighten up the house and let's get out a patrol."[48] Being a life saver wasn't for the weak or faint-hearted.

On occasion, local reaction to a daring and successful rescue was tumultuous. For example, on May 19, 1894, in the midst of a northeast gale, the schooner *William Shape* went up on a bar five miles north of Port Huron. A desperate attempt to save the crew by five local men in a yawl resulted in the capsizing of the boat and death of four would-be rescuers. The nearest Life-Saving Service crew was at Sand Point, 70 miles distant. A frantic telegram asking for help set the wheels of rescue into motion. A train was quickly assembled by the Flint, Pere Marquette Railroad, the lifeboat lashed on a flatcar and Captain Plough and his crew loaded into the caboose. With the tracks ahead cleared and the "wild Irishman," Thomas Hour, at the throttle, the train barreled down the rails for Port Huron setting a new speed record en route. Once on the scene, the Sand Point crew rapidly made their way out to the wreck and plucked the sailors off the rigging. They had been stranded there for 24 long hours. Within 20 minutes of reaching the beach, the schooner went to pieces. Port Huron exploded in celebration. Captain Plough and his men were the guests of honor at a city-wide banquet. A contemporary newspaper reported that night a life saver's money was no good in Port Huron. The following day another special train returned the crew to Sand Point, but at a much slower speed.[49]

Off Duty Hours

The life savers were required to be prepared to respond to the call for help 24 hours a day. But the Service recognized the need for flexibility in allowing the men to depart the station grounds. Keepers were authorized to allow the men to leave the station between sunrise and sunset to hunt and fish, provided they did not violate the game laws or trespass on private land. In addition, they were not allowed to go beyond signal distance in the event a quick recall was needed.[50]

A July 23, 1899, incident at the Point aux Barques Station illustrated the seriousness with which unauthorized absences were treated. A surfman named Pease left the station without the keeper's permission and was gone more than an hour, not returning until 8:30 p.m. He did not respond to the alarm bell until after 20 minutes had passed. When he did return, he stated he was escorting a lady friend home since she was afraid to drive home alone at night. When the matter came to Kimball's attention, he initially considered it serious enough to dismiss Pease immediately. He later relented, offering him a period of leave without pay as punishment.[51]

The keeper was also allowed, at his discre-

FIGURE 91
Life savers at Eagle Harbor at leisure.

Jack Deo
Superior View Studio

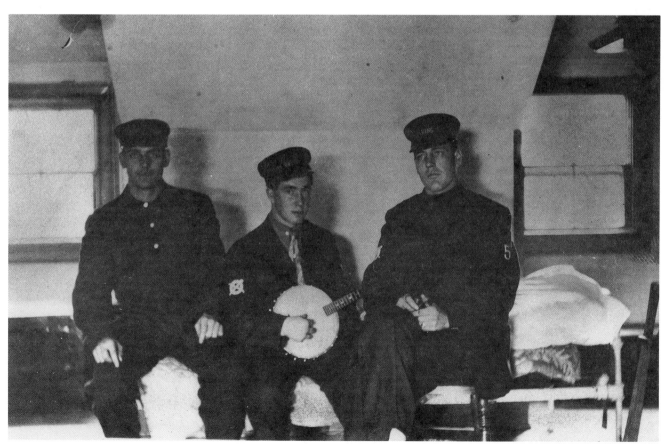

FIGURE 92
Living quarters at the Eagle Harbor Life-Saving Station, circa 1913. Note the "cheese cake" picture on the wall.

Jack Deo
Superior View Studio

On application to the general superintendent, an unpaid leave of absence could be granted. Requests were required to be very detailed, outlining closely exactly why the leave was needed. If granted, substitutes were employed.[53]

There were opportunities for genuine relaxation. Captain J.H. Merryman, the Service's Inspector, related one such instance.

"In fine, clear weather, when the wind is offshore, and there is little occasion for anxiety, the surfman gather in the mess-room and while away the time rehearing the legends of the coast, spinning yarns, singing or listening to the tuneful strains of violin or flute. Now and then, when the moon is full, there is a 'surprise party' at the station. From the mainland or neighboring set-

tion, to permit one member at a time, in turn, liberty not to exceed 24 hours. Liberty always ended not later than noon the following day. Typically the liberty started between dawn and noon at the keeper's discretion. If the weather turned bad, he had to return immediately. This privilege could not be given to the same man more than once a week. Keepers had more flexi-

FIGURE 93
The specific circumstances of this photo of keeper John Anderson and his crew are unknown, but it is believed to show his Two-Heart River crew during a special occasion, perhaps Thanksgiving dinner. His wife, Caroline, is on his right.

Don Nelson Collection

bility concerning their own absences. Like other men, they could be gone from the station once a week between sunrise and sunset in good weather. But they also had the option of being absent for a full 24 hours once a week, providing the No. 1 surfman was left in charge and the keeper furnished a competent substitute.[52]

tlements come men and women, the friends and relatives of the surfmen, bringing cakes and pastries, and other good things from their homes. Then all joy is unconfined; the boat-room is cleared of carriage and cart, and the merry dance goes round. Do not imagine, however, that in these festivities the patrol is relaxed. Not at all; the rule is inflexible, and its violation would be discovered. Indeed, who knows that the beach watch is not then doubled and that, with wife or sweetheart to share his vigils, the patrolman yearns not for the pleasures at the station?"[54]

The arrival of a life saving crew at small isolated communities often added significantly to local society. When Keeper William Walker arrived from Grand Haven to open the Sleeping Bear Point Station he brought not only his six-

man crew, but also wife, mother, step-father and two sisters. The crew became an integral part of the community. Parties and social activities were commonplace.[55]

At Hammond Bay get-togethers attracted people from the entire area. "A wooden dance floor referred to as the bowery was set up near the station and great quantities of food were brought in for the dining." Homemade ice cream topped the treats.[56]

The Point aux Barques station grounds, in combination with the light station, was a popular spot for picnics by area Masonic groups. The life savers usually provided a demonstration drill or two to delight the revelers.

Even when on liberty, a life saver was not allowed to become drunk. In a 1904 letter from the Assistant Inspector of the Twelfth District (Lake Michigan) to the Keeper at Point Betsy it was stated, "...any drunkenness or intoxication on the part of anyone connected with a station cannot be tolerated, and that proof of such drunkenness or intoxication will be deemed sufficient grounds for recommending immedi-

ate dismissal." Although a man might be on liberty, he was still subject to recall in the event of threatening weather. He had to always be able to perform his duties without the influence of intoxicating liquors.[57]

A popular event in the Ninth District (lakes Erie and Ontario) for many years was the "Life-Savers Ball." Hosted by the Oswego and Big Sandy Stations, the ball committee had representatives from stations at Niagara, Ashtabula, Charlotte and Fairport. The ball was held in Ellisburg every January after the season was over. Tickets including supper and dancing to an orchestra were $1. The ball always drew a large crowd and was the culmination of several days of socializing.[58]

On at least one occasion, December 19, 1893, Port Huron political leaders hosted a life savers banquet. Besides a grand buffet and the obligatory political speeches, an orchestra provided the background for an evening of dancing and celebration by the life savers and their ladies. Every Lake Huron station plus two from Lake Superior were represented.[59]

Some crews also participated in organized athletics. The Huron City Sluggers, a popular baseball team in Michigan's Thumb area during the turn of the century, was chiefly made up of the Point aux Barques crew. The only thing different from a normal team was that they had to play all their games at home on the station grounds.

Equipment Maintenance

Particular care was paid to maintaining station equipment. Regulations required that after a boat was used it was to be returned to the boathouse quickly. On the first good day after use, it was to be brought outside and allowed to dry completely. Any damage was to be immediately repaired. If such repair was beyond the crew's ability, a competent workman was to be hired and the bill forwarded to the district superintendent.[60]

FIGURE 94
The life savers could certainly take advantage of their surroundings. This crew at Two-Heart shows off a fine catch of lake trout. Keeper John Anderson is in the peaked hat at right.

Anderson Collection
Marquette
Maritime Museum

FIGURE 95
The life saver's cemetery at Two-Heart today. Soon the forest will obscure all trace of it.

Author's Collection

FIGURE 96
The Two-Heart cemetery, circa 1930. There is no evidence of the wooded fence today.

Rainbow Lodge

cal arrangement. The Service always was concerned with cost.[63]

The keepers of volunteer stations were required to live close to the station and during thick or stormy weather were directed by regulation to "keep a sharp lookout upon the coast for distressed vessels." If a wreck was discovered during daylight, the day recall signal for the volunteers was flown from the flagpole. The night recall signal was the Lyle gun fired twice in quick succession. Keepers were also encouraged to be innovative in using other means as well. The bottom line was getting the crew to the station as fast as possible. Should a volunteer not be able to reach the station, or a regular surfman be ill or unable to respond, the keeper was to engage a competent substitute or volunteer at the established rate.[64]

The same strict maintenance was applied to the beach apparatus. After its use, whether rescue or drill, every part was carefully cleaned and returned to the equipment house. All metal surfaces were to be wiped dry. At the first opportunity of good weather, all lines and hawsers were completely dried.[61]

The damp was the constant enemy of the station buildings and equipment. Keepers were directed to open all doors and windows frequently during fair weather to help drive out the dampness and moisture. Special attention was paid to keeping the various lines and hawsers dry.[62]

Actions On Discovering a Wreck

When a wreck or vessel in distress was discovered, the life savers sprang to action. Whether notified by the watchman in the tower, or by signal from a patrolman, the crew responded by immediately preparing the boats or beach apparatus as needed. If he felt it necessary, the keeper was authorized to hire horses, carts or tug boats to help move his crew and equipment to the wreck site. When possible the Service encouraged him to make "permanent arrangements" with local owners at "reasonable rates," instead of on a case-by-case basis, feeling the former was a more economi-

The keeper's primary concern was always the saving of life over property. Regulation required that "on boarding wrecks by boat, the preservation of life will be the keeper's first consideration (or that of the person in charge of the boat for the time being), and he will on no account take in goods or merchandise which may endanger the safety of the boat and lives of those intrusted to his charge; and should any-

thing of the kind be put in against his remonstrance, he is fully authorized to throw it overboard."[65]

Keepers were to render all possible assistance to masters of stranded vessels in attempts to refloat them. However, the beach apparatus lines and hawsers were to be used only in landing passengers and crew. If the master of the stranded vessel contracted with a wrecking company to refloat the ship or dismantle it, or with an agent of the underwriters or owner, the responsibility of the life savers ceased. If the

Superintendent Jerome Kiah, who was at the station on a visit, solved the problem by holding the crew in readiness at the station, but placed a surfman with a horse opposite each

FIGURE 97
The Two-Heart cemetery sits on this hill overlooking the old station.
Author's Collection

vessel got into trouble later of course, the life savers were still required to help. Life savers working on a stranded vessel were often in a dangerous situation and had to keep a keen eye out for deteriorating weather.[66]

In the unusual event that a vessel wrecked after the station closed for the season, the keeper was expected to still gather the crew and complete a rescue. If regular surfmen were not available, volunteers were to be used.[67] Again, the critical point was that the rescue had to be accomplished despite the difficulty.

The innovations used by crews to be prepared for wrecks were considerable. During a September 9, 1885, gale, the Sand Beach watch sighted two schooners potentially in distress. Unable to enter the harbor, each came to anchor about two miles offshore. But one was five mile north of the station and the other five miles south of it. During the day, both vessels could be kept under watch from the tower, but at night neither would be visible. Since both had an equal likelihood of needing the life savers help, the crew was in a quandary where they should go. Normally they would move their equipment to the beach opposite the vessel and stand by. If they choose the wrong vessel, they would be far out of position for the other.

vessel throughout the night. If a schooner signaled for help, the surfman could quickly gallop to the station and set the wheels of rescue in motion. As events played out, one of the vessels did require their services.[68]

Once the rescue was completed the keeper was expected to notify the general superintendent by telegraph or telephone. Ever concerned with cost, keepers were instructed to be complete in all details, but to be as brief as possible.[69]

The Bodies

Dealing with the bodies of the drowned became a routine activity for the life savers. Regulations called for the dead to be properly cared for. When they could not be identified, a complete description was to be entered in the journal with a copy sent to the superintendent. Any jewelry or items found on the body that could aid in identification were recovered and turned over to the district superintendent.[70] At isolated stations, bodies were often temporarily interned nearby to await final instructions for their disposition. Temporary burials often became permanent when no claims for the bodies were made.

The cemetery at Lake Superior's Two-Heart

River Station is in a small swale midway up a hill to the southwestward of the station. The site, which overlooks both the station grounds and the lake, was the final resting place for

Bedraggled and near death, he alone struggled to shore. Spotted by a sharp-eyed life saver, he was brought to the station. After stimulants, he told his sad tale.

FIGURE 98
A grave depression at Two-Heart partly outlined with birch logs. It is the only grave with a marking of any kind.
Author's Collection

Keeper Albert Ocha's first wife and two of his children as well as a surfman and numerous shipwreck victims. Although at once well maintained and surrounded by a wooden picket fence, when the author located it in the fall of 1992, it was overgrown by the forest. With the exception of one grave marked by a rough cross and partially outlined in birch logs, only old grave depressions indicated that the cemetery was present.

It was not uncommon for a station to recover a score of bodies after a major wreck. An example of the problems of recovering bodies was provided by the loss of the 301-foot steel steamer *Western Reserve.* The big freighter was upbound for the ore docks at Two Harbors, Minnesota, when she broke in two in a gale and sank on August 30, 1892. The disaster occurred about 35 miles northwest of Deer Park Station. All 27 passengers and crew perished, except the wheelsman.

All of the steamer's crew of 21 and six passengers, including the owner, his wife and their two small children, managed to abandon the ship safely in two yawl boats. Within minutes one of the yawls capsized. Only one of its occupants reached the second boat that now carried 19 souls. For 10 long hours the small yawl blew before the fury of wind and wave. By 7 a.m. it was about a mile offshore when breaking waves on an outer sandbar capsized the boat. Of all those aboard, only the wheelsman reached the beach alive.

The Deer Park keeper knew the bodies from the second yawl soon would be coming ashore. Had they drown offshore, as in the instance of the first boat, the chances were they never would be found, adding more truth to the old saying, "Lake Superior never gives up its

FIGURE 99
The 301-foot steamer *Western Reserve.* She sank off Deer Park with the loss of 26 of 27 aboard.

dead." The old life saving captains were not only experts at rescue, but also recovery. They knew when and where the lost ones would come up. Most bodies from the *Western Reserve* came ashore in about two weeks and were in good condition, several being described as "perfectly natural." All those found were within a 12-mile stretch of beach. To keep the roaming wolves off, the life savers increased their patrols. In the words of the station keeper, "The little girl, 12 years of age, was found in a perfect state of preservation and beautiful even in death. Tears filled my eyes so that I could scarcely see; she lay there alone on that desolate shore with her skirts and hair partly covered with sand, as through she had been a little angel hovering over the scene of desolation and sorrow and had lost her way and had been cast ashore.

"We knew that relatives would come to claim their bodies, so in arranging for their burial, we took the measurement of each one, and made a note of the manner of clothes, color of hair and eyes, and general features and complexion, and name if found on papers; indeed, anything by which they could be identified. Then we placed them in separate graves in the dry sand up a safe distance from the beach. Somehow we could not bury any of them without a prayer, and you know that is not in my line, but I believe in God all the same. Well, what I could not do some of the men could, and they helped me out, so we managed among us to have a little prayer over each one that we buried."[71]

Records show that the keeper's optimism concerning the bodies being claimed was misplaced. Of the 16 located, only four, apparently the owner and his family, were returned to Cleveland. The rest remained where the life savers buried them.[72]

Although the life savers were prepared for it, the experience of finding a body was always disconcerting. W.H. Law in his book *The Life-Savers in the Great Lakes* described it well. "The most trying experience of the night patrol is finding a dead body washed up on the beach. They sometimes hear wolves howl in the timber along the shore, that terrifies a dog that they may have with them for company, until he cowers at their feet, but this does not bother them. They keep close to the water and feel safe, knowing that wolves have a dread of water. But it is not so for a dead body; something has to be done with it, no matter what condition it is in. A man requires nerves of steel to brace up and approach a body lying on the beach in order to ascertain whether it is man or beast, so that he may report to the captain."[73]

26 Life Savers making connection with sub-marine cable on Government Service Telephone Line, Grand Marais, Mich.

Minor Operations

After the turn of the century, the life savers, especially those stationed at major cities and towns, became increasingly involved in rendering aid to small craft. Where previously only skilled seamen and fishermen ventured on the water, the recent advent of more leisure time, coupled with the availability of the new gasoline or napha-powered launches, opened up the world of recreational boating to the public. Frequently the life savers found themselves "rescuing" inept would-be sailors, not only in launches, but also canoes, sailboats and rowboats. Despite the size of the craft, the Service responded with professionalism. A rescue is a rescue, whether an 18-foot launch or 500-foot ore carrier.

Missions not only included towing disabled small craft back to the dock, but also rescuing people from overturned boats and fetching those blown offshore by a freshening breeze.

FIGURE 100
Crews sometimes engaged in non-life saving activities. The Grand Marais crew is helping to bury a government submarine cable.
Michigan State Archives

The life savers often exercised some prudence is rushing to the aid of small craft. As the keeper at Duluth stated, "Some of the most expert yachtsmen need help occasionally however. They become too anxious and enthusiastic to win a race, perhaps, and keep on too much sail in a stiff breeze, or their running board hits a bar, or some other accident befalls them in their eagerness to come in ahead.

"Quite often we have to tow in launches whose engines will not work. Launch owners hate to admit that they have to be towed in, considering it something of a disgrace. We let them alone usually until we see they clearly cannot get out of trouble themselves, unless they fly the signal of distress and make it evident that our services are really wanted. Of course if the weather is bad we go to their help the moment we see the engine is out of commission. This week we were called eight or 10 miles out into the lake by a launch whose engine was not working. A wind was blowing offshore and the boat was drifting down the lake."[74]

Instead of tying up the big lifeboat or surfboats for such simple duty, they often used smaller craft such as a 22-foot power launch or a "dinkey." In 1908 the Duluth Station had two powered launches. One was the 34-foot lifeboat *Intrepid* with a 25-horsepower engine and the second a 22-foot surfboat with a six-horsepower motor. For accidents close to the station, the dinkey was often the first on the scene. For rescues of 400 yards or less, it was quicker for two men to row out than to go through the drill of starting the power boats![75]

Some duties were more pleasant. For the July 1909 Chicago-Mackinac sailboat race, the Point Betsy Station crew was tasked to keep a sharp lookout for the racers. As they passed the station, the life savers were to telegraph both the Chicago Yacht Club offices and the race committee on Mackinac Island.[76]

At isolated stations the crews often performed a variety of non-traditional tasks. At South Manitou Island the keeper several times sailed to the mainland to summon aid for sick and injured islanders.[77] At Hammond Bay one of the surfmen was a skilled cobbler and had the additional job of keeping everyone well shod.[78]

Uniforms

When originally organized, the Life-Saving Service was not uniformed. The practice is believed to have started on the Great Lakes where many crews adopted uniforms of their own design as a symbol of esprit de corps. In the early 1880s, Captain Dobbins, the Ninth District Superintendent, outfitted his crews in a basic sailor uniform with the letters, "U.S.L.S.S." and the station number on the cap ribbon. One or two stations of the district used white shirts with blue trim. However, the surfmen disliked the flat sailor caps that gave no protection for the eyes. Captain Kiah, the Tenth District Superintendent, had his crews wear straw hats that were "held in great contempt by the old backwoodsmen of the upper stations."

Initially Captain Dobbins allowed his crews to wear uniforms of their own choosing. The result was not the professional look he had in mind. One crew elected to dress like railway conductors. Another selected red shirts and white breeches resembling firemen, while a third wore gold lace and buttons "gorgeous as naval commodores." Enough was enough and Dobbins soon standardized uniforms in the district.[79]

All agreed that having an official uniform had great merit, and various ideas were considered. On August 5, 1889, the Life-Saving Service issued a circular establishing a formal uniform requirement. Instead of raising enthusiasm, it generated only resentment since it required the members to pay for them out of their salaries. The uniforms were not an issue item. Although the uniform regulations were amended on April 5, 1895, the members were still required to purchase them. It was the responsibility of the assistant inspectors to order the uniforms including sending the payment to the manufacturer.[80]

There were several reasons that the Service felt that uniforms were important. At first, most stations were located at remote sites, but as time passed settlements grew up around the stations and new stations were established in populated areas. Frequently the beaches opposite a wreck crowded with spectators, many wearing clothing common to workmen, fishermen and other local citizens. During the confusion of the rescue it was imperative that the keeper be able instantly to identify his men in order to properly control and direct them. Distinctive uniforms would allow him to do just that. Uniforms also allowed the crews to be quickly identified as life savers when boarding wrecked craft. This avoided any suspicion of being salvagers or other "ne'er-do-wells." Last of all, the Service felt that the uniforms inspired the respect of the public and fostered habits of neatness and a sense of responsibility, self respect and esprit de corps.

There were only two basic uniforms, a keeper's and a surfman's. The keeper's was made of a dark blue kersey or flannel. It had a double breasted coat with a rolling collar and five gilt Life-Saving Service emblem buttons for each breast. Two more small gilt buttons were on each plain cuff. A seven-button vest was also worn. A pea jacket style overcoat was used for cold weather. The cap was made of dark blue cloth with the top being slightly larger than the base and a leather bill. The Life-Saving Service emblem was embroidered in gold just above the bill. A white shirt and blue trousers completed the uniform. All buttons were emblazoned with the Life-Saving Service symbol. The price for the basic outfit was about $18.25 and the pea jacket $17. The full kit including optional items and storm suit cost $52.15.

FIGURE 102
Manistee station crew wearing white jumpers. Note the child perched on the lifeboat.
Manistee County Historical Society

Surfmen had a coat similar to that of the keeper but single breasted and with only four medium plain black buttons. A two-inch pleat ran down from each shoulder on front and back. A cloth belt went through the pleats at the waist. An embroidered Life-Saving Service emblem was on the right sleeve and the seniority number embroidered on white silk on the left. The cap was identical to the keeper's except there was no device and the band said, "United States Life-Saving Service." Blue trousers were also part of the uniform. Sailor type jumpers and coveralls were also authorized. A surfman's basic uniform cost about $15.65. The overcoat was an additional $11.50. A full outfit including storm gear cost $33.55.[81]

In 1902 the uniform was changed again. Crew members were to be all dressed alike at all times. They were to wear the same kind of shoes, white canvas or black leather and identi-

FIGURE 103
Life saving dress. Popular
in the early days, it looked
more effective than it was.
Author's Collection

cal shirts and ties if worn. Dark blue flannel shirts were recommended for the winter and light blue for the summer. Ties were to be black.[82]

A storm suit made of brown rubberized cloth or cotton duck was also authorized. As long as they conformed to standards, civilian suits could be used. The station name was stenciled on the back. A classic black southwester hat with the station name in white letters and "L.S.S." in an arc above was also included as part of the outfit.[83] Later the storm gear was modified such that crewmen wore light colored suits while the keeper's was dark. As with the distinctive uniforms, the special colors aided identifying the keeper from the men during the turmoil of rescue.[84]

Early life savers were equipped with a special life saving outfit. Invented by Clark Merriman in 1852 and known as a "Merriman suit" or "life saving dress," it consisted of "footed pantaloons of India-rubber, and above the waist of a double ply of the same material covering all but the face, and inflated severally in the breast, back and head, between the plies, by three rubber tubes."[85] Enclosed much as a modern diver in a dry suit, the wearer was buoyant and impervious to cold air and water. It was intended to help surfmen working in the surf and provide protection when working aboard wrecks.

To the uninitiated, a life saver's sudden appearance in the dress could have a startling

around like a yearlin' calf in a two-acre medder, a yellin' and a-screechin' all the time as loud as I could holler, and ye'd jest orter seen them fellers scoot for the cedars. I guess they's runnin' yit." When asked about the hunters' guns, he replied, "Pshaw! Them fellers never knowed they had no guns."[86]

Although dramatic, the life saving dress was not a great success. After initial issue, they were never resupplied. The suits were expensive and the rubber tended to deteriorate rapidly. They also were not generally popular with the men.[87] As time passed, the Service examined other alternatives including the "Dobbins water-proof dress of surfmen" in 1883. The Dobbins dress was judged "valuable in cases where the crew has to work in the surf, or in going off to a wreck to superintend the sending ashore of shipwrecked persons." The men were allowed to purchase such suits for their own use, but apparently none did.[88]

The Service considered the regular storm

effect. One old story well illustrates the point. A surfman moving from an outlying area had just crossed a swamp and, appearing suddenly in the tall grass, saw two snipe hunters. "I seen they was mighty skeered," said the life saver, "and took me for the devil or some other sea varmint, so I beginned to cut up and prance

FIGURE 104
The North Manitou Island crew in full storm gear.
Sleeping Bear Dunes National Lakeshore

suits to meet all requirements. Special gear was simply not necessary. As with all clothing, the men were required to purchase them from their own pockets.

Lifebelts also received the same short shrift when first introduced. The men preferred to rely on their own skill as swimmers without having to manage with a cumbersome cork jacket. The jacket weighed approximately four and a half pounds and consisted of a series of small pieces of cork strung together on a canvas vest. There was also a degree of pride that prevented them from wearing anything that might suggest the least appearance of a faint heart. Only the loss of an entire East Coast crew while not wearing jackets brought home the point strongly enough that they also were accepted as a necessary item of equipment.[89] Keepers were strictly charged that each crewman wear his lifebelt when in the boats for any reason.

Medals

The 1874 act also provided for the award of medals of honor to persons who endangered "their own lives in saving or endeavoring to save the lives of others from the perils of the sea within the United States or upon any American vessel."[90] Eligibility was not limited to members of the Service. The majority of medals were awarded to citizens at large.

Initially there were two classes of medals: first class for "cases of extreme and heroic daring" and second class for "cases not so distinguished."[91] Originally the second class medal could only be awarded to persons who actually endangered their lives in saving the shipwrecked. The 1878 Act, however, allowed its awarding to persons making "signal exertions in succoring the shipwrecked and saving the drowned."[92] An 1882 act of Congress redesignated the medals as gold and silver. In addition it stipulated that should anyone be authorized a second award of either medal, the award would be in the form of an inscribed bar of the same material as the original medal. The bar would be hung with a ribbon from the original medal.

Subsequent awards would continue to be in the form of bars.[93]

The Director of the Mint was charged by Congress to prepare the medals. After a strong competition, a design by Anthony C. Paquet was selected for the first class medal. The gold medal was two inches in diameter and one-eighth-inch thick. The front had a surfboat and crew in a heavy sea. Around the edge was inscribed "Life-Saving Medal of the First Class, United States of America." On the reverse was a pedestal intended to bear the appropriate inscription. Based on the excellence of the design, he was also employed to design the second class medal.[94] The first medals were struck at the Philadelphia Mint.

A special committee consisting of the general superintendent, the Chief of the Division of Internal Revenue and Navigation and the Chief of the Division of Revenue Marine was formed to examine all applications for the award of either medal. Their recommendations were forwarded to the Secretary of the Treasury for approval.[95]

Awards were not made based simply on eyewitness accounts. Affidavits describing in detail all of the facets and circumstances were required. They had to clearly show exactly how life was risked or "signal exertions" made. The affidavits were also required to be sworn before an authorizing officer and be accompanied by a certificate from a collector of customs or the U.S. District Attorney showing the affiants to be credible persons.[96]

The initial award of the first class medal was to three brothers from Marblehead, Ohio, Lucien, Hubbard and A.J. Clemons. They received the awards for their remarkable heroism in rescuing two crewmen from the 450-ton schooner *Consuelo,* wrecked two miles north of Marblehead on May 1, 1875. Lucien was in his house watching the small schooner battling her way through a gale when, to his horror, he saw it capsize. Quickly he called his brothers and together they launched a 12-foot flat-bottomed skiff and made for the area where the schooner

FIGURES 105 & 106 (NEXT PAGE) Existing gold life saving medals are very rare. This one was given to surfman Chester O. Tucker for his role in the dramatic rescue of the *L.C. Waldo* crew in November 1913.

Michigan Historical Museum Fort Wilkins Complex

went over. The families of the Clemons brothers n e r v o u s l y watched in gut-wrenching fear as time and again the small boat disappeared in the rolling lake only to reappear and continue for the schooner. Eventually they were able to haul aboard the mate and another sailor. Unable to reach shore, the rescuers and rescued alike were saved by the tug *Winslow*. The tug had seen their plight from nearby Kelley's Island and come out to help. Five of the schooner's crew perished. When the Life-Saving Station at Marblehead was established the following year, Lucien became the keeper. He remained in the Service until March 31, 1897.[97]

A rare example of an award of a life saving medal to a woman was the case of Edith Morgan, the daughter of the keeper at the Grand Point Au Sable Station. She received a silver medal for aiding during two separate rescues. On March 23, 1878, two men capsized in a small boat about three miles off shore. A heavy sea was running, and the weather was frigid. Since the station was not yet in operation for the year, Captain Morgan used his own family to form an ad hoc crew. With his youngest son at the tiller, Morgan, Edith and the other son rowed for the pair seen still clinging to the bottom of their boat. Unable to make it over the breakers on the bar, the Morgan boat swamped and was driven back. Sending his youngest son to town to gather a volunteer crew, Edith and Morgan cleared away a mass of driftwood and logs from the beach to speed the launch of the surfboat. The volunteers eventu-

ally made the rescue.

On December 21, 1879, the passenger steamer *City of Toldeo* grounded during a roaring gale 200 yards off the beach and a mile south of the station. Battered by the waves, the next morning the steamer resembled a massive ice berg. Attempts by the life savers to reach the wreck with the surfboat were futile when ice clogged the oar locks. Eventually they used the Lyle gun to rig a hauling line to the vessel. After making the painter of the surfboat fast to the whip, the surfmen were able to pull the boat out to the wreck. Using this desperate measure, all 18 of the steamer's crew were saved. The key to the rescue were the men and the woman who worked the lines ashore. Strong backs were in short supply and Edith proved to be the key member of the hauling crew. For six hours she stood 18 inches deep in snow and slush, braving the worst of the nordic blasts. Witnesses testified that but for Edith, some of the steamer's crew surely would have perished.[98]

The Start-Of-Season Examination

Although the provisions of the Act of 1874 in theory assured that only competent men were hired as keepers and surfmen and that politics would not be part of the selection process, in practice this proved not to be always true.

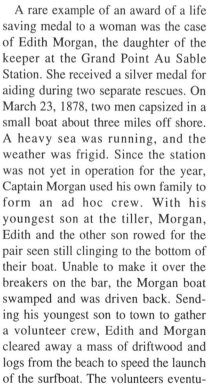

FIGURE 107
Surfman Chester O. Tucker.
Michigan Historical Museum Fort Wilkins Complex

At the beginning of each active season a board of examining officers consisting of two Revenue Marine Officers (including the inspector) and a medical officer from the Marine Hospital Service, visited each station to examine the professional competence of each keeper and crew and their medical condition. The Service stated the

FIGURE 108
W.H. Law.
Author's Collection

inspectors were of the "greatest use, not only in weeding out unworthy members of the crews but in bracing and animating the others for the serious and arduous duties required of them as sentinels of the winter coast and guardians of the lives of stranded sea-farers."[99]

As the result of their inspection, keepers and surfmen were dismissed for many reasons, including a lack of knowledge of duties and experience, surfmen being members of the keeper's family, drunkenness, absence from the station and physical disabilities. For example, in the fiscal year ending June 30, 1876, of 396 keepers and surfmen examined in three East Coast districts, 67 men were dismissed, 17 of them keepers.[100] While the comparatively large number of men dismissed as the result of the examination process reflected a failure in the selection process, it also represented a success in the maintenance of high standards. Simply put, the Service would do all it could to assure that the regulations were followed to the letter and that only the best men available were hired.

The examiner's application of the rules was sometimes harsh. In one instance they arrived at an East Coast station about dark on Thanksgiving Day only to find the station locked and the crew gone. They eventually discovered the crew to be at the village holiday celebration. While the wind was blowing offshore and thus it was unlikely a wreck would occur, the failure to man the lookout and run the patrol was considered inexcusable. Despite the fact that the crew had previously been an excellent one, they were all summarily dismissed.[101]

The first year that the Great Lakes districts were examined was 1877. Because of the large number of lifeboat stations with their volunteer crews and the failure of the law at the time to provide drill pay for calling crews in for an examination, none of the volunteer crews were examined other than the keepers. Of 21 keepers examined, however, five were "deemed unsuit-

able," two for "indifferently conducting affairs of their stations," one in personal qualifications, one physically disabled and one for "intemperate habits." The last keeper had originally been selected for his position because of the great courage and skill he showed during several rescues before joining the Service. For his daring and leadership he had won the praise and commendations of maritime associations and city governments as well as medals of honor, including the first class medal awarded by the Secretary of the Treasury. In view of these circumstances and his promise to reform, he was permitted to remain. All of the full-time surfmen, except one

FIGURE 109
The bethel house.
Author's Collection

physically disqualified, were found acceptable.[102]

Because there was no tradition of life saving on the Lakes, unlike that of the Atlantic coast, the keepers and superintendents had little practical knowledge of how the various apparatus worked. They could handle the boats with the best of the Service crews, but the mortars were a mystery. Due to this deficiency, the general superintendent or the inspector took special pains during this first trip to instruct them so they in turn could train their crews.[103]

and the pure force of his personality, he was able to gain their financial support for his various projects.

Besides doing missionary work in the local area, Law ranged far about the Lakes, often vis-

FIGURE 110
The original Evanston station was built with a stone foundation, brick superstructure and slate roof. It was far more imposing than the typical Great Lakes station and fit in better with the overall campus architecture.

Northwestern University Archives

W.H. Law

One of the shadowy figures who operated on the fringe of the Service was the Reverend William Hainstock Law. He was more popularly known by his initials W.H. Born in 1852 in Claremont, Ontario, he briefly taught school before becoming a Protestant minister. In 1854 he settled with his family in the Les Cheneaux area of Michigan's Upper Peninsula, which had only recently opened for homesteading. Reportedly he was the first Protestant missionary to locate in the northern Lake Huron area. Eventually he established a "bethel house" near Hessel. The structure was three stories high with a four-story tower and served as a church, home, hospital or hotel, whatever was needed at the time. The clientele were sick or destitute fishermen, sailors and lumberjacks.[104]

It is my impression that had he lived today, Law would been an extremely effective "televangelist." He was always stumping for donations and had a golden touch. The money to pay for his mission did not come from the sparse settlers of the north woods. However, the area was a frequent retreat among monied interests from the Midwest and East. The Cheneaux Club was doubtlessly a favorite haunt for Law and his philanthropic activities. By his acts as an unofficial hunting and fishing guide

iting isolated lighthouse and life saving stations on Superior, Huron and Michigan, including them as part of his unofficial ministry. He also established station libraries. For his travels he first used his naptha launch *Pittsburg.* Presented to him in 1889 by admirers, it had a canopy top and was a common sight in the area.[105] Later he used his yacht *Dream.* Described as "beautiful and staunch," it was 40 feet overall and included a 13-foot upholstered cabin complete with galley and lavatory. It was reportedly also paid for by subscriptions from well-to-do friends.

In 1902 Law moved from Hessel to Detroit. A fire in 1907 destroyed the bethel house. Law related his experiences in a number of books and pamphlets (see bibliography). Although of the "storm warrior" tradition, they do provide excellent insight into the activities of the Service. He died in 1928.[106]

Medical Care

Authorized medical care for life savers for practical purposes did not exist. The exception was the Marine-Hospital Service. Keepers and surfman were authorized care at these facilities. It was required that the men present themselves at the hospital with a certificate signed by the keeper, district superintendent or assistant inspector testifying to their entitlement to care.

In the Great Lakes, hospitals were at Cairo and Chicago, Illinois, Cincinnati, Ohio, Detroit, Michigan, and Louisville, Kentucky. Considering the great distances from the stations, medical care was generally unavailable.[107]

For the great majority of illnesses and injuries the remedies came either from the station medicine chest or such local physicians as were available. At Hammond Bay one of the surfmen filled the role of station "doctor," a job normally done by the keeper. His skills could be called on for a variety of problems. In one instance he reattached a severed toe, which surprisingly turned out successfully. Liberal doses of castor oil were the most common remedy provided to the sick. His ministrations were also available to the community at large. The nearest doctor, at Rogers City 15 miles away, was only called in the most serious cases.[108]

Flood Duty

All rescues by Great Lakes crews were not made on the Great Lakes. In March and April 1913 numerous crews were employed in flood service throughout the Midwest. The floods extended generally over Ohio and Indiana as well as parts of Kentucky, West Virginia, Illinois, Missouri and Tennessee. The rampaging waters were devastating. In Ohio alone 454 people were killed, 100,000 made homeless and $250,000 in property lost. Dayton suffered 150 deaths.

Seven Great Lakes crews were sent to the disaster areas; the Louisville[109] crew to Dayton, Ohio, and Covington, Kentucky; the Cleveland crew to Dayton; the Lorain crew to Delaware, Ohio, and Covington; the Old Chicago crew to Fort Wayne and Terra Haute, Indiana, and Cairo, Illinois; the Michigan City crew to Peru, Illinois; and the Evanston and Jackson Park crews to Cairo. Additional crews from Erie, Ashtabula, Fairport, Marblehead, Kenosha and South Chicago as well as Ocean City, Maryland, and Virginia Beach, Vir-

ginia, were placed on alert, but not deployed.

Before the Cleveland crew received orders to Dayton they had already been on flood duty for several days, including a continuous 30-hour stretch. The Cuyahoga River had overflowed its banks, and a good part of Cleveland was underwater. When keeper H.J. Hansen and his crew finished in Cleveland they had rescued 100 persons. They snatched people from buildings, factories and the top of locomotives.

Getting to the flooded areas was difficult. Train tracks were flooded and bridges washed out requiring long detours. Rail cars were short, necessitating delay. Once in the flood zones, civil officials were confused and unsure of what needed to be done.

In the flooded areas, the life savers performed a variety of tasks including rescuing stranded people, delivering food or other supplies and transporting medical personnel.

When the work was finished, the life savers left behind a tremendous amount of good will. The people in the affected areas were genuinely grateful for their aid. All told, the crews rescued 3,509 people.[110]

The Student Crew

No book on the life savers of the Great Lakes would be complete without explaining the famous "student crew" at Evanston, Illinois. This crew was unique in the Service. Located on the campus of Northwestern University, it was entirely composed of college students.

The Evanston Life-Saving Station crew was

FIGURE 111
The student crew launches the surfboat during a drill. When done with "Norwegian steam" as illustrated, it was hard work.
Northwestern University Archives

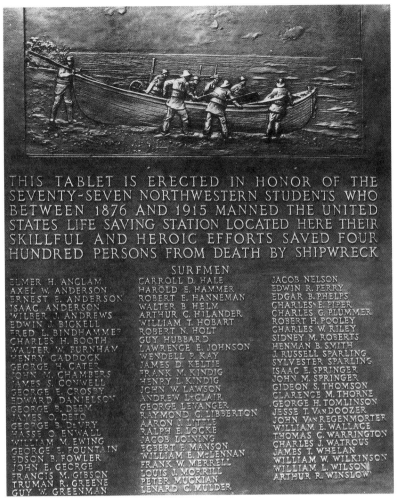

THIS TABLET IS ERECTED IN HONOR OF THE
SEVENTY-SEVEN NORTHWESTERN STUDENTS WHO
BETWEEN 1876 AND 1915 MANNED THE UNITED
STATES LIFE SAVING STATION LOCATED HERE THEIR
SKILLFUL AND HEROIC EFFORTS SAVED FOUR
HUNDRED PERSONS FROM DEATH BY SHIPWRECK

SURFMEN

ELMER H. ANGLAM	CARROLL D. HALE	JACOB NELSON
AXEL W. ANDERSON	HAROLD E. HAMMER	EDWIN R. PERRY
ERNEST E. ANDERSON	ROBERT E. HANNEMAN	EDGAR B. PHELPS
ISAAC ANDERSON	WALTER B. HELM	CHARLES E. PIPER
WILBER J. ANDREWS	ARTHUR C. HILANDER	CHARLES G. PLUMMER
EDWIN J. BICKELL	WILLIAM T. HOBART	ROBERT H. POOLEY
FRED L. BINDHAMMER	ROBERT N. HOLT	CHARLES W. RILEY
CHARLES H. BOOTH	GUY HUBBARD	SIDNEY M. ROBERTS
WALTER W. BURNHAM	LAWRENCE E. JOHNSON	HENMAN B. SMITH
HENRY CADDOCK	WENDELL P. KAY	J. RUSSELL SPARLING
GEORGE H. CATER	JAMES D. KELTIE	SYLVESTER SPARLING
JOHN W. CHAMBERS	FRANK M. KINDIG	ISAAC E. SPRINGER
JAMES S. CONWELL	HENRY L. KINDIG	JOHN M. SPRINGER
GEORGE E. CROSBY	JOHN W. LAWSON	GIDEON S. THOMSON
EDWARD DANIELSON	ANDREW LeCLAIR	CLARENCE M. THORNE
GEORGE B. DEEM	GEORGE LEVANGER	GEORGE H. TOMLINSON
JAMES O. DETO	RAYMOND G. LIBBERTON	JESSE T. VanDOOZER
GEORGE B. DeVRY	AARON J. LITTLE	JOHN VanREGENMORTER
HASSE O. ENWALL	RALPH E. LOCKE	WILLIAM E. WALLACE
WILLIAM M. EWING	JACOB LOINING	THOMAS C. WARRINGTON
GEORGE E. FOUNTAIN	EGBERT E. MANSON	CHARLES J. WATROUS
EDSON B. FOWLER	WILLIAM E. McLENNAN	JAMES T. WHELAN
JOHN E. GEORGE	FRANK W. MERRELL	WILLIAM W. WILKINSON
FRANCIS M. GIBSON	LOUIS J. MORRILL	WILLIAM L. WILSON
TRUMAN R. GREENE	PETER MUCKIAN	ARTHUR R. WINSLOW
GUY W. GREENMAN	LENARD G. MULDER	

FIGURE 112
This memorial plaque was dedicated to the student crews of Northwestern on June 14, 1947.
Northwestern University Archives

that the manning requirement was greater than one class could handle. To solve the problem, each class was charged to provide four volunteers. From this select group, the faculty picked a captain and crew. When the Life-Saving Service moved to the Lakes in earnest and the Evanston Station was built, the crew was already in place.

Although the students, now with the help of the district superintendent, did their best to train themselves, and considering the district superintendent at one point pronounced them the "best drilled and equipped crew on Lake Michigan," it was obvious that the keeper position should be held by a professional mariner. The constant turnover of student captains caused by graduation, regardless of their dedication, was just too difficult a problem to overcome. The search started for an experienced keeper.

The individual selected was Lawrence O. Lawson, a veteran seaman of both ocean and Lakes. On July 17, 1880, he assumed command of the most noteworthy crew in the Service. It was at first feared that the coming of an outsider, especially a rough and tumble sailor, would drive a wedge between the university and station. Quite the reverse happened. The keeper easily won over both the students and faculty and became a respected member of the university community.

The Evanston crew had the distinction of causing more "ghost" reports than any other station. Part of the beach patrol route ran past the cavalry cemetery. When the patrol went out in their white summer uniforms, local citizens often reported seeing ghosts, especially on gloomy nights.

The crews contained a mixture of students; Phi Beta Kappas, athletes, newspaper editors, debaters all took a turn at the oars. Under the expert tutelage of Lawson, boys were molded into men.

During the period 1880-1890 it was claimed that the Northwestern crew assisted 35 vessels and rescued 175 lives. For the entire period of their existence from 1877 to 1915, they were credited with saving more than 400 lives. The brilliant rescue of the victims of the *Calumet* wreck in November 1889 resulted in each member of the crew receiving a gold medal. The student crews of Northwestern won a special place in the annals of the history of the Service.[111]

actually formed before the official establishment of a station in 1877. The impetus was the September 8, 1860, wreck of the steamer *Lady Elgin* just northwest of the campus with the loss of approximately 287 lives. As the result of the disaster, city leaders appealed to the government to have a lifeboat located on the university grounds. The wheels of the bureaucracy moved slowly, but on October 1, 1871, it was announced by a representative of the Navy that a lifeboat would be given if the university would provide the crew. Implicit in the offer was the understanding that the university crew would train themselves and be ready to assist should a wreck occur in their area. No boathouse or other equipment was provided.

In a formal ceremony, the lifeboat was committed by the university president to the class of 1872. For several years each succeeding senior class manned the boat as a special responsibility, however there was no call for its use during this period. It soon became apparent

t, U.S. Life-Saving Service, 1885, p. 33.
. 26, NARA.
1891, Institute for Great Lakes Research.

nd Hammond: Detroit, 1902), p. 17.

aptain Albert Ocha," *Nor'Easter,* January-February 1992, p. 9.

1899, RG 26, NARA.

ions, p. 61.

Association, 1902, RG 26, NARA.
," *Inland Seas,* Summer 1968, p. 111.

pp. 20-21; *1909,* pp. 26-27; *Chronicle* (Marquette, Michigan) May 11, 1909 .
tsy Station, n.d., IGLR.
Rough Riders of the World," 1901, RG 26, NARA.
New Monthly Magazine, Vol. LXIV, No. CCCLXXXI (February 1882) p. 360.

t Betsy Station, February 24, 1903; Rev. W.H. Law. *The Life-Savers on the Great Lakes*
-15.

RG 26, NARA.

42. O'Conner, p. 191.
43. *Annual Report, U.S. Life-Saving Service, 1913,* p. 30.
44. Journal of the Life-Saving Station at South Manitou Island, June 10, 1910, RG 26, NARA.
45. *Detroit Free Press,* August 16, 1908.
46. Kimball, *Organization and Methods,* p. 20.
47. Kimball, *Organization and Methods,* p. 30; *Annual Report, U.S. Life-Saving Service, 1878,* p. 53; Lamb, "American Life-Saving Service," pp. 372-373; Darrell Hevence Smith and Fred Wilbur Powell, *The Coast Guard, It's History, Activities and Organization* (Washington, D.C.: Brookings Institute, 1929) pp. 34-35.
48. Doughty, "Life at a Life-Saving Station," p. 520.
49. R.E. Prescott, *Vol. V, Historical Tales of the Huron Shore Region and Rhymes (Alcona County Herald,* 1939), pp. 29-30.
50. *Revised Regulations,* pp. 49-50.
51. Letter, S.I. Kimball to keeper, Point Aux Barques Station, August 1, 1899, RG 26, NARA.
52. *Circular 119,* December 16, 1905, U.S. Life-Saving Service, RG 26, NARA; *Revised Regulations,* pp. 49-50.
53. *Circular 110,* December 16, 1905, U.S. Life-Saving Service, RG 26, NARA.
54. Captain J.H. Merryman, "The United States Life-Saving Service – 1880," *Harpers Magazine,* 1882, p. 22.
55. Weeks, *Sleeping Bear,* pp. 114-116.
56. Rilla, "The Years at Hammond Bay."
57. Letter, Assistant Inspector, Twelfth District to keeper, Point Betsy Station, September 27, 1901, IGLR.
58. Advertisement, "Life-Savers Ball," January 31, 1900, Dossin Great Lakes Museum.
59. *Port Huron Tribune,* December 20, 1893.
60. *Revised Regulations,* pp. 53-54.

61. *Revised Regulations,* p. 53.
62. *Revised Regulations,* p. 54.
63. *Revised Regulations,* pp. 52-53.
64. *Revised Regulations,* p. 53.
65. *Revised Regulations,* p. 53.
66. *Revised Regulations,* p. 56.
67. *Revised Regulations,* p. 56.
68. Letter, Superintendent 10th District to S.I. Kimball, September 11, 1885, RG 26, NARA.
69. *Circular 16,* U.S. Life-Saving Service, February 2, 1893, RG 26, NARA.
70. *Revised Regulations,* p. 66.
71. Rev. W.H. Law, *Heroes of the Great Lakes* (Detroit, 1906), pp. 41-42.
72. Frederick Stonehouse, *Lake Superior's Shipwreck Coast* (Au Train, Michigan: Avery Studios, 1985), p. 66.
73. Law, *The Life-Savers on the Great Lakes,* p. 17.
74. *Duluth Evening Herald,* August 8, 1908.
75. *Duluth Evening Herald,* August 8, 1908.
76. Letter, Assistant Inspector Twelfth District to Keeper, Point Betsy Station, July 27, 1909.
77. Vent, *South Manitou Island,* pp. 65-66.
78. Rilla, "The Years at Hammond Bay,".
79. Bibb, "Life-Saving Service on the Great Lakes," p. 390.
80. *Circular 70,* U.S.L.S.S., April 15, 1895, RG 26, NARA; O'Brien, *Guardians of the Eighth Sea,* p. 43.
81. *Circular 70,* April 5, 1895, U.S.L.S.S., RG 26, NARA.
82. Letter, Assistant Inspector, Eleventh District to Keeper, Point Betsy Station, July 27, 1904, IGLR.
83. O'Brien, *Guardians of the Eighth Sea,* p. 43.
84. *Annual Report of the U.S. Life-Saving Service, 1897,* p. 481.
85. Lamb, "The American Life-Saving Service," p. 360; O'Connor, p. 194.
86. Merryman, "The United States Life-Saving Service – 1880," p. 21.
87. *Annual Report, U.S. Life-Saving Service, 1890,* p. 555.
88. *Annual Report, U.S. Life-Saving Service, 1883,* p. 413.
89. *Circular 39,* U.S. Life-Saving Service, March 27, 1876; Merryman, "The United States Life-Saving Service – 1880," p. 21.
90. *Annual Report, U.S. Life-Saving Service, 1876,* p. 855.
91. *Annual Report, U.S. Life-Saving Service, 1876,* p. 855.
92. *Annual Report, U.S. Life-Saving Service, 1879,* p. 54.
93. *Revised Regulations,* pp. 24-25.
94. *Annual Report, U.S. Life-Saving Service, 1876,* p. 855; *Portrait and Biographical Album of Huron County* (Chicago: Chapman Brothers, 1884), p. 483.
95. Kimball, *Organization and Methods,* p. 39.
96. *Life-Saving Service Circular 66. Award of Life Saving Medals,* Treasury Department, June 24, 1889; *Life-Saving Service Circular 200, Award of Life Saving Medals,* Treasury Department, December 26, 1894, RG 26, NARA.
97. *Annual Report, U.S. Life-Saving Service, 1876,* p. 829; Merlin D. Wolcott, "Heroism at Marblehead," *Inland Seas,* Vol. 16, No. 4. Winter 1960, pp. 268-274.
98. *Annual Report, U.S. Life-Saving Service, 1880,* pp. 38-39.
99. *Annual Report, U.S. Life-Saving Service, 1877,* p. 33.
100. *Annual Report, U.S. Life-Saving Service, 1876,* p. 828.
101. *Annual Report, U.S. Life-Saving Service, 1878,* p. 21.
102. *Annual Report, U.S. Life-Saving Service, 1878,* pp. 33-34.
103. *Annual Report, U.S. Life-Saving Service, 1877,* p. 36.
104. Philip McM Pittman, *The Les Cheneaux Chronicles* (Charlevoix, MI: Les Cheneaux Centennial Committee, 1984), p. 322.
105. John A. Markstrum, *Les Cheneaux Pioneers* (Detroit: John A. Markstrum, 1973), p. 46.
106. W.H. Law, "W.H. Law," *Les Cheneaux Breezes,* 1953, pp. 50-54; Pittman, *Les Cheneaux Chronicles,* p. 322; *South Haven Tribune- Messenger,* August 21, 1903.
107. *Circular 128,* U.S.M.H.S., August 31, 1894, RG 26, NARA.
108. Rilla, "The Years at Hammond Bay."
109. Although the Louisville crew is listed as a Great Lakes crew, with this exception I did not consider as such for this book.
110. *Annual Report, U.S. Life-Saving Service, 1913,* pp. 277-292.
111. Lifesaving Files, Northwestern University Archives.

Equipment

The Board of Life-Saving Appliances

Early in the organization of the Life-Saving Service it was realized that a proper mechanism was needed to evaluate life saving equipment. To accomplish this task, a commission consisting of Navy officers, Treasury Department representatives and various experts in maritime activities and life saving operations was formed. It met for the first time in May 1872 at the station at Seabright, New Jersey. Its purpose was to assess the merits of various equipment including surfboats, signaling devices, rockets, mortars and liferafts. Based on their recommendations, particular items were selected for Service-wide use.[1]

At the specific request of Kimball, language was inserted into the Act of June 18, 1878, to make it part of the general superintendent's responsibility to "cause to be properly investigated all plans, devices and inventions for the improvement of life saving apparatus, for use at the stations, which may appear to be meritori-

ous and available."

To meet this requirement, Kimball formed an official Board of Life-Saving Appliances. Although the composition changed periodically, in 1884 it consisted of Revenue-Marine Captain James H. Merryman, Inspector of the Life-Saving Stations; Captain David A. Lyle, Ordnance Department, U.S. Army; Revenue-Marine Lieutenant Thomas D. Walker, Assistant Inspector; Benjamin C. Sparrow, Superintendent, Second District; David P. Dobbins, Superintendent, Ninth District and John C. Patterson, Keeper of the Shark River, New Jersey, Station, Fourth District. It was a veritable who's who of the early Service. By regulation, the Board was charged to examine two broad classes of equipment: wreck ordnance such as guns, shot-lines, faking boxes, etc. and miscellaneous apparatus, to include boats, signals, life preservers and such other items as the general superintendent may refer.[2]

The Board met at the call of its president to

FIGURE 113
This classic photo of the Marquette crew shows the differences between a lifeboat on the left and a surfboat on the right. Note the careful stowage of gear in the surfboat. Cleary is at the helm of the lifeboat.
Marquette Maritime Museum

test, examine and report on the apparatus referred to it by Kimball. It was forbidden from "entering into protracted discussions with inventors or their agents as to the principals involved, in methods of improvement in plans

superintendent whether the Board would evaluate any particular device.

Devices that fell into the category of the "strange" included "Richl's Life-Saving Kite" and the "Fox Vacum Gun of 82." The kite was intended to carry a line to a vessel wrecked offshore replacing the need for a Lyle gun. The second device was truly creative. It was essentially a monster vacuum gun intended to "shoot" a small partially enclosed boat from the beach to an offshore vessel in distress. The projectile boat in which a life saver was seated would leap "from crest to crest of every angry wave and heaving swell...to carry the glad tidings of help and hope to the ill-fated passengers and crew." As the manned projectile was "skipping" to the wreck, it trailed a rope that unraveled from a spool kept ashore. It was expected that those aboard the vessel, seeing the life saver com-

FIGURE 114
Early illustration of the English-style lifeboat on a beach carriage.
Author's Collection

submitted or how defects may be remedied."[3]

The evaluation periods were closed to the public. Only Board members, their employees and the inventor or his agent were permitted. Perhaps as the result of Captain Lyle's cautious influence, any gun, rocket or other device using an explosive charge was required to be fired at least three times at maximum charge by the inventor as a safety test before submission. Exhibitors were allowed to demonstrate their inventions before the Board and the results would be noted, but any official tests had to be conducted only by the Board. Once the device was submitted, it had to stand or fall on its own merits and in the hands of real life savers. All shipping and test expenses, to include ammunition, had to be borne by the inventor. The Board was to incur no expense of this nature.[4]

Any request for the Board to evaluate a life saving invention had to be submitted to the general superintendent. Requests were to be extremely detailed, include relevant patents, construction, materials used, drawings and plans, weights and description of use. It was strictly up to the judgement of the general

ing, would jump into the water to await rescue. To help those in the water, the life saver had "in the boat a long cord, to which is attached a bundle of rubber bags containing compressed air, each having a tube and stopper, and these he cuts off rapidly with his jack-knife as soon as they are pulled out of the hatchway; he then throws them quickly about to the drowning people. By placing the ends of these tubes in their mouths, many of the passengers are enabled to breath, and are thus kept alive until they reach the escape line which fastens the boat to the shore. By this line the little boat is hauled in, when the sailor hoists his flag – the signal of "pull the passengers to shore."[5]

The Board made a special effort to evaluate new technologies. For example, in 1897 and 1902 they examined various portable electric searchlights. Although they decided that while lights would have value at a wreck site, the great weight, roughly 600 to 700 pounds including a generator or batteries, was simply too ponderous for Service applications. This technology would have to wait for either smaller power plants or a better means of moving them along the shore than the wreck cart.[6]

Ideas for new devices came from a variety of sources: the general public, Revenue-Marine officers, keepers and regular surfmen; all had suggestions for new or improved equipment. Each was evaluated with the inventor receiving a detailed reply from the Board. Great Lakes crews were particularly active in suggesting new ideas, including electric signaling devices and reindeer hair life preservers.

Until the end of the Life-Saving Service in 1915, the Board of Life-Saving Appliances appraised the relative merits of thousands of items of life saving gear. Some proved valuable additions to the life saver's armory. Others were dangerous and were rejected out of hand. Most, however, fell somewhere in the middle, perhaps only a marginal improvement over existing gear or too expensive to be economical. Nonetheless, the Board dutifully evaluated them all.

The Boats

The Life-Saving Service used two distinctive types of boats, a heavy lifeboat and a light surfboat. Each had special characteristics and was designed and used for specific applications. The same general use factors applied when both craft were eventually motorized.

It appears that most boat repairs were completed by the crews without commercial assistance. In addressing the repair of a boat at the Point Betsy Station, the district superintendent wrote the keeper, "I am sure yourself and crew can do a better job on the boat than any boat builder I can employ."[7] Kimball later sent detailed instructions outlining exactly how the repair was to be made. Self repair was also very economical, doubtless an important consideration for the Service. Many life savers were skilled boat builders and constructed and repaired private vessels in their off time.

Boats of all types, including their wagons, were transferred between stations as requirements dictated. Thus while it is true that stations always had a lifeboat and a surfboat, they may well have had more, especially as the Service grew and new models introduced.

The Lifeboat

The lifeboat proper was invented in Great Britain in 1785 by Lionel Lukin, a London coach maker. Modified several times, it became the standard craft of the famous Royal National Lifeboat Institution. Recognizing that the English lifeboat was the best available, in 1872 Kimball purchased one of the smaller boats for the fledgling United States organization to use as a basis for study and perhaps further development. The boat, including carriage and all equipment, cost $1,600. The English boat was 30 feet overall, 7 feet 1 inch in beam, 3 feet 6 inches in depth and weighed almost 4,000 pounds. The hull was double planked mahogany. Four relieving valves would drain her of water in 24 seconds. After evaluation by Captain Merryman, the Life-Saving Service Inspector, it was determined that the boat was

FIGURE 115
A lifeboat under sail. Sails were frequently used on both lifeboats and some surfboats.

Institute for Great Lakes Research

FIGURE 116
The English model lifeboat
was popular on the Lakes.
The boat pictured is from
Grand Marais.
Michigan Maritime Museum

too big and heavy for most American applications.[8]

The self-bailing and self-righting lifeboat, as it eventually reached its design maturity, was a compromise of conflicting capabilities and construction. For every design advantage, there was an offsetting disadvantage. It had great stability in the water as the result of the large beam and heavy iron keel and ballast, but the weight impaired speed. The buoyancy was maintained by air-tight cases both fore and aft and along the sides. The bulk of the cases lessened the number of passengers that could be carried. The cork ballast below decks helped it float even if stove, but added more weight, further slowing it down. When the sails were rigged, speed increased, but stability decreased. The heavy keel, ballast and air tanks all made the boat self-righting, but required increased sheer, which exposed more of the side to the force of the wind. The strength of the boat's construction allowed it to batter through tremendous seas, but also added more weight. Other than the strength and stability that enabled it to remain stable and together in the worst of seas, the great advantage of the lifeboat was its ability constantly to right itself and self-bail.[9]

The self-bailing ability was provided by the

insertion of a deck a few inches above the water line in which several tubes extended through to the bottom of the boat. Each tube was fitted on the top with a valve that opened downward by the pressure of any water in the boat and closed when the pressure lessened. When the boat flooded, the water automatically drained through the tubes, making it self-bailing.[10]

Lifeboats could be sailed as well as rowed. Typically they were equipped with removable main and foremasts that allowed the use of a jib as a third sail. Some lifeboats were also equipped with a centerboard. Rowing oars were 13 to 14 feet in length while the steering oar was 19 feet.[11]

The most expeditious method of using a lifeboat was to have a tug or steamer tow it to the general area of operations. This left the crew fresh for the exertions required for the rescue proper.

The large English lifeboats were as long as 40 feet, with a beam of 10 feet 4 inches and 5 feet in depth. Keels weighed 600 to 1,500 pounds with an equal amount of ballast. Built of mahogany, they weighed at least 4,000 pounds and required a carriage weighing a ton.

Based on the 30-foot English model, in 1874 Merryman submitted plans to the Secretary of the Treasury for a 26-foot 8-inch self-bailing, self-righting wooden lifeboat. Its beam was 7 feet 3¼ inches and draft 21 inches. The hull was double planked ⅜-inch mahogany. All fittings and relieving tubes were copper. The iron keel weighed 688 pounds. Copper air cases were built in at the bow and stern and five canvas-covered wooden cases along each side under the battens. Three compartments beneath the main deck were filled with cork. Merryman also submitted plans for a similar boat made of galvanized iron. One boat of each design was produced. Of the two, the wooden boat proved superior and became the model for subsequent Service lifeboats.[12] Because of the reliance on the original English lifeboat design, these boats were usually called "English" lifeboats within the Service.

During the period 1876-1897, an estimated 77 Merryman lifeboats were built, 80 percent of which went to Great Lakes stations. Major East Coast builders were Frederic C. Beebe of Greenport, Long Island, New York, and A. B. Wood of New York City. Beebe built seven boats, all for the Lakes, and Wood built eight, seven of which were for the Lakes. Great Lakes builders included Thomas Bagley of Chicago, the Detroit Boat Works and the Wolverine Dry Dock Company of Port Huron. Bagley built three boats, Wolverine Dry Dock and the Detroit Boat Works another 13. All were assigned to the Lakes.[13] Other builders' lifeboats destined for the Lakes included the New York firms of Samuel Ayers, Blackburn and Company, Stephen Roberts and B. Frank Wood.[14] Costs varied widely. In 1881 a Roberts lifeboat cost $1,135. Seven years later an Ayers-built English lifeboat cost $1,575. In 1894 a Wolverine boat was $491.[15]

In the Life-Saving Service, lifeboats were confined to those stations where they could be launched directly into sheltered harbors. There were no roads on the beaches and the great wagons hauling the boats would easily bog down in the fine sand. To have any chance at pulling them, four-horse teams were needed, usually unavailable at remote stations. When the surf was washing high on the beaches, often the only route open was over the dunes themselves, a hopeless endeavor. Even if the life savers reached the wreck site, the deep draft of the lifeboat made it impossible to launch in the shoal water common to many American (including the Great Lakes) beaches.[16]

The lifeboat stations on the Great Lakes (as of 1876) were all located near harbors or sheltered areas to allow the boats to be launched directly into calm waters. Most casualties, usually in the form of collisions, also occurred near these congested shipping lanes. To run out of the harbor and make the rescue was the ideal mission for the heavy lifeboat.[17]

Between 1876 and 1889, 37 of the 26-foot lifeboats based on the English model were placed into service. During this period, they made 474 trips, saving 584 persons, capsizing only once with the loss of five lives.[18]

The big lifeboats gained a tremendous amount of respect for their prowess in heavy seas. The Superintendent of the Tenth District (Lake Michigan) reported that some of his crews provided assistance to vessels in conditions so severe that the most powerful tugs and steamers refused to leave the safety of the harbor. In one instance thousands of people watched from shore as a crew in a lifeboat performed a rescue under storm conditions so bad that the crowd thought "nothing made by man could go out through the surf and sea then raging and return." Adding that, "people here are

FIGURE 117
The Point aux Barques crew in a 26-foot English model lifeboat. Note the drogue rigged on the stern quarter for quick use.
Ted Richardson Collection

beginning to regard the self-righting and self-bailing lifeboat as one of the wonders of the world." To those aboard a sinking vessel, watching one plow toward them through a gale-whipped lake, it surely was![19]

The Ninth District (lakes Superior and Huron) superintendent stated, "There is only one of the large lifeboats in this district (at Thunder Bay Island), and the keeper and crew of that station have had so much practical experience with it that it would be impossible to instill in them any more confidence than they possess already. They regard the boat as something almost supernatural."[20]

The Superintendent of the Eighth District commented on the lifeboat by stating, "I have seen considerable service on lifeboats; have been instrumental, when commanding the Francis lifeboat, in saving the remnants of three dif-

ferent crews, and knowing that neither keeper nor crew of the station had any experience with this class of lifeboats, I felt the importance of the moment, volunteered to go and assumed command. We ran along in three or four fathoms of water some seven miles with wind and sea on the starboard bow; the sea was unusually heavy and broke continually. The boat filled with water several times, and was on her beam ends five times. She would right herself, and be ready for the next comber. It was a severe test and proved the boat to be a perfect lifeboat, and I am of the opinion there has never been and never will be a sea upon the lakes which the lifeboat cannot safely encounter. There probably never has been a heavier sea on the lakes than that of Saturday last."[21]

The Service also used two other varieties of lifeboat, the Richardson and the Dobbins. Both were modifications of the English lifeboat and considerably lighter.

The Dobbins lifeboat was especially interesting. It was designed by Captain David Porter Dobbins, an experienced Great Lakes mariner. Dobbins was a character of the first order. Born in Erie in 1821, at age 13 he was sailing on the steamer *William Penn.* By age 18 he was owner and master of the schooner *Marie Antoinette.* He continued to sail the Lakes in a variety of positions until 1851 when he became a marine insurance inspector in Buffalo. He first became involved in life saving in October 1853 when he organized a boat crew of vessel captains to go to the aid of the wreck of the *Oneida* at Point Albino near Buffalo. After strenuous efforts they were able to save one crewman lashed to the rigging. The others had all perished. In recognition of their efforts, the citizens of Buffalo presented each rescuer with an inscribed gold watch. In 1860 Dobbins assisted in the rescue of the crew of the schooner *Comet* ashore also near Buffalo. A Francis corrugated iron lifeboat was used in the endeavor that although successful, resulted in the destruction of the boat. The Francis boat was placed at Buffalo as part of the initial government effort to provide lifeboats to prominent locations on the Lakes. He was one of two men in charge of the boat.[22]

On January 29, 1876, he was appointed as Superintendent of the Ninth District (lakes Erie and Ontario). Dobbins became interested in the problem of lifeboats and developed an improved version that was not only self-righting and self-bailing but also self-ballasting. This last innovation allowed his boat to weigh a

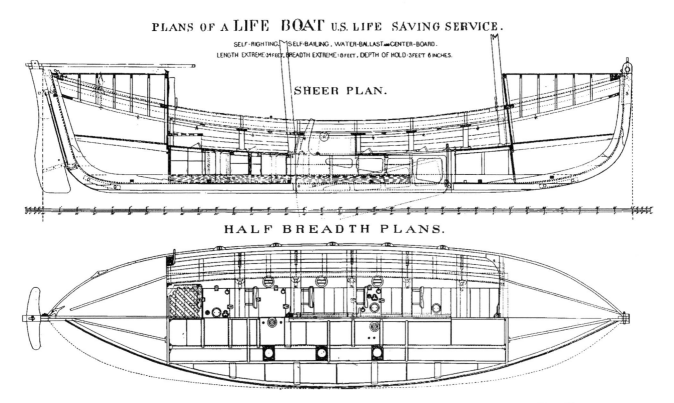

PLANS OF A LIFE BOAT U.S. LIFE SAVING SERVICE.

SELF-RIGHTING. SELF-BAILING. WATER-BALLAST AND CENTER-BOARD.
LENGTH EXTREME 34 FEET. BREADTH EXTREME: 8 FEET. DEPTH OF HOLD 3 FEET 6 INCHES.

SHEER PLAN.

HALF BREADTH PLANS.

FIGURE 119
Plans and specifications for a 34-foot lifeboat.
National Archives

mere 1,600 to 2,000 pounds, less than half that of the 4,000 pounds for the English model lifeboat. Being lighter gave the Dobbins boat improved maneuverability. It could respond quicker to the oars, thus was able to dodge large waves easier than the heavier English boat. In 1881 his prototype was evaluated by the Tenth District crew at Point aux Barques Station. They gave it excellent marks. An improved version was provided in 1883 to nine stations in the Ninth District. Two more were given to the Canadian Life-Saving Service.[23] All of the U.S. and Canadian stations endorsed the boat strongly.[24] Those with experience with the heavy English style boats reportedly appreciated the superiority of the Dobbins.

Comments from the keepers were laudatory. Keeper William Clark of the Erie Station said, "The Dobbins boat we hold in reserve for extraordinary wrecking service....We, of course, have great confidence in her, and much prefer to use her in rough, broken water than any open boat that was ever built." Keeper Thomas Williams of the Buffalo Station said that the boat "...is capable of facing any surf or sea she is liable to encounter without the risk of swamping, foundering or sinking. This boat has the entire confidence of all hands."[25]

The Dobbins lifeboats had some unique features other than being self-ballasting. The hold was filled solid with 500 pounds of cork sheets

dipped in hot paraffin, set vertically sheet to sheet and tree nailed together. The water-proofed cork prevented flooding if the hull was pierced and could be used as rough floats should the lifeboat ever break up. The fore and aft air chambers were not sealed, but had water-tight manholes to allow their use as temporary quarters for shipwreck victims. Six to eight invalids, women or children could be squeezed into each compartment. The scuppers were also spring loaded, decreasing the self-bailing time. The Dobbins was considerably cheaper than the English boat costing $500-$700, instead of $1,500.[26]

There were also other variations of the Dobbins. The boat assigned to the Crisp's Point Station in 1888 is listed as having a length of 26-feet 6 inches and a beam of 5 feet 11 inches.[27]

After an evaluation at Buffalo in 1883, the Board of Life-Saving Appliances reported, "This self-righting and self-bailing lifeboat has the good qualities possessed by the English lifeboat obtained with much lighter weight by a very good method of construction....The model is fair but can be improved in the future boats built upon this plan." The Board further recommended that it be tested on the Atlantic to learn its potential for beach launching.[28]

A 1885 Service evaluation of a Dobbins at Buffalo was extremely complimentary. The

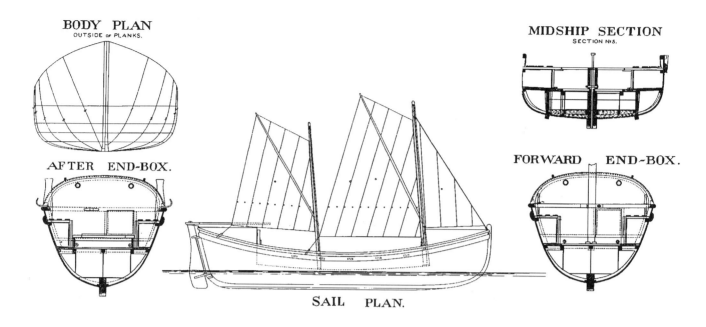

BODY PLAN
OUTSIDE or PLANKS.

MIDSHIP SECTION
SECTION Nº5.

AFTER END-BOX.

FORWARD END-BOX.

SAIL PLAN.

FIGURE 120
Plans and specifications for
a 34-foot lifeboat.
National Archives

boat had a 24-foot length, 6-foot beam and a depth of 2 feet 4 inches. The frames, keelson, stem, stern post and gunwale were white oak. The planking, decks and air case bulkheads were Lake Superior cork pine. The knees were tamarack and thwarts white ash. Four-foot air cases were in the turtle-backed bow and stern. The self-bailing capability was provided by six spring-loaded waist port scuppers each 2 feet by 5 inches, and six 2½-inch ball valve scuppers. Two small pumps were located amidships to handle any water accumulating between the cork and sheathing. Either a rudder or sweep oar steered the boat.

The Board reached numerous conclusions regarding the Dobbins. It considered her "practically insubmersible." After capsizing, the test boat righted herself almost immediately and freed itself of water in a mere ten seconds! When a self-righting but not self-bailing lifeboat was capsized simultaneously, it was estimated it would have taken the crew 15 minutes to bail it out even in calm seas. The Dobbins could safely carry 33 persons. When compared to the 43 carried by the English lifeboats with a 33-foot length and 8-foot beam, the smaller Dobbins had distinct advantages.[29]

Dobbins lifeboats were built by only three contractors: in Buffalo by David P. Dobbins or William Hingston and Son and in Erie, Pennsylvania, by W.H. Loomis. The cost was far less than the standard English boats. In 1887 a boat for the Grand Point Au Sable Station cost $500.[30]

There was some controversy regarding the

Dobbins lifeboat. Captain Dobbins obviously was very enthusiastic concerning it and advocated it strongly. The evaluations of the district stations need to be viewed with some degree of skepticism. After all, Dobbins was the Ninth District Superintendent and it was his pet project. Under those circumstances, for a keeper not to provide a strong testimonial would be remarkable. To a degree the Board of Life-Saving Appliances may have tempered their evaluations. While they agreed that the boat had value, it was not accepted for Service-wide use. That it was a good boat there is little doubt. But whether it was as good as its advocates claimed is open to speculation. The design was a compromise, and as is often the case in such situations, it did not fully meet all of its objectives.

The Richardson lifeboat was designed by Captain John M. Richardson, superintendent of the First District. Instead of the 4,000 pounds in weight and 22 inches in draft of the big English boat, his weighed only 3,600 pounds and drew a comparatively mere 18 inches. The weight savings was achieved by substituting cedar planking on oak frames instead of mahogany. Although the Service was pleased with the weight reduction and general performance, it felt further improvements could be made.[31]

In 1891 a larger 34-foot lifeboat was introduced in the Service. Very close to the original Merryman-English model, it was self-bailing and self-righting. Added capabilities included self-ballasting and a centerboard. An estimated 24 were built, nearly all by Great Lakes builders. The majority were assigned to Lakes stations.[32]

The standard 34-footer had three cross and two longitudinal bulkheads below decks. Eighty-two copper air tanks filled the empty spaces. Additional air cases were in the bow and stern and along the sides. Together the cases provided 1½ tons of buoyancy. When tested, a load of 44 men only brought the scuppers awash. The boat was so stable that 3,300 pounds of pig lead on the gunwale was needed to bring it awash. The gun metal keel weighed 1,050 pounds, metal center board 750 pounds and copper air tanks 900 pounds. When turned upside down, this great weight helped roll the boat upright. As in the special Columbian Exposition boat, white oak was used for the frames, stem and stern posts and two layers of clear ³/₈-inch Honduras mahogany laid diagonally formed the hull planking. Between each layer was a covering of 10-ounce cotton duck treated with white lead and oil. The planking was riveted throughout. The deck was also mahogany. Two hollow spruce spars provided for sails as required.[33]

A 34-footer was expressly built for the 1893 Columbian Exposition. The workmanship was considered superlative. The hull and woodwork was made of the clearest mahogany and the keel was entirely brass. The crew who worked on her at the fair claimed that she was harder to roll than the regular lifeboats; doubtlessly her 11,000 pound weight helped her stability. At the conclusion of the exposition the special

boat was sent to the Thunder Bay Island Station.[34]

Some maritime authorities consider that the lifeboat as used by the U.S. Life-Saving Service was the finest small craft ever built. All of the frames were made from the best white oak available and the planking from Pacific Northwest Port Orford cedar. Fittings were either brass or bronze, eliminating any chance of corrosion or rust. Each boat was closely inspected and tested before being accepted by the Serv-

FIGURE 121
The special 34-foot lifeboat built for the 1893 Columbian Exposition in Chicago was later sent to Thunder Bay Island.
Jesse Besser Museum

FIGURE 122
The author's conjecture is that these remains are of the *Valorous* or "Centennial" lifeboat. The boat was built in 1876 by Blackburn and Company of New York to exhibit at the Centennial Exposition in Philadelphia. After the show it was sent to Oswego. In 1880 it was transferred to Portage, in May 1891 to the new Marquette station, in November 1891 to Hammonds Bay and finally in September 1892 to Thunder Bay Island. Based on its age, it was likely condemned on the island.
Jesse Besser Museum

ice. Men's lives would depend on it being as seaworthy as human hands could make it.[35]

By any measure, the lifeboat was a tremendous rescue craft. But its advantages of strength, stability, self-righting and self-bailing were balanced by the weight. It was indeed a compromise.

The Surfboat

The other boat used by the Life-Saving Service was the surfboat. Unlike the lifeboat adopted from Great Britain, the surfboat was a uniquely American invention.

The idea for the original design was taken from the small craft used by New Jersey coastal fishermen and wreckers. This hardy breed of surfmen earned their living by launching their boats regularly through the breaking surf and over outlying sandbars. This activity called for both outstanding boat handling and a very special type of craft.

In 1858 several models of Jersey surfboats were tested by the Department of Treasury. Wardell's surfboat and Green's surfboat were described as clinker built of cedar, square stern and without air chambers. Their length was 26 feet with a seven-foot beam. The weight was

950 pounds. Bunker's surfboat was also clinker built of cedar. Square-sterned, she had air chambers fore and aft and under the thwarts. Slightly smaller at 24 feet 8 inches overall and six feet in beam, she was also lighter at approximately 700 pounds. Although all three boats performed well, especially in the hands of their expert crews, the Bunker boat proved particularly adept for life saving use.[36]

By 1889 three varieties of surfboat were in common use: the Beebe, the Higgins and Gifford, and the famous Beebe-McLellan. All were double ended constructed of white cedar with white oak frames and measured 25 to 27 feet in length, 6½ to 7 feet in beam and 2 feet 3 inches to 2 feet 6 inches in depth amidships. Their bottoms were flat with little or no keel. Typically they drew 6 to 7 inches of water and weighed 700 to 1,100 pounds. Air compartments were at the bow and stern and under the thwarts. Lifelines were festooned along each side. Rowed by six men, they were designed to carry 10 to 12 shipwreck victims, but often held as many as 15. Each boat cost between $210 and $275. The Beebe and the Higgins and Gifford were nearly identical except that the former had more sheer and was clinker built while

FIGURE 123
A "Long Branch" or "Jersey" surfboat on a beach wagon. Note the characteristic "squared" stern.
Author's Collection

the latter was carvel built. The Beebe-McLellan was a Beebe with a self-bailing capability added.[37] Early surfboats were not self-bailing or self-righting.

A fourth variety was the 23-foot Monomoy. Although this model was most commonly used on the East Coast, particularly in Massachusetts, a Monomoy was assigned to the South Manitou Island Station. It was equipped with a centerboard and sail rig.[38]

A fifth variety that saw limited use on the Great Lakes was known as an "old red Jersey" or "Long Branch." Made of cedar and oak, they were made by any of several New Jersey boat builders. It has been observed that no two of the Jersey boats were exactly the same, regardless of model or builder. In size they ranged from 25 to 27 feet in length and 5½ to 7 feet in beam. Their square sterns distinguish them in the old photographs. The original surfboats provided to Crisp's, Two-Heart and Vermilion Stations were of this variety. At $175 each they were also relatively inexpensive. Those Francis

of a Life-Saving Service officer.[40]

Surfboats were made by many different contractors. Major ones included Higgins and Gifford of Gloucester, Massachusetts, Frederick

Beebe of Greenport, New York, Thomas Bagley of Chicago, Stephen Roberts and D. Blackburn of New York City. Others included Gordon of Detroit, Lawrence B. Newman, Charles H. Huff and Henry C. Lane of East

FIGURE 124
The Holland crew prepares to launch what appears to be a Beebe surfboat. The bow of a small supply boat is in the foreground.
Van Ingren Collection
Michigan Maritime Museum

FIGURE 125
This 1890 photo of the Two Rivers station clearly shows a "Long Branch" surfboat on the left and a Merryman lifeboat on the right.
Ted Richardson Collection

metallic surfboats still serviceable often found their way into early use.[39]

Surfboats were typically painted white with green bottoms. Official specifications called for all materials to be of "first quality" and "workmanship to be of the first quality in every respect." All work was subject to the approval

Long Branch, New Jersey, and Charles W. Herbert of Manasquan, New Jersey.[41]

The greatest advantage of the surfboat was its lightness. Using the carriage, it could easily be hauled on the loose sand of the beach to reach the wreck site and launched in very shallow water. The mechanics of launching the surfboat

Beebe-McLellan Self-Bailing, Water-Ballast Surfboat, 1900.

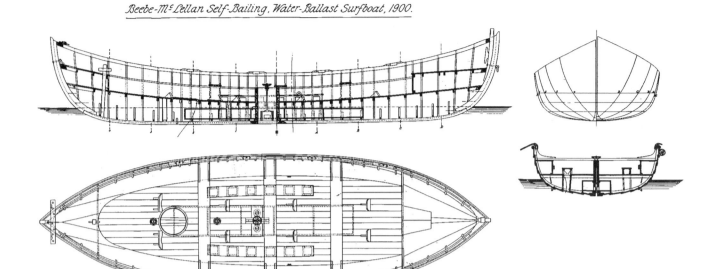

was described by a 1893 writer as "the surfboat is brought down to the water (using a team of horses) on its carriage. The carriage is backed in as far as possible, the crew takes their seats and when the right moment arrives, at the word of command, the carriage is jerked out and the boat is shot, bow on into the water."[42]

In the hands of the experienced surfmen of the Service the boat maneuvered through the breakers and combers with marvelous ease. Where the heavy lifeboat battered through the seas, the light surfboat darted across the dangerous crests of the heaving waves with great suppleness. The lifeboat was powerful but slow; the surfboat nimble and fast. Its wonderful handling characteristics were a great advantage when working near wrecks. The nimbleness enabled it to avoid floating wreckage and quickly slip under the lee of a vessel at an opportune moment and take off the stranded crew.

Kimball described the use of the surfboat as follows: "The keeper steers with a long steering oar, and with the aid of his trained surfmen, intent upon his every look and command, maneuvers his buoyant craft through the surf with masterly skill. He is usually able to avoid a direct encounter with the heaviest breakers, but if he is obligated to receive their onset meets them directly 'head on.' His practiced hand immediately perceives any excess of weight thrown against either bow and instantly counteracts its force with his oar as instinctively and unerringly as the skilled musician presses the proper key of his instrument. He thus keeps his boat from broaching-to and avoids a threatened capsize."[43]

Eventually nearly all of the stations in the

Service had both a lifeboat and surfboat, including the original Great Lakes lifeboat-only stations. Life savers preferred the surfboat for short trips when the number of victims was small. In addition, they were very handy when providing miscellaneous assistance to casualties such as running out lines to tugs and transporting officials. One keeper stated that the surfboat "cannot be surpassed, and that in her he will go upon any sea in which any lifeboat can live."[44]

Between 1871 and 1889, Service-wide, surfboats were launched for rescue 6,730 times, bringing ashore 6,735 victims. During this period the boats capsized 14 times, drowning 41 people, 27 being lifesavers and 14 shipwreck survivors.[45]

The Service was justly very proud of their surfboats. A special surfboat, the *Excelsior,* was built and exhibited at the London Fisheries Exposition in 1884. Following the show it was shipped back to the United States and sent to the Grand Point Au Sable Station.[46]

The Tenth District (Lake Michigan) superin-

tendent spoke of the surfboat enthusiastically. "The keepers and crews of the other stations are continually recounting the wonderful qualities of their particular boat in heavy surf. They all have been thoroughly tried. I must give you my experience in the surfboat, upon my last trip to Lake Superior. I was at station No. 6. I had walked 16 miles the day before, and must get to Whitefish Point that day to catch the steamer, or be detained four days. I was not able to walk

FIGURE 128
Two Rivers life saving crew under the command of keeper George E. Sogge taking the surfboat to the wreck of the steamer *Francis Hinton* November 16, 1909.
Ted Richardson Collection

FIGURE 129
Captain Trudell exercises the Grand Marais crew in the surfboat. Practicing in rough water was normal.
Michigan State Archives

and the wind was blowing a gale directly off the lake. The surf was very high and furious. I ordered the surfboat out. The keeper could not believe me in earnest; but was soon convinced that I was. The boat was taken to the beach, headed out, two men placed in the bows, the rest strung along her sides; and when a favorable opportunity came, the order to launch was given; but the effort was a failure; the boat was thrown ashore with a half pitch-pole. The second attempt ended like the first; but the third time the men were mad and determined, and she was successfully taken through the surf,

FIGURE 130
This rare photo shows a lifeboat being delivered aboard a schooner.
Manistee Historical Museum

and from there to the Point (eight miles). She did not ship two barrels of water. This crew will stake all they have on that boat. The men at all the stations are anxious for occasions to distinguish themselves."[47]

Until the advent of the motorized craft, Great Lakes boats were not named except for those in the Ninth District (lakes Ontario and Erie) during the period David Dobbins was district superintendent. A partial listing follows:

Oswego	lifeboat	*Dreadnought, Valorous*
	surfboat	*Resolute*
Charlotte	lifeboat	*Volunteer*
	surfboat	*Diligent*
Buffalo	lifeboat	*Discovery, Vindicator*
	surfboat	*Restless*
	16-ft. dingy	*Success*
	18-ft. firescow	*Firebug*
Erie	lifeboat	*Defiance, Venture*
Fairport	lifeboat	*Viking*
	surfboat	*Refuge*
Cleveland	lifeboat	*Vigorous, Dictator*
Marblehead	lifeboat	*Diadern*
	surfboat	*Retriever*
	supply boat	*Voyager*
Grand Pt. Au Sable	surfboat	*Excelsior*

The *Valorous,* an English model lifeboat, was exhibited at the 1876 Philadelphia Centennial Exposition. The *Excelsior,* a Higgins and Gifford surfboat, was shown at the 1884 London Fisheries Exposition. Later it was shipped to the Grand Point Au Sable Station.[48]

Superintending Construction

Of all the equipment purchased or manufactured for the Service, lifeboats and surfboats were considered the most critical. To be certain the boats were properly built and tested, the Service appointed a Revenue-Marine officer as superintendent of construction of boats. Functioning under the inspector, he was posted in New York City, a major center of boat building, to take the fullest advantage of improvements in design and construction of the boats and later motors and related equipment. The officer was also responsible to work with potential bidders for new construction and to assist in obtaining repair parts for engines and motors as needed. He was involved in determining the design and specifications as well as drawings for all types of boats, boat wagons and beach apparatus.[49] The officer was required to be present during the construction to assure that all material and workmanship were in full compliance with the specifications. Deviation of any nature without prior approval of the Secretary of the Treasury was not allowed. He also tested the boats before acceptance.[50]

The first superintendent of construction was Captain J.H. Merryman appointed in 1872. In 1873 he was promoted to become the Inspector of the Service. He held the position until his death in 1890. The construction position was later assumed by Captain McLellan.

Onboard Gear

The Service paid special attention to how gear was stowed in both the lifeboat and surfboat. They felt that not only the success of the rescue mission depended on it but also the safety of the boat crew. All items had to be placed to be readily available for action, but not hinder the quick movements of the crew.

For a lifeboat such gear included the anchor, heaving line and grapnel, hatchet, drogue and rope, various lines and sheets, life buoy, heaving line and tub, spare masts, oars and steering oar, boat hooks and lantern.

There were two critical principles that were never to be violated. The first was that every item ordinarily required should always be kept aboard. The Service recognized that during the heat of a call for rescue, critical items could be easily left ashore. By storing them aboard, human error was eliminated. The second principle was that every article must be stowed in the same place and in the same way every time without fail. This was absolutely necessary to allow the crew to work the boat without hindrance. To have to row with even the smallest avoidable inefficiency in a heavy sea could spell disaster. For example, if the ropes were not properly coiled and stowed beneath the thwarts and clear from the foot boards, the surfmen's legs could cramp; muscles in the back, shoulder and arms also would not work properly causing discomfort, strain and early fatigue. As a result the rescue effort could fail. The rescue and boat would be needlessly in peril. If the

DECK-PLAN OF A SELF-RIGHTING LIFE-BOAT, SHOWING THE MANNER IN WHICH THE GEAR IS STOWED.

Boat and Gear.   *List of Articles Shown.*

1. Anchor.
2. Cable.
3. Bow heaving-line or grapnel-rope and grapnel.
4. Drogue-rope.
5. Stern heaving-line.
6. } Veering lines.
7. }
8. Jib outhaul or tack.
9. Mizzen-sheets.
10. Drogue.
11. Life-buoy.
12. Loaded cane, heaving-line, and tub.
13. Tailed block.
14. Pump-well hatch.
15. } Deck ventilating-hatches.
16. }
17. Foot-boards for rowers.
18. Side air-cases.
19. Relieving tubes and valves.
20. Samson's post.
21. Thwarts.
22. Central batten, to which the masts and boat-hooks are lashed.

FIGURE 131
Plan for equipment stowage on a self-righting lifeboat. It was critical everything be in proper position.
National Archives

FIGURE 132
Onboard gear was always stored to be ready for action at a moment's notice as this photo of the Fairport crew and their surfboat shows.
Ted Richardson Collection

FIGURE 133
The author believes this photo shows the initial installation at Marquette of a Lake Shore engine in a surfboat. Notice the extensive hull changes required to accommodate the propeller.

*Marquette
Maritime Museum*

lifeboat's masts, normally lashed amidships between the oarsmen, were improperly secured, and the boat was thrown on its beam ends, the masts could trap the men on the lee side preventing them from getting free to right the boat. Disaster could be the result.[51]

Righting lines were especially important. Beside each oarlock a light line was secured with a small wood float at the bitter end. When the boat capsized, the float brought the line free. When the lines were thrown over the hull of the overturned boat, the crew used them to "walk" up the hull, righting the boat as they went.

The Service strongly emphasized every article must be stored properly in the assigned location and ready for instant use. Inspectors were to pay particular attention to assuring that the gear was aboard all boats and ready for action.

Motorized Boats

As is evident by the work of the Board of Life-Saving Appliances, the Service was deeply concerned with capitalizing on the latest technical innovations. Motorizing lifeboats and surfboats was one of the more important improvements made.

The initial experiments were conducted by the Marquette Life-Saving crew in 1899. In April of that year a 12-horsepower, two-cylinder gasoline engine manufactured by the city's Lake Shore Iron Works was installed in a 34-foot self-righting and self-bailing centerboard lifeboat. The engine was water cooled and used a "make and break" spark ignition. The motor was placed in the after air chamber without dis-

turbing any of the boat's original construction. Results were so successful that another engine was installed with some minor modifications in a second boat.[52]

The Lake Shore Iron Company was the manufacturer of the "Superior" marine engine. The company started in the 1850s as a builder of mine equipment and steam engines for mine hoists.

By the 1890s many of their "Superior" engines were in use about the harbor.[53] The Service selected the Lake Shore engine because of its "lightness per horsepower, simplicity of construction, compactness and its unfailing ability to run under adverse conditions."[54]

The lifeboat the engine was installed in was not the Marquette Station's regular boat. It was a special lifeboat shipped in from the Monmouth Beach, New Jersey, station. Originally one was to be sent from the Grand Haven, Michigan, depot, but none was available.

The contract with Lake Shore stated that if the trial was a success and the government kept the engine, the company would receive $1,000. If the Service decided not to retain the engine, then Lake Shore would remove it and return the boat to the original condition in return for the sum of $250.[55]

Although the Marquette station had used the motorized lifeboat under varying conditions, it's most severe storm test occurred in November 1900. As reported in the city's *Daily Mining Journal,* "Captain Cleary and his sturdy crew put in a couple of hours of the roughest kind of work yesterday afternoon. They did not enact the roles of life savers but were engaged with the more prosaic task of giving their gasoline engine-propelled lifeboat a thorough test in the teeth of the heaviest blow that has been experienced here this fall. For upwards of two hours they sported around in huge seas which washed over the breakwater as if it were a log boom. When their craft had been tried in every possible manner they returned to the calm waters of the inner harbor entirely satisfied and pleased with the test.

"Up town the movements and antics of the lifeboat as it braved the fierce wind and waves were attentively watched from all points of vantage. Many people, not initiated in the crew's skill in riding out severe storms, were astonished at its temerity in venturing outside the breakwater and many were the 'ohs' and 'ahs' as the lifeboat would plunge from the crest of a wave completely out of sight. The stability and buoyancy of the craft were remarkable. It rode the seas like a duck although at times it would be fairly hidden from sight by huge masses of spray. When headed into the very teeth of the storm it

tion was closely examined. Although effective to a degree, the steamers sacrificed the self-righting capability, an unacceptable concession in the eyes of the Service.

The Service considered electric power, but the great weight of the batteries made the boat too heavy for transport and caused it to draw too much water to maneuver over shallow sand bars. Compressed air as well as carbonic acid

appeared to be making about six miles an hour, a remarkable speed considering the unusual size of the rollers and the great velocity of the wind. Against these a craft propelled by oars in the hands of the members of the crew would have been unable to make the slightest headway. Many people observing the wonderful work of the boat, expressed their surprise that gas engines were not used in all life saving craft in the service."[56]

To fully evaluate both the concept of motorized boats and their practical application, the Service appointed a special commission chaired by C.H. Peabody, the President of the Board of Life-Saving Appliances and a professor of naval architecture and marine engineering at the Massachusetts Institute of Technology.

Steam had earlier been considered as a power source, and the experience of steam lifeboats in Great Britain's Royal National Lifeboat Institu-

reaction engines also proved impractical.[57]

After due course, the commission recommended gasoline engines be installed in other large lifeboats and that some special modifications in terms of raised decks and heavier keels be provided. In addition, two entirely new lifeboats were built incorporating the improvements. The Inspector of the Life-Saving Service, Captain C.H. McLellan, Revenue Cutter Service, continued to evaluate the performance of motorized boats. McLellan originally worked with Marquette's Captain Cleary installing the original test engine in the Marquette boat.[58]

As the advantages of the motorized craft became obvious, more were added to the Service. Engine power also increased as larger power plants became available. In addition, both surfboats and lifeboats continued to evolve in response to engine capability. The new craft

FIGURE 134
Captain Cleary and the Marquette crew prepare to launch their newly motorized surfboat.

Marquette Maritime Museum

were constantly being evaluated, both by the Board of Life-Saving Appliances and selected stations. In 1909, the Two-Heart River Station (Lake Superior) tested the new Beebe-McLel-

FIGURE 135
This later version of a motorized surfboat shows an improved skeg and rudder over the original Marquette installation.
Ted Richardson Collection

lan self-bailing power surfboat with excellent results.[59] The motors were enclosed in watertight compartments. If the boat capsized, a unique circular circuit breaker automatically stopped the engine. Once the boat self-righted and self-bailed, it could be restarted and the mission continued.[60]

Although the gas-powered boats increased capability, there was a significant penalty. In 1900 the lightest 12-horsepower engine togeth-

er with fittings weighed 1,500 pounds. However, by 1906 technology improved such that a 25-horsepower engine weighed less than half of the old model. A 75-gallon main full tank was located in the bottom of the forward air case and an auxiliary 25-gallon tank in the top of the case. The gas was gravity fed to the engine from the top tank. As needed, fuel was pumped from the bottom tank to the top, thus assuring the bulk of the weight was always low.[61]

In 1909, 44 of the 34-foot lifeboats and six of the new 36-footers were motorized. By 1914, there were 147 power lifeboats and surfboats in use. Lifeboats generally had 35- to 40-horsepower engines and surfboats 12-horsepower ones.[62]

The big powered lifeboats were given names by the crews befitting the nature of their work. The boat at Grand Marais, Michigan, was called *Audacity,* while that at Duluth was *Intrepid.* The Harbor Beach boat was *Fearless,* Marquette's *Tempest,* Eagle Harbor's *Loyal,* Lorain's *Advance,* Sturgeon Bay's *Restless* and *Willing,* Frankfort's *Daring,* Thunder Bay Island's *Preserver* and Marblehead's *Brave.*[63]

The motorized boats more than doubled the scope and range of operations at the stations where they were provided. The life savers were

FIGURE 136
Captain Henry Cleary and his 34-foot motor lifeboat *Tempest* under way. A drogue is rigged on the stern quarter.
Ted Richardson Collection

able not only to reach the scene of disaster faster, but also in much better physical condition than before. In 1907, before motorized boats were in common use, 2,158 persons

additional boats to handle the more mundane tasks of daily operations. Moving supplies from the Revenue-Cutters or just ferrying surfmen across the harbor were typical jobs. Listed in the records simply as "supply boats," they were often old surfboats no longer considered fit for the stress of storm work. As late as 1899 the stations at Crisp's Point and Vermilion used outmoded Francis metallic surfboats to fill the workboat requirement. Sheboygan used their Francis until 1887.

Sometimes the boats were built by the crews. The Ship Canal Station crew built a 15-foot rowboat and 16-foot supply boat in 1887.

FIGURE 137
Through the waves, a motor lifeboat under way. The big boats were extremely seaworthy.

*Institute of
Great Lakes Research*

(Service-wide) were carried to safety in their boats. The average during the period 1908 to 1911 was 2,852, clearly showing an increase in capability.[64]

Other Boats

While as a rule most stations had both a lifeboat and a surfboat, they often also had

Material for the first cost $6 and the second $10.65! The rowboat was needed to allow the patrol to cross the canal. In 1882 Quinton Morgan, the original keeper at Deer Park, built a 32-foot supply boat out of Norway pine for the Two-Heart Station. Supply boats were also constructed by the same firms that built the lifeboats and surfboats. These manufactured

FIGURE 138
Five station boats are in view in this photo of the Grand Haven station.
Michigan State Archives

FIGURE 139
A life saver's beach cart. Note the tally board in the front, hawser reel and shot-line boxes. A drogue is hanging on the left. The cart is on display at the Sleeping Bear Point Maritime Museum at Glen Haven, Michigan.
Author's Collection

craft were also more expensive than the crew-built ones. A 18-footer from Thomas Bagley of Chicago cost $53. A 16-footer was $43.[65]

Beach Apparatus

The term beach apparatus was used to refer to the specific items of equipment carried on the station's two-wheeled beach cart. Normally it consisted of a $5\frac{1}{2}$-inch eprouvette (Manby) mortar with bed and three balls (360 pounds). The more effective and lighter Lyle gun was later substituted; one shotline with faking box (80 pounds); one $2\frac{1}{2}$-inch hauling line on a whip, 250 fathoms with block (300 pounds); one $4\frac{1}{2}$-inch hawser (600 pounds); one crotch and sand anchors, picks and shovels (125 pounds). If the lifecar was included, another 225 pounds was added, bringing the weight to nearly 1,700 pounds.

This was a considerable weight when it was realized that it had to be hauled by the crew by hand from the station to the point on the beach opposite the wreck. Invariably this had to be done in the worst weather, through mud, storm and soft sand. It was common for the crews to be utterly exhausted when they arrived, just at the time when their greatest strength would be needed.

When ready for action the cart looked like a junk man's wagon with gear seemingly piled on top of gear. In reality it was a master work of planning and loading. Not an article was superfluous or a necessary one omitted. There were two slightly different carts used. They can be identified by the wheels, one having a single iron wearing band and the other two thin bands.

Unless it was absolutely needed, it became common practice on the Great Lakes to leave the lifecar at the station and rely instead on the lighter breeches buoy. The difference in weight between the lifecar and the breeches buoy, including the much lighter hawsers and lines, was nearly 550 pounds. Sometimes, when it was imperative to reduce the cart weight to the greatest possible extent, the heavy hawser was left behind at the station and the entire rescue was accomplished with the lighter whip.[66]

If it were later necessary to bring the lifecar, it was hoped that the crew of an adjacent station would be available to haul it.

Invariably, the breeches buoy was sufficient for Great Lakes rescues. The vessels driven ashore usually were crewed by five to 10 people, a number more appropriate for the one-at-a-time breeches buoy than the heavy five-per-trip lifecar.

The breeches buoy was simple in the extreme, nothing more than a pair of canvas

breeches attached to a cork life ring 7¹/₂ feet in circumference. The ring in turn attached with four rope lanyards to a block or metal hook that in turn was rigged to a heavy line running from the vessel to the shore. Although when or how the breeches buoy was invented is unknown, it is believed it evolved from the bosun's chair. This was a canvas seat or wooden plank attached to a line and pulleys that enabled the sailor to be raised or lowered to different locations on the vessel to work. The breeches buoy weighed a mere 21 pounds making it easily transportable. It also stood the test of time, remaining in service with the Coast Guard well into the 1950s.

The last Great Lakes rescue using the Lyle gun and breeches buoy was on September 12, 1953. The 530-foot steamer *Maryland* blew ashore east of Marquette during a north gale. Using the old Lyle gun, the Marquette Coast Guard removed 24 of her crew before the hawser snapped. In a sign of times to come, the remaining 11 were recovered by a helicopter.[67]

Although in theory simple, the actual procedure for performing a rescue with the beach apparatus and breeches buoy was very complicated. All actions were under the explicit direction of the keeper.

After hauling the cart from the station to the wreck site, the crew care-

fully positioned it on the beach opposite the vessel and a few yards to windward. The front faced the surf. The keeper removed the leather haversack containing the cartridges, primers, lanyards and gun level from the cart and placed it around his waist.

The sand anchor was buried to the rear and a few yards downwind by the No. 4, 5 and 6 surfmen. Normal depth was two feet. The gun was positioned four paces to the windward of the cart by the keeper and No. 1. The shotline or faking box was posted a yard to the windward of it by Nos. 2 and 3.[68] The box was turned upside down and the pegs removed, thus leaving the line on the open box, properly coiled and ready to deploy. The box was canted on an angle of about 45 degrees. If a second shot was necessary using the same shotline, a tarpaulin was spread out on the beach and the line was laid out in large loops called "French faking." The shotline box was about 3 feet long, 1¹/₂ feet wide and 1 foot deep. From 500 to 700 yards of line was in the box, depending on its size.[69]

The keeper and No. 1 loaded the gun with the

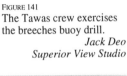

PRACTICE, IN THE LIFE SAVING SERVICE. EAST TAWAS MICH COPYRIGHT 1909 BY
RESCUING WITH THE LIFE-BUOY. Brodohau Photog AUSABLE MICH.

cartridge and shot while No. 2 attached the shotline, taking care that there was no slack between the shot and faking box. Nos. 1 and 2 positioned themselves on their knees on the left and right side of the gun. Under the direction of

luck the line arced across the wreck. This was far easier said than done. The projectile was affected by both the weight of the following shotline as well as the force of the wind. The ship was also a small target. Should the wind be gusting or quartering, it was difficult to aim a shot such as to cause the line to drop neatly over the deck. Although the shot could drop cleanly and true on the far side of the vessel, the line could blow or float clear of the wreck and fall into the lake.

While the gun was readied, No. 4 unloaded the crotch, brought it to a suitable location and opened it. The preferable site was high on a sand bank. He made a second trip to the cart to bring the breeches buoy and the end of the hawser, placing both just to the front of the crotch. Nos. 3 and 4 ran

FIGURES 142 & 143
The drill manual carefully prescribed every man's job and position during the breeches buoy drill.
Author's Collection

the keeper, they trained the muzzle using the rear handles. Once the lateral direction was set taking due allowance for the wind, the keeper adjusted the elevation, inserted the primer and set the lanyard. Standing to the weather side, he gave the cautionary command "Ready," and at the best opportunity fired.

Behind the shot trailed the shotline. With

the tackle from the sand anchor to the crotch, leaving it ready to be attached. Using the shotline, the crew aboard the wreck hauled the whip line (continuous line) with a tail block to the wreck. Normally the shotline would be cut to minimize the amount of line to be hauled aboard the wreck. Sometimes not cutting the line could result in the shipwreck crew having

FIGURE 144
A Great Lakes crew erecting the crotch. Contrary to normal drill procedures, the keeper is assisting.
Sleeping Bear Dunes National Lakeshore

to drag an extra 200 to 300 yards aboard. However, if, in the judgement of the keeper, there was no imminent danger of the wreck going to pieces, the line was not cut and the full length taken aboard. The life savers helped by assuring that the line ran free and with minimum stress. Once aboard the wreck, the crew secured the line as high as possible, preferably on a mast. A wooden placard or "tally board" attached to the whip provided detailed, illustrated instructions in both English and French. Despite this precaution, in more than one example crewmen were unable to understand the simple actions required of them. In one instance the vessel captain looked dumbly at the French side of the instructions, utterly unable to comprehend them. In the confusion of the wreck, he failed to realize that English instructions were on the reverse side.

Once the whip was secured to the wreck, the free end ashore was rove through a block on the sand anchor pennant by No. 4 and the two ends joined by No. 3 with a double fisherman's bend. Following this action, Nos. 1 and 2 used a rolling hitch to bend the lee side of the whip onto the hawser as near the water as possible. Nos. 2, 3, 4, 5 and 7 pulled the weather side of the whip to haul the hawser to the wreck. The keeper worked to hold the hawser free while No. 1 did the same for the lee whip. When the hawser was secured to the wreck, No. 6 snatched the bight into the sand anchor block.

The whip was cast off and Nos. 1 and 2 hauled it back to shore until the bend was

reached. A travel block was snapped onto the hawser and to the ends of the whip bend onto the strap of the breeches buoy block. Simultaneously the keeper, Nos. 3, 4, 5, 6 and 7 hauled through the hawser slack by hand, attached the tackle using a cat's paw in the hawser, pulled the hawser "moderately" tight and raised the crotch making the hawser fully taut. Securing the tackle, the breeches buoy was now ready for use. In action Nos. 1 and 2 manned the left and right sides of the whip and Nos. 2, 4, 5, 6 and 7 shifted the breeches buoy. The keeper supervised and assisted as needed.

In some circumstances, if a man from an adjacent crew was available, he would be sent

FIGURE 145
The Ashtabula crew practices under the close supervision of the keeper.
Jack Deo Superior View Studio

out to the wreck on the first breeches buoy run to help the victims and coordinate the rescue. Other crewmen from the second station would assist from shore by hauling and helping victims. Keepers were cautioned never to allow

thus preventing needless damage to the equipment. It may be needed for another rescue or the vessel might be breaking up. To remove the hawser, a special device known as a "hawser cutter" was used. Resembling an open block, it

FIGURE 146
One of the crew of the car ferry *Pere Marquette 16* rides the breeches buoy ashore after wrecking off Ludington on December 27, 1906. The life savers successfully removed 36 of the crew.

Author's Collection

interference in the management of the rescue from outsiders, but they could aid in hauling lines or the like.[70]

It was not uncommon during gale and storm for a strong current to run between the beach and outer bar. Called a "set" or "cut," combined with surf action, it could twist and tangle the lines during the attempt to haul them from shore to ship. Occasionally, when the beach apparatus was fully established, the motion of the wreck as it rolled in the seas or shifted was powerful enough to break the lines. Equally true, if the vessel's crew allowed the lines to chafe against the wreck, lines would part. In extreme cold, the lines froze stiff or ice jammed the blocks. Unless proper care was taken, the speed at which ropes ran through the blocks could generate enough friction to set them on fire.[71]

Once the crew from the stranded vessel was safely on the beach, it was often necessary to quickly recover the hawser from the wreck,

attached to the hawser and was hauled out as close to the mast as possible using the whip. When tripped by a pull on the return end of the whip, internal knives on the hawser cutter cut the hawser allowing it to be hauled ashore.[72]

The Rev. W.H. Law in his book *Heroes of the Great Lakes* recounts this story of the breeches buoy in action. "On one occasion, when a life-saving crew was taking people off a wreck, the breeches buoy was used, bringing one after another to the shore. After landing several, the captain noticed that the breeches buoy was coming in apparently empty. Nothing was visible in it except but the top of a little boy's head. In helping him out the captain spoke to him kindly and in a playful way remarked, 'Why little man I was beginning to think we had nothing in the buoy this time. What a little mite you are, not much bigger than a pint of cider, are you?' The little fellow looked up and smiled, and feeling himself safe on land, his normal condition returned, and with it a spirit of mirthfulness, and he said, 'Say cap, you will have load enough next time you send out the old breeches.' Lo and behold you, when the breeches buoy sent out returned, it brought back the little boy's mother, who weighed over two hundred pounds, filling the buoy, causing it to sag on the line, until her feet, sticking through, almost dipped in the water. You can't blame the captain for doubling up with laughter every time he tells this story, as he calls to remembrance that boy passing a joke on his fat mother."[73]

The Service considered the reloading of the cart after use to be extremely important. Like the boats, regulations clearly established where every item was to be placed and secured. For example, the hawser was always coiled right handed from the outside toward the center. Subsequent layers required the bight to be carried to the outside and the process repeated. This detailed process meant that in use the hawser would always run from the center, thus minimizing the potential for fouling. The loops of the shovel handles were placed over the upper horn of the pick, with the shovel blades to the right and secured by a line spliced around the right rear of the cart and brought up and over the handles.

The Lyle gun was to be set athwart the hawser directly over the axle with the muzzle to the right. Three-foot rope stops held it firmly in place. Shotline boxes were placed between it and the tailboard. They were also secured with three-foot stops. The sand anchor was rigged to the tailgate. The keeper's haversack containing three 6-ounce, three 5-ounce and three 4-ounce cartridges and a dozen primers was placed on the gun. Regulations detailed where every item was to be placed and secured without deviation.[74]

Properly loaded, the cart should balance perfectly, thus making it as easy as possible to haul to the wreck site. Regulations identified that if it didn't balance, the most likely cause was a slightly different sized crotch and sand anchor. Moving the gun a few inches fore or aft would reinstate the balance. This minor movement of the gun was the only deviation allowed.[75]

For the time carts were considered expensive. In 1899 each cart together with double reels as built by the Racine Wagon and Carriage Company in Racine, Wisconsin, cost $57.[76]

Lifecar

During the early years of the Service, although mostly on the East Coast, the lifecar was a commonly used appliance. There is a fair degree of confusion concerning who invented the device. Congress at different times recognized the claims of two men, Joseph Francis and Douglas Ottinger. Francis was also the inventor of many patented life saving devices, including metal-

FIGURES 147 & 148
The hawser cutter open and closed. A sharp pull on the lower lines closed the steel blades cutting the hawser.
Author's Collection

FIGURE 149
The Lyle gun fires for the *Argo* rescue.
Ted Richardson Collection

lic lifeboats and special folding life preservers. His Novelty Iron Works also provided the metal lifeboats for the original life saving stations. Ottinger was a Revenue-Marine captain who was extensively involved in establishing the early New Jersey stations. Relations between the two men were acrimonious at best, each latter accusing the other of stealing "his" invention. Since the records are unclear, it is suspected that the two worked together in developing the lifecar, but Francis, being a businessman, ended up with the patent rights and therefore the right to claim the invention.

Kimball was careful to steer the middle ground between the two claimants. When asked he simply said that details were contained in the Congressional Record. He also "exercised the utmost care to make every statement exactly correct" regarding the controversy. There was no gain to the Service in alienating either faction.[77]

Congress at different times recognized both men. In 1859 it voted Ottinger $10,000 in consideration of the lifecar's service to humanity. In 1887 another Congress awarded a gold medal to Francis for the same reason.[78]

FIGURE 150
The *Argo* was driven ashore off Holland during the great November 1913 storm. The crew aboard was unable to correctly rig the breeches buoy. Seeing the trouble, one of the surfmen tied off a line to his waist, and after sending the other end to the vessel, had the crew of the *Argo* haul him aboard through the surf. Once on the deck of the *Argo,* he quickly directed the setup of the breeches buoy.
Ted Richardson Collection

Although he claims that he conceived the idea in 1838, Francis did not begin work on the lifecar until 1841. His intention was to build a

covered lifeboat that was strong enough to withstand the blows of the most powerful waves. Using a hawser from ship to shore, it could be drawn through the surf bringing victims to safety. The first efforts used wood as the material, but he could not overcome the problems of weight. To make the lifecar strong enough to withstand the pounding of laying alongside a wreck, or contact with the rocks of a beach, made it too heavy for easy use. The required frames and knees needed to stiffen it only added to the weight problem as well as made it difficult to find room for passengers.

In a burst of inspiration, Francis decided to try sheet iron. After building a set of wooden dies representing the lifecar, he attempted to press an iron sheet against them thus molding a hull. However, after every attempt, once the pressure was released, the iron sheet sprang back into its original shape. It was only after discovering the principle of corrugating metal that Francis was able to make the sheet hold the pressed shape. After a long series of experiments, Francis was able to make what he considered the perfect lifecar in 1847.[79]

The Francis lifecars were manufactured using cast iron dies weighing three tons and costing $6,000. This was very expensive for the time. The iron sheets were formed into shape with a large hydraulic press exerting 800 tons of force. A rounded iron deck was added that was not corrugated. A deck hatch allowed the passengers, normally four, to enter. When closed the

hatch was sufficiently watertight to keep the occupants dry. An iron "trip cylinder" ran above the top of the deck. Its purpose was to assure that if the lifecar overturned, it would quickly right itself. Fresh air entered through a series of small holes along the top.[80]

Although intended for the lifecar, the half-hull sections when joined formed a type of lifeboat without the requirement of knees or other internal bracing. Altering the dies allowed Francis to produce metallic lifeboats for a variety of uses. Many were used by early lifeboat stations as well as shipboard applications on commercial and naval vessels.[81]

Francis lifecars were provided in 1849 to the original New Jersey stations. Although they had not been practically tested, great faith was placed in them.[82] The test came on January 17, 1850, when the British ship *Ayrshire* with 201 souls on board was driven on a reef near the Squan Beach (New Jersey) Station. The conventional lifeboats then available were incapable of making it through the boiling surf. However, the Francis lifecar could and did, rescuing 200 of the 201 on board. The lone casualty was caused when a victim, unable to get into

FIGURE 151
Joseph Francis, considered by many to be the inventor of the lifecar.
Author's Collection

FIGURE 152
The Francis boat press.
Author's Collection

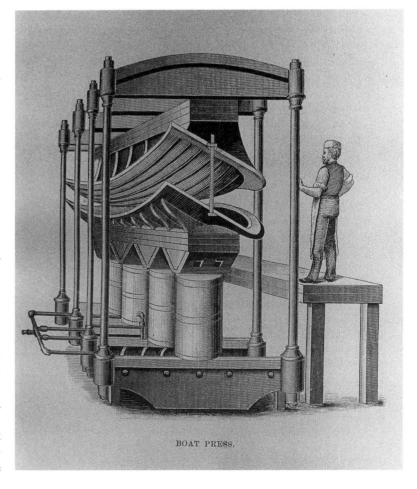

BOAT PRESS.

TWO HUNDRED LIVES SAVED FROM THE WRECK OF THE SHIP AYRSHIRE, JANUARY 12, 1850, BY FRANCIS' PATENT CORRUGATED LIFE-CAR.

FIGURE 153
The *Ayrshire* rescue on
January 12, 1850.
Author's Collection

the car with his family, jumped on the outside as it started in to the beach. He was almost instantly washed off and drowned.[83] The car used in the rescue was later sent to Washington and displayed in the capitol rotunda.[84]

It also became a featured exhibit at various national and international expositions. Included in the display was the Manby mortar and projectile used during the rescue.[85]

The original version of the Francis lifecar traveled on a hawser run through rings on two chains fore and aft. Later models used large hoops mounted directly on the car's hull. The original lifecar was also comparatively light and easy to manage. "Improved" versions designed by others were larger, heavier and more awkward. Francis always believed his original was the best.[86]

The rigging for the lifecar was much the same as the breeches buoy, except that instead of the victims being hauled one at a time above the waves in a teetering canvas contraption, the metal lifecar was used. While the breeches buoy ride may have been terrifying, the lifecar must have been doubly so. Passengers were stuffed into it like sardines, often lying on top

of one another. There were no windows. It was utterly black and without ventilation of any kind. The sounds of the waves crashing into it and the howl of the wind must have made the passengers wish for the flimsy breeches buoy. Later designs provided for more headroom, at least enough to allow the occupants to sit upright.

Remembering the lifecar, an old keeper stated, "Well sir, there's curious things seen on the beach on nights of shipwreck. I'm no hand at describing. Some men stagger out of the car sick, some crying or praying, some as cool as they'd just stepped off a tram."[87]

By 1890 the use of the lifecar had declined greatly. Shipwrecks had decreased in frequency and the competence of the life saving crews increased such that boat rescues were more common. The breeches buoy was also far lighter to haul across the shore to the wreck site. Since newer vessels were stronger, they broke up slower, allowing more time for a one-at-a-time rescue with the breeches buoy.[88]

Despite the declining popularity, the Service continued to buy lifecars. In 1899, 10 were purchased from the Continental Iron Works at a cost of $230 each. However, instead of being directly issued, they were stored until needed.[89]

The Lyle Gun

The Life-Saving Service originally used a mortar to fire a line to a stranded vessel. The

pellant. They were also expensive, a drawback the Service wanted to avoid.

In 1854 Navy Lieutenant John A. Dahlgren conducted a series of experiments at the Washington Navy Yard to develop a more efficient line-throwing device. The result was described

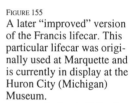

FIGURE 154
A Francis lifecar, possibly the original of *Ayrshire* fame, is on display at the Smithsonian Institution in Washington, D.C.
Author's Collection

mortar was a Manby or "eprouvette" mortar, originally developed in 1807 by Captain G.W. Manby, a British merchant master. It had a 5½-inch bore and a range of 421 yards.[90] Weighing with shot approximately 360 pounds, it was a heavy and awkward device. In addition, the design of the iron bed gave them a tendency to overturn when fired in soft sand. Should the bed break, a new casting was required, thus negating any chance of quick, cheap or local repair. An inherent problem with mortars was the high angle of fire required. This meant very long shotlines were needed which in turn increased problems with fouling. Manby mortars were the issue mortar for the original Great Lakes stations. A Manby was also used to fire the line to the *Ayrshire* wreck, allowing the Francis lifecar to prove its unique capability. Rockets saw some use as line-carrying devices, mostly in Europe, but generally proved to be inaccurate and suffered from unstable pro-

as a "...howitzer capable of throwing a ball with the line attached 370 yards,...twice the distance thrown by the mortar now in use."[91] The records are unclear regarding the fate of Dahlgren's howitzer. It may have been used in

FIGURE 155
A later "improved" version of the Francis lifecar. This particular lifecar was originally used at Marquette and is currently in display at the Huron City (Michigan) Museum.
Author's Collection

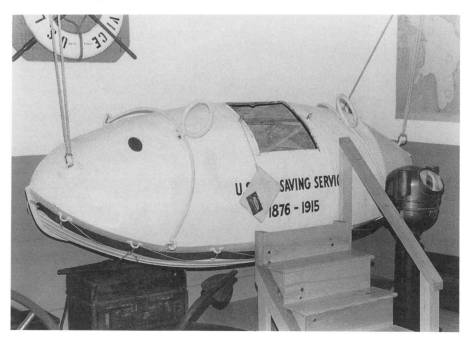

limited numbers but never achieved the acceptance of the Manby. Dahlgren was an extraordinary ordnance officer. He is remembered not for his work with a line-throwing gun but instead as the developer of large bore Civil War guns. During the war his creations, some with bores as large as 15 inches, weighing 10 tons and firing 1,000-pound shells, were known as "Dahlgrens."

Recognizing the deficiencies of the existing mortars and rockets, one of Kimball's first actions on appointment as general superintendent was to find a better line-throwing device. Initially, experiments with a 3-inch caliber smooth-bore mortar designed by the famous Civil War gun designer Robert P. Parrott were promising. Made of cast iron and lined with a steel barrel, it weighed a hefty 201 pounds. The carriage was made of ash and added another $65\frac{1}{2}$ pounds to the system for a total of 267 pounds. The projectile was 15 inches long and weighed 22 pounds. A total of seven shots were fired by the Parrott mortar during the June 1877 trials at the West Point Foundry, Cold Spring, New York. The results were not auspicious. The shotline broke during two firings. In six,

the mortar recoil described as "very violent" was strong enough to turn it upside down, upset the carriage or blow it back more than six feet! Both Superintendent Kimball and Captain Merryman were present for the tests. Despite the problems, a range of 473 yards was obtained, and since there was no better alternative, the Service ordered 25 of the mortars.[92]

Parrott also built two larger mortars for two Cape Cod stations. These monsters weighed an incredible 522 pounds (300 pounds for the mortar and 222 pounds for the bed) and fired a 33-pound projectile up to 496 yards.[93]

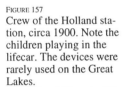

Realizing that he needed to tap the best artillery expertise available, Kimball recruited the aid of the Army Board of Ordnance. After due consideration, on June 6, 1877, the Chief of Ordnance assigned Lieutenant David A. Lyle to the job of conducting experiments to evaluate the best guns for the Life-Saving Service.

The objectives of the experiments were manifold: to extend the range of guns; determine the best kind, size and caliber; reduce the overall weight to the greatest extent possible; find the best type and size of shotline; find the best powder and determine appropriate charges; secure the best faking box and find the best relative position of the gun and box.[94]

The Lyle experiments were conducted initially during the fall of 1877 at an improvised range near the National Armory at Springfield, Massachusetts. A second series of tests was conducted at the U.S. Army Ordnance proving ground at Sandy Hook, New Jersey, in the Spring of 1878.[95]

Lieutenant Lyle initially tested a 3-inch muzzle-loading rifled mortar, but quickly found it unsuitable for use. It was complicated to load and fire and the spinning of the projectile induced by the rifling decreased the range and twisted the shotline. He decided his efforts should be concentrated on smooth-bore guns.

Lyle manufactured his experimental guns from bronze, a material he considered superior

guns were easy to keep clean, especially the bores and prime holes. Lastly, the guns could be recast if required, and if condemned from further use still had scrap value. Bronze had long been out of fashion for artillery field pieces because of its propensity to quickly deteriorate under the pressures of rapid firing. However, the life saving guns were used sparingly and then with comparatively light charges. The original test guns were cast with Lake Superior copper, from the Quincy mine, and German tin.[96]

The guns were mounted on small wooden carriages. Iron handles were on either side of the carriage. The gun could be easily dismounted and carried by one man on his shoulder while a second took the carriage.[97]

Lyle found that three sizes of gun were appropriate for Service use. For ranges of 300

FIGURE 158
Colonel David Lyle, the inventor of the Lyle gun.
Author's Collection

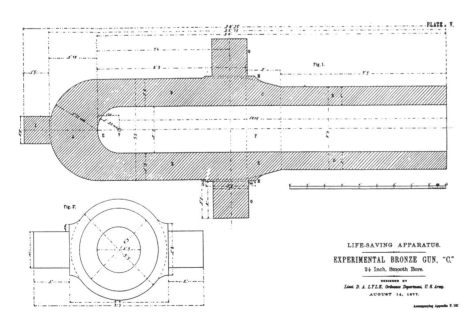

LIFE-SAVING APPARATUS.

EXPERIMENTAL BRONZE GUN, "C."
2½ Inch, Smooth Bore.

DESIGNED BY
Lieut. D. A. LYLE, Ordnance Department, U. S. Army.
AUGUST 14, 1877.

FIGURE 159
Experimental gun "C" eventually became the famous Lyle gun.
Author's Collection

for Service use. It was strong but comparatively light in weight. It was not affected by corrosion from exposure to salt air as steel or iron was and was not liable to sudden bursting. Bronze

yards or less with heavy shotlines (No. 7), a 3-inch gun was best; ranges of 400 yards and less with braided lines (No. 4-7) a 2½-inch gun was adequate; for ranges of 250 yards and less with

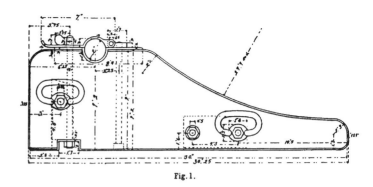

Fig.1.

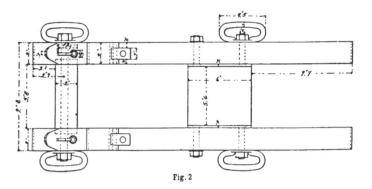

Fig. 2

service lines (No. 4 and 7), a 2-inch gun was acceptable. The 2½-inch gun weighed 158 pounds (108 for the gun and 50 for the carriage) and the 2-inch 89 pounds (54 for the gun and 35 for the carriage). The 3-inch gun weighed only slightly more than the 2½-inch. The weight difference between any of the Lyle guns and the old 360-pound mortar was considerable.[98] It was the 2½-inch gun that became the Service standard. This gun was a mere 24¼ inches in length.

The projectiles for all three bronze guns were cast iron and of the same general design, differing only in size and weight. All had a wrought iron eye bolt screwed into the base as an attachment point for the shotline. The 2½-inch projectile was 15¾ inches long and 19 pounds, the 2-inch was 15 inches long and 13 pounds and the 3-inch was 13¾ inches long and 23 pounds.[99]

The eye of the shank to which the shotline was attached projected out of the mouth of the gun far enough to prevent the line from burning. The shotline was also protected by the very tight fit of the projectile into the bore. The clearance was called windage, and Lyle had his projectiles machined to practically eliminate it. The exact tolerances were between .002 and .015 inches.[100] After firing, the shot rotated such that the eye bolt was trailing. Any charge of powder, up to 8 ounces, could be used with the gun.[101]

The recoil from the gun was terrific. During drill the standard charge of 1½ ounces of powder was sufficient to knock the gun back six feet. A maximum rescue charge of eight ounces meant that the crew "probably had to go hunting for it."[102]

The large recoil was a direct cause of the light weight and resulting portability. Normally the weight of a cannon partially absorbed the recoil of firing. Lyle however felt the important criterion was portability, the ability to move the gun anywhere quickly. As long as the shot went true, the gun could easily be recovered.

The powder used was important. Although all powder at the time was a variation

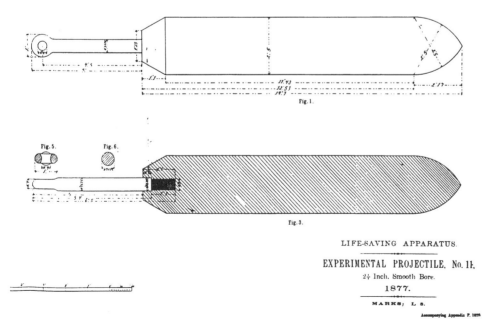

Fig.1.

Fig. 5.   Fig. 6.

Fig. 3.

LIFE-SAVING APPARATUS.

EXPERIMENTAL PROJECTILE. No. 1¼.

2¼ Inch. Smooth Bore.

1877.

MARKS; L 8.

Accompanying Appendix P. 1878

of black powder, the grain size could be considerably different and could greatly affect the performance of the gun. Lyle eventually concluded that a powder made by the Hazard Powder Company of Hazardville, Connecticut, which later became part of Dupont, was the best. The powder later was marketed as Hazard's Life-Saving Service Powder and Dupont Life-Saving Powder. Lyle recommended charges of 4 to 6 ounces for Nos. 4 and 4½ lines and 4 to 8 ounces for Nos. 6 and 7 lines.[103] Hazard Life-Saving Service Powder came in 10-pound kegs. In 1885 each cost $2.70.[104]

Lyle found that the shotlines were just as critical to the task as the gun. Hemp was too brittle, and while braided linen was usable, the best was waterproofed braided linen line. It cut through the air better and provided increased range. He noted that all new lines were stiff and difficult to properly fake. They all needed to be fired several times with light charges to make them more flexible when faked. Only new lines should be used over wrecks.[105]

Three sized shotlines were standard in the Service, Nos. 4, 7 and 9 being respectively ⁴/₃₂, ⁷/₃₂ and ⁹/₃₂ of an inch in diameter. The smaller the line, the greater the range. No. 4 line was only used when the wreck was at extreme range. It was too light to directly haul the whip line aboard. Instead an intermediate line was required, which meant more effort on the part of the shipwrecked crew and the life savers. The smaller line was also more difficult to handle, especially with half frozen hands in the

midst of a roaring Great Lakes gale.[106]

Faking, the skill of artfully coiling the shot line into the faking box, was absolutely critical

FIGURE 162
With a cloud of powder smoke, a Lyle gun fires during a drill.
Weckler Collection
Michigan Maritime Museum

to the success of the shot.

Lyle recommended that keepers frequently hold faking drills to teach all of the surfmen "not only how to fake, but how to do it well and rapidly." He felt that "an ordinary faker with two good assistants can put 600 yards of No. 7 line in from 25 to 28 minutes. A clumsy man will generally be from 40 to 50 minutes

FIGURE 163
The Lyle gun was built to be versatile. The special hinges allowed the barrel to be quickly removed from the carriage for transport over difficult terrain.
Author's Collection

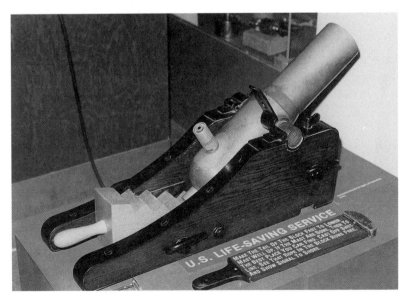

putting up the same line. It must be remarked that the more rapidly the faking, the greater the danger of getting it too tight upon the pins."[107]

If it was necessary to fire a second shot and a

FIGURE 164
Lyle considered the art of
faking to be critical.
National Archives

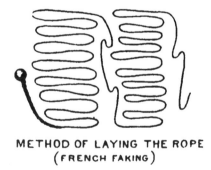

**METHOD OF LAYING THE ROPE
(FRENCH FAKING)**

FIGURE 165
French faking was used
when time to fake the shotline back into a box wasn't
available.
Author's Collection

boxed line was not available, the original was "French faked." This procedure required laying out the line in large loops on a tarpaulin spread on the beach. This was at best an extreme measure. Because the line was wet and invariably sand-covered, its performance was severely degraded.[108]

Lyle noted that in evaluating various guns and rockets, range was often the criterion considered most important. Accuracy was considered next most critical. Lyle found that while the deviation of the projectile was usually not excessive, the drift of the line could be "out of all proportion." He questioned what value range was if "at every shot the line falls clear of the vessel by perhaps many yards, due to the lateral drift of the line from the effect of wind." The lighter the line, the greater the drift. Using a very light No. 3 1/2 linen line and a 3-inch gun, he reached a remarkable distance of 694 3/4 yards. The greatest range previously obtained with the much heavier mortar in earlier tests was 631 yards. A distance of 400 yards was considered the maximum requirement for a life saving mortar.[109] Beyond this distance it was considered impossible to pull a hawser tight enough to avoid it dragging in the surf.

Lyle noticed that during storms, there were frequent temporary lulls of the wind, ranging of from 7 to 20 seconds. A line-carrying projectile was normally airborne for 8 1/2 seconds and it took another 5 to 15 seconds for the line to settle. For extreme cases 25 seconds was needed to fire the gun and allow the line to fall over the wreck. Commonly, it only took half as long. With these facts in mind, Lyle recommended that the gun be prepared for firing and the keeper wait with the lanyard taut for a lull before firing, thus giving his shot the greatest chance of success. It took skill and experience to gauge just the right moment to let fly.[110]

Some use was made of the Hunt gun developed by Edmund S. Hunt of Massachusetts. This gun was also used by the Massachusetts Humane Society. The Hunt gun had a longer range and was provided to Atlantic stations where the outlying bars were beyond the range of the Lyle gun. The intention was not to be able to use the beach apparatus at such an extreme range, but instead to be able to run a line that could help a boat or lifecar reach the wreck. The gun was similar to the Lyle gun with the exception of an increase in the bore of one inch and a different carriage mounting and projectile. Initially the No. 4 shotline deployed from a metal can placed near the gun. When it emptied, the remainder of the line came from the projectile itself that contained 320 yards tightly coiled within the body. The range of the Hunt gun was 40 yards more than that of the Lyle gun. The Service made only limited use of the Hunt gun because the line was too light for all but extreme circumstances, and after each firing the projectile had to be returned to the manufacturer for refilling. This was an added expense the Service did not want.[111]

The Cunningham rocket system also saw very limited use. Similar to the Hunt gun in that it combined a shore-based line can with a line packed in the rocket body proper, it was capable of 700- to 1000-yard ranges. As with the Hunt gun, the line was only No. 4, and the system itself was expensive.[112]

Without a doubt, the Lyle gun was the life saver's system of choice. It was inexpensive. Without projectiles, it cost only $87.83. The only recurring operational expense was for powder, estimated at 5 cents a shot. When the large number of drill iterations was considered, the Lyle gun was very economical. The gun was easily handled and prepared for use, night or day. In cold weather, a common condition on the lakes, gloves could be worn without loss of speed. The small gun was also extremely versatile. For example: to rescue the crew of a vessel wrecked on an offshore island, one East Coast keeper loaded the gun and equipment in a surfboat, rowed to the wreck and anchored some distance out from it. With the gun lashed to the after thwart and the faking box placed on the stern, he used a one-ounce charge to drop a line cleanly to the men on the vessel. As the result of his initiative and the Lyle gun's unique capabilities, all were saved. In another instance, a crew fired the gun from the upper window of a fish house to reach a wreck. Using the breeches buoy, the lifesavers hauled the crew to safety through the same window.[113]

The first production Lyle guns were made at the Parrott West Point Foundry in 1879. Additional runs followed in 1894 and 1896. The American Ordnance Company in Bridgeford, Connecticut, manufactured 105 in 1900. Production appeared to have ceased about 1930.[114]

David A. Lyle was a remarkable man. Born in Ohio in 1845, he graduated from West Point in 1869. Before his work with the life savers, he soldiered in Alaska, assisted in a geographic survey of Death Valley and taught at West Point. His work evaluating and developing life saving guns was so successful that he remained a member of the Board of Life-Saving Appliances for the remainder of his career. His expertise stood the Board in good stead on many occasions. Lyle later received a degree in mining engineering from the Massachusetts Institute of Technology, served as an inspector of ordnance and retired in 1909 as the commander of the arsenal at Augusta, Georgia, as a full colonel. He died in 1937 at the age of 92.[115]

Figure 24. Coston flares.

By 1885 most stations had been equipped with a second set of breeches buoy apparatus including hawsers and hauling lines. The second set was intended to speed rescue in those instances when large numbers of persons were aboard the wreck. The lifecar was still considered too heavy and cumbersome for general use. The Service felt that once the crew had set up the first breeches buoy, it could be operated by a gang improvised from spectators usually present at a wreck, although an experienced surfman would be required to supervise. If a crew from an adjacent station were on hand, they would operate it. The first crew then proceeded to establish a second breeches buoy.[116]

FIGURE 166
In the hands of the beach patrol, Coston flares warned many vessels of danger as well as signal to the station lookout.
Author's Collection

Coston Signals

Although small in size, Coston signals were a critical part of the life savers' equipment. The idea of a hand-held, brightly burning colored flare that could be used for signalling at night was originally engineered by Benjamin Franklin Coston. Described as a true genius, for a time Coston worked as the chief scientist at the Washington Navy Yard Laboratory. When a promised promotion did not come through, Coston resigned his position in 1857 and moved to private industry becoming the president of a Boston gas company. Within a year he was dead of a fever.[117]

Before dying, he told his wife about a box containing an extremely valuable invention. Investigating the contents after his death, she discovered the instructions for mixing chemicals and a new code for signalling at night. Eventually recovering the prototypes from the Navy, the widow discovered that the chemicals

had deteriorated with time and were useless. After recruiting special assistance from fireworks experts, with the greatest of difficulty she reconstructed her husband's invention, formed a company, manufactured and marketed the unique signals world wide. The term "Coston" became synonymous with any hand-held flare. The best available device when the Life-Saving Service was formed, it was only natural it became a staple of the organization.[118]

The signals were visible for 20 miles and burned clean and bright with either red, white or blue light. Used in sequence with the special code, messages could be sent at night. The Navy used them for fleet signaling as well as the life savers. The Coston signal remained in use well into the 1930s.[119]

The actual use of the Coston signal has been described as follows. "In one end there is a socket where he places a Coston, a sort of cartridge, about three inches and a half long and an inch and a half thick, of dark color. He holds this wooden thing in his left hand, and shoves a spring that protrudes in the way of a button from the other end, with his right hand, which causes a sharp point to pierce the cartridge or Coston, and it goes off with a sizzling noise and with a red light that continues about two minutes."[120]

Telephones

Always concerned with technological innovation, the Service was quick to adopt the telephone for life saving purposes. For example, a March 3, 1903, act of Congress authorized a line from the mainland on the east side of Green Bay, Wisconsin, across Death's Door to the Plum Island Life-Saving Station, continuing to Washington Island, Wisconsin, then to the lighthouse on Rock Island. Other stations in remote areas were connected by short land lines and cables which were often maintained jointly by the Weather Bureau and the Service. These lines usually ran to local exchanges.

By 1894 nearly all Lake stations located in ports were at least wired to local exchanges. The Service considered the telephone lines to be "one of the most important features of the Life-Saving Establishment."[121] It was so critical to the Service that the position of superintendent of telephone lines was eventually established.[122]

Every effort was made to make the connections as economically as possible. The Point Betsy Station was originally connected to Bell Telephone in Frankfort through a local lumber company line. When the company closed down, the Service arranged to continue to use the poles but only at no cost to the government.[123]

Economy measures included how poles were obtained. In 1899 the Service was granted permission by the Light House Board to cut 132 poles from timber on the Sturgeon Point Light House Reservation. The poles were needed to establish a telephone line between the Sturgeon Point Life-Saving Station and Harrisville. The life saving keeper at Sturgeon Point was directed to perform the work and authorized up to $8 to pay for hauling the poles to the beach.[124]

The telephone system proved an invaluable aid to prompt and efficient life saving operations. When necessary, two or more crews could be quickly brought together for mutual support. Tugs or other help could be summoned and various maritime associations could be notified as required. Of course the use of the telephone was restricted to official business only. Personal calls, regardless of their nature, were strictly prohibited. However it is fair to assume they were still made, especially on dark and lonely nights when the lines ran station to station and not through a local exchange.

1. Nalty, *Wrecks*, p. xxxvii-xxxviii.

2. *Revised Regulations*, pp. 90-92.

3. *Revised Regulations*, p. 92.

4. *Revised Regulations*, pp. 93-94.

5. *Annual Report, U.S. Life-Saving Service, 1882*, pp. 484-487; *1906*, p. 426.

6. *Annual Report, U.S. Life-Saving Service, 1897*, pp. 480-481; *1902*, p. 448.

7. Letter, District Superintendent, Twelfth District to keeper, Point Betsy Station, September 3, 1895, Institute for Great Lakes Research.

8. William D. Wilkinson, *Nineteenth-Century Coast Lifeboats in the Collections of the Mariners' Museum* (Newport News: 1992), pp. 5, 10, 12.

9. *Annual Report, U.S. Life-Saving Service, 1879*, p. 42.

10. Merryman, "The United States Life-Saving Service – 1880," p. 17.

11. U.S. Life-Saving Service, *Specifications and Drawings for a Thirty-Four Foot Self-Righting and Self-Bailing Lifeboat with Centerboard, 1900*, pp. 20-21.

12. Wilkinson, *Nineteenth-Century*, pp. 15-16.

13. Wilkinson, *Nineteenth-Century*, p. 8.

14. "Record of Boats," U.S. Life-Saving Service, RG 26, NARA.

15. "Record of Boats," U.S. Life-Saving Service, RG 26, NARA.

16. *Annual Report, U.S. Life-Saving Service, 1877*, p. 42.

17. *Annual Report, U.S. Life-Saving Service, 1876*, p. 823.

18. Kimball, *Organization and Methods*, pp. 22-23; Letter, William D. Wilkinson to author, November 20, 1992; Kimball in *Organization and Methods* refers to these boats as 29-footers. It is believed that this was a misprint and he actually meant the 26-footer.

19. *Annual Report, U.S. Life-Saving Service, 1877*, p. 49.

20. *Annual Report, U.S. Life-Saving Service, 1877*, p. 43.

21. *Annual Report, U.S. Life-Saving Service, 1877*, p. 43

22. David Porter Dobbins, *The Dobbins Life-Boat* (Buffalo: 1886), pp. 42-45; Theodore Johnson, "The Life-Saving Service of the Lakes – The Relation of Captain Dobbins Thereto," *Magazine of Western History*, Vol. 4 (June 1886), pp. 238-239.

23. Commander William E. Ehrman, "They Had to Go Out, But the Dobbins Brought Them Back," *Inland Seas*, Winter 1986, p. 238.

24. The U.S. Stations were Cleveland, Fairport, Erie, Buffalo, Big Sandy, Salmon Creek, Oswego, Charlotte and Point Aux Barques. The Canadian stations were Point Traverse and Wellington in Prince Edward County. (Dobbins, pp. 26-39); in 1866 the Canadian firm of William Marton built six Dobbins boats for the Canadian life savers (Mansfield, p.384).

25. Dobbins, pp. 34-35.

26. Ehrman, "They Had to go Out," pp. 239-240. Dobbins, pp. 20, 24-25.

27. "Record of Boats," U.S. Life-Saving Service, RG 26, NARA.

28. *Annual Report, United States Life-Saving Service, 1883*, p. 422.

29. Dobbins, pp. 29-31.

30. "Record of Boats," U.S. Life-Saving Service, RG 26, NARA.

31. *Annual Report, U.S. Life-Saving Service, 1876*, pp. 826-827.

32. Wilkinson, *Nineteenth-Century*, p. 20.

33. Captain C.H. McLellan, "The Evolution of the Lifeboat," *Marine Engineering*, January 1906, pp. 7-11.

34. *Alpena Argus*, January 24, March 4, 1894.

35. Dossin Great Lakes Museum Archives.

36. Peter J. Guthorn, *The Sea Bright Skiff and Other Jersey Shore Boats* (New Brunswick, NJ: Rutgers University Press, 1971), pp. 82-83.

37. Kimball, *Organization and Methods*, pp. 20-21.

38. Journal of the Life-Saving Station at South Manitou Island, November 5, 1902, RG 26, NARA; Letter, S.I. Kimball, RG 26, NARA.

39. "Record of Boats," U.S. Life-Saving Service, RG 26, NARA.

40. U.S. Life-Saving Service, *Specifications of the Beebe Surfboat, 1890*, p. 6.

41. "Record of Boats," U.S. Life-Saving Service, RG 26, NARA.

42. T.J.A. Freeman, "The United States Life-Saving Service," *American Catholic Quarterly Review*, Volume 18, July 1893, pp. 663-664.

43. Kimball, *Organization and Methods*, p. 23.

44. *Annual Report, U.S. Life-Saving Service, 1877*, p. 43.

45. Kimball, *Organization and Methods*, p. 21.

46. "Record of Boats," U.S. Life-Saving Service, RG 26, NARA.

47. *Annual Report, U.S. Life-Saving Service, 1877*, pp. 43-44.

48. "Record of Boats," U.S. Life-Saving Service, RG 26, NARA.

49. Letter, S.I. Kimball to C.D. Hilles, Assistant Secretary of the Treasury, December 19, 1910, RG 26, NARA.

50. Letter, S.I. Kimball to Inspector, June 26, 1899.

51. *Revised Regulations*, p. 101.

52. *Annual Report, U.S. Life-Saving Service, 1906*, p. 18; *1900*, p. 421.

53. Ernest H. Rankin, "Captain Henry J. Cleary, Life Saver Showman," *Inland Seas*, summer 1977, p. 139.

54. *Annual Report, U.S. Life-Saving Service, 1900*, p. 421.

55. Letters, Horace L. Piper, Acting General Superintendent to Lieutenant C.H. McLellan, April 6, 1899, April 13, 1899, RG 26, NARA.

56. *Daily Mining Journal* (Marquette, Michigan), November 9, 1900.

57. Freeman, "The U.S. Life-Saving Service," p. 661.

58. *Annual Report, U.S. Life-Saving Service, 1906,* p. 18.

59. *Annual Report, U.S. Life-Saving Service, 1909,* p. 283.

60. Charles A. Harbaugh, "The U.S. Life-Saving Service," *The Aetna,* February 1911, p. 35.

61. McLellan, "The Evolution of the Lifeboat," p. 10.

62. *Annual Report, U.S. Life-Saving Service, 1914,* p. 283.

63. *Annual Report, U.S. Life-Saving Service, 1913,* p. 124; Notes, Ted Richardson, August 12, 1992.

64. *Annual Report, U.S. Life-Saving Service, 1911,* p. 21.

65. "Record of Boats," U.S. Life-Saving Service, RG 26, NARA.

66. *Annual Report, U.S. Life-Saving Service, 1895,* p. 420.

67. Frederick Stonehouse, *Marquette Shipwrecks* (Au Train, Michigan: Avery Studios, 1977), pp. 75-76.

68. *Revised Regulations,* p. 67.

69. O'Connor, pp. 187-188.

70. *Revised Regulations,* pp. 69-77; U.S. Life-Saving Service, *Beach Apparatus Drill,* 1890, pp. 3-24.

71. Merryman, "The Unites States Life-Saving Service – 1880, " pp. 13-14.

72. *Beach Apparatus Drill,* pp. 21-22.

73. Rev. W.H. Law. *Heroes of the Great Lakes* (Detroit, 1906), p. 11.

74. *Beach Apparatus Drill,* pp. 19-22.

75. *Revised Regulations,* pp. 77-79.

76. Letter, S.I. Kimball to Racine Wagon and Carriage Company, November 13, 1899, RG 26, NARA.

77. Letter, S.I. Kimball to John R. Spears, June 6, 1899, RG 26, NARA.

78. Piper, "The Life-Saving Service," pp. 1-2.

79. James L. Pond, Compiler, *History of Life-Saving Appliances. and Military and Naval Constructions* (New York: E.D. Slater, 1885), pp. 32-36.

80. Pond, p. 36.

81. Pond, pp. 36, 42, 72.

82. Robert F. Bennett, *Surfboats,* pp. 24 -26.

83. Pond, pp. 43, 51, 107.

84. Miles Imlay, RADM, U.S.C.G., "The Story of the Lifecar," *Alumni Association Bulletin,* Vol. XX, No. 3-4, p. 57.

85. Piper, "The Life-Saving Service," pp. 1-2.

86. Joseph Francis, *Metallic Life-Boat Corporation* (New York: William C. Bryant, 1853), p. 20.

87. Davis, "Life-Saving Service," p. 310.

88. Nalty, *Wrecks,* p. 46.

89. Letter, Horace L. Piper, Acting General Superintendent to Inspector, June 30, 1899, RG 26, NARA.

90. Bennett, *Surfboats,* pp. 44-45.

91. Letter, John Gutherie to J.N. Shillinger, January 1, 1855, RG 26, NARA.

92. *Annual Report, U.S. Life-Saving Service, 1878,* pp. 342-345; *1877,* pp. 39-40.

93. *Annual Report, U.S. Life-Saving Service, 1878,* p. 343.

94. *Annual Report, U.S. Life-Saving Service, 1878,* p. 236.

95. *Annual Report, U.S. Life-Saving Service, 1878,* pp. 309-319.

96. *Annual Report, U.S. Life-Saving Service, 1878,* pp. 236-238; *1880,* p. 275; *1901,* p. 442.

97. *Annual Report, U.S. Life-Saving Service, 1878,* pp. 236-238.

98. *Annual Report, U.S. Life-Saving Service, 1878,* pp. 246-248.

99. *Annual Report, U.S. Life-Saving Service, 1878,* pp. 248-249.

100. J.P. Barnett, *The Lifesaving Guns of David Lyle* (South Bend: South Bend Replicas, 1976), pp. 15, 67.

101. Kimball, *Organization and Methods,* p. 25.

102. Heckman Powell, *What the Citizen Should Know About the Coast Guard* (New York: W.W. Norton, 1939), p. 100.

103. Barnett, pp. 72-74.

104. Voucher for Purchases, Form 1814, September 1, 1885, Hazard Powder Company, RG 26, NARA.

105. *Annual Report, U.S. Life-Saving Service, 1878,* p. 242.

106. Kimball, *Organization and Methods,* p. 25.

107. *Annual Report, U.S. Life-Saving Service, 1878,* p. 254.

108. W.D. O'Connor, "The U.S. Life-Saving Service," *Popular Science Monthly,* Vol. 15, (June 1879) p. 188.

109. *Annual Report, U.S. Life-Saving Service, 1878,* p. 244.

110. *Annual Report, U.S. Life-Saving Service, 1878,* p. 245.

111. Kimball, *Organization and Methods,* pp. 25-26.

112. Kimball, *Organization and Methods,* p. 26.

113. Kimball, *Organization and Methods,* p. 27.

114. Barnett, pp. 18-19.

115. Barnett, pp. 1-2.

116. *Annual Report, U.S. Life-Saving Service, 1885,* p. 33.

117. Martha J. Coston, *Signal Success, The Work and Travels of Mrs. Martha Coston* (New York: J.p. Lippencott Company, pp. 27-28.

118. Coston, *Signal Success,* pp. 35-52, 294-298.

119. *Annual Report, U.S. Life-Saving Service, 1901,* p. 423; Nalty, *Wrecks* pp. 1-2.

120. Law, "The Life-Savers on the Great Lakes," p. 16.

121. *Annual Report, U.S. Life-Saving Service, 1889,* p. 63; *1894,* p. 68; *1904,* pp. 45-46.

122. Smith and Powell, *The Coast Guard,* p. 36.

123. Letter, General Superintendent to keeper, Point Betsy Station, August 1, 1891; Institute for Great Lakes Research.

124. Letter, S.I. Kimball, to Superintendent 10th District, November 10, 1899, RG 26, NARA.

FIGURE 168
This 1895 circa photo of Lake Huron and Lake Superior district keepers shows the men that manned the sweep oar. It is thought it was taken during winter conference in Port Huron. Several of the Lake Superior keepers are not present, and it is surmised they were held back by weather. Left to right from the rear: Albert Ocha, J.W. Plough, J.H. Frame, Henry Gill, Thomas H. McCormick, E.P. Motley, Benjamin Trudell, Joseph Valentine, J.E. Henderson, James Scott, M.A. McLennan, J.A. Carpenter, J.H. Persons, H.D. Ferris, James McCaw, R.M. Small. Superintendent Jerome Kiah is in civilian attire in the center.
Ted Richardson Collection

By all accounts, Great Lakes keepers were characters of the first order. The mold was broken once they were made. The names of these brave men can now only be found in the dusty journals on deposit in the National Archives or in the yellowed pages of old newspapers. The exploits of Trudell, McCormick, Small, Carpenter, Crisp, Bernier, Griesser, Plough, Persons, Sogge, Ocha and so many others all led their crews into the pages of history.

Although every keeper in the Service was a unique individual, the following ones well epitomize the courage, steadfastness, skill and innovation that characterized the men who held the steering oar.

Morgan, with hatchet and gun

A.B. Bibb, the Service architect, in his 1882 article describes a visit with Captain Quinton Morgan, the keeper of the Sucker River (Muskalonge Lake/Deer Park) Lake Superior station. "A fish supper having been duly dispatched, we sat in the door, smoking the captain's cigars and chatting. Gently the night came down and we sat and watched the wonderful tone of gray stealing over the sea and sky. The old captain was spinning a long yarn about life at No. 12, his wife helping him now and then with a leaf out of her experience.

"He told us how he had passed winters here when the snow lay six feet on the level, and reached almost to the top of the house, blowing in off the ice-bound lake and lodging in a big drift under the hill. He had pitched his wigwam upon Muskalonge Lake and sat within many a long day, fishing through the ice, the cat, dog and cow his only companions. When he could he worked in the woods, felling trees in this clearing which we saw. Now and then he heard from the outer world, when Fechette passed up the shore with his dog-train to Grand Marais, and down again for the Sault. The cow, the dog and the cat marched about with him every-where. When the spring opened and the crew

FIGURE 169
Captain Lawrence O. Law-son, the keeper of the Evanston station after his retirement.
Northwestern University Archives

came back to the station, these animals, for a long time, would go on tramp with the patrol at night; the cow especially, was slow to give up the habit.

"Mrs. Morgan had not been within here in the winters; he was entirely alone. His crews had been drawn from rough material – the lumber camps back in the woods, in the early fall. There was one camp of 80 men now 13 miles up Sucker River. They would soon be out when he anticipated trouble with his men, already discontented. One of his first crews had jumped him on the beach one night and intended to

hang him, but he got 'the drop' on the crowd, and drove them up the beach and back to duty at the muzzle of their own revolver. Chartier (the keeper of the Two-Heart River Station) was with him, having known of the row, and came up to back him.[1]

"Thus he told his story, not in such words, but mostly in figurative nautical lingo, plentiful-ly enriched with exple-tives. We slept in the captain's room, on the upper floor of the sta-tion, that night, and cer-tainly no more comfort-able quarters could be desired. Such a home in the wilderness seemed doubly enjoyable. In the morning a great din arose under the window. Looking out, we saw the captain blowing on a tin fog horn, and the great dogs seated on their haunches about him, baying in deep and dis-mal tones. These ani-mals are worked in the sleds during the winter. They are large, sinewy brutes, of great strength and endurance. Fechette makes the run with them from Grand Marais to Sault Ste. Marie in two days. He goes himself on snowshoes, some-times riding on the sled, and stopping at intervals to rest and eat.

"Captain Morgan has trained them to travel the beach on foggy nights, baying in their deep voices. The sound carries far to sea, he says.

"Our visit to Captain Morgan's station was accompanied by the unpleasant feature of a sort of mutiny among the crew. They were at log-gerheads with their keeper. The trouble seemed to have arisen out of the keeper's insistence on discipline and a strict performance of duty. This was irksome to these wild, free spirits of the forest, and they were making things very uncomfortable for the keeper. Some nasty threats had been muttered. They refused at first to get into the surfboat when Captain Morgan ordered it for our departure. When we did get off, the old captain carried a pistol in his shirt, and a hatchet in the stern beside him. He told us he feared their attacking him after we had gone. It was a specimen of the kind of life he has always led at this place."[2]

Lawson of Northwestern

Another of the old keepers was Lawrence Oscar Lawson of the Evanston, Illinois, station. Lawson was born on September 11, 1842, in Kalmar, Sweden. He did not go to sea until the age of 18 when he shipped out as a seaman under his stepfather. His father, a blacksmith and mill owner, had died four years earlier.

He first reached the United States in 1861, the beginning of the Civil War. During the next four years he sailed from New York as a common seaman, trading to France, Cuba, Key West, Porto Rico and other coastal ports. He was on the first merchant vessel to enter New Orleans after it was freed by Union troops.

During the course of sailing from New York he "got religion." While attending a camp meeting in Sing Sing, New York, he experienced a religious awakening. Later he frequently attended services in a "bethel ship" in New York harbor. It was later said his deep religious conviction was an impressive part of his personality.

In 1864 he sailed fresh water, reaching Buffalo in the spring of the year. He had apparently heard that the pay and working conditions were far better than the harsh conditions prevalent on salt water. Reportedly shipboard meals even included ham and eggs! By December he had made his way to Chicago in the schooner *Tanner*. With his small savings he purchased land in the Woodlawn area and started a small commercial fishing operation. When business slowed, he continued to sail in such vessels as the *Christina Nelson* and *Clara Parker*, among others. In 1864 he sold his land to the park commission at a considerable profit and moved to Evanston where he built a shanty on the beach near the lumber docks.

Lawson also became a trustee of the Evanston Swedish Methodist church. At the time, the number of Swedish Methodists was so small that they worshiped with the Danish and Norwegian Methodists. There were problems with this arrangement that must have taxed Lawson's patience. Hymns were always sung in Swedish and response readings given in Norwegian. The Danes just had to do the best they could. Eventually the ethnic groups grew large enough to form their own churches.

In 1876 he married Petrine Wold of Chicago, another Swedish immigrant. The couple would have nine children. Initially the couple settled in Ludington, Michigan, and started a commercial fishing operation. After a fierce storm destroyed his nets and boats, Lawson returned to Evanston. He may have been wiped out, but he was not defeated. He simply began again.

When the need arose for a professional keeper at the Evanston station, Lawson immediately came to mind. He was well known in the area and about the only experienced seaman locally available. It was an excellent choice. Lawson was an immediate success, and the students looked up to and respected him greatly.

To provide a suitable dwelling, Lawson moved his old shanty to the station grounds. Gradually over a 10-year period in his spare time he built a new home on the site. As he finished each room, in turn his growing family moved into it.

It was 1883 before he led his student crew on their first rescue. The victim was the schooner *Katherine Howard*, wrecked in a powerful squall directly off the station. With Lawson at the sweep, the surfboat nimbly danced over the breakers and returned with the schooner's crew. Other wrecks followed. On August 2, 1885, the schooner *Jamaica* went on an offshore reef near Glencoe during a north gale. The crew quickly fled to the rigging to await rescue. Word of the wreck was slow to reach the station. It was only after the mist thinned in the morning and Lawson was able to climb the light tower to see for himself that was it clear just where the schooner was. The life savers removed the crew of 10 including two women and a boy using the breeches buoy. Soon after the vessel went to pieces.

Lawson was nearly killed during the rescue of the crew of the schooner *Halstead*. On Thanksgiving 1887 a northeast gale drove the schooner on a bar off Glencoe. After bringing the surfboat by wagon to the scene, Lawson and his crew launched and headed for the wreck. Fifty yards out from the beach the steering oar, against which the keeper was leaning heavily, snapped, throwing him into the raging lake. Driven under the boat, he surfaced on the other side and grabbed the stroke oar. Knocked off course by the sudden loss of steering, the boat lost way and filled with water from breaking seas. Slowly, with Lawson still hanging precariously to the oar, the powerful waves forced the boat back to the shore. It had been a near thing for the old Swede. On the beach Lawson directed his crew in hauling out the boat, bailing it and finally launching again. After two trips the schooner's sailors were safely ashore.

FIGURE 170
Lawson was looked on by many of his students as a second father.

U.S. Coast Guard

1889 was Lawson's busiest year. As the result of an October storm the steam barge *Ballentyne* with the schooner *Ironton* and tug *Protection* were driven ashore at Wilmette. All crews were recovered by the Evanston surfmen. November 28 saw the steamer *Calumet* driven on a bar off Highland Park during a terrific northeast storm. The wreck was 12 miles to the north of the station, and just getting there took a Herculean effort on the part of Lawson and his crew. The route was through broken country; thick brush obstructed their progress and deep ravines challenged their strength. When they came close to reaching the area of the wreck, the Army garrison at Fort Sheridan provided the final impetus to carry the surfboat to the beach. It took three trips but Lawson was able to rescue all 18 men from the steamer.

For their remarkable demonstration of courage and tenacity, the entire crew received gold life saving medals. The official presentation ceremony was several weeks later. A large audience of local people, students and faculty crowded the event. The front of the hall was decorated with the implements of the life savers: oars, signal flags, Lyle gun, etc. Lawson and the crew wore their blue uniforms and sat in the first row of seats. The local congressman presented the medals and other officials spoke testifying to the crew's steadfastness and courage. For a time Lawson's medal was displayed in a local store front.

Lawson continued to cheat death. During a rescue in 1895 of the crews of the barges *Owen, Michigan* and *Nicholson* aground off Glencoe, he and his crew brought 36 sailors to safety. During one of the trips a monster wave struck the surfboat with such force that Lawson was thrown from the stern clear to the bow, completely over the crew seated below. The old Swede managed to grab the bow just in the nick of time before being thrown into the icy water. Only the quick reaction of the stroke oar to the loss of the keeper's steady steering kept the boat from capsizing in the tumultuous waves and averted disaster for all.

Another near miss occurred during the winter of 1895. Ice had jammed the intake of the city water works, and Lawson and two volunteers took a small boat to try to clear it. The intake was a mile out; a strong offshore wind was blowing. The trio soon got stuck in an ice floe and, unable to free themselves, were being blown out into the lake. Luckily, they attracted attention by waving their coats. A rescue party was able to haul them to shore. It had been another near thing.

On July 16, 1903, Lawson retired as keeper. To say he retired was a bit of a euphemism in that he left the Service voluntarily, but as with all keepers received no pension at all. He was 61 years old and had captained the crew for 23 years. Although he still felt as strong as ever, the job required a younger, more agile man. It was claimed that during his tenure he rescued 337 persons from 35 vessels. To the students at

Northwestern it was the end of an era. He taught his crews courage and thoroughness in the performance of their duties. His strong Christian faith inspired them to overcome the odds. His classroom was the station and his laboratory the open lake. His crews were not normal surfmen with relatively focussed experience and ambitions. They were life savers who would become doctors, lawyers, businessmen, the leaders of their communities, states and nation. He was a rare influence on these gifted students. To many of his young surfmen he was nearly a father. He started with boys and made them men!

After retirement, Lawson continued to fish and serve as a leader in his church. He remained a respected and valued member of Evanston. Small boys often gathered around him, asking the old life saver to tell the stories of past glories. On October 29, 1912, the old Swede died of cancer. A brilliant star in Kimball's galaxy of keepers was gone.[3]

Ocha – Buried by his crew

Dedication to the Service was the hallmark of keeper Albert Ocha. Born in 1863, he spent his early life in Port Hope, Michigan, on the west shore of Lake Huron. On March 21, 1882, at the age of 18, he joined the Service as surfman at the Ottawa Point (Tawas) Station. It was obvious that he learned his craft well since on October 4, 1886, a bare 23 years old, he was appointed keeper of the Portage Station on

Lake Superior.[4]

While at Portage he led his crew on many spectacular missions, including the 1886 rescue of the crews of the steamer *Robert Wallace* and schooner-barge *David Wallace* and the 1887 rescue of the crew of the schooner *Alva Bradley*. All three vessels wrecked near Marquette, which required transporting the life savers and their boat on a special train from Houghton, a distance of 110 miles. Barreling along the tracks at breakneck speed, Ocha and his crew were able to reach the scene quickly enough to save the day. These efforts were considered among the most striking ever performed by the Service and made the young keeper a legend along the Superior shore.

Perhaps it was due to his relative youth, but the records show that Ocha seemed to have an inordinate amount of trouble keeping a crew during his duty at the Ship Canal Station. Of 43 men employed during his tenure as keeper October 4, 1886, to September 30, 1891, three deserted, 16 resigned, two transferred to other stations and 22, more than half, were discharged for various causes. The resignations were for all of the typical reasons: ill health, personal business, other work and discontent. Also included was one man who resigned because he refused to take demotion to a lower number. Discharges included refusal to work, drunk on patrol, bad character, poor surfmanship, calling the watch too early, tampering with the patrol clock and threatening the keep-

FIGURE 171
The Evanston station was dwarfed by the university campus.
Ted Richardson Collection

FIGURE 172
Albert Ocha, a legend on
the south shore of Lake
Superior.
Author's Collection

er. Whether Ocha simply had a poor lot of men to deal with or his inexperience caused his own problems is unknown, but his crew turnover was high.

On September 20, 1890, Ocha received a letter of reprimand from Kimball. It seems that during a routine investigation into the discharge of a crewman, the assistant inspector discovered that on the night of July 4th the keeper and one of his men visited a local saloon staying until well after midnight. Worse, the inspector determined that Ocha and his men had stopped at the same tavern previously while on duty. Only after considering Ocha's previously exemplary record did Kimball make an exception and not dismiss him outright. The reprimand had the desired effect. The lapse was not repeated.[5]

Ocha's crew problems continued to plague him. On September 24, 1891, one of his men returned from town drunk and too late to make his patrol. When confronted by Ocha, the man ran upstairs to the bunkroom and returned with a revolver threatening to shoot the keeper. No shots were fired; the county sheriff was needed to cart the miscreant off to the lockup. On September 30, 1891, Ocha resigned from the Service for unspecified reasons.[6] Perhaps he had just had enough of dealing with difficult crews. As none of the crew was considered capable of assuming the keepers position, it was given to George A. Smith.

On July 1, 1892, Ocha was back in the Service and appointed as the No. 2 surfman at the Grand Point Au Sable Station on Lake Huron. Then, for unknown reasons he left the Service on December 5, 1893.[7] During this period there was a financial panic on the Lakes and an estimated 30 percent of the life saving

crews resigned. It's probable that he left to find a better paying job to support his family.

For Ocha, life saving was in his blood and in late 1894 he returned to the Service. Because of his earlier resignation, he was forced to start again as a surfman, finding a position at the Ashtabula, Ohio, station. In 1896 he transferred to Crisp's Point on Lake Superior. In 1900 he was appointed keeper of the nearby Two-Heart River Station.

Ocha transferred in the fall of 1912 to the new Eagle Harbor Station on Michigan's rugged Keweenaw Peninsula. To move his household goods, he constructed a 50 x 22-foot flat-bottomed barge. Unable to tow it with his own boat, a 36-footer with a 12-horsepower engine, one of his friends towed it up to Eagle Harbor with a tug. Moving the goods normally, by wagon and train, was too expensive for a poorly paid life saver. Ocha left part of his life at the Two-Heart Station.[8] In the little cemetery on the hill overlooking the river were the graves of his wife and several of his children. Life at the remote stations was always hard, but it had been especially so for Ocha.[9]

The death of Mrs. Ocha well illustrates the terrible isolation of the lonely Lake Superior stations. When taken ill, it was utterly impossible to bring a doctor to her. The roads were impassable, still covered with deep snow. A raging storm closed off the route along the beach. After she died, the same difficulties prevented bringing the body out for a proper viewing, funeral and burial. It took a dog sled and a relay of strong men three days to bring a casket into the station. Although they couldn't get his wife's body out, Ocha was held in such high respect that friends within a radius of 20 miles braved the cold and snow to make their way to the station for the modest funeral. With simple ceremony, she was laid to rest in the station cemetery.[10]

In mid-October, Ocha brought his family from Two-Heart River to the new station in his 36-footer. A second boat towed along behind. The fall weather was far from good, but for a tough old life saver it was just one more obstacle to be overcome.

"We left Marquette at 9 a.m. It blew quite hard when we left, but the wind was partly after us, and a heavy dead sea running from the North. The wind increased to a 55-mile gale, but we had to keep right on....The worst of the whole trip was crossing Keweenaw Bay from Point Abbey to the entry. I had to head into the wind to keep from rolling over. Had all the weight in the stern and then the seas would come on top of the covering and drench me and the engine. It is the greatest wonder in the world that it did not stop....If it hadn't been for the cover on the power boat, she would have surely sunk. She dove clear under and was nearly half full when we got to the Portage."[11]

After apparently aggravating long standing liver problems as the result of his strenuous efforts to open the new station, train a new crew and relocate his family, on November 22, 1912, Ocha died. He was 49 years old. He had dedicated nearly his entire working life, 31 years, to the Service. With his crew as pall bearers, Albert Ocha was buried in the Eagle Harbor cemetery.[12] To help provide for his children, a public subscription was circulated in his hometown of Tawas, Michigan.[13]

Today no marker can be found identifying Ocha's grave or commemorating his heroic life. Although the cemetery records are not complete, they do not even list him as being buried there. Based on his poor financial circumstances at the time of his death as evidenced by the necessity for a public subscription for his family, there likely was no headstone placed, or it was so insubstantial that it is now illegible. A true Great Lakes hero lies in an unknown grave on Lake Superior's lonely shore.

Albert's brother Frank was also a life saver. He was the keeper at Tawas when he performed what some called the perfect "fade out." On an October 1896 evening he left the station in his private boat for East Tawas to see

FIGURE 173
Frank Ocha, Albert's brother, simply faded out.
Iosco County Historical Museum

his family. Since there was no easy road between the station and town, it was far faster to row along the shore than to tramp through the woods. After visiting at home, he left for the station, but never arrived. The boat was discovered still tied to the pier and his hat floating in the lake. Although foul play was feared, an

FIGURE 174
Henry Cleary, the trainer of life savers.
Grand Haven Library

extensive search found nothing. No body or evidence of wrongdoing was revealed. Frank Ocha was simply gone. After the requisite seven years passed, his wife received his insurance. To some, though, Frank had just "faded out."[14]

Cleary – He trained the best

Henry J. Cleary, the longtime keeper of the Marquette Station, was a life saver of a little different twist. Superbly competent as a traditional boat handler, he proved his capability during the September 21, 1895, rescue of the crew of the steamer *Charles J. Kershaw*. In the midst of a roaring gale, the steamer went aground on a rock reef just east of Marquette. Thousands of city residents watched in awe as Cleary and his crew went about their dangerous business. After a harrowing beach

launch with the surfboat he deftly plucked nine of the shipwrecked crew off the steamer. During the second launch to remove the four still aboard, the surfboat was damaged and several life savers disabled. Returning to Marquette with a crew partly made up of volunteers, he launched the big lifeboat and rowed down to the wreck. Reaching the beleaguered steamer, he quickly ducked under her stern and removed the crew. Within minutes all were safe on the beach. It was called the greatest Lake Superior rescue of the 1890s.

Born in Port Hope, Michigan, in 1862, he sailed commercially on a schooner for several years until he joined the Service in 1881 at the age of 19. Cleary was one of 11 children. His father, Maine-born William G. Cleary, served as a ship's carpenter to Commodore Matthew Perry. Eventually settling in Port Hope, he built fishing boats and farmed.[15] In his early days he was a fishermen and sailor. At age 17 he commanded a small schooner. Henry Cleary's first station was Point aux Barques on Lake Huron. Later he served at Grindstone and Tawas. In March 1885, at the age of 23, he was appointed keeper of the Deer Park, Lake Superior Station. He stayed at Deer Park until coming to Marquette to open its station on April 1, 1891.

Cleary's strongest ability was as a trainer of life saving crews. As a mark of how well he was regarded by the Service, he was selected above all other keepers to take a demonstration

FIGURE 175
A young Henry Cleary sits on the station porch with his Marquette crew.
Marquette Maritime Museum

FIGURE 176
This 1912 photo shows
Cleary in Marquette at the
helm of his personal boat.
Ted Richardson Collection

crew of surfmen to the 1893 Chicago Worlds Fair. Implicit in the assignment was the requirement to train the crew to a razor's edge of proficiency. The crew was not a regular crew from a single station. It was composed of picked men from many stations across the Service. Although each was highly competent, it was critically important to mold them into a perfect team. Every drill the crew demonstrated had to be accomplished to the highest standard possible. Cleary did his job so well that he took crews to all of the important fairs and expositions: the Trans-Mississippi in Omaha in 1898, the Pan-American Exposition in Buffalo in 1901, the Louisiana Purchase Exposition in St. Louis in 1904, the Jamestown Exposition in Hampton Roads in 1907 and the Alaska-Yukon-Pacific Exposition in Seattle in 1909.[16]

Cleary also had a good sense of humor. During the 1898 Omaha show, one of the men complained to him about the daily dunking in the uncomfortably warm water of the lagoon. The keeper told him that the water was just fine. When another said, "Well, captain how will it be in October?" Cleary answered, "Oh, it will be about like Lake Superior then."[17]

During his last exposition in Seattle, Cleary remained nimble enough to be able to offer his crew an expensive dinner, if during the boat capsizing drills they were able to get him wet above the knees. They never did get the old life saver wet, and he never bought dinner.[18]

The *Marquette Chronicle* summed up his experiences. "Captain Cleary had without question taken a more active part on world shows than any other man in the city or in Michigan. He has perhaps met more of the world's celebrities in diplomatic, military and marine circles than any other man in the state as his duties as officer in charge of the United States life saving exhibit at five great exhibitions have brought him in touch with these notables. Presidents have shaken the captain's hand and taken rides about the lagoons on the grounds of the various shows in the United States life saving boat. At the Jamestown exposition the Marquette man met naval officers high in command of the world's fleets and no doubt the meeting was a mutual pleasure. At the St. Louis exposition Geronimo, the famous Apache outlaw, took a fancy to the captain and often rode with him in the government launch."[19]

Cleary also showed a decided mechanical bent. When the Service decided to test the idea of motorizing lifeboats, it was Cleary with his Marquette Station crew that led the way. In 1899, working with an engine provided by the city's Lake Shore Iron Company, the crew performed a series of extensive tests, the results of which proved the desirability of motorizing the Service boats.[20]

Captain Cleary died of pneumonia at his station on April 10, 1916. He was 54 years old and had been in the Service for 37 years, 25 of them in Marquette. He was buried in the Gore Township cemetery just north of Port Hope.[21]

From the Little Big Horn to the 12th District

Life savers were always men of long experience, but usually it was of the nautical variety. Charles Morton was the exception. When he died in Grand Haven on July 7, 1913, he was

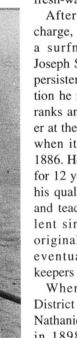

FIGURE 177
Cleary at the steering oar in 1914. Known as the showman keeper, he died in the saddle in 1916.

Marquette Maritime Museum

serving as the Superintendent for the Twelfth District, a remarkable career change for a man who soldiered at the Little Big Horn with Custer and the 7th Cavalry!

Morton was born in Ireland on July 12, 1853, and at a young age immigrated to America. Part of his early life was spent in the Pennsylvania coal fields. Eventually, like many Irishmen, he joined the Army where he spent most of his five-year hitch in Indian Country.

When Custer was massacred by the Indians at the Little Big Horn, Morton was a trooper in Major Marcus Reno's command. To fight his last battle, Custer split the regiment into three battalions, giving one to Major Reno and one to Captain Frederick Benteen, retaining the third under his direct command. When the Indians tore into Custer, Reno could plainly hear the sound of the fighting. But ignoring Napoleon's maxim of always marching to the sound of the guns, Reno stood fast despite the pleas of his officers to help their companions. Custer's column was wiped out to the man. Reno was later court-martialed for his cowardice and

deplorable leadership.

During his years on the Plains, Morton was said to have met many of the personalities of the old West. While stationed at Fort Brady in the Soo, he saw the steamer *Nyack,* then the most magnificent passenger steamer on the Lakes, lock through on her maiden voyage. This event might well have compelled him to a fresh-water career.

After his Army discharge, Morton became a surfman at the St. Joseph Station. Through persistence and application he rose through the ranks and became keeper at the Holland Station when it was opened in 1886. He remained there for 12 years. Apparently his qualities as a trainer and teacher were excellent since four of his original Holland crew eventually became keepers themselves.

When the Twelfth District Superintendent, Nathaniel Robbins, died in 1898, Morton was appointed to his position. Reportedly his ability to "see matters at all angles" made him successful as superintendent. He enjoyed great popularity with the surfmen who knew he was one of them.[22]

B.G. Cameron

Life saving medals were awarded for persons who endangered "their own lives in saving or endeavoring to save the lives of others from the perils of the sea within the United States or upon any American Vessel." In March 1899 a silver life saving medal was awarded to Keeper Benjamin G. Cameron not for a single act of courage, but rather to honor 22 years of heroic deeds.

Cameron was born in Holton, on the banks of the St. John River between Maine and New Brunswick. In 1841 he moved with his parents to Chicago. At the age of 10 he started a sailing career as a cook on a schooner. For the next 30 years he sailed the Great Lakes, working in nearly every capacity. When the Kenosha Station opened in 1880, he was appointed keeper.

The silver medal was awarded in recognition

of his actions in rescuing life and property in not less than eight wrecks! The first rescue occurred before he even became a life saver. On December 10, 1875, the schooner *William H. Hinsdale* stranded about three miles south of Kenosha in a severe northwest blizzard. A March 16, 1899, letter from the Secretary of the Treasury to Cameron stated, "The crew of four men were lashed to the rigging, covered with ice and barely alive. As soon as she was discovered, you procured a boat and caused it to be transported to the shore abreast of her, where you and other volunteers launched it over a formidable ice barrier several feet in height, in the face of a very dangerous sea, and pushed bravely out to the rescue. Upon reaching the vessel you mounted the rigging, with your own hands unlashed the imperiled men and passed them one by one into the boat below, which under your command, conveyed them to the shore. "...It is highly probable that except for your prompt and efficient conduct, some, if not all of them, would have perished."

During the October 28, 1879 wreck of the steamer *Amazon* near Grand Haven, Cameron also assisted in the rescue. On November 12, 1881, Cameron and his Kenosha crew rescued the crew of seven from the waterlogged schooner *E.T. Royce,* 10 miles offshore. The captain of the schooner stated, "Without (his) aid, all aboard would probably have perished."

Two years later, Cameron again led his men 10 miles offshore to make a rescue, on November 13, 1883, saving the crew of the schooner *Rockaway.* The schooner's crew was nearly frozen and had been without food or rest for 48 hours.

On November 24, 1887, in the midst of a blinding snowstorm and roaring gale, Cameron and his crew pulled 12 men from the steamer *Solon H. Johnson*

and its scow. Both were ashore 10 miles south of the station. According to eyewitnesses, had the life savers arrived an hour later, the sailors would have been dead.

December 2, 1890, again brought Cameron and his men into action. During snow and gale, they recovered the crew of the steamer *A.C. Van Raalte,* wrecked two miles south of the station.

During the wind-whipped night of December 2, 1895, Cameron used a volunteer crew to rescue the crew of the scow *Harry Johnson,* ashore at the mouth of Kenosha harbor. Cameron initially tried to reach the scow in the surfboat launched from the station. But ice built up so quickly on the crew, oars and bottom of the boat that he was forced back. Carrying the boat to the breakwater, Cameron and his men,

FIGURE 178
Keeper Charles Morton, a veteran on Custer's 7th Cavalry, finished his days as the Twelfth District Superintendent.
Michigan Maritime Museum

with great difficulty, launched it to the water eight feet below and completed the job. On April 16, 1897, Cameron and his crew rescued the crew of the schooner *Congress,* wrecked south of the Kenosha piers.

During his entire career, Cameron never received a gold life saving medal. No single rescue was so extraordinarily dangerous to merit this pinnacle of awards. He had to be satisfied with his silver medal. But his bravery, tenacity and leadership well illustrate the rare breed of men that were keepers.[23]

1. Mose Chartier, born in Canada in 1847, appointed keeper Two-Heart River Station March 17, 1877, discharged June 24, 1889.

2. Bibb, "Life-Saving Service on the Great Lakes," pp. 397-398.

3. Dennis Noble, *Great Lakes, A Brief History of the United States Coast Guard Operations:* Commandants Bulletin Bicentennial Series, p. 9; Life-Saving Files, Northwestern University Archives.

4. "Record of Employees," U.S. Life-Saving Service, RG 26, NARA.

5. Letter, S.I. Kimball to Albert Ocha, RG 26, NARA.

6. "Record of Employees," U.S. Life-Saving Service, RG 26, NARA.

7. "Record of Employees," U.S. Life-Saving Service, RG 26, NARA.

8. Al Miller, "Lake Superior Sentinel, The Life and Times of Captain Albert Ocha," *Nor'Easter,* January-February 1992, p. 8.

9. Dr. Julius F. Wolff Jr., "A Lake Superior Life-Saver Reminisces," *Inland Seas,* Summer 1968, p. 113.

10. *Grand Marais Herald,* March 19, 1910.

11. Miller, "Lake Superior Sentinel," pp. 1-9.

12. Miller, "Lake Superior Sentinel," pp. 1-9.

13. Neil Thorton, *Around the Bay* (Tawas City, MI: Printers Devil Press, 1991), p. 131.

14. Thorton, *Around the Bay,* pp. 130-131.

15. *Portrait and Bibliographic Album of Huron County,* p. 139.

16. *Daily Mining Journal* (Marquette), April 15, 1916.

17. *Port Huron Daily Times,* nd, 1898.

18. *Seattle Post-Intelligence,* June 5, 1909.

19. *Marquette Chronicle* May 11, 1909.

20. Ernest H. Rankin Sr.,"Captain Henry J. Cleary Lifesaver-Showman," *Inland Seas,* Spring 1977, pp. 4-11; Summer 1977, pp. 128-141.

21. *Daily Mining Journal* (Marquette), April 15, 1916.

22. *Grand Haven Daily Tribune,* July 8, 1913.

23. Rev. W.H. Law, "A Hero of the Great Lakes," *The Sailors Magazine,* March 1901, pp. 2-4.

Tables

The tables in this chapter are presented to quantify in real terms the work of the Life-Saving Service on the Great Lakes and compare it to the Service as a whole.

The figures are extracted from the *Annual Reports* for the years indicated. Thus the figures under 1878 reflect the fiscal year July 1, 1877-June 30, 1878.

For ease of explanation, the districts were not identified by number but by the Lakes they encompassed. The "Great Lakes Total" columns represent the totals for all of the Lakes. The "Life-Saving Service Total" is the sum of all districts, including the Lakes.

The Life-Saving Service was careful to state, "It should not be understood that the entire amount represented by these figures was saved by the Service. A considerable portion was saved by salvage companies, wrecking tugs and other instrumentalities, often working in conjunction with the surfman. It is manifestly impossible to apportion the relative results accomplished. It is equally impossible to give even an approximate estimate of the number of lives saved by the station crews. It would be preposterous to assume that all those on board vessels suffering disaster who escaped would have been lost but for the aid of the life-savers; yet the number of persons taken ashore by the lifeboats and other appliances by no means indicates the sum total saved by the service. In many instances where vessels are released from stranding or other perilous situations by the life saving crews, both the vessels and those on board are saved, although the people are not actually taken ashore, and frequently the vessels and crews escaping disaster entirely are undoubtedly saved by the warning signals of the patrolmen, while in numerous cases, either where vessels suffer actual disaster or where they are only warned from disaster, no loss of life would have ensued even though no aid had been rendered. The number of disasters, the property involved, the amounts saved and lost, the number of persons on board and the number lost are known, and the facts are all that can be expressed statistically with reasonable accuracy."[1]

However, in an attempt to quantify results, I used the column "No. Persons Saved" to represent the difference between the number on board, less those lost. I feel this represents a reasonable measure of the life savers' success.

An analysis of the data in terms of relative comparisons does present some interesting results. Remember, however, the data only represents actions within the scope of Service operations, not commerce at large.

At the zenith of the Life-Saving Service, there were 271 stations, divided into 13 districts.

District Number	Area	Number of Stations
1	Maine & New Hampshire	15
2	Massachusetts	32
3	Rhode Island, New York Fishers Island, New York	10
4	Long Island, New York	30
5	New Jersey	41
6	Delaware, Maryland & Virginia North of Chesapeake Bay	19
7	Virginia, South of Chesapeake Bay & North Carolina	34
8	South Carolina, Georgia & East Coast of Florida	1-8[2]
9	Gulf of Mexico	8
10	Lake Ontario & Lake Erie Louisville, Kentucky	12
11	Lake Huron & Lake Superior	19
12	Lake Michigan	31
13	Pacific Coast	19[3]

The 61 Great Lakes stations represented 22.5 percent of the Services assets.[4] All things being equal, it could be expected that the Great Lakes

LAKES ERIE & ONTARIO	1877	1878	1879	1880
No. of Disasters		24	25	55
Value of Vessels		$84,190	$121,520	$298,040
Value of Cargoes		$59,019	$19,845	$87,537
Total Value of Property		$142,209	$141,465	$385,577
No. of Persons on Board		102	128	273
No. of Persons Saved		102	126	272
No. of Persons Lost		0	2	1
No. of Shipwrecked Persons Sheltered at Stations		8	8	54
No. of Days Shelter Provided		9	10	75
Value of Property Saved		$78,874	$105,733	$313,902
Value of Property Lost		$63,335	$35,732	$71,675
No. Disasters, Total Loss Vessel & Cargo		3	2	5

LAKES HURON & SUPERIOR	1877	1878	1879	1880
No. of Disasters	5	8	7	16
Value of Vessels	$114,000	$82,000	$63,400	$156,050
Value of Cargoes	$31,000	$32,324	$13,400	$73,775
Total Value of Property	$145,000	$114,394	$76,800	$229,825
No. of Persons on Board	85	57	62	169
No. of Persons Saved	85	52	62	169
No. of Persons Lost	0	5	0	0
No. of Shipwrecked Persons Sheltered at Stations	0	9	5	0
No. of Days Shelter Provided	0	9	7	0
Value of Property Saved	$126,800	$80,294	$74,250	$156,515
Value of Property Lost	$18,200	$34,100	$2,550	$73,310
No. Disasters, Total Loss Vessel & Cargo	0	2	1	4

LAKE MICHIGAN	1877	1878	1879	1880
No. of Disasters	9	7	21	65
Value of Vessels	$36,500	$36,300	$194,195	$606,880
Value of Cargoes	$13,580	$12,450	$122,865	$247,452
Total Value of Property	$50,080	$48,750	$316,685	$854,332
No. of Persons on Board	38	37	185	465
No. of Persons Saved	38	27	181	465
No. of Persons Lost	0	10	4	0
No. of Shipwrecked Persons Sheltered at Stations	0	4	15	47
No. of Days Shelter Provided	0	14	15	96
Value of Property Saved	$25,080	$9,600	$188,090	$440,139
Value of Property Lost	$2,500	$39,150	$128,775	$414,193
No. Disasters, Total Loss Vessel & Cargo	2	4	2	9

GREAT LAKES TOTAL	1877	1878	1879	1880
No. of Disasters	14	39	53	136
Value of Vessels	$150,500	$202,490	$379,115	$1,060,970
Value of Cargoes	$44,580	$103,793	$156,110	$408,764
Total value of Property	$195,080	$305,353	$534,950	$1,469,734
No. of Persons on Board	123	196	375	907
No. of Persons Saved	123	181	369	906
No. of Persons Lost	0	15	6	1
No. of Shipwrecked Persons Sheltered at Stations	0	21	28	101
No. of Days Shelter Provided	0	32	32	171
Value of Property Saved	$151,880	$168,768	$368,073	$910,556
Value of Property Lost	$20,700	$136,585	$167,057	$559,178
No. Disasters, Total Loss Vessel & Cargo	2	9	5	18

LIFE-SAVING SERVICE TOTAL	1877	1878	1879	1880
No. of Disasters	134	171	219	300
Value of Vessels	$1,986,744	$1,879,063	$1,922,276	$2,616,340
Value of Cargoes	$1,306,588	$745,672	$965,610	$1,195,368
Total Value of Property	$3,293,332	$2,624,735	$2,887,886	$3,811,708
No. of Persons on Board	1500	1557	2105	1989
No. of Persons Saved	1461	1331	2049	1980
No. of Persons Lost	39	226	56	9
No. of Shipwrecked Persons Sheltered at Stations	368	423	371	449
No. of Days Shelter Provided	963	849	1074	1202
Value of Property Saved	$1,713,647	$1,097,375	$1,445,086	$2,619,807
Value of Property Lost	$1,579,685	$1,527,360	$1,442,800	$1,191,901
No. Disasters, Total Loss Vessel & Cargo	34	59	54	67

FIGURE 179
Table of annual activities.

1881	1882	1883	1884	1885	1886	1887	1888
46	61	78	61	58	74	53	62
$454,410	$689,980	$447,310	$575,610	$342,460	$484,540	$172,565	$345,225
$151,227	$371,865	$252,435	$218,192	$57,905	$131,210	$48,265	$59,295
$605,637	$1,061,845	$699,745	$793,802	$400,365	$615,750	$220,830	$404,520
333	665	915	399	409	455	271	264
332	665	914	399	409	454	268	263
1	0	1	0	0	1	3	1
34	25	12	39	10	24	10	20
44	74	15	43	21	27	10	22
$459,139	$927,810	$581,725	$706,695	$384,140	$588,490	$190,060	$379,365
$146,498	$134,035	$118,020	$87,107	$16,225	$27,260	$30,770	$25,155
11	6	5	6	4	4	2	1
1881	1882	1883	1884	1885	1886	1887	1888
9	18	31	35	24	27	39	63
$76,100	$161,465	$421,680	$729,300	$395,140	$280,490	$581,650	$995,810
$17,375	$18,250	$72,040	$329,848	$71,465	$123,300	$235,240	$298,250
$93,475	$179,715	$493,720	$1,059,148	$466,605	$403,850	$816,890	$1,294,060
85	106	195	334	207	301	255	517
85	106	195	334	207	301	255	517
0	0	0	0	0	0	0	0
7	10	9	58	9	11	26	75
14	16	15	148	22	11	46	201
$68,902	$163,995	$465,235	$881,890	$458,270	$376,930	$664,315	$983,105
$24,573	$15,720		$177,258	$8,335	$26,920	$152,575	$310,955
3	0	0	1	0	1	1	7
1881	1882	1883	1884	1885	1886	1887	1888
39	61	78	61	56	60	94	109
$460,207	$395,615	$457,945	$412,725	$441,020	$472,340	$514,355	$1,023,175
$196,957	$85,160	$149,305	$185,620	$85,160	$133,050	$173,170	$389,840
$656,957	$481,160	$607,250	$598,345	$526,180	$606,050	$687,525	$1,413,015
297	311	403	339	287	335	472	746
294	309	392	338	285	332	472	740
3	2	11	1	2	3	0	6
42	58	75	51	6	36	32	71
54	132	161	83	6	45	45	159
$537,432	$388,985	$478,140	$406,860	$453,915	$500,650	$639,905	$1,271,690
$119,525	$92,175	$129,110	$191,485	$72,254	$105,400	$47,620	$141,325
8	6	13	8	3	6	8	0
1881	1882	1883	1884	1885	1886	1887	1888
94	140	187	157	138	161	186	234
$990,717	$1,247,060	$1,326,935	$1,717,635	$1,178,620	$1,237,370	$1,268,570	$2,364,210
$365,559	$475,275	$473,780	$733,660	$214,530	$387,560	$456,675	$747,385
$1,356,069	$1,722,720	$1,800,715	$2,451,295	$1,393,150	$1,625,650	$1,725,245	$3,111,595
715	1082	1513	1072	903	1091	998	1527
711	1080	1501	1071	901	1087	995	1520
4	2	12	1	2	4	3	7
83	93	96	148	25	71	68	166
112	222	191	274	49	83	101	382
$1,065,473	$1,480,790	$1,525,100	$1,995,445	$1,296,325	$1,466,070	$1,494,280	$2,634,160
$290,596	$241,930	$247,130	$455,850	$96,814	$159,580	$230,965	$477,435
22	12	18	15	7	11	11	8
1881	1882	1883	1884	1885	1886	1887	1888
250	345	416	439	371	467	467	544
$2,744,247	$3,272,585	$5,165,795	$7,143,960	$3,544,475	$4,523,420	$4,876,465	$6,114,690
$1,310,505	$1,493,642	$2,076,925	$3,463,980	$1,089,905	$2,090,135	$2,296,065	$3,638,530
$4,054,752	$4,766,227	$7,242,720	$10,607,940	$4,634,380	$6,613,555	$7,172,530	$9,753,220
1878	2398	4040	4432	2439	3074	6601	3950
1854	2386	4021	4412	2428	3045	6543	3933
24	12	19	20	11	29	58	17
407	468	651	532	568	807	737	743
1060	1379	1879	1319	1686	2000	1894	1898
$2,828,680	$3,106,457	$5,671,700	$9,161,354	$3,379,583	$5,171,328	$5,881,735	$7,966,660
$1,226,072	$1,659,770	$1,571,020	$1,446,586	$1,254,797	$1,442,227	$1,290,795	$1,786,560
66	67	68	64	56	88	72	71

1889	1890	1891	1892	1893	1894	1895	1896
67	65	73	76	70	80	75	69
$245,285	$670,990	$340,040	$362,345	$782,120	$425,835	$566,635	$350,280
$33,355	$67,860	$229,225	$111,240	$68,705	$81,490	$60,690	$144,940
$278,640	$738,850	$569,265	$473,585	$796,825	$507,325	$627,325	$495,220
193	487	344	269	439	368	582	325
192	487	338	265	433	367	579	316
1	0	6	4	6	1	3	9
15	18	17	14	35	9	34	4
47	26	17	16	63	9	99	4
$221,155	$686,810	$482,215	$458,135	$744,565	$405,315	$522,605	$484,830
$57,485	$52,040	$87,050	$15,450	$52,260	$102,010	$104,720	$10,390
0	2	4	0	3	4	3	0
1889	1890	1891	1892	1893	1894	1895	1896
53	38	47	53	64	54	50	75
$1,012,610	$524,265	$1,059,505	$1,037,645	$1,073,960	$934,545	$908,900	$1,615,085
$458,610	$137,675	$264,730	$551,130	$244,385	$269,425	$455,385	$479,500
$1,471,220	$661,940	$1,324,235	$1,588,775	$1,318,345	$1,203,970	$1,364,285	$2,094,585
399	317	581	414	592	418	744	584
393	316	576	414	591	418	744	583
6	1	5	0	1	0	0	1
13	47	46	27	47	14	76	13
13	127	128	27	94	14	127	24
$1,299,395	$541,030	$1,222,655	$1,431,150	$1,206,785	$1,113,940	$1,112,920	$1,806,725
$171,825	$120,910	$101,580	$157,625	$111,560	$90,030	$251,365	$287,860
6	5	4	1	8	4	3	5
1889	1890	1891	1892	1893	1894	1895	1896
93	85	85	88	94	131	107	104
$1,019,915	$1,002,430	$849,065	$755,110	$1,160,530	$1,067,095	$1,932,440	$1,355,715
$159,155	$362,955	$118,785	$114,315	$301,655	$387,310	$218,380	$129,630
$1,179,070	$1,365,385	$967,850	$869,425	$1,452,185	$1,454,405	$2,150,820	$1,485,345
728	584	396	474	721	723	1163	1184
728	577	395	470	720	707	1156	1184
0	7	1	4	1	16	7	0
36	4	39	34	22	63	56	40
62	4	47	73	61	83	65	45
$1,144,565	$1,108,770	$942,200	$805,205	$1,334,600	$1,198,645	$1,980,995	$1,357,595
$34,505	$256,615	$25,650	$64,220	$127,585	$255,760	$169,825	$127,750
3	4	3	4	4	18	5	6
1889	1890	1891	1892	1893	1894	1895	1896
213	188	205	217	228	265	232	248
$2,277,810	$2,197,685	$2,248,610	$2,155,100	$3,016,610	$2,427,475	$3,407,975	$3,321,080
$651,120	$568,490	$612,740	$776,685	$614,745	$738,225	$734,455	$754,070
$2,928,930	$2,766,175	$2,861,350	$2,931,785	$3,567,355	$3,165,700	$4,142,430	$4,075,150
1320	1388	1321	1157	1752	1509	2489	2093
1313	1380	1309	1149	1744	1492	2479	2083
7	8	12	8	8	17	10	10
64	69	102	75	104	86	166	57
122	157	192	116	218	106	291	73
$2,665,115	$2,336,610	$2,647,070	$2,694,490	$3,285,950	$2,717,900	$3,616,520	$3,649,150
$263,815	$429,565	$214,280	$237,295	$291,405	$447,800	$525,910	$426,000
9	11	11	5	15	26	11	11
1889	1890	1891	1892	1893	1894	1895	1896
527	529	491	507	581	596	675	680
$4,748,515	$5,326,905	$4,921,690	$5,646,090	$6,537,570	$6,975,725	$8,075,075	$8,992,405
$1,688,230	$2,290,530	$2,099,115	$2,706,245	$1,713,540	$2,979,645	$2,650,100	$3,853,380
$6,416,745	$7,617,435	$7,020,805	$8,352,335	$8,251,110	$9,955,370	$10,725,175	$12,845,735
3422	3496	3491	2923	3892	4491	5823	5205
3383	3448	3441	2896	3863	4423	5797	5185
39	48	50	27	29	68	26	20
787	788	551	658	663	647	803	613
1732	1881	1516	1754	1659	1474	2232	1436
$5,045,425	$5,510,945	$5,783,960	$7,174,475	$5,470,850	$7,729,475	$9,220,265	$11,408,685
$1,362,320	$2,106,490	$1,236,845	$1,177,860	$1,680,260	$2,225,895	$1,504,910	$1,437,100
63	76	62	60	88	91	73	67

1897	1898	1899	1900	1901	1902	1903	1904
104	82	79	77	87	60	57	55
$530,410	$372,970	$635,745	$574,475	$163,755	$219,685	$809,270	$100,555
$211,965	$61,195	$80,945	$188,100	$31,090	$19,100	$83,630	$16,500
$742,375	$434,165	$734,690	$762,575	$194,845	$238,785	$892,900	$117,505
426	287	455	422	303	205	336	214
425	285	453	420	300	204	335	214
1	2	2	2	3	1	1	0
31	11	9	50	14	5	27	9
37	11	9	53	14	5	27	9
$702,890	$431,805	$558,125	$676,750	$153,040	$216,180	$746,060	$60,685
$39,485	$2,360	$176,565	$85,825	$41,805	$22,605	$148,840	$56,820
1	0	1	3	2	0	4	2
1897	**1898**	**1899**	**1900**	**1901**	**1902**	**1903**	**1904**
55	62	69	75	82	84	62	74
$545,285	$837,530	$1,162,505	$1,697,935	$999,485	$2,688,885	$1,228,445	$916,065
$167,540	$149,660	$282,650	$375,410	$405,350	$474,760	$283,540	$306,045
$712,825	$987,190	$1,445,155	$2,073,345	$1,404,835	$3,163,645	$1,511,985	$1,222,110
391	303	354	487	425	563	320	295
391	300	354	486	425	553	319	295
0	3	0	1	0	10	1	0
25	10	45	28	81	39	51	49
49	11	50	34	136	112	83	74
$663,850	$899,970	$1,275,930	$2,038,910	$1,363,465	$2,848,315	$1,453,940	$868,650
$48,975	$87,220	$169,225	$34,435	$41,370	$315,330	$58,045	$353,460
1	3	5	3	0	5	3	3
1897	**1898**	**1899**	**1900**	**1901**	**1902**	**1903**	**1904**
117	99	115	102	116	108	107	120
$771,275	$958,315	$1,040,580	$696,410	$741,025	$1,322,845	$851,145	$520,145
$167,855	$217,435	$356,955	$132,765	$168,015	$137,420	$352,855	$131,945
$939,130	$1,175,750	$1,397,535	$829,175	$909,040	$1,460,265	$1,204,000	$652,090
515	559	645	424	508	606	521	405
511	557	644	423	505	604	520	399
4	2	1	1	3	2	1	6
57	88	98	25	28	61	24	57
86	99	115	25	30	89	52	234
$891,010	$1,012,465	$1,075,170	$804,280	$866,480	$1,283,850	$1,160,145	$514,455
$48,120	$163,285	$322,365	$24,895	$42,560	$176,415	$43,855	$137,635
6	6	9	2	0	5	3	7
1897	**1898**	**1899**	**1900**	**1901**	**1902**	**1903**	**1904**
276	243	263	254	285	252	226	249
$1,846,970	$2,168,815	$2,838,830	$2,968,820	$1,904,265	$4,231,415	$2,888,860	$1,536,765
$547,360	$428,290	$720,550	$696,275	$604,455	$631,280	$720,025	$454,490
$2,394,330	$2,597,105	$3,577,380	$3,665,095	$2,508,720	$4,862,695	$3,608,885	$1,991,705
1332	1149	1454	1333	1236	1374	1177	914
1327	1142	1451	1329	1230	1361	1174	908
5	7	3	4	6	13	3	6
113	109	152	103	123	105	102	115
172	121	174	112	180	206	162	317
$2,257,750	$2,344,240	$2,909,225	$3,519,940	$2,382,985	$4,348,345	$3,360,145	$1,443,790
$136,580	$252,865	$668,155	$145,155	$125,735	$514,350	$250,740	$547,915
8	9	15	8	2	10	10	12
1897	**1898**	**1899**	**1900**	**1901**	**1902**	**1903**	**1904**
699	767	722	693	770	746	697	770
$5,242,755	$6,054,895	$6,194,225	$6,361,155	$5,470,095	$9,425,330	$7,300,955	$4,928,240
$1,986,615	$1,313,200	$2,048,950	$3,376,105	$2,097,445	$5,141,800	$1,750,195	$1,777,290
$7,329,570	$7,368,095	$8,243,175	$9,737,260	$7,567,540	$14,567,130	$9,051,150	$6,705,530
4443	3987	4574	3436	3775	4220	4337	3328
4390	3965	4511	3383	3758	4195	4313	3294
53	22	63	53	17	25	24	34
587	663	751	675	647	712	1086	659
1082	1328	1460	1447	1214	1272	2414	1311
$5,291,175	$6,588,355	$6,391,185	$7,491,460	$6,565,275	$12,292,795	$7,882,045	$5,330,080
$2,038,395	$779,740	$1,851,990	$2,245,800	$1,002,265	$2,274,335	$1,169,105	$1,375,450
54	59	72	61	43	51	57	50

1905	1906	1907	1908	1909	1910	1911
59	84	80	8	124	140	154
$151,610	$597,630	$668,225	$371,900	$710,030	$680,555	$963,720
$3,005	$159,090	$64,190	$1,200	$128,390	$30,310	$10,110
$154,615	$756,720	$652,415	$373,100	$838,420	$710,865	$973,685
191	586	621	63	595	622	703
190	581	619	63	584	622	700
1	5	2	0	11	0	3
6	30	37	1	16	57	17
6	30	45	1	16	59	17
$139,310	$658,505	$630,900	$350,450	$790,595	$602,600	$965,685
$15,305	$98,215	$121,515	$22,650	$47,825	$108,265	$8,145
1	6	3	2	4	5	1
1905	1906	1907	1908	1909	1910	1911
91	112	111	21	145	148	112
$1,749,405	$2,208,425	$822,880	$1,076,700	$3,462,690	$1,845,675	$857,965
$274,250	$381,600	$129,025	$483,825	$722,005	$504,615	$100,435
$2,023,655	$2,590,025	$951,905	$1,560,525	$4,184,695	$2,350,290	$958,400
461	649	391	261	807	551	387
460	637	388	255	807	551	387
1	12	3	6	0	0	0
45	44	74	23	72	26	15
67	46	90	34	96	55	19
$1,903,230	$2,293,330	$873,650	$1,422,700	$3,906,830	$2,242,655	$497,820
$120,425	$296,695	$70,255	$137,825	$277,865	$107,635	$460,580
1	5	3	2	5	3	1
1905	1906	1907	1908	1909	1910	1911
110	155	122	43	256	234	263
$3,144,800	$1,779,255	$1,233,420	$1,665,000	$2,317,365	$913,240	$2,250,745
$656,950	$346,745	$140,420	$474,505	$322,655	$428,040	$438,120
$3,801,750	$2,126,000	$1,373,840	$2,139,505	$2,640,020	$1,341,280	$2,688,865
1183	1000	1103	640	1363	988	1046
1179	998	1088	638	1358	987	1045
4	2	15	2	5	1	1
91	49	149	18	35	55	33
132	82	149	34	59	68	45
$3,547,550	$1,784,940	$1,263,400	$2,056,515	$2,548,090	$1,217,760	$2,469,760
$254,200	$341,060	$110,440	$82,990	$91,930	$123,520	$219,105
9	7	4	4	10	7	6
1905	1906	1907	1908	1909	1910	1911
260	351	313	72	525	522	529
$5,045,815	$4,585,310	$2,724,525	$3,113,600	$6,490,085	$3,439,470	$4,072,430
$934,205	$887,435	$333,635	$959,530	$1,173,050	$962,965	$548,665
$5,980,020	$5,472,745	$2,978,160	$4,073,130	$7,663,135	$4,402,435	$4,620,950
1835	2235	2115	964	2765	2161	2136
1829	2216	2095	956	2749	2160	2132
6	19	20	8	16	1	4
142	123	260	42	123	138	65
205	158	284	69	171	182	81
$5,590,090	$4,736,775	$2,767,950	$3,829,665	$7,245,515	$4,063,015	$3,933,265
$389,930	$735,970	$302,210	$243,465	$417,620	$339,420	$687,830
11	18	10	8	19	15	8
1905	1906	1907	1908	1909	1910	1911
785	848	838	1094	1376	1463	1461
$7,997,225	$10,482,365	$7,002,000	$10,390,955	$13,143,610	$8,742,135	$9,865,380
$2,588,125	$4,558,775	$1,830,585	$3,139,270	$2,962,470	$3,138,430	$2,123,235
$10,585,350	$15,041,140	$8,832,585	$13,530,225	$16,106,080	$11,880,565	$11,988,615
5044	5320	5112	5712	8900	6661	8846
5007	5291	5069	5690	8870	6608	8809
37	29	45	22	30	53	37
624	811	807	562	613	664	449
1510	1727	1140	1000	1050	1171	739
$8,175,410	$12,266,100	$7,432,985	$11,666,435	$13,810,700	$10,051,160	$10,086,975
$2,409,940	$2,775,040	$1,399,600	$1,863,790	$2,295,380	$1,829,405	$1,901,640
63	49	55	56	72	74	52

1912	1913	1914	Total
166	136	214	2938
$591,165	$890,135	$2,404,905	$19,196,120
$171,425	$88,945	$205,415	$3,808,905
$762,590	$979,080	$2,610,320	$22,888,430
607	1251	923	16031
605	1249	921	15951
2	2	2	80
26	7	56	799
92	7	80	1149
$662,480	$938,510	$2,415,995	$20,422,128
$100,110	$40,570	$194,325	$2,568,447
4	6	5	115
1912	1913	1914	Total
126	130	137	2412
$843,215	$2,455,875	$3,486,940	$41,109,505
$79,435	$472,995	$952,255	$10,722,502
$922,650	$2,928,870	$4,439,195	$51,832,137
381	624	717	14789
381	624	716	14732
0	0	1	57
19	12	34	1194
27	17	76	2119
$868,440	$2,849,210	$3,107,245	$45,613,241
$54,210	$79,660	$1,331,950	$6,182,411
3	3	5	110
1912	1913	1914	Total
300	248	351	4413
$2,159,475	$1,847,480	$1,967,260	$40,373,337
$287,400	$179,335	$162,585	$8,688,794
$2,446,875	$2,026,815	$2,129,845	$49,052,594
1071	1019	1610	25094
1071	1009	1610	24956
0	10	0	138
40	16	31	1686
62	18	29	2658
$2,321,060	$1,938,705	$2,034,795	$44,003,491
$125,815	$88,110	$95,050	$5,036,772
4	4	6	215
1912	1913	1914	Total
592	514	702	9763
$3,593,855	$5,193,490	$7,859,105	$100,678,962
$538,260	$741,275	$1,320,255	$23,220,201
$4,132,115	$5,934,765	$9,179,360	$123,773,161
2059	2894	3250	55914
2057	2882	3247	55639
2	12	3	275
85	35	121	3679
181	42	185	5926
$3,851,980	$5,726,425	$7,558,035	$110,038,860
$280,135	$208,340	$1,621,325	$13,787,630
11	13	16	440
1912	1913	1914	Total
1730	1743	1937	27848
$10,710,900	$13,080,380	$17,304,840	$256,711,475
$2,537,405	$2,542,770	$4,203,020	$90,769,395
$13,248,305	$15,623,150	$21,507,860	$347,561,020
7193	9041	9296	171931
7144	8954	9258	170388
16	87	38	1512
444	437	430	23655
814	756	744	53066
$11,155,170	$13,860,000	$18,783,200	$282,507,997
$2,093,135	$1,763,150	$2,724,660	$63,944,073
59	69	82	2424

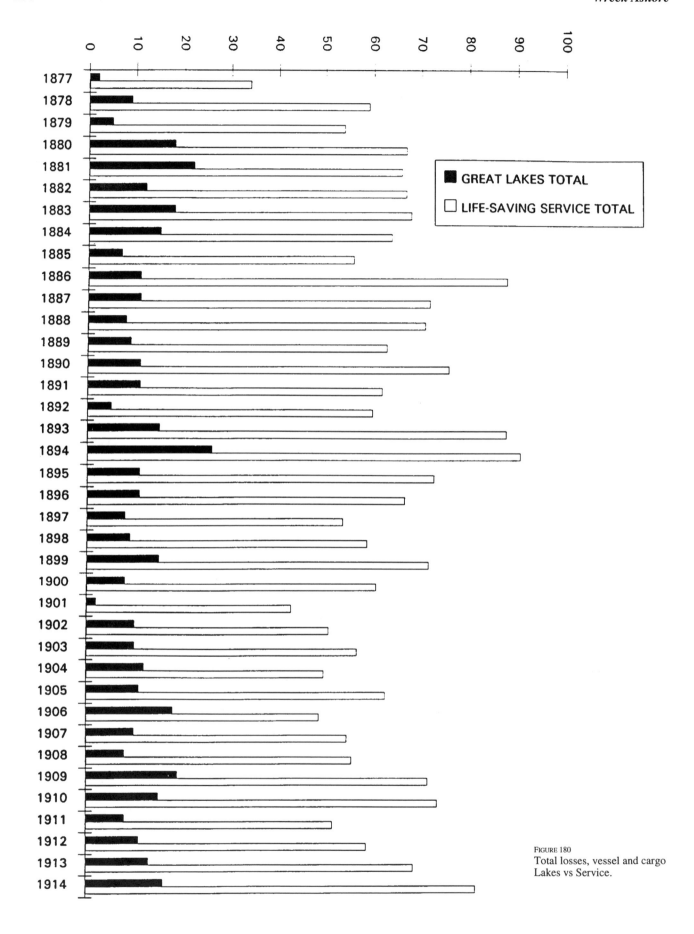

FIGURE 180
Total losses, vessel and cargo
Lakes vs Service.

NUMBER OF PERSONS LOST

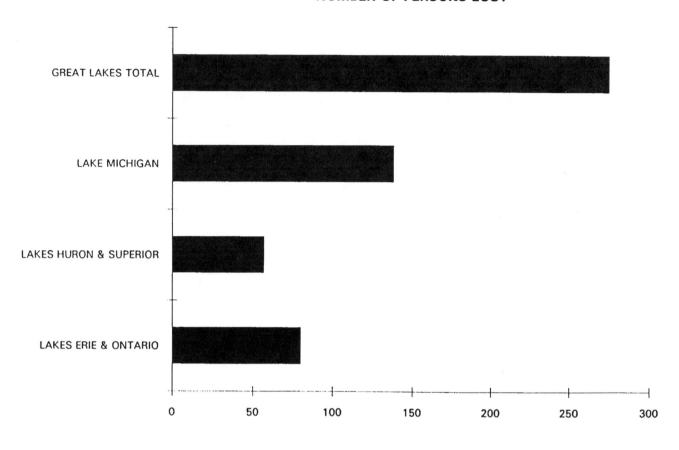

Figure 181
Number of persons lost.

would have approximately the same percent of the wrecks and rescues. This was not the case. Compared to the Service as a whole, the Lakes experienced:

35 percent of the disasters

18 percent of the number of persons lost

21.5 percent of the value of property (vessel and cargo) lost

32.6 percent of the persons rescued.[5]

We can conclude that the Lakes, at least in terms of those areas covered by the operations of the Life-Saving Service, suffered more wrecks, but with less total loss than should be expected. The need for the Service on the lakes was well demonstrated in fact as well as anecdotal accounts.

A look at the situation within the Lakes is most revealing.

	Erie/Ontario	Huron/Superior	Michigan
No. of Disasters			
	2938 (30.1%)	2412 (24.7%)	4413 (45.2%)
No. Persons Lost			
	80 (29.1%)	57 (20.7%)	138 (50.2%)
Value Property Lost			
	$2,568,447 (18.6%)	$6,182,411 (44.8%)	$5,036,772 (36.5%)
No. Total Losses			
	115 (26.1%)	110 (25%)	215 (48.9%)

It is clear that Lake Michigan was the most important area of Service operations. There were more wrecks with greater loss of life in

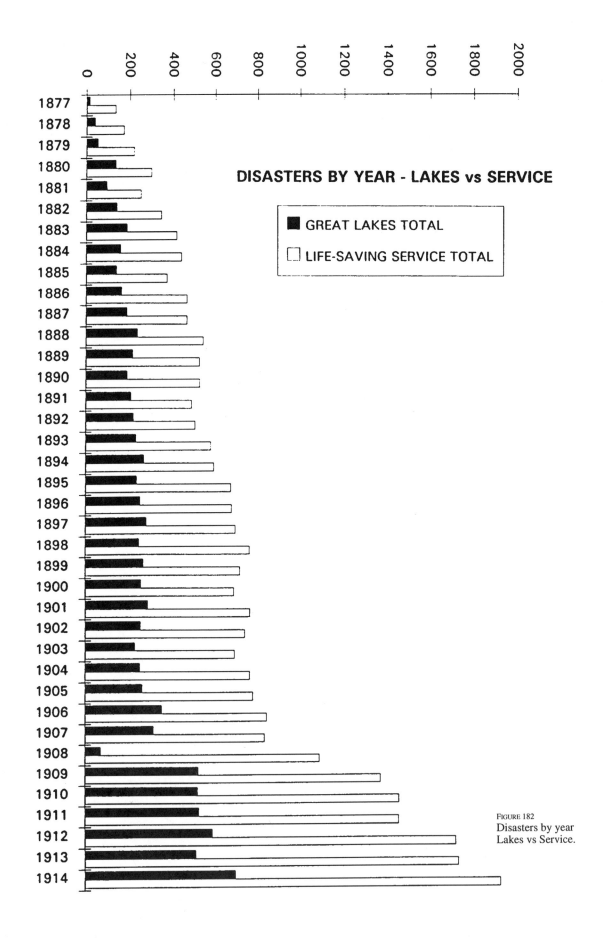

FIGURE 182
Disasters by year
Lakes vs Service.

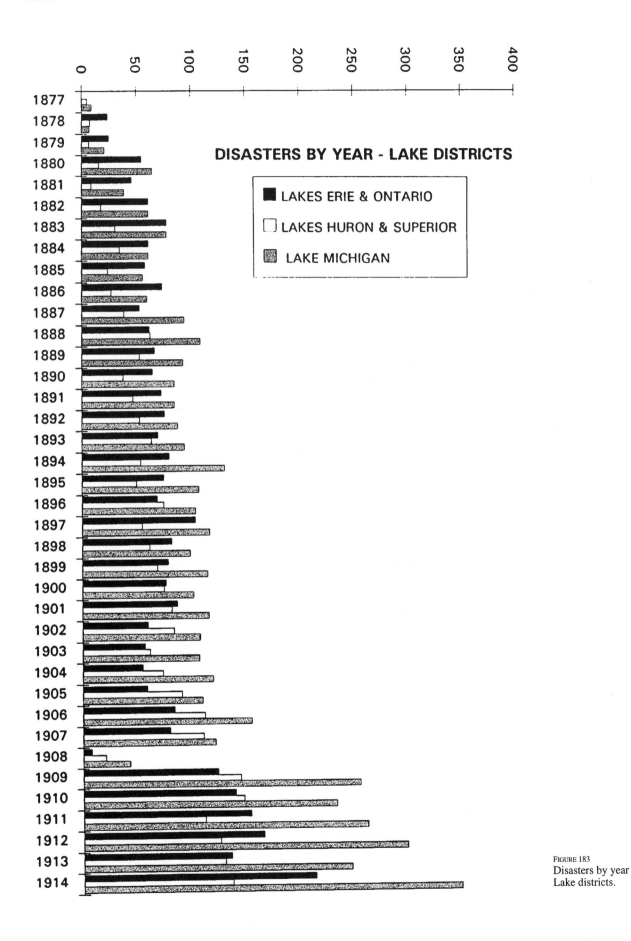

DISASTERS BY YEAR - LAKE DISTRICTS

■ LAKES ERIE & ONTARIO

□ LAKES HURON & SUPERIOR

▨ LAKE MICHIGAN

FIGURE 183
Disasters by year
Lake districts.

this district than any other. Interestingly, the Superior-Huron district wrecks represented greater monetary value, perhaps due to the comparatively expensive vessels engaged in the ore trade.

It is noteworthy that the sharp rise in num-

bers of disasters starting in the *Annual Report* for 1909 was the result of the tremendous increase in gasoline motor boats. The majority of these were small undocumented pleasure craft.

FIGURE 184
Value of property lost
Lakes vs Service.

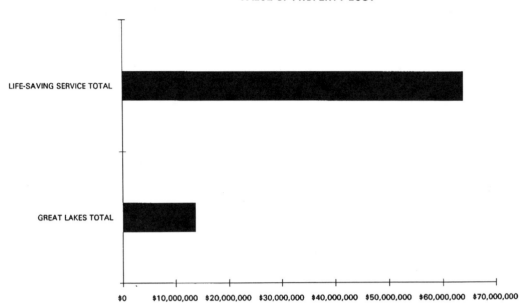

FIGURE 185
Value of property lost
Lake districts.

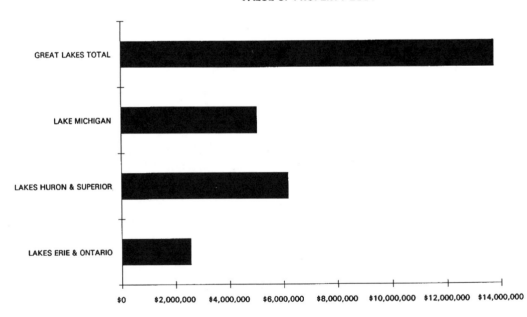

1. *Annual Report, U.S. Life-Saving Service, 1912,* p. 12.
2. One station, eight Houses of Refuge.
3. *Register of the U.S. Life-Saving Service, July 1, 1914,* Government Printing Office, pp. 6-25.
4. Less Louisville.
5. Figures include Louisville.

Part III

The Rescues

The following stories were selected because each illustrates a particular part of the life saver's rescue operations. Some stress equipment, demonstrating the surfboat or lifeboat in action, the use of the beach apparatus with the breeches buoy or lifecar. Others show combinations of gear. All of the stories attempt to put the equipment into context to exhibit its use under actual conditions. With the exception of the incident of the shame of the Holland crew, all clearly illustrate the life savers' perseverance, the will to overcome, to conquer the elements and make the rescue despite the difficulties. They show the relentlessness of both the life saving crews and nature.

Chapter 13
Grand Haven, Five In A Day

Although the Life-Saving Service crews are more commonly thought of in terms of performing heroic rescues of only one wreck at a time, the crew of the Grand Haven, Michigan, station on November 1, 1878, set a new standard when they rendered aid to five vessels and saved 29 sailors in a single day. This feat was all the more remarkable considering that it was not a full-time crew, but a volunteer one!

Particularly laudable were the efforts that the volunteer crew made in performing beach patrols. Patrol duty was not required of volunteers. They were expected to show up only when an actual rescue was in the offing. Regulations allowed them to be paid for the rescue, but not for other duties. Nonetheless, many volunteer crews often initiated patrols when the weather

turned foul. For the two weeks before the wrecks of November 1, the Grand Haven crew had been actively patrolling in anticipation of being needed. The facts of the remarkable day were recorded in the *Annual Report* of 1879.

"At eleven o'clock in the morning, the district superintendent at Grand Haven received a telegram stating that the bark *L.C. Woodruff* of Cleveland, Ohio, was ashore at White Lake Harbor, 42 miles distant, sunk in 13 feet of water, with the crew all in the rigging. Keeper Connell, of Station No. 5, started at 12 p.m. by special train to the rescue, with the life-car and apparatus and four of his men, the other four remaining for service at Grand Haven, and arrived abreast of the wreck in two hours, having to change cars once and transfer the crew and apparatus again from the cars to a tugboat, which carried him six miles further by inland water to the scene of the wreck. The vessel lay 150 yards from the shore with the seas making a clean breach over her, two of her masts gone, her crew of ten men in the fore-rigging and hundreds of excited spectators looking on. Seven of the crew were saved, but three were unfortunately lost.

"During the preparations for the departure for part of the crew for the wreck of the *Woodruff,* the schooner *Australia,* of Muskegon, Michigan, in attempting to make an entrance between the piers, which is about 400 feet wide, was swept aside by the heavy sea and strong current, and struck the end of the north pier, staving in her starboard bow. One man jumped from her upon the pier, and another, in attempting to do so, was carried overboard, by the heavy seas that now swept her decks, and was lost. The vessel continued to thump the pier, but finally worked nearly alongside and grounded when the life-saving men threw their heaving stick and line to her, and getting her lines made them fast, thus preventing her from swinging broadside to the beach and becoming a total wreck. The remainder of the crew, six in number, was then taken off and brought to the station.

"The remanent of the volunteer life-saving crew was now in charge of Surfman John De Young, the keeper having gone with the others to the *L.C. Woodruff.* Anticipating disaster from the heavy weather, Surfman De Young had the surfboat hauled down to the beach. Soon after, about twelve o'clock, the schooner *America,* of Chicago, went ashore north of the piers, and he and his men launched the lifeboat, and after a hard pull reached the vessel and brought her crew of eight men safely ashore.

"At three o'clock the schooner *Elvina,* of Oswego, New York, came ashore between the north pier and the *America,* her stern swinging against the latter's bow. The life-boat crew waded out into the breakers as far as they could, and succeeded in getting a line from her, which they made fast to the pier, thereby preventing the vessel from beating against the other schooner. They went out in the surf-boat and brought the captain ashore at his request.

"Shortly afterward, the schooner *Monplier,* of Detroit, in attempting to run into the harbor, struck the outer bar, fell off to leeward, and grounded on the wreck of the steamer *Orion,* knocking a hole in her bottom and filling immediately. The seas at once swept over her, and her men took to the rigging. The life-saving

crew immediately launched the surf-boat and with great toil and difficulty succeeded in reaching the vessel, from which they rescued seven men and a woman."[1]

Because the first wreck, the *Woodruff,* involved loss of life, the Service was required to perform a full investigation. The results clearly indicated problems with the management of the actual rescue and a lack of the professionalism that would later characterize the Service. It was simply more than could be expected of a volunteer crew.

"On the 31st of October this vessel was at anchor in Lake Michigan, off White Lake, a body of water making inland therefrom. The evening previous all of her sails, except her main staysail, had been carried away in a northwest blow, together with her jibboom, foretopmast and mizzen mast; the latter, however, still held upright by the rigging. About midnight of the 31st, the vessel dragged her anchors toward shore, that by four o'clock in the morning on November 1, her stern was in the outer breakers. Here she held until daylight, when she began to drag again, and by eight o'clock in the morning, she fetched up on a bar in 13 feet of water, when her mizzen mast went over the side. At nine o'clock the gale had grown so violent, that the crew of the vessel were obliged to take to the fore-rigging, the decks being swept by furious seas, and the situation had become alarming.

"The position of the bark was half a mile north of the piers at the entrance to White Lake, and opposite a sawmill, in front of which, protruding upon the water, was a ugly bank 12 feet high, consisting of slabs, edgings, and refuse stuff, the whole being covered with sawdust. The ends of the edgings bristled out all over the bank. Between the vessel and the bank was an old sunken wreck, an obstruction increased by an accumulation of refuse stuff from the sawmill. Within a hundred yards was a beach of sand, on which and on the bank an excited crowd of spectators had gathered from the neighborhood, and from ten to twelve vessels windbound at White Lake. The captains and men of those vessels made repeated attempts to launch from the beach a yawl belonging to the schooner *Ellen Ellinwood,* and go out to the relief of the crew of the *Woodruff,* but the boat was swamped at every effort. Finally, at about nine o'clock in the morning, it was decided to telegraph from Whitehall, at the head of White Lake, to Grand Haven, for the assistance of the life-boat crew.

"The telegram arrived about eleven o'clock, and by noon Keeper Connell, of Station No. 9, with a crew of four men, all that could be spared from wreck service then requisite at Grand Haven, started for the rescue by special train, taking with him the wreck ordnance and life-car. The distance was 42 miles, the route taken being by train to Whitehall, where the life-boat crew, with their apparatus, were transferred to a tugboat, which carried them across the inland waters of White Lake to the scene of the wreck, at which they arrived by two o'clock in the afternoon.

"The vessel lay within 150 yards of the shore, with a terrible running sea breaking over her, and her crew of ten men up in the rigging, under the eyes of the throng on land. Keeper Connell planted the wreck gun on the bank, and at the first shot sent a line over the vessel just abaft of the main rigging. A tail-block with a one-and-a-half-inch double line was next bent on the shot-line, and the men on the wreck began hauling it off. An awful sea was then breaking against the bank and a strong parallel with the shore was running rapidly. This current caused one part of the whip-line to sag to leeward, and when the tail-block at the end was about 40 yards from shore, the line unfortunately became entangled in the sunken wreck, while at the same time another part of it fouled in the jagged *chevaux-de-frise* of the protruding edgings. While an effort was made to clear the line, the hauling on the wreck continued, and the shot-line parted. In the midst of a scene of intense excitement and confusion on the part of the spectators, the whip-line was hauled in by the life-boat crew and operations were recommenced.

"The second shot fell short, the line being wet; but a third, carrying a dry line, was successful, and the line was seized by the men in the rigging. The keeper, in view of the experience of the former trial, judiciously determined to now send out the tail-block with a single part of the whip-line rove through it, having a bowline in the end to which another shot-line was bent on for the purpose of hauling the end of the whip through the block back to shore after the block should be secured to the wreck. The tail-block reached the wreck, and was made fast, but unluckily in hauling the end of the whip-line ashore the shot-line fouled in a sunken obstruction. In the midst of an attempt to set it free, the excited crowd insisted, despite remonstrance, upon a volunteer attempt to reach the wreck by working out the yawl, attached by a painter to the whip-line suspend-

ed between the wreck and the shore, an attempt which resulted in the boat being capsized, and the five volunteers who had undertaken to haul themselves out in this way being thrown into the water, from whence they were rescued with great difficulty, but fortunately without loss.

"The efforts of keeper and crew, impeded by these accidents and interruptions, had up to this time resulted only in getting a single rope stretched between the wreck and the shore, and it was now beginning to grow dark. In his sworn testimony, obtained in the official investigation of this disaster, the keeper, sustained by the testimony of his crew, states that at this point he proceeded to make ready the life-car, with the intention of having it hauled out to the wreck by the suspended whip-line in the hands of the men on board, arriving at which it could be drawn back by those on shore. Had this maneuver been executed, there is no doubt that all on board could have been quickly and easily landed. It appears, however, that the captain and some of the men on the wreck, despairing, in the growing darkness, of help from the shore, and unaware of any further attempt being made for their relief, had resolved, at this stage, to endeavor to work themselves along the whip-line to land, and the keeper while engaged, as he states, at the life-car, looking up as he heard a shout from the crowd, saw four of the men from the *Woodruff* in the water making their way along the rope. He at once rushed for the shore end of the whip-line, but at least fifty excited men had hold of it, and without listening or heeding, possessed with the one thought of dragging the sailors to land, they ran pell-mell up the bank, straining the line until it snapped near the tail-block on the wreck, thus severing the connection which had been affected with so much difficulty, and continued their headlong course, hauling the four sailors rapidly through and beneath the water until the capsized yawl, still attached to the whip-line, was reached, when boat and men came all together, over and under, in a terrible manner, to the shore. The captain, when the yawl was reached, contrived to seize and hold on to it, and came in scathless, but the three men were perfectly insensible when jerked up the bank from the sea, not only being nearly drowned by their sub-marine transit, but having suffered the extreme pounding of the boat, as it thrashed and tumbled with them through the water. The keeper at once went to work and succeeded in restoring them to consciousness by the practice of the method of resuscitation in use by the service, but one of them, the mate, died subsequently from his injuries.

"The mainmast of the vessel now went over the side, and her stern began to break up. All connection with the shore being severed, the six men remaining on the wreck hastily made rafts of the floating deck planks, on which they endeavored to land. One sank and was drowned about 100 feet from the vessel. One came ashore safely a mile and a half up the beach, and another two miles and a half. Two others got to the bank abreast of the wreck. The sixth man perished obscurely, not having even been seen to leave the vessel. Thus of the ten men on board, two were drowned and one died of injuries incident to his rescue.

"The result must be deeply regretted; yet it is difficult to see how it could have been otherwise. The recital of the disaster afforded by the evidence shows that the keeper and his men were victims of a series of adverse circumstances, which appear to have been incapable of mastery, and which baffled measures certainly well taken for the deliverance of those aboard the wreck."[2]

Chapter 14
"Poor Boys, They Are All Gone"

There was never a doubt that life saving was a dangerous job. The tragic loss of the entire Point aux Barques crew, save for the keeper, on April 23, 1879, is a case in point. At this time in the history of the Service, it was only the second time a crew had been lost. The first was in 1876 when a North Carolina crew perished in an attempt to rescue the crew of an Italian bark. It is believed the loss was caused when the panic-stricken sailors jumped into the surfboat en mass, capsizing it.

The almost elegant story of the Point aux Barques disaster is that contained in the *Annual Report* for 1880. The published investigation was performed by the district superintendent, Captain Joseph Sawyer. Ironically Sawyer would be drowned within the year.

"I arrived at Sand Beach the evening of the 24th, and learned there that the life-saving crew were lost in their attempt to reach a vessel in distress off their station, and that the vessel had afterwards got out of trouble and was then lying at the breakwater at Sand Beach. As the steamer on which I was going up was to remain there a little while, I went out and saw the master of the vessel and got his statement, which is substantially as follows:

"'I am the master and owner of the scow *J.H. Magruder,* of Port Huron. Her tonnage is 136.71. The crew consists of myself and four men, namely, Frank Cox, Thomas Purvis, Eddy Hendricks and Thomas Stewart. I have my wife and two little children aboard. I left Alcona with a load of 187,000 feet of lumber for Detroit at noon the 22d instant, wind north, fresh. Sighted Point aux Barques light at ten o'clock that night, wind east, light, but breezing up. Took gaff-top-sails in at eleven o'clock. When abreast of the light we commenced listing bad to starboard. Saw we were making great leeway and the lee rail underwater. Discovered here for the first time that the vessel was leaking badly, with two feet of water in the hold. About midnight was laboring very heavy, with high wind and heavy sea. I feared we would roll over and was satisfied we could not weather the reef. Got both anchors ready and let go about 2 a.m. the 23d, when she immediately righted. Had fourteen feet of water under the stern, and at every heavy surge on the chains she would drag anchor, the seas breaking over her bows. Hung a red lantern in the main rigging, as a signal of distress to the life-saving station. I certainly feared the vessel would be lost, and that our lives were in great danger, if assistance was not rendered. The vessel would strike bottom between every heavy sea. At daybreak I displayed my ensign at half mast, union down, and about seven a.m. observed the answering signal from the station. About eight o'clock saw the surf-boat coming out. We were about three miles southeast from the station. Lost sight of surf-boat in a few moments; thought the seas was too heavy for her, and that she had gone back, but in about 1½ hours (9.30) saw her again about one mile north of us, pulling to the eastward, to get out of the breakers on the reef. In a short time I saw her down in the troughs of a very heavy sea, and when she came up we saw she had capsized. We saw them right her and bail out, when she again started to pull for us. In about twenty minutes she again capsized. Saw several men clinging to her, for some time, but finally saw only one. Our boat was in good condition. She is 16 feet long.

Did not think of launching her. No ordinary yawl-boat could live in such a sea. I thought the life-saving crew used good judgement in crossing the reef were they did. I then commenced throwing my deck load overboard and at noon, the wind shifting to the northeast, we made all sail and started, cleared the reef, and arrived in Sand Beach all safe, but leaking badly. The weather was piercing cold, and all that day the spray would freeze as it came aboard us.'"

The superintendent continues: "I arrived at Huron City at one o'clock Sunday morning (25th). The two dead bodies of surfmen Petherbridge and Nantau were put aboard of the steamer here, and sent down to Detroit, by direction of their friends. I arrived at the station at 3 a.m., and found Keeper Kiah in a very bad condition, both mentally and physically. The sad story of his experience, and the loss of his brave crew is as follows:

"'A little before sunrise on the morning of the 23d, James Nantau, on watch on the lookout, reported a vessel showing signal. I got up, and saw a small vessel about three miles from the station, bearing about east and by south. She was flying signal-of-distress flag at half mast. I saw that she was at anchor close outside the reef. All hands were immediately called; ran the boat out on the dock; and, when ready to launch, surfman Deegan, on patrol north, came running to the station, having discovered the vessel from McGuire's Point, 1½ miles north from the station. At this time a warm cup of coffee was ready, of which we all hastily partook, and a little after sunrise (5.15 by our time) we launched the boat. Wind east, fresh, sea running northeast, surf moderately heavy. We pulled out northeast until clear of the shore surf, and then I headed to cross the reef where I knew there was sufficient water on it to cross without striking bottom. We crossed the reef handsomely and found the sea outside heavier

FIGURE 187
Keeper Jerome Kiah was the sole survivor of the Point aux Barques crew.
Author's Collection

than we had expected, but still not so heavy as we had experienced on other occasions. After getting clear from the breakers of the reef, the boys were in excellent spirits, and we were congratulating ourselves on how nicely we got over. I then bore down towards the vessel, heading her up whenever I saw a heavy sea coming. When heading direct for the vessel, the sea was about two points of the compass forward of our port beam, and for the heaviest seas I frequently had to head the boat directly for, or dodge them. When about a quarter of a mile from the vessel, and half a mile outside the reef, and very nearly one mile from the nearest point of land, I saw a tremendous breaker coming for us. I had barely time to head her for it, when it broke over our stern and filled us. I ordered the boys to bail her out before the sea had got clear of her stern, but it became apparent at once that we could not free her from the water, as the gunwales were considerably underwater amidships, and two or three minutes after she was capsized. We righted her a second time but with the same result. I believe she several times capsized and righted herself after that, but I cannot distinctly remember. As near as I can judge, we filled about one hour after leaving the station. For about three-quarters of an hour we all clung to the boat, the seas occasionally washing us away, but having our cork jackets on, we easily got back again. At this time Pottenger gave out, perished from the cold, dropped his face in the water, let go his hold, and we drifted slowly away from him. We were either holding on the life-lines or the bottom of the boat, the latter position difficult to maintain owing to the seas washing us off. Had it been possible for us all to remain on the bottom of the boat, we would have all been saved, for in this position she was buoyant enough to float us all clear from the water. My hope was that we would all hold out until we got inside the reef where the water was still. I encouraged the men all I could, reminded them that there were others, their wives and children, that they should think of, and to strive for their sakes to keep up, but the cold was too much for them, and one after another each gave out as did the first. Very little was said by any of the men; it was very hard for any of us to speak at all. I attributed my own safety to the fact that I was not heated up when we filled. The men had been rowing hard and were very warm, and the sudden chill seemed to strike them to the heart. In corroboration of this theory I would say that Deegan, who did the least rowing, was the last to give out. All six perished before we had drifted to the reef. I have a faint recollection of the boat grating or striking the reef as she passed over it, and from that time until I was taken to the station, I have but little recollection of what transpired. I was conscious only at brief intervals. I was not suffering, had no pain, had no sense of feeling in my hands, felt tired, sleepy and numb. At times I could scarcely see. I remember screeching several times, not to attract attention, but thought it would help the circulation of the blood. I would pound my hands and feet on the boat whenever I was conscious. I have a faint recollection of when I got on the bottom of the boat, which must have been after she crossed the reef. I remember too in the same dreamy way of when I reached shore; remember of falling down twice, and it seems as if I walked a long distance between the two falls, but I could not have done so, as I was found within thirty feet of the boat. I must have reached the shore about 9.30 a.m., so that I was about 3½ hours in the water. I was helped to the station by Mr. Shaw, lightkeeper, and Mr. McFarland; was given restoratives, dry clothes were put on, my limbs were dressed, and I was put to bed. I slept till noon (two hours), when my wife called me, saying that Deegan and Nantau, had drifted ashore, and were in the boat-room. My memory from this time is clear. I thought possibly these two men might be brought to life, and, under my instructions, had Mr. Shaw and Mr. Peters work at Deegan for over an hour, while I worked over Nantau for the same time, but without success. I then telegraphed to the superintendent and the friends of the crew. The four other men were picked up between 1 and 2 p.m., all having come ashore within a quarter of a mile from the station. The surf-boat and myself came ashore about one mile south of the station, the bodies drifting in the direction of the wind, and the boat with the sea. I ordered coffins for all. On the 24th, Hiram Walker, of Detroit, telegraphed to ship the bodies of Petherbridge and Nantau to Detroit, which I did, together with their effects. The other four men were delivered to their friends, all residents of this county.

"'The following are the names of the lost crew: William I. Sayres, Robert Morison, James Pottenger, Dennis Deegan, James Nantau, and Walter Petherbridge. Sayres and Morison were widowers. Sayres leaves five children, the youngest eight years old. Morison leaves three children, the youngest six years old. This would be the third season for these men at the station. Pottinger and Deegan each leave a wife and four children, the youngest two months old each. This was the second season for these two men at the station. Nantau and Petherbridge were single men and this was their first season at the station.'

"Mr. Samuel McFarland makes the following statement:

"'I am a farmer, and was working on the farm about one-fourth of a mile from where the surf-boat came ashore, when I heard gulls screeching, as I supposed, several times, but paid no attention to it. Presently my two dogs started to run for the cliff, and thinking that somebody might be calling for help from the shore, I went to the edge of the high cliffs overlooking the lake, and saw a boat bottom up about 100 rods from shore, with one man on it. Not knowing that the station crew were out, started to notify them of what I saw. Upon getting to the station, about 9 o'clock, and learning that they were out, concluded it was the surf-boat I had seen, and went to the light-house after Mr. Shaw to accompany me to where the boat was drifting in. When we got there the boat was ashore, and Captain Kiah was standing on the beach about 30 feet from the boat, with one hand holding on to the root of a fallen tree, and with the other hand steadying himself with a lath-stack, and swaying his body to and fro, as if in the act of walking, but not stirring his feet. He did not seem to realize our presence. His face was so black and swollen, with a white froth issuing from his mouth and nose, that we did not at first know who he was. We took him between us, and with great difficulty walked him to the station. Several times on the way he would murmur "Poor boys, they are all gone." At one time he straightened out his legs, his head dropped back, and we thought he was dying, but he soon recovered again. Upon reaching the station he was given restoratives, his clothes removed, and he was put to bed. His legs from above the knees were much swollen, bruised and black.'

"Mr. Shaw corroborates this statement from the time he took part in it.

"'I attended the funerals of Deegan and Pottenger, the 25th, and hope I may be spared from ever again witnessing such a scene. The wives of these two brave men were almost crazed by their great loss, and the cries of the poor children left fatherless, were heart-rending in the extreme. It is sincerely to be hoped that the bill now pending in Congress, granting pensions to the families of surfmen who lose their lives in the discharge of their duty, will become a law, so that the families of these truly brave men may be compensated to the extent of its provisions.

"'In conclusion I would state that I feel very keenly the loss of this crew, but I can lay the blame at no one's door. It was one of those unfortunate accidents that are liable to occur twice in a lifetime. Had the boat been two seconds earlier or later, the seas would have broken ahead of her, or she would have passed over it before breaking; but upon straightening up the boat there was no time left to back or dodge. The sea broke when she lay in the most critical position to take it. Certainly it was the duty of the crew to answer the signal of distress, and certainly they responded most promptly. There was no discord here; there was more than a friendly feeling existing between the keeper and crew. They had together made a good record at their station, and when duty called each strove to be foremost in the boat.'

"I have conversed with several who have served with Keeper Kiah, and all speak in the highest praise of him as a man, and of his superior skill in handling a surf-boat. He has the sympathy of the entire community, including the friends and relatives of his dead crew, in his present trouble.

"The closing incident in the Point aux Barques tragedy was the resignation of the staunch keeper, too shattered in mind and body, for the time at least, to retain his position. Thus the heroic station was by a day's experience left at once vacant of its crew, who, this very year, had saved nearly a hundred lives."[3]

In recognition of the "sturdy bravery" and his "intrepidity, fortitude and tenderness which marked the calamity which befell him and his crew," Captain Jerome G. Kiah received the Service's gold medal.[4]

In consequence of the loss, Congress provided $1,000 to be divided among the families of the five crewmen. It is important to note that the action had to be taken as part of an appropriations bill. The law itself provided no provision for automatic death payments.[5]

Kiah's career as a life saver was far from over. After the drowning death of district superintendent Joseph Sawyer on October 20, 1880, Kiah, now fully recovered, was appointed in his place. He served in this position for 35 years, finally retiring on March 19, 1915, at the age of 72 when the creation of the new Coast Guard provided for pensions.[6]

Chapter 15
"Her Condition Was Dreadful"

A characteristic of a life saving crew was not quitting – always trying to overcome against all odds. In the November 20, 1879, rescue of the crew of the schooner *Mercury,* the Ludington crew wasn't even formed, but it still didn't quit! The *Annual Report* of 1880 relates the details.

"On Tuesday, November 18, the three-masted schooner *Mercury*, of Grand Haven, Michigan, laden with 251,000 feet of pine planking, left the harbor of Ludington, Michigan, at noon, bound for Chicago. She was commanded by Captain Louis Sterling, and had a crew of seven men, including a man cook. Off Little Point au Sable, the wind shifted to the southwest and blew a gale, compelling the vessel to sail off her course and make for the Manitous. By ten o'clock in the forenoon of Wednesday, November 19, she reached Point Betsy, and by noon the winds hauled to the northwest, blowing with fearful violence, and accompanied by a blinding snow storm, and the vessel lost a part of her canvas, her yawl-boat, a portion of

her cargo, shipped several heavy seas, and became water-logged. Her captain handled her with the foresail as well as possible, but could not prevent her from often falling into the trough of the sea and taking in great floods of water. An attempt to run her under Grand Point au Sable failed, and finally, about nine o'clock on Thursday morning, November 20, she drifted ashore two miles south of Pentwater. Her condition was then dreadful. She was covered with ice, already beginning to go to pieces, and the furious seas so constantly broke over her that her crew were unable to keep on deck, and took refuge in the cabin. Here the water was over knee deep, and the wretched men, in momentary expectation of their doom and unable to make any effort to reach the shore, were in danger of perishing from the cold before the breaking up of the vessel. They finally succeeded in getting the stove up on the cabin table and lighting a fire in it, up around which they huddled, thereby keeping themselves from freezing. They were almost famished, and their condition could hardly have been more deplorable. Several futile efforts for their rescue were meanwhile made by persons residing near Pentwater, the final effort being the launch of a yawl by three volunteers, which resulted in the boat being capsized in the breakers, and one of the noble fellows, a man named Hawkins, being drowned. The nearest life-boat station was at Ludington, nearly fifteen miles distant, but the wires between that place and Pentwater were down, and it was not until seven o'clock that evening that a dispatch was got to Capt. Joshua J. Brown, the keeper, that the *Mercury* was ashore and crew perishing.

"The station (No. 7, Ludington, Michigan, Lake Michigan, Eleventh District) was then in process of erection, and not, of course, ready for service. No crew had been enrolled, but fortunately a portion of the appliances, including the life-boat, had been sent and were in store. The scene of the wreck was far beyond the sphere of the operations of the station, but the keeper, without a moment's hesitation, ran to collect a crew. It went like a fire through the community that Captain Sterling had many times faced danger on Lake Michigan to save the lives of others, and there was a general desire that no effort should be spared to rescue him and his men. Nevertheless, the sea and the storm were so terrible that when it became known that the services of a tug were necessary to get out the life-boat, as without such aid the boat could not have got even out of the harbor, the regular tugs all refused to go, their owners knowing that the enterprise involved the probable destruction of their vessels. Finally the keeper applied to Captain Smith, of the little steamer *Magnet,* and this gallant man instantly accepted the hazard, started for the steamer, and in half an hour had her fires up and steam on.

"Keeper Brown meanwhile had to rush up town and find the owner of the warehouse, where the oars and other appliances were under lock and key, they hurry to the boom which temporarily held the self-righting and self-bailing life-boat, and get the latter equipped for service. These preparations, including the muster of a crew, though made in desperate haste, consumed time, but by nine o'clock all was accomplished, and the little steamer, with the life-boat in tow behind her, ploughed out into the darkness on her perilous voyage. The dangers and terrors of the expedition, like the daring of the men who undertook it, are unreportable. The official statements show that in assuming the task of convoy, Captain Smith took into account the probable foundering of his steamer, and only ran the risk on the consideration that he would have a life-boat in tow, which, in the event of his vessel being overwhelmed, might give him and his men a chance for their lives. The distance from Ludington piers to the wreck was, as previously stated, nearly fifteen miles, and all the way the sea flew incessantly over the steamer, and lashed her decks as she waded and staggered on her course, each sea making her captain question whether she would stand the next. Those who peered across her stern through the darkness and spray could only at times see the life-boat, which the seas appeared to cover entirely, and whose safety was only assured to the anxious gazers at intervals when she rose from the burying waters.

"For five miles of the distance between Ludington and Pentwater the lakeshore is composed of precipitous clay banks, against which in storms the surf directly beats, making landing or refuge alike impossible. If by any accident, the tow-line had parted anywhere along this extent, the life-boat, which could hardly have been sufficiently controlled by her oars in such a storm, would have been hurled upon this inaccessible wall of clay and dashed to pieces, while all aboard would as surely have perished. The steamer, however, survived the ordeal, weathering every danger, and after two terrible hours of her rough combat she arrived a mile to windward of the locality where the *Mercury* was supposed to be and let slip the life-boat.

"The boat was at once pulled towards the land. Two large fires, struggling in the wind on the shore disclosed, as they approached, the broken and ice-clad wreck. There was no sight nor sound of life on board as the life-saving crew rowed up under the little lee her stern afforded, and there was no response to their shouts and calls. After a few minutes' laborious efforts to hold the boat in contiguity to the wreck, which was stranded in ten feet of water, the heavy wind and sea, and the over-mastering undertow, swept her away. The crew bent to their oars and soon brought the boat back under the lee of the stern, and renewed their hails. They were again carried from the wreck, and it was not until the fourth attempt that faint cries were heard responding to their halloos, and a few dark figures appeared on the deck. The men had been huddled together, half insensible, on their perch in the cabin, and had only now been aroused to the consciousness that other beings were near them. The astounding sight of the life-boat alongside of them in the dead of the night and in the height of the storm seemed to put new life into their famished and half frozen frames; the heaving-line cast by the life-saving crew was at once made fast to the mizzen rigging, and in a few minutes they had thrown their baggage into the boat. In their eagerness to follow, the first man missed the boat and fell overboard, but was fortunately caught by some of the life-boat men and dragged in. The transfer of others from the wreck then proceeded with more caution and in a short time all were taken off without further accident, and the life-boat let go her line.

"The saved men were pitiably weak, but the gale and the sea were so violent, and the difficulty and danger of the return trip to the steamer so great, that the keeper made every man who could pull a pound, take hold of an oar, and after a hard row to windward of about a mile the life-boat reached the *Magnet*. An attempt was now made to get the rescued men on board the steamer, but owing to their

exhausted condition and the fury of the sea it failed, and to prevent them from freezing, the life-boat was headed for Pentwater, where it arrived together with the steamer a little after midnight. In the excitement and activity of the hour consumed in the direct rescue, the state of the men taken from the wreck was not fully comprehended, and it was not until the arrival at Pentwater that the keeper and his crew realized how nearly perished they were. The little help they gave at the oars had expended the feeble remnant of their strength, and upon landing they had to be lifted into the wagons which conveyed them to a neighboring hotel, where they were soon made as comfortable as their miserable condition permitted. They were all badly frozen, and it is plain could not have survived their sufferings much beyond the hour at which the life-boat came to the rescue.

"The life-boat, upon examination, was found to have passed through the ordeal of the daring enterprise with some damage – not, however material."[7]

Chapter 16
"Where's The Woman"

Although the lifecar was rarely used on the Lakes, the wreck of the schooner *J.H. Hartzell* was an exception. The *Hartzell* rescue also illustrates the incredible difficulties life saving crews had to overcome just to get to a wreck. The following is extracted from the *Annual Report* of 1881.

"The first wreck of the year within the range of the Life-Saving Service, which involved loss of life, was that of the schooner *J.H. Hartzell,* and occurred about a mile south of the harbor of Frankfort, Lake Michigan, on the 16th of October, 1880. The scene of this occasion was in every respect extraordinary, and few narratives could surpass in interest the soberest recital of what took place that day abreast of and upon the wooded steeps in the neighborhood of one of our western towns.

"The schooner belonged at Detroit and left L'Anse, Lake Superior, on Monday, October 11, with a cargo of four hundred and ninety-five tons of iron-ore for the Frankfort Furnace Company. She was commanded by Captain William A. Jones. Her crew consisted of six men, named, respectively, John Cassidy, (mate,) Mark Maham, William Hyde, Edward Biddlesome, Charles Coursie and George

Hyde. There was also on board a woman cook, named Lydia Dale, who had shipped at Buffalo, but is supposed to have belonged in Toledo, Ohio. The vessel made a good run, with favoring winds, and arrived off Frankfort about 3 o'clock on Saturday morning, October 16. Her captain concluded to wait until daylight before entering the harbor, and she lay off and on in the fresh southeast breeze until about six o'clock, when the wind suddenly shifted to the southwest, and began to blow a hard gale, with squalls of hail, snow and rain. She was then rather close to the shore, and about two miles south of the piers. An attempt was at once made to wear ship, but in the growing fury of the wind and sea, the vessel would not obey her helm, and began to drift in; seeing which her master let go both anchors and set his signal of distress. She still continued to drag, and soon struck upon the middle bar, about three hundred yards from shore. Directly abeam of her was a range of wooded sand-hills or bluffs, almost precipitous, and several hundred feet high, known as Big and Little Bald Hills. As soon as she struck, the captain slipped the anchors, and she swung around, bow to the shore. Hard aground, the seas at once crashed over her, and the awful staving and rending usual in such cases began. The yawl was carried away, the deck cabin wrenched asunder and scattered to the breakers, and the vessel began to founder. In a couple of hours all that remained for her crew was to take to the rigging. The cook, Lydia Dale, had been seriously ill. She was very weak, and it took the united efforts of four men to get her aloft into the cross-trees of the foremast, across which planks had been nailed. Upon this species of platform she lay, wrapped up as well as possible, with her head supported on the knees of one of the sailors, and as they stated, rapidly grew delirious. A little while after the men had got aloft, the vessel sank in sixteen feet of water, the stern resting upon the bar and the forward part in deeper water. Later the mainmast gave way and went over, remaining attached to the foundered hulk by some of the cordage, and thrashing and plunging alongside with every rush of the seas. The foremast, with the men upon it – one of them, the captain, clinging to the ratlines, about ten feet above the water; the remainder fifty feet aloft in the cross-trees, with the recumbent woman – swayed and creaked ominously, some of the wedges having become loosened, and seemed likely to go over at any moment. It was a horrible feature of this shipwreck that the vessel, now and utterly ruined, had a short time before been loitering to and fro in the fresh breeze, with no anticipation of disaster, waiting only for daylight to drop into her harbor, near at hand. So suddenly and fiercely had the tempest risen that within an hour destroyed her, and placed in deadly jeopardy, the lives of the wretched company that clung to her one tottering spar.

"The vessel was seen from the town shortly after she struck. One of the earliest to observe her was a little boy, the son of a fisherman named Joseph Robeior, who lived with his parents in a cabin on the hill near the south pier, and who, looking through the sheeting rain and hail, saw her plunging in the breakers. The lad at once told his father, who ran without delay to the village of South Frankfort with the alarm, and, accompanied by some fifteen or twenty citizens, cut across the hills and got abreast of the wreck near 8 o'clock. Other persons continued to arrive, and at length the crowd built a fire and laid pieces of driftwood along so as to form in huge rude letters, black against the white ground of the bluff, the words 'LIFE-BOAT COMING.' Eager signals from the sailors announced that they could read this gigantic telegram. Meanwhile, a gallant young citizen named Woodward had started on horseback for the nearest life-saving station (No. 4, Eleventh District), at Point au Bec Scies, ten miles distant, by a sandy and hilly road, mostly lying through the woods. The young man galloped furiously through the tempest, which was constantly increasing in violence, tearing along the difficult highway to such good purpose that by half-past 8 o'clock he dashed up to the station with the news of the wreck. The keeper, Captain Thomas E. Matthews, at once ordered out the mortar-cart and beach apparatus. In a few minutes, the cart, loaded with the Lyle gun, the breeches-buoy, hawser and hauling lines, and other appurtenances, left the station, dragged by the horse, which young Woodward hitched on, the hauling being aided by himself and the station-men, Marvin LaCour, J.W. Stokes, Martin L. Barney, Leonard Rohr and J. Manuel. One of the surfman, Charles LaRue, was away on the south patrol when the start was made, and followed his comrades to the scene of the wreck subsequently.

"The expedition had set out upon a terrible journey. The Point au Bec Scies station is upon the lake-shore, north of Frankfort, south of which town the wreck lay, and the intervening river and the harbor piers making out into the lake from the town made it impossible, in any case, to arrive at the wreck by following the line of the coast. The only way was to make a circuit through the woods and around the rear of the town, where the bisecting river could be crossed by a bridge in that locality, and the beach south of Frankfort gained. The shortest route, not less than seven or eight miles long, was by a road which led off the beach to an intersecting road leading to the town, but to gain this it was necessary to travel two miles from Point au Bec Scies along the beach, and the beach was now submerged by a swashing flood constantly bursting against and washing away the steep banks of the lake-shore, battering the escarpment with intertangled masses of logs, stumps and trees, and of course, rendering the way impassable. The expedition was therefore compelled to lengthen the detour by taking an old trail or cart-track, which had been pioneered by the Point au Bec Scies light-house construction party several years before for the transportation of materials. This road wandered through the woods, along winding ravines and up steep, soggy sand-hills. Across these activities the way was so difficult that the men and the horse, tugging and straining at the cart together, could only make ten or fifteen yards and a pull without pausing. This violent toil was pursued amidst the roaring of the gale, which now blew almost a hurricane, and the rushing of the storm, until about a mile's distance from the station had been accomplished. By this time the men, despite the bitter cold, were hot and wet with their efforts, and the horse, steaming with exertion, trembled on his limbs and could scarcely draw. There were at least nine miles more of there disheartening journey before them, and as the party were already sorely spent. The difficulties of an ordinary country road, in the rougher regions of the west, are quite indescribable, and thus far the way was not even a road, but a rude cart-trail, made years before, already half-choked with a dense undergrowth, and cumbered here and there with fallen trunks of trees. The load the horse and men had to drag through its rugged and mushy ruts weighed not less than a thousand pounds, and it is needless to say that the labors of hauling this burden were not lightened by the frightful blasts which fitfully burst through the pines upon the gang as they strained and bent at their toil, nor by the incessant pelting of the driven hail and rain, which lashed and stung their faces.

"Fortunately some relief was at hand. The State road had been gained, and a light buggy came hurrying along with Mr. Rennie Averill, who, at the solicitation of Mr. Burmeister, the marine correspondent of the *Chicago Inter-Ocean,* had nobly undertaken the task, from which several persons had recoiled on account of the severity of the storm and the dreadful condition of the roads, of bearing the wreck alarm to the station, not knowing that this had been done by Mr. Woodward. With the aim of getting help for the hauling, the keeper jumped into the buggy and rode on with Mr. Averill, ahead of the crew. Before long, they met another brave citizen, named Samuel Benton, who was also hastening to the station with a double team to give the alarm. He reported another team behind him, on the road, and, at Captain Mathews' request, which showed wise forethought, he pushed on to the station to bring up the life-car and Merriman suit, taking with him, by the keeper's order, Surfman LaCour, as he passed the cart on the way. The keeper also requested Mr. Benton to bring back Surfman LaRue, whom he judged to have reached the station by this time from his patrol. It is noticeable, and it is due to Captain Mathews to say, that his conduct of operations, from the begin-

ning to the end of this laborious and difficult enterprise, was in the highest degree praiseworthy, no step being omitted or forgotten which could facilitate the rescue.

"The life-saving crew had got on with their load some half a mile further when they were met by another citizen with a team of stout horses, sent on by the keeper to aid the hauling. A more rapid progress was now assured. The State road upon which they were traveling was a great improvement on the trail they had left, although fearfully rough. It lay four or five miles straight to Frankfort through dense timber, broken as it neared that place by an occasional farm clearing. The lower part of the town traversed, the road continued along the inner basin which forms the harbor, leading to a bridge spanning the river which feeds this place of anchorage. The bridge crossed, the track went on for some miles further through a dense growth of woods to the neighborhood of the wreck. Nearly the whole way was a series of steep up-grades, plentifully strewn with pitchholes. Along such a course the expedition valiantly struggled, arrived at and rushed through Frankfort, emerged again upon the rugged country road, crossed the river, plunged into the woods, and finally, about half-past 10 o'clock, reached the rear base of the bastion of high hills which separated them from the lake where the wreck lay. The ardor of the rushing march of this train of men and horses is shown by the fact that they conquered the rough stretch of ten miles in about two hours.

"The keeper had driven on to an elevated farm, known as Greenwood's, from whence he could overlook the lake, and saw about a quarter of a mile to the north, the wreck with the stormy water flying over her. He was returning toward the cart of apparatus, with the idea that the road to Greenwood's must be taken, when a citizen named Miller, mounted on horseback, rode up to him crying out, 'Follow me and I'll show you a short cut.' The party followed him through a ravine about a quarter of a mile. The way then led up the overhanging hillside through the brush, and the tug with the loaded cart was terrible. So steep was the ascent that man and beast had fairly to climb, and almost to hoist the cart after them. Nothing could have been done but for the aid of a crowd of sturdy townsfolk, who had assembled there, and anticipating the arrival of the life-saving party, had cleared away with axes and handspikes a great deal of the undergrowth and fallen trees. Even with these impediments removed, so precipitous was the acclivity, that it took the united efforts of twenty-seven brawny men, by actual count, and a span of stout horses, to gain the summit, only about twenty feet being made at a time. By these accounts, worthy of giants, the top of the hill was reached; but the crowd were now brought up all standing by a belt of woods, as yet unpierced, which bristled along the crest of the eminence, and in which lay fallen trees half buried in brush and dense undergrowth. The obstacle seemed to inspire all present with a saddened electric energy, and gave occasion for a striking and admirable scene. In an instant, and as by a simultaneous impulse, all hands, citizens and crew, flung themselves upon the wood with axes and handspikes, and a work began which resembled a combat. The hill-top resounded with the blows of the implements, the heavy thuds of fallen timber lifted and flung aside, and the shouts of the brigade of pioneers mingled with the howling of the wind and the hissing of the descending hail and rain. The wood seemed tumbling asunder, and its rapidly opening depths were alive with rude figures in every variety of fiery action. In some places, men were showering terrible blows with axes upon standing timber. In others they were prying and lifting aside great fallen trees with all their branches, shouting in chorus. Groups here and there, with frantic activity, were uprooting and rending away masses of brush and undergrowth. Sometimes ten men would fling themselves in a mass upon a young tree or a sapling, pull it down and tear it away in an instant. In an incredibly short space of time the way through the wood was cleared, and the mortar-cart loaded with apparatus was dragged forward to the brow of the hill.

"The gap cloven by this heroic onset disclosed a strange and dreadful diorama. The concourse of life-savers, fifty or sixty in number, were upon the summit of a precipitous bluff nearly three hundred feet above the sea. This bluff was composed of sand, covered near the top with a yellow sandy loam, with here and there a patch of clay upon its slanted surface. The mass not being compact, owing to the nature of the substance, yielded readily to any force brought to bear upon it, and the gale, which was now blowing with fury, beating upon the acclivity like a simoon, flung up the sand for ten or twelve feet high upon the face of the slop, so that, to the gazer looking down, the whole surface appeared in rapid and violent motion. Above the dusky layer of this sand-storm was an air thick and blurred with snow

and rain, and the crowd looking through, saw far below, looming with a sort of misty distinctness from the terrific confusion of the waters, the nearly sunken wreck, its two masts still standing, resembling grotesque dishevelled steeples made up of spar and cordage. This object had the effect of rendering all this subsidiary to itself – the immensity of livid and lowering atmosphere in which it was central – the ragged undulations of surf, bursting into foam, which flung themselves around it with furious celerity, and seemed racing toward it from the farthest sea. The hull was well smothered up in the breakers, but at intervals between seas it appeared for a moment black and streaming as the surf on the bar fell away. Standing in the spreading ladders of the lower rigging, a few feet above the water, was a diminished figure with upturned face, watching the people of the summit of the bluff. This was the captain. The monstrous waves curled and broke above his feet, and covered him with their spray. Forty feet above him could be seen, lessened by distance, a bundle of faces, peering at the crowd on shore from the swaying cross-trees. These were the faces of the crew. The fore-top rose above them and the gaff-topsail, partially unfurled, bulged and flapped over them in the tempest. This frightful spectacle, seen by the crowd on the heights through the weird curtain of the tempest, amidst the uproar of the wind and sea, had something of the vivid unreality of the scenery of a vision.

"What the crowd could not see, owing to the distance, was fraught with deeper elements of pity and terror. The captain of the vessel, who had but recently recovered from a fever, stood covered with frozen snow and rain in the ratlines, stiffened and discolored with exposure to the storm. High above him, on the giddy and unstable perch, the six men crouched, blue in the face with cold. The fury of the wind in this tottering eyrie was such that when one of the group had occasion to communicate with another, he could only do so by shouting through hollowed hands into his ear. Amidst all the dim of gale and sea, the unhappy men could hear the harsh creaking of the mast as the vessel swayed to and fro. They expected every moment to go over. The poor women lay among them in the narrow space the elevation afforded, her lower limbs, swathed in a weft of canvas which one of the men, Edward Biddlecomb, had cut out of the gaff-topsail above and roped around them, hanging down through the orifice in the deck of the cross-trees, and her head on the knees of the sailor, William Hyde, who kept her face covered from the storm. She had become very cold and numb, and from time to time the men nearest to her chafed her hands and arms in the effort to revive her. She gave no heed to these attentions. The delirium, which the sailors aver in their testimony, marked her first hours aloft, had, as they state, yielded to unconsciousness.

"No time was lost by the life-saving crew and citizens in commencing operations for the rescue. The prospect was discouraging in almost the last degree. It was a long distance from the summit of the hill to the wreck, and the slope of the sandy hill-side, as has been said, was almost a precipice. Anxiously surveying the ground, Captain Mathews descried, about two hundred and fifty feet beneath him, a narrow ledge or plateau, some ten or twelve feet wide, and at once determined that the cart must be lowered to this foothold as the place of operation. A portion of the whip-line was unwound from the reel and fastened to the body of the loaded vehicle as a drag-rope, the other end being taken to a fallen tree as a loggerhead or snubbing post. Surfmen Barney and Stokes and citizen Woodward placed themselves in the shafts to guide the cart; the rest of the crew and citizens seized the rope to lower away, and the perilous descent of the nearly perpendicular bluff was begun. At every step the yellow slope gave way in masses, instantly caught up in the whirl of the blasts that burst incessantly upon the acclivity. The descent continued steadily, without accident, to a point when it was found that the line employed was too short to enable the cart to gain the plateau. An audacious expedient was at once entered upon. The line was cast off from the fallen tree, and held by the crowd, each man sitting and laying back with his feet braced in the sand, and acting as a drag upon the burden. In this way the men slid down the bluff behind the cart load, ploughing and tearing their way amidst an augmented storm of sand and dirt: some of them being jerked down the bank head-foremost, but most of them maintaining their position. In a few minutes, panting and sweating with their effort, and looking like the dirtiest of brick-makers, they stood around the cart on the narrow ledge, the tremendous surf, thick with flood-wood, bursting in foam and spray a few feet below them.

"The cart was at once unloaded, the lines made ready, and the Lyle gun planted and fired. It was then a little before 11 o'clock. The charge was seven ounces, and at the first fire the shot, directed with great judgement on the part of the keeper, flew almost directly across the wind about two hundred yards beyond the vessel, carrying the line along her starboard broadside as she lay nearly head on to the shore, and letting it fall right upon her weather-rigging, fore and aft, where it was instantly caught by her captain. Unfortunately, the slack of the line was immediately swept by the wind and current under the head-gear of the wreck, where it fouled and could not be cleared by the people on board.

The first effort to establish line communication with the wreck therefore proved a failure, and the shot-line was hauled in and faked for another trial. This time, with the view of overcoming the added weight of the line, which was wet and clogged with sand, the keeper used an eight ounce charge. He also trained the gun a little nearer the vessel, aiming to make the line fall higher against the rigging and to prevent if possible, its fouling with the wreckage. His calculations were superbly accurate. Before the echoes of the report of the gun had ceased along the bluff, the line, flying aloft its full length, had fallen directly across the fore-rigging, where it was caught by the men in the cross-trees.

"It wanted at this time a few minutes of noon, and the shipwrecked sailors were in possession of a line from the shore. The anxious question now was, whether this line would stand the strain of hauling out the double rope, or whip, running through a tail-block, which was at once bent on to it. As allowance had to be made for the slack caused by the distance and the tremendous current, there was a vast length of this double line to be paid out between ship and shore. It was manned by at least fifty men, who strung themselves along up the face of the bluff with the aim of keeping as much as possible out of the sea, where it was endangered by the drift-stuff and wreckage. At times the force of the current would carry both parts of the whip far to leeward, and the sailors would fail to haul in an inch, and could only take a turn with the shot-line around the heel of the foretop mast. Then the men upon the slope of the bluff would raise and straighten out the whip as much as possible, and at a signal from the keeper below, suddenly slack, giving the sailors in the cross-trees, working in concert with them, a chance to haul in a few feet at a time. These maneuvers were regulated by the keeper solely in pantomime, for such was the uproar of the gale that his voice could not have been heard beyond the distance of a few feet, even through a speaking trumpet.

"The strain on the slender shot-line increased as it took out more and more of the whip-line, and every moment the toilers on the slant of the acclivity, timing their labor to the gestures of the grimy figure below them, felt, with him, the dread that the strands would part; but the tough braided linen held, and after more than two hours of such exertions as make the muscles tremble, they had the satisfaction of seeing the whip arrive, and the tail-block properly fastened around the lower mast-head and heel of the topmast, the block hanging forward over the cross-trees.

"A new obstacle, involving a terrible discouragement, had gradually been developed as the further end of the whip-line rose from the water up the mast. The whole length of this double rope, hanging between the tail-block at the mast-head and the shore, was seen to be twisted, one part over the other, and full of turns. Every effort had been made to prevent this result; the files of men that paid out the rope had been kept widely apart, with members of the life-saving crew judiciously stationed at certain points among them; and two experienced surfmen had tended the reel on the cart which gave off the whip to the sea. But the trouble had commenced when the rope first struck the water. The tail-block then immediately began to spin, showing that the rope, dragged upon by the current and unequally soaked by the sea, was curling and twisting as it ran. Presently a large tree, with all its branches, lying in the wash of the surf, had fouled with the whip, increasing the difficulty, and the line was only released by the keeper and several of the crowd rushing down the bank and jumping into the frothing surf, waist-deep to clear it. Besides, in assisting the sailors to overcome the current by hauling in the slack, and then rapidly paying out, the tangle had been constantly increased, the sea taking advantage of each delivery to roll and twist the line before it could be tautened. It now stretched in the condition, in a sagging double, between the unsteady mast and the hands of the files of men along the storm-strewn surface of the bluff.

"The ardent throng of citizen co-workers with the life-saving crew, were reasonably enough struck with consternation at this incident. A volley of excited questions began to shower upon the keeper in regard to what he was going to do to save the men. Every other second anxious interrogations or expressions of dejection or despair were shouted at him through the uproar of the storm, and for a few minutes his position was exceedingly trying. The crowd however, were good natured and obedient in the highest degree, and presently every man rushed to his place under the keeper's orders, and all fell to work clearing the line. This was done by fastening one end to a tree on the brow of the hill and hauling it taut, then untwisting or dipping the other part around it, tautening up both parts from time to time while maintaining the operation. Finally, after fully an hour's work the last of the turns were out, and the line was clear.

"The breeches-buoy was at once rigged on. As the slope was constantly giving way, several small landslides, half-burying the men below, having already occurred, no sand-anchor was planted, the keeper relying on the force he had under command to hold and handle the line. Surfman LaCour was stationed at the summit to tend the slack, which he did by taking a turn with the line around a fallen tree. The buoy then went out toward the wreck, urged by the eager arms of the haulers.

"As the men who worked the line were compelled by the steepness of the bank to stand in constrained positions, half upright, half reclining, upon ground constantly giving way, and were also greatly hindered by the blinding sand and buffeting wind, the outward progress of the buoy was slow, but at length it arrived at the mast. After some little delay, as though the people in the cross-trees hesitated, a man was seen through the dim atmosphere to get into the buoy, which was at once hauled back to the shore. The hauling was done under such difficulties that the passage of the buoy to the shore occupied seventeen minutes by the watch of one of the bystanders. At it approached, several persons rushed down the bank into the surf, and the man was pulled out and helped up to the little plateau. It was the first mate, John Cassidy. His jaws were set, his eyes vacantly fixed, and the expression of his face dazed and frightened. A citizen, Mr. Burmeister, gave him a draught of brandy. This seemed to revive him, and presently he said, 'Save the others.' Two or three questions were asked him in regard to the vessel and the persons on board, which he answered faintly, and he was then led away towards the town, supported on either side by two citizens.

"In reply to one interrogation, he had been understood by the keeper to say that the woman in the cross-trees did not want to come ashore in the buoy, and as he left, the keeper was notified by Surfman LaCour that the tree to which the whip-line was secured was slowly giving way, and the bank coming down under the strain. This circumstance, and the mate's declaration, decided the keeper to substitute the life-car for the buoy, partly because the car could be towed out like a boat until it reached the mast, thus relieving the latter of a certain amount of tension upon it, while its use also dispensed with the fallen tree and spared the pull upon the bank; partly also, because its employment might facilitate the rescue by landing a greater number of the shipwrecked at each trip. The car was accordingly ordered forward, and the keeper, with his own hands, attached it to the lines.

"Every face blazed with excitement as the hauling began. The life-car, as soon as it entered the surf, was dashed about like a cockle-shell. In the second line of breakers, owing to the men not paying out rapidly enough to allow it to tail into the current, it was suddenly tossed bottom up, but righted again immediately, and continued violently lurching on its way. Gradually it grew steadier as it got further from the shore. After protracted effort on the part of the haulers, it had at length reached the wreck, when, all at once, the jagged mainmast, which had fallen sometime before, and was swinging along side with other wreckage, rose on the summit of a huge breaker, and lunging like a battering-ram, struck the car such a blow that it tossed it spinning twelve or fifteen feet into the air. Although every one's heart leaped into his mouth, the life-savers took swift advantage of the momentary lightening of the line to haul in the slack, and rowse the car up, where it hung almost perpendicularly some twelve feet below the mast-head. Without the least delay, two of the men, William Hyde and Edward Biddlecomb, were successively lowered from the cross-trees by ropes around their bodies, and got in. A third man was lowered in the same way, who secured the door, and was then hauled back again by his companions. All hands then fell to work on the hillside, and the car approached the shore. As it drew near, floundering in the surf, the keeper and several men rushed down waist deep into the foaming flood, seized and dragged in the car, unclasped the door, and liberated the two sailors. Mr. Burmeister at once gave them brandy from his flask. They were then helped up the bank, and as the crowd, in their eagerness to assist, gathered rather too thickly for a soil which seemed

to vie with the sea in instability, the bank suddenly gave way, and the whole mass were within a hair's breath of being precipitated into the tumbling sea below them. They were clutched and pulled out by those above them, and after a violent scramble along the steeps, succeeded in gaining a narrow strip of level ground to the northward. Upon being interrogated about the woman, the two men appear to have given evasive answers, to the general effect that she would come ashore in the next trip of the car. They were led away by Mr. Burmeister, until a team near by was reached, which conveyed them to the place of shelter and succor they sorely needed.

"The life-car received some damage around the hatchway and cover from the blow of the mast and the battering wreckage. It was speedily hammered into shape and again set out on the lines. The haulers had learned by their first experience how to handle the ropes, and the car pursued its course through the broken water without capsizing. From time to time during the strenuous hauling bursts of sand on the slope indicated the moments when the ground gave way under the feet of the files of devoted men toiling in the heart of the gale, and who could be seen on these occasions to slide and stagger as they pulled, struggling to preserve their foothold or escape engulfment. The tempest continued to scourge the escarpment with unabated violence, and the air of the waning afternoon was thicker than ever with the wind-blown rain, snow, and hail, driven in alternate gusts, and interblent with the driving substance of the hills. Amidst this continued fury the car slowly worked on towards the wreck.

"The captain of the sunken vessel meanwhile crept up from his place in the lower rigging toward the men above. He was so exhausted by long standing and exposure that he was unable to climb over the futtock-shrouds on to the cross-trees, and was prevented from ascending through the orifice which had been left in the platform, as the lower limbs of the woman, swathed in their wrappings of canvas, hung through the opening. By the efforts of the sailors, aided by his own, the inert body was drawn away and lashed by the bent knees to the Jacob's ladder. He then mounted through the opening, and endeavored, as he testifies, to rouse the woman into some signs of life. The life-car soon hung again in mid-air below them, and the second mate and captain clambered slowly down and got in. In the beginning of the creeping darkness the car arrived from the sea, and was torn open by a dozen eager hands. The crowd were confident that the woman would be brought this time, and were stupefied when only the two men appeared. There was an instant burst of fierce interrogations, to which the captain and mate appear, like their predecessors, to have rendered equivocal answers. The effect of their replies was that the woman was the same as dead, and that she would be, or might be, brought to shore at the next trip. These rejoinders were received with sullen looks and angry murmurs from the crowd. These was no time, however, for parley, as approaching night was fast darkening the storm, and the two man were led to a team near by, which drove away with them, while the life-car was hastily repaired, and once more hauled upon its way.

"The first breaker flung the car upside down, and it remained so the entire trip. It was nearly dark by the time it rose again from the sea to the neighborhood of the cross-trees, and the anxieties of the keeper became intense lest some shocking accident should mar the closing act of rescue. He could only barely see that the car had reached the proper place. The glasses merely enabled him to discern shadowy objects moving about the mast-head, and he vainly endeavored to determine whether the two sailors were engaged in lowering the woman from the cross-trees. To give them every opportunity to save her, he kept the car a long time out, fearful all the time that the crowd, from which every now and then burst expressions of impatience, might suddenly become uncontrollable, and madly haul away, possibly at the very moment when the sailors were descending with their burden through mid-air. An admirable instinct of obedience, however, from first to last pervaded these volunteers, and they remained under command. Finally it grew so dark that the car became utterly invisible, and the keeper at length gave the signal to haul. A frenzy of activity at once fell upon the hillside. The common consciousness that the woman was at last coming in the car with the remainder of the men on the wreck, and that the tremendous hardship and effort of many hours were about to bear full fruit, gave a furious alertness to the cordons of obscure figures on the ghostly front of the bluff, and the rope of the life-car slid swiftly through the darkness. The night had fairly set in on this sustained labor, when the life-car was seen emerging from the gloom over the riot of the breakers. It had made the trip bottom up, and presently grounded in this position on the edge of the shore. The voice of the keeper at once rang out to those around him. 'Now, boys,' he cried, 'jump down and roll that car over and get that woman out as soon as you can.' A dozen men rushed down the slope, waist deep in the surf, and lugged the car up out of the swash and floodwood. In a moment the car was rolled over, and the hatch snatched off. A man instantly sprang out quite nimbly. It was the sailor, George Hyde. Another figure, stiff and halting rose in the opening, and was helped from the car. This was the other sailor, Charles Coursie. A cry of many voices then rose. 'Where's the woman?' It was followed by a momentary silence, in which men were seen bent over the open hatch and groping about with their arms inside the car. Then some one shouted to the crowd in a terrible voice, 'They haven't brought the woman!' The announcement was received with a savage burst of imprecations. The dark air resounded with a roar of curses, and amidst the din men were heard yelling that they never would have laid hands to the hauling lines if they had known that the woman was to be left upon the wreck to perish. Amidst the turmoil, the keeper took aside the sailor, George Hyde and demanded, looking him right in the eyes, 'Why didn't you bring that woman?' Hyde faced him, and replied, 'The woman is dead.' 'Be careful now,' retorted the keeper. 'If you don't know for certain that she's dead, say so; and if you do know, say so.' 'The woman is dead and stiff as a board,' returned the sailor, adding, 'She's been dead for sometime.' The keeper then wheeled about to the sailor Coursie, and sternly demanded, 'Is that woman dead?' Coursie replied, 'Oh, yes; she's been dead for quite a while.'

"It is probable that the feeling that the sailors spoke the truth – at all events, that the doubt as to what the truth was – mixed in either case with the horrible sense of irremediable tragedy – had its influence upon the generous men who had toiled so long at the wreck and gradually stilled them. What is known is, that their rough fury soon settled into sullen quietude. It is, and doubtless will always be, an open question in what condition the hapless woman was left upon the mast. Whether alive or dead, her desertion caused great excitement at Frankfort for some time afterward, and it is certain that on this topic opinion was considerably divided. No common conclusion appears to have been reached, nor is it likely that such unanimity would be possible from the evidence. A coroner's inquest held upon her body, which was washed ashore seventeen days afterward, found that she came to her death by drowning, leaving it to be inferred that she was left upon the wreck alive, and perished upon the subsequent fall of the mast into the sea. None of the sailors appear to have been present at this inquest, they having all left the neighborhood soon after the disaster; and the strongest evidence against them seems to have been the depositions of certain witnesses as to the admissions made by two or three of their number. On the other hand, the concurrent testimony of the last four men upon the wreck, given in the form of affidavits immediately after the occurrence, is that the woman was, at the time of their departure, quite dead. If this statement can be accepted, it is not without support from some antecedent circumstances. It does not seem to be questioned that she had soon become unconscious after her removal to the staging of the cross-trees, and was in a failing condition for hours before the last man was brought ashore. Her death, therefore, from previous illness and current exhaustion, is not unlikely, and if dead, the men perched aloft with her upon a mast rocking in its step, and every moment likely to fall, must have felt it useless, as it would have been physically impossible, to have lowered the heavy and inert burden of her corpse twelve feet down into the car and felt also that their every exertion was justly due to their own preservation. Another possibility is, that when they left she was not dead, but insensible or in a dying condition, and that they felt that her insensibility would make it impossible to save her. It this case their failure to make the effort would hardly be less than criminal. Its only extenuation would be the consideration of the terrible and perhaps insurmountable difficulties of the task. She was a heavy woman, and lay, an utter weight, powerless to help herself, on the narrow ledge of the cross-tree planking, sixty feet above the rush of the waters. It will be remembered that the sailors had to descend from this shaken perch, a distance of twelve feet, to gain the life-car, each man partly availing himself of the broken shrouds which flapped around the mast, and partly lowered from above by a rope in the hands of comrades. It was like the descent of a spider who hangs in mid-air by a tread while he catches at the filaments of his broken web to guide his way downward. To each man, a certain and considerable amount of self-help, in such a descent, was possible, but far otherwise in the case of an inert mass, lowered from a swaying spar,

toward the mouth of a life-car swinging at random, almost perpendicular, and well-nigh inaccessible. At all events, it remains, and will doubtless always remain, a mystery, whether, as the coroner's jury substantially found, the poor woman was needlessly sacrificed; whether she was abandoned in her insensibility because her companions felt the impossibility of lowering her to the car; or whether she was left behind because she was dead, and could not therefore be saved.

"The keeper stood for a few minutes gazing into the stormy darkness and debating with himself whether anything could be done for the recovery of the body. Had there been any daylight left, he would have called for volunteers to go out to the wreck in the life-car and make the effort. But he realized that he would have no control of the movements of his volunteers after they left the shore. He would not be able to guard the car from the wreckage alongside the sunken hull, nor know when he had reached the mast-head. He would not know when to lower it for the return trip; he might let it down while the hatch was still open, and spill his men into the sea, or he might haul home and leave one of the men on the cross-trees. More than all, as the rickety mast might fall at any moment, he would be guilty of risking the destruction of the bold men who undertook the enterprise. The only course left open to him was to suspend operations and endeavor to get the body in the morning, if the mast was left standing, and this he resolved to do.

"In a few minutes the whip was unreeved, the apparatus secured high up on the bank, and the sullen crowd, bitterly disappointed at the loss of the woman, though they had saved seven men, dispersed and straggled away to the town. They had eaten nothing all day and were much spent by their exertions. The life-saving crew were too exhausted to attempt to return to their station that night, and scattered around at different houses, with instructions to reassemble at the scene of the wreck early in the morning. Surfman LaCour, who had fared rather harder than the others, having been in charge of the landing of the car, and had been repeatedly thrown down in the surf, was compelled to halt on the way to town, and spent the night at a house near the beach. Before long the vague slopes, beaten by the tempest, were left in utter solitude, and nothing that was human remained on the scene except the body of the woman, lashed to the rude tressels on the mast, out in the sightless darkness.

"In the night the mast fell. The keeper, up at 4 o'clock in the morning, found that it was gone. Visiting the wreck as soon afterward as possible, he recovered his shot and shot-line from the fallen spar which was there, but found the cross-trees vacant. Seventeen days later, however, as had been stated, the body of the woman was discovered on the beach near Frankfort, where it had drifted ashore."[8]

The storm that sank the *Hartzell* was a devastating one. The 70 mph blow wrecked or damaged 94 vessels, killing an estimated 118 people. The greatest loss of life, 70 to 80 people, occurred on the sidewheeler *Alpena*. She "went missing" on Lake Michigan.[9]

The *Hartzell* rescue illustrates key points often ignored by Great Lakes writers. The local townspeople, some 50 to 60 in number, assisted fully in the effort. They freely provided both the labor and resources in the form of horses, teams, wagons and the shelter of their homes. The life savers were there in their official capacity. They were paid to endure the cold and wet. The townspeople were there of their own free will. Hour after hour, they stood by to help wherever they could. Without their assistance the life savers never would have reached the wreck, been able to work the beach apparatus or get the victims to quick shelter. The life savers provided the brains, the technical know how of what must be done and how to do it, but the people supplied the muscle. It was an unbeatable combination.

Chapter 17
The Wreck of the *Morning Light*

The schooner *Morning Light,* with her crew of seven, was bound from Manistee, Michigan, to Chicago with a load of lumber when she was forced to anchor by a northwest gale. Buffeted by the wind, she dragged her anchors, and at 5 a.m. November 24, 1882, went aground south of the Ludington Station and 200 yards offshore. At 7:30 a.m. the beach patrol found her and notified the station. The keeper and crew were on the verge of leaving for her with the beach apparatus when a citizen reported that all except one man aboard were dead. Although the information was not true, the keeper believed it. Since several strong men would be required onboard the wreck to haul the lines out for the breeches buoy, he changed his plans and left the apparatus at the station. Instead he would try the rescue with the lifeboat.

The sea was tremendous with waves breaking across the harbor from pier to pier. A local tug, however, risked the waves and towed the lifeboat to within one-half mile of the wreck before releasing it. The life savers pulled down to the first line of breakers and dropped anchor, intending to use it as a pivot to allow the lifeboat to get within working distance of the schooner. Seen in the clear light of day, the *Morning Light* was a disaster. The pounding seas had nearly battered it to pieces. Several hours earlier, the mainmast toppled overboard but was still held to the vessel by the stays to the foremast which threatened to fall at anytime. This made the lee of the vessel a very dangerous place for the life savers to work. If the mast fell, they would be crushed!

It took several attempts before the crew was able to work close enough to the *Morning Light* to reach it with the hand grapple, catching on the jib-topsail stay. They discovered that the crew was still aboard and very much alive. After removing two of the stranded sailors, the jib boom gave way, forcing the life savers to move the lifeboat back from the wreck. While attempting to return to the schooner a "terrific sea rose, like a shoulder, and threw the boat end over end." Ponderously, the great lifeboat righted itself. But those aboard were seriously injured. Several had been struck either by the oars or other loose gear, or hit the gunwales when she rolled. Quickly the crew clawed their way back aboard, hauling the two *Morning Light* men with them. The episode had left the life savers too exhausted to make another attempt to reach the sailors still on the schooner. Reluctantly they cut their anchor cable and headed the lifeboat for the beach. Before they landed, the remaining mast came down with a crash, striking just where the lifeboat had been. Had they not left, they likely would have been killed by the falling spars.

When the life savers reached the beach, the keeper sent one man back to the station to get a team and bring the surfboat back. The rest of the surfmen waited on the beach. They kept busy by protecting the lifeboat from floating debris and preparing to help any survivors that either washed off the wreck or attempted to reach the shore on their own. One sailor decided to chance it. After jumping into the seething waves he battled his way into the breakers just shy of the beach before the undertow pulled him under. Just in the nick of time, several brave surfmen waded into the boiling surf and pulled him to safety.

When the surfman reached the station, he discovered that an ad hoc crew of fishermen had just launched the surfboat. The sea had started to subside and it was now possible to run the boat from the station to the wreck.

Although injured when the lifeboat struck his head during the capsize, half frozen and drenched, the life saver took charge of the surfboat. Again a tug was used to tow it to the vicinity of the wreck. The *Morning Light* was now breaking up quickly. Nimbly and expertly, the surfboat dropped down through a field of floating debris and picked up the remaining four sailors from the wreck. All returned to the safety of the Ludington Station.

It was a gallant rescue by the Ludington crew, ably showing their skill and tenacity. Failing once, they tried again until successful.[10]

Chapter 18
Throttle to the Firewall

Transporting a life saving crew and their equipment by train to make a rescue wasn't unheard of. But the 110-mile run of the Portage, Lake Superior, crew to Marquette stands as an epic in the history of the Service.

Starting early on November 17, 1886, Lake Superior was plummeted by a wild northeast storm. It blew for three days, accompanied by thick squalls of snow and driving sleet. Shipping was brutalized by the ferocity of the blow. More than 30 vessels were damaged, with a loss of more than $500,000 and almost 40 lives. The winds were so fierce, docked vessels snapped their lines.

Marquette was hit especially hard. Storm waves broke completely over the breakwater. Normally calm waters of the harbor were whipped into frothy turbulence. The strong wooden lighthouse at the end of the breakwater was washed off, eventually to end up on the beach. The terrible tempest was so awe inspiring that people came out of safe shelter just to watch the wild unleashed power of the lake in action.

Their bravery was rewarded. In midafternoon a schooner, later identified as the *Eliza Gerlach,* was seen making her way through the gale-blown lake toward Marquette. Close reefed, she bounded wildly through the grey seas. To those ashore it was plain that if she kept her course she would smash into the breakwater. Without waiting to be called, Captain John Frink and the tug *Gillett* headed out for her. He knew what needed to be done, and he did it! Showing great seamanship, Frink managed to get a line aboard *Gerlach* and tow the schooner clear, averting certain disaster.

The *Gillett* had no sooner brought the *Gerlach* into the bay than the steamer *Iron Chief* signaled that she had caught brief sight of another schooner in trouble. The unknown schooner, which turned out to be the *Florida,* had sailed into the harbor in the midst of a snow squall,

FIGURE 188
During the tremendous November 1886 storm, the Marquette breakwater light was washed off, ending up on the beach.
Marquette Maritime Museum

having navigated strictly by fog signals. Unable to see, she ran in too close to the beach. Without room to come about, all she could do was drop both anchors and pray. Driven by the northeast blasts, her hooks dragged. It was only a matter of time before she would smash on the rocks off Whetstone Brook.

After quickly coaling, Frink and the *Gillett* headed across the harbor to the area indicated by the *Iron Chief.* Seeing the schooner's terrible predicament, Captain Frink of the *Gillett* ran his tug close under her quarter and yelled for the crew to jump. Eight of the men aboard the schooner successfully leaped to the tug. The ninth misjudged the jump and landed in the water between the two vessels where he was crushed to death between the surging hulls. The tug returned to the comparative safety of the merchandise dock and unloaded the survivors. The rescue moved the local paper, the *Mining Journal,* to comment, "If ever a man deserves the government's life-saving medal...John Frink is the man!"

The northeaster continued to blow through the dark night and into the morning of the 18th. When dawn broke, the grey light revealed the lake as a mass of breakers churned white by the fury of the storm. Local damage was severe. All of the wooden planking had been torn off the breakwater; spray from the crashing waves was flying 40 feet high. Destruction was everywhere. Snow showers continued to pelt the area.

Between squalls, the dim outline of two vessels could be just seen six miles to the east. They appeared to be fast on the outer bar off the Chocolay River. Word soon reached the city that they were the 209-foot steamer *Robert Wallace* and her consort, the 216-foot, four-masted schooner-barge *David Wallace.* Both were stern on, and about 400 yards offshore. The schooner was slightly nearer to the beach. Her aft cabin had been swept off and she appeared broken.

Both vessels were bound from Duluth to Buffalo with wheat when the storm struck them at 4 p.m. on the 17th. Instead of bucking into the teeth of the storm, the captain of the steamer decided to run before it. Unsure of his whereabouts in the blinding snow, at midnight he checked his engines down and proceed slowly. An hour later he went aground. The steamer had a crew of 15 and the schooner nine.

Immense waves swept over both vessels. A boarding sea had rolled down the deck of the steamer and smashed into the engine room causing huge clouds of steam when the cold

water hit the boiler. Momentarily freed by the seas, the schooner started to run up on the steamer, but swung off toward shore. The crew of the steamer fled to the captain's cabin forward to escape the smashing waves on the stern. Throughout the long dark night the terrified crew waited, certain that the vessel was going to pieces. As long as the pressure held, the whistle sounded, but the roar of the gale was so strong that the men in the nearby schooner couldn't hear it, let alone anyone else.

By 11 a.m. Marquette residents had loaded a yawl onto a wagon and set out for the wrecks. The volunteers included sailors from many vessels in the harbor, including five from the wrecked *Florida.* When they arrived at the beach opposite the vessels they saw the full fury of Lake Superior. Waves were breaking on

FIGURE 189
The schooner *Florida* several days after wrecking in Marquette harbor.
Author's Collection

the besieged ships with unrelenting cadence. The steamer appeared totally wrecked. The deck was at water level with waves sweeping over her end to end. The crew could be seen peering out from the safety of the captain's cabin and wheelhouse. The schooner was in better shape. Closer to shore, she was only damaged forward and her masts still stood.

Five of the volunteers manned the yawl and launched through the crashing surf. They intended to row out to the steamer while trailing a line behind, planning to use it as a lifeline to the beach. Almost immediately they were driven back to the shore. A second try was made which, against all odds, got about halfway before a wave nearly swamped the yawl. Signaling to shore, they were hauled back by the rope. Another attempt with a skiff also failed. Seeing the failure, the men on the wrecks tried to float lines ashore using water barrels. Each time the current carried the lines away.

During the day the crowd on the beach continued to increase. Sympathy for the shipwrecked sailors grew throughout the community. Snow flurries periodically obscured the wrecks.

With the failure of the yawl, a team was sent to the Marquette Powder Mill to get an old mortar that was stored there. The mortar, however, was spiked, which meant the touch hole had to be redrilled at a local iron shop. To

encourage the sailors, the crowd started five large bonfires on the beach. In addition, they coiled lines in preparation for the mortar. When the wagon carrying the heavy mortar reached the beach, it was after 6 p.m. and darkness had fallen. The dancing flames cast an unearthly glow over the entire scene as the mortar was unloaded and set up. The crowd cheered heartily, knowing that rescue was not far off.

Under the direction of Captain James Freeman of the *Gillett* the mortar was quickly prepared for use. When all was ready it was fired, but the projectile barely carried 50 feet. Rapidly the line was recoiled and the mortar loaded with a much heavier charge of powder. For the second time the old mortar fired, but this time it burst, sending iron fragments screaming past the rescuers' ears. Incredibly, no one was injured. After the mortar failed, the crowd was dejected, believing that all was lost. To have the sailors perish just offshore was more than could be accepted.

Earlier in the day, John Frink realized professional help was needed. He telegraphed the life savers at the Portage (Ship Canal) Station, telling them of the situation and asking for their aid. The actual message was received in Houghton, then delivered to the station six miles up the canal by the tug *Croze,* reaching there at 4 p.m. on the 17th.

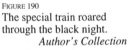

FIGURE 190
The special train roared through the black night.
Author's Collection

Keeper Albert Ocha and his crew immediately sprang into action. They loaded the lifeboat, beach apparatus and other equipment onto the tug and headed for Houghton. There they transferred their equipment onto a special train consisting of an engine, coach and two flatcars. Many citizens eagerly helped with the transfer. At 7:45 p.m. the special got under way.

In the locomotive, engineer Henry Jackson rammed the throttle of old No. 39 to the firewall. Literally blowing aside snow drifts as they went, the special Marquette, Houghton and Ontonagon Railroad train flew along the tracks for Marquette. The snow-covered train roared through gale and snow, rattling and clanking on the rails. Inside the coach the life savers tried to rest, knowing that their ordeal was yet to come. The 110 miles was covered in 3 hours 10 minutes, including several necessary stops for switching. When the train pulled into Marquette at 10:55 p.m., an enthusiastic crowd was waiting at the station. The *Annual Report* for 1887 reported that the throng saw "something white, shapeless, deformed, monstrous and enormous, come snorting and clanging into the depot. It was the delivering train, nearly buried in accumulated snow."

One of the stops made while en route was just before Michigamme where Keeper Ocha wired ahead to Captain Frink. Ocha alerted Frink to have teams standing by to bring the equipment to the wreck site and to have a good supply of lanterns at the ready. Frink followed Ocha's instructions and in addition collected food from local merchants for the half-starved sailors when they came ashore.

After loading additional men, the train took the life savers as close to the beach as the line ran. There they loaded the equipment on wagons and sleighs. It was hard traveling along the dark lakeshore, over treacherous ground and driftwood. They arrived at the beach at 1 a.m. on November 19th. The bonfires continued to cast an erie spell-like glow over the area, making the night beyond the fire's glow intensely dark. Although the gale still blew, the snow had stopped. Despite the lateness of the hour, a large crowd of 400 people still was waiting on the gale-swept shore.

In removing the lifeboat from the carriage, the rudder was damaged. Exactly how it happened was never clear, but Ocha thought it was a case of "too many hands" helping. Deciding not to fight the terrible waves in a damaged boat, Ocha elected to use the beach apparatus. Soon the Lyle gun roared and a shotline neatly

dropped across the steamer's midships. But the crew forward would not brave the open wave-swept deck to recover the line.

Ocha had no option but to make an attempt in the lifeboat. At 2 a.m., in the hellish black-

ness of a full Lake Superior nor'easter, he launched. By the time he crossed the first of two bars, he had shipped three seas, the irons of the rudder were bent and timber split. He had no choice but to return to shore for repairs. While some of his men worked to repair the rudder, the rest helped with the Lyle gun. Another shotline was dropped on the steamer, but again the crew took no action to secure it. They would not leave the safety of the captain's cabin.

At daybreak, the lifeboat temporarily repaired, Ocha launched again. The crew pulled

FIGURE 191
With Ocha at the steering oar, the Portage crew bravely rowed for the wreck.

Author's Collection

for all they were worth in a desperate fight to reach the beleaguered steamer. Twice seas were shipped, but each time the lifeboat continued on, eventually crossing both reefs and reaching the steamer's lee. The lifeboat was a remarkable sight. As the result of the spray and waves, it was heavily coated in ice. She was so weighed down, instead of taking all 15 of the crew aboard, Ocha could only take nine. Any more might have swamped her! Safely depositing the first load ashore, the life savers returned for the rest. A succession of waves filled the boat, but she persisted and reached the steamer. The second load also landed safely. The life savers suffered badly. Each man had been drenched with icy water and their storm suits were frozen stiff.

About 7 a.m., Ocha and his men headed out a third time, now to try for the schooner. By now the wind had dropped, but the waves were still tremendous. Time after time, the lifeboat filled with surging water, each time it self-bailed and continued for the schooner. Crossing the second bar, a huge wave reared up and almost threw them end over end. The rudder split a

second time and Ocha was forced to break out the steering oar, a doubly difficult technique, especially in such dreadful conditions. After nearly an hour's battle, the life savers pulled up to the schooner and loaded the nine sailors aboard. Again Ocha safely landed his charges on the beach.

As each boatload of survivors landed, they were hustled to the warmth of the fires and given hot food and drink. Those from the steamer were far the worse off, half frozen and without food for nearly two days. All were taken to Marquette's European Hotel to recover.

The life savers returned to their station the following day. The story of their thrilling ride on a high-balling special through storm and snow and the remarkable rescue became part of the legend of the life savers.

Both vessels were later recovered and returned to service. The *Robert Wallace* eventually sank off Two Harbors in Lake Superior in 1902 when she broke her stern post. The *David Wallace* was lost in a gale off the Maine coast in 1915.

Ocha's 110-mile dash was not a one-of-a-

FIGURE 192
The *David Wallace* and *Robert Wallace* aground off Marquette several days following the dramatic rescue.

Marquette Maritime Museum

FIGURE 193
Ocha and his crew in their
lifeboat the morning after
the rescue.

*Marquette
Maritime Museum*

kind incident. Less than a
year later, in October 1887,
he made another desperate
run to Marquette to rescue
the crew of the schooner-
barge *Alva Bradley.* It was
this second run that helped
convince the Service to establish a Life-Saving Station
in the city.[11]

Chapter 19

"She's All Right, The Flag is Way Up"

The loss of a surfman for any reason was always a terrible tragedy. But a death as the result of a mistake in deciding whether a vessel was in distress or not was truly meaningless. That's exactly what happened to the crew of the Grand Point Au Sable Station.

At 7 a.m., November 29, 1886, the station lookout spotted a schooner under reefed sails rounding Big Sable Point to the north of the station. Since the wind was strong from the north and a high sea running, the life savers were on alert for vessels experiencing problems. The storm had been blowing for a day and the temperature was hovering near zero. Notified that a vessel was sighted, the keeper made his way to the tower and closely examined her through his glass. About two miles out and abreast of the station, the schooner started to raise a flag up to the top of the main but stopped half way. Apparently the unknown schooner had made a traditional half-mast signal indicating distress. Combined with the storm, the keeper believed her to be in distress and called his men to the surfboat.

The boat was launched without incident, although the surf was running high. While rowing to the vessel, one of the surfman glanced over his shoulder and noticed that the flag was now up at the trunk and that the schooner was continuing on course. He commented to the man opposite that, "she is all right; the flag is up." Apparently the keeper did not hear the remark or notice the flag change. The life savers pulled on for the schooner. When the boat reached the outer bar, however, a breaking wave stopped the forward motion and partly flooded it. Before the bow could be swung back into the waves, another crest struck it, knocking the keeper into the bottom of the boat. Caught in the trough of the waves, within five seconds the surfboat capsized. The crew, except surfman John Smith, landed clear of the boat. Swimming back to the boat they held tight to the life lines. Smith surfaced beneath the overturned boat. Although he yelled to the men outside that he was fine, an hour later, when the boat was partially righted by a comber, his lifeless body washed out.

After half an hour the boat had nearly washed ashore, coming close enough that one of the men was able to swim to the beach. More bad luck intervened. Within a hundred yards of the Hamlin Harbor piers, a current carried the overturned boat offshore. This was probably to the crew's advantage since the force of the waves striking the piers, would have killed them. Once past the piers, the current died and the half-frozen life savers reached the relatively calm water behind the south pier. Paddling with one oar, hands and arms, they managed to work the boat close enough to the beach to make a desperate effort to save themselves. Three of the crew made it to shore safely. The keeper was seen to reach shallow water and stand up. A following wave knocked him down and he didn't get up again. His inert form was hauled out by another of the crew. One man, too weak to swim, stayed with the boat. When it finally grounded on the shore, he was unconscious and had to be cut free of the life lines.

The three life savers still standing, exhausted almost to the point of collapse, their clothes frozen stiff, now tried to fight their way over the snow-covered beach for help. Luckily a search party of four local citizens soon reached them and hustled the survivors to shelter at a nearby home. The party returned as quickly as possible for the keeper and unconscious surfman. Both died soon after being carried to the house.

It was later determined that the schooner was the *A.J. Dewey.* She had been bound from Pierpont for Manistee in tow of a tug when within three miles of her destination the towline broke, fouling the tug's propeller. The tug was later blown ashore and the crew rescued by the Manistee station. Under the circumstances, the *Dewey* had no option but to raise a head sail and run before the wind. When she rounded Big Sable Point she tried to signal for a tug, but the halyards fouled, resulting in a U.S. flag suspended at half mast, a traditional signal of distress. It took about a half hour to clear the mess and by then the surfboat was on the way.

As the result of the confusion, a keeper and two valiant life savers lost their lives. In addition, two women became widows, two children fatherless and an "aged mother disconsolate and destitute."[12]

Chapter 20

"Trusting To The Qualities Of The Surf Boat"

At 8:30 a.m., October 24, 1887, the crew of the Cleveland Station was alerted that a three-masted schooner was ashore 14 miles to the east of the station. The *Annual Report* of 1888 reported the rescue.

"A heavy westerly gale prevailed with a rough sea. Speedy action was necessary as the condition of the vessel was unknown and the delay that would be caused by an attempt to reach the scene by a boat might be fatal to the imperiled men. An appeal for transportation was made to the Lake Shore Railroad Company. It promptly placed at the disposal of Keeper Goodwin two flat cars and an engine which were run down close to the station. On one car the beach apparatus was hastily placed, on another, the life-boat and launching cart. The crew leaped quickly aboard and a short run was made to Noble, the station nearest to the scene of the accident. The wreck was yet two miles away, but the news of the arrival of the life-saving crew quickly spread, and with instant and ready sympathy many eager hands were ready to help in unloading the boat and the gear. Horses were at once obtained and a start made for the wreck. No road led to the shore, the way being over the highly cultivated land of this region, through plowed fields, thickets of underbrush where it was necessary to cut a passage, over fences, dikes, brooks and other obstacles. With an ardor and haste inspired by the thought of the human lives at stake, this toilsome march was begun. An absolutely new road was required for the heavy carts. For quickly making this, where the advance was sometimes by foot, the surfmen alone could hardly have sufficed. A band of volunteers from the neighboring farm-houses, some with axes, some with other implements, some with their hands alone, organized an effective assistance, proceeding ahead, now tearing down fences, now clearing down shrubbery, now cutting through their own well-kept vineyards, all actuated by a common impulse to get forward help for the men who were clinging for their lives to the wreck. Arriving early at the goal, where those most advanced among the accompanying throng could already see the masts of a vessel, a momentary dismay was caused by the breaking of the axle of the apparatus cart, but it was lifted up and almost carried along by the enthusiastic crowd. At half past 10 o'clock the cortege reached the edge of a steep bluff sixty feet high opposite which the ill-fated vessel could be seen. She was the *Zach Chandler,* of Cleveland, Ohio, with a cargo of coal from Ashtabula, for Escanaba, Michigan. In the gale of the previous night her sails had blown away and she became unmanageable. To prevent her, if possible, from going ashore two anchors were let go, but they failed to hold and she slowly dragged towards the beach and finally struck. From the crew of ten, six men had in the early morning effected a landing in the schooner's boat, but the sea had so increased that it had been impossible for them to return for the rescue of their comrades, who could be seen, drenched by the dashing of the ice-cold waves, clinging to the deck. As it seemed a hopeless task to get the boat down the cliff and every moment was precious, the beach apparatus was at once placed in position. The vessel had not struck broadside on, but for some cause, perhaps the partial holding of one of the anchors, had so drifted in that only her stern was presented to the shore. She was, besides, at least four hundred yards from the bluff, and to the assembled crowd it seemed impossible that a line could be thrown over an object presenting so little extent so great a distance away. The rapid and prompt preparations of the surfmen were watched with bated breath, and when the gun was discharged and the line went whizzing through the air fairly over the mizzentop, delighted shouts hailed the successful shot. With painful effort one of the half frozen crew went aloft, brought down the line, and with the assistance of his comrades attempted to haul it aboard. It soon became evident, however, that they were too much exhausted to do this; at one moment they would seem to be slightly gaining, then the waves and current would remorselessly drag back what they had obtained. About half an hour was spent in these vain efforts. The sea was still increasing and the icy gale chilling and benumbing the four perishing men. Whatever was to be done must be effected at once. The life-boat was upon its carriage a short distance back in a thicket. There was no chance to properly launch it as the beach could only be reached down a precipitous descent of nearly sixty feet. It seemed next to impossible to place this heavy boat, weighing at least sixteen hundred pounds, in a position where it could be of service. No time, however, was spent in deliberation. Seizing the boat, the surfmen, assisted by scores of willing arms, lifted it bodily from its carriage, transported it to the edge of the bluff, and lowered it to the narrow margin of the rocky beach below where the surf was thundering in. Swiftly it was manned and shoved out into the breakers, when all at once it was lifted by a huge inrushing billow and thrown upon a jagged rock, staving two holes in its bottom. Not daunted, trusting to the qualities of the life-boat, Keeper Goodwin commanded his crew to go ahead. His confidence was not misplaced; the boat kept afloat. Soon they were alongside the wreck and the four men, nearly dead with cold and exhaustion, were taken onboard. They were landed without further mishap, stimulants were administered, and they were kindly cared for at a neighboring farm-house until they were sufficiently recovered to reach their homes. The successful issue of this difficult case was due in great degree to the assistance rendered by the people of the vicinity who placed themselves under the orders of the keeper and efficiently seconded the attempts of the crew at rescue. The schooner was subsequently pulled off, in a badly damaged condition, by two steam-tugs and taken to Cleveland."[13]

Chapter 21

"Discharged On The Spot"

Instant obedience to the keeper's commands was crucial to the success of a rescue. Should a surfman not obey or refuse an order, he was instantly dismissed. A case in point was the capsizing of the schooner *Reed Case*'s yawl on October 20, 1888.

The *Reed Case* was bound light from Duluth to Portage Lake, Michigan, with a crew of eight. A heavy sea was running, accompanied by a strong southwest gale when she reached the vicinity of the Keweenaw Upper Entry on the 19th. Instead of laying out for the weather to improve, her captain attempted to run between the piers. Seeing his intention, Keeper Albert Ocha of the Portage Station, prepared his crew to go out if necessary. One of the finest keepers on the Great Lakes, 25-year-old Ocha was on his way to becoming a legend along Lake Superior's south shore.

The *Reed Case* continued to make for the entry and just as surely, the wind blew her off to leeward. She struck the end of the east pier hard enough to punch a hole in her port bow. Bouncing off the pier once, a wave slammed her against it again. Managing to get clear, she worked her way a short distance out into the lake and quickly anchored. Immediately one chain broke and the other anchor dragged. The gusting wind blew her four miles to the northeast before the remaining anchor finally caught, holding her about half a mile offshore.

Ocha launched his lifeboat at 9 a.m. and rowed to a point just inside the piers where he streamed a five gallon can of oil from the bow and another from the stern. The slow drip of oil would help dampen the waves. Using oil to calm storm waters was an old sailor's trick. To work, the oil used had to be vegetable or animal rather than mineral. The oil's viscosity formed a film on the surface that acted as a shield between the water and the wind. The oil's slick prevented the wind from getting traction on the water, thus inhibiting the wind from piling the water into waves. On larger craft, the oil was applied over the weather side, usually through the hawse hole or by bags or barrels hung from a cathead. Ocha's use of oil cans was different from the normal method which involved the use of a canvas sack filled with cotton waste, oakum or similar material. Oil was poured into the bag and the top tightly tied to prevent it coming out too fast. The sack was punctured several times with a sail needle to allow a slow but steady drip. As long as the vessel stayed in the slick, the worst effect of the waves could be avoided.

With the oil cans out, Ocha rigged a reefed foresail and slipped out from the shelter of the piers into the wild lake and headed for the schooner. The wind was blowing hard enough that even the reefed sail was too much, and soon it came down. Ocha continued under oars. When the life savers reached the schooner it was "rolling and pitching heavily."

The *Reed Case*'s captain called down to Ocha in the lifeboat that he was leaking badly and wanted a tug. Ocha replied that in such weather no tug in the harbor would come out and that he would standby. The captain however was adamant and began to lower his yawl boat intending to send his steward ashore for a tug. Seeing the seas where far too rough for a yawl to survive and wishing to avoid needless loss of life, Ocha agreed to run the steward onto a nearby sandy beach. After nearly capsizing in a wave trough, Ocha realized that the beach he wanted to land at was impossible to reach. Instead he worked his way to a site down the coast protected by a 30-foot bluff and an offshore reef. But when the lifeboat was crossing the reef, a large wave knocked a surfmen from his seat and swept away his oar. As the

result, at the critical moment the boat slewed, causing it to strike the beach at the wrong angle. Another wave forced it broadside, partially stoving it. After the life savers hauled the damaged boat ashore, the shaken steward left to try to find a tug.

Leaving the lifeboat on the beach, Ocha and his crew returned to the station to get the beach apparatus. He knew a rescue would be required. It was now 1 p.m. and the wind had shifted strong to the north. Heavy snow squalls were occasionally blotting out visibility. With great trouble, the beach cart was pulled to a point opposite the *Reed Case*. Although a team of horses was used, hauling the apparatus cart over snow, slush, tree roots and driftwood was difficult. Accompanied by a roaring bonfire, the life savers kept a close watch on the schooner and patiently waited. The steward returned to the beach at 2 p.m. As Ocha had said earlier, no tug would come out. When dawn broke it was plain that the *Reed Case* was in a bad way. To Ocha's expert eye it looked like she would soon go over on her beam ends. He tried to reach her with the Lyle gun, but it was at extreme range and against the power of the howling north wind. The shotline fell short.

Ocha's only option was the surfboat, and he and his crew returned to the station to get it. The lake was running too high to chance a trip down from the entry so, like the beach cart, the crew used a horse team to haul the wagon and surfboat overland. Assisted by the crew from the steamer *City of Fremont,* they managed to pull the wagon to a point a half mile short of the schooner, where it became hopelessly stuck. Taking the boat out of the wagon, they dragged it on the ground the rest of the way, which resulted in tearing a hole in the bottom.

Ocha meanwhile had gone on ahead to select the best site to launch from. When he came in view of the schooner he was startled to see that the yawl was being lowered. Running to the beach cart he ripped off the canvas cover and wrote on it "BOAT IS COMING." He tied the canvas up between two trees so it was visible to the schooners' crew. He hoped they would see it and stay aboard! Ocha ran quickly back down the trail to urge on the surfboat crew. Arriving at the beach with the boat only five minutes later he saw the yawl swamped in the waves near shore with two men clinging desperately to it. All the surfman except one who remained with the equipment hurried to the beach to try to help bring the survivors to safety. No sooner had the crew left, than the lone surfman saw another man in the water some distance from the yawl. He turned away to grab two lifebelts. When he looked around again the man was gone. Joining hands, the life savers waded into the surf and hauled the yawl, with the two survivors still numbly clinging to it, to shore.

Half frozen and utterly unable even to walk, the sailors were carried to the warmth of the bonfire. Removing their clothes, the life savers gave the bedraggled men their own. The stalwart station medicine chest provided the required stimulants. Another surfman was sent back to the station to get warm, dry clothing and a wagon to transport the sailors to shelter.

Since it would soon be night and the situation aboard the *Reed Case* was deteriorating quickly, Ocha decided he had to try to reach it with the surfboat even though it was damaged. Using a line on the stern they lowered the boat down the steep bank to the edge of the water. As they prepared to launch, Ocha ordered surfman Jeremiah Hanly to climb into the bow and prepare to use his oar to keep her from going broadside in the waves. As stated in the *Annual Report,* "This Hanly refused to do, saying that he would not endanger his life in such a sea. He was promptly discharged on the spot by the keeper...."

Already short the man he sent back to the sta-

tion for the clothes and wagon, Ocha was now down two. He still pressed on. At the first chance the crew launched and rowed clear of the shore. A breaking wave promptly half-flooded the boat, but bravely they kept on while one man bailed. Because of the hole in the bottom, bailing proved fruitless and was abandoned. Rowing hard and trusting their boat, they pulled for the schooner. Reaching it, they removed the four remaining men, returned to the beach and made a safe landing. Even half full of water the surfboat brought them through! The spectators who had braved the storm to watch the crew in action were treated to a rare feat of bravery.

When the wagon arrived, the shipwrecked sailors were quickly brought to the station and given warm clothes, food and shelter. The rescue may have been completed but the life savers' work was far from finished. All the equipment that was so laboriously brought to the beach had to be returned to the station and repaired for another day. The sailor briefly sighted struggling in the water away from the yawl was the captain. His body was recovered the next day. The *Reed Case* became a total loss. Filling with water, she eventually rolled and was destroyed by the relentless storm waves of Lake Superior.[14]

Chapter 22
Cleary To The Rescue

As discussed in the chapter on keepers, Henry Cleary, the longtime keeper at Marquette, was a life saver of rare ability and cool leadership. The best example of his talents was the rescue of the crew of the wooden steamer *Charles J. Kershaw* on September 29, 1895. This writer considers it one of the finest small boat rescues performed by the Service on the Lakes during the decade of the '90s.

Early on the morning of September 28, 1895, the 223-foot, 1,324-ton *Kershaw* was upbound on Lake Superior with the schooner-barges *Moonlight* and *Kent.* On the bridge of the steamer, Captain Robert Pringle could sense a change in the weather. There definitely was a storm brewing. From long experience, he knew it would be a bad one.

By noon the storm had not yet arrived. The wind persisted from the south and the *Kershaw* and her consorts continued for Marquette. The longer the weather stayed good, the quicker

they would reach port. At 10 p.m. the wind shifted suddenly to the northeast and began to blow with a vengeance. The easy sailing was over. Now it would be a fight all the way.

Cold gray seas slammed into the steamer's quarter with powerful regularity. Waves ran the length of the weather deck. Behind, the schooners followed obediently, but strained at the tow cable. Captain Pringle rang to the engine room for more steam to keep the *Kershaw* safely offshore. Sheets of rain blotted out visibility.

Down in the engine room there was a problem. A steam pipe had cracked and although the chief engineer had wrapped a chain tight around it, steam still whistled from the break. It would hold for a while, but too much pressure and it would burst, rendering the steamer powerless.

At 2:40 a.m., September 29, the *Kershaw* and her tows were turning to port to enter Marquette Harbor. They almost made it, but precisely at this moment the cracked steam pipe let go with a roar. Helpless, the three vessels were driven shoreward by the gale. Captain Pringle raised his distress signals and cut the tow cables. With luck the schooners might be able to get a staysail up and claw off the beach. If

FIGURE 194
The *Charles J. Kershaw* before being wrecked on the Chocolay Reef.
Author's Collection

not, they would be no worse off than keeping their tow lines.

At 3 a.m. the steamer struck hard on Chocolay Reef, about three-quarters of a mile east of Marquette. Huge waves rolled over the *Kershaw,* slowly starting to batter her to pieces. The crew fled to the stern where they were momentarily safe. Both schooners fetched up on the sand beach further down the coast. They were driven so far ashore, the crews were able to jump to safety without getting their feet wet.

Shortly after the steam pipe burst, the lookout in the tower at Marquette Station saw the distress signals through a gap in the squalls. He sounded the alarm, swinging the life savers into action. Cleary quickly ordered the surfboat loaded into the wagon and sent for a team. Once the horses arrived, the life savers were on the way. By 6 a.m. they were on site and after deciding the schooners were safe, began assembling their gear on the beach opposite the reef. In the dim light they could just make out the dying steamer. With the first glimmer of dawn they could see that she was jammed tight on the reef and the sea had opened a huge hole in her bow.

The life savers carefully prepared their surf-

boat for a launch. The lake was churned to a boiling rage. In the words of Captain Cleary, "The surf was furious and filled with wreckage, logs and stumps." Each was potentially deadly to the frail surfboat.

The actions in launching either surfboat or lifeboat off the beach were substantially the same. For the *Kershaw* rescue, Cleary used the standard Service technique. With the boat pointing into the surf, the carriage was backed into the water until it was in deep enough to assure that the surfboat would float when launched. Either horses or the crew provided the backing power. When all was in readiness, the crew climbed aboard and took their places on the thwarts, oars in hand. Bystanders manned several long ropes attached to the carriage. If sufficient manpower was not available, the ropes were made fast to a horse. After carefully judging the waves and at precisely the right moment, the keeper gave the command to launch. A stern securing line was dropped off and the men on the launching ropes ran up the beach as fast as possible. The boat, now supported only on the carriage's keel rollers, shot off the wagon and into the water. Instantly the crew gave way with their oars to try to get the boat under way before the waves could beat her back to the beach.

Once off the carriage, the real difficulty was just beginning. Speed was imperative for a boat rowing into a heavy surf. The safety of the boat depended on that speed as well as the skill of the crew. If the waves were large and accompanied by a strong onshore wind, only by the greatest efforts of the crew could headway be made. Every man had to row for all he was worth!

The danger faced by the boat was that the wave would carry it away on the wave front and force it to broach or turn broadside and capsize. In either case, the result was fatal. If the boat had sufficient way on her, however, she could meet the wave head on and it would pass safely beneath.

When the waves were large but the wind was light or offshore, care needed to be taken that the boat was not rowed so fast that it crested a wave and fell too heavily on the backside. It may be necessary to "check" it just before meeting the wave. Only long experience taught the keeper just how much speed was needed for each circumstance. Sharp-eyed keepers also tried to dodge the sea, to avoid meeting a wave precisely at the moment of breaking.

At 7 a.m. Cleary made his first launch into this maelstrom of death. Several times breaking waves filled the boat, but each time she freed herself and continued. Avoiding the floating debris as best he could, he steered for the wreck. Eventually he reached the lee of the stern where nine of her crew slid down a rope and into the bouncing surfboat. The rest would have to wait for a second trip. To take them now would overload the boat.

The run to shore was just as difficult as the run out. Three times the surfboat filled with water when waves flooded over the stern. Each time she self-bailed. The log jam of wreckage in the surf was so thick, Cleary could not bring her straight in. The crew had to jump into the surging water and clear a safe path through the logs to the beach. One surfman, Joe Greenwood, was badly injured when he was crushed between a log and the boat.

Landing a boat through surf was far more complicated than just rowing it to the beach. It was an extremely dangerous exercise involving considerable skill by the keeper and crew. There was always the very serious danger of broaching or pitch-poling. Broaching occurred when the boat was traveling in the same direction as the seas, but without sufficient resistance and was carried forward by the force of the wave. When a wave overtook a boat the first effect was to force up the stern and depress the bow. As the wave passed beneath her, the boat first leveled then depressed her stern and raised the bow. This was the desirable outcome. If a boat had enough inertia into the wave, it would safely pass beneath her. However, if a boat had insufficient inertia, the overtaking wave would raise her stern high and carry it before it. If the boat was carefully steered, it could run a considerable distance, literally "surfing" before the wave passed beneath. But if the bow dug in, then the boat could be thrown end over end or broach. Service boats, with their large air chambers fore and aft, tended to broach rather than pitch-pole. Pitch-poling happened when the stern was thrown over the bow, in a kind of half somersault.

FIGURE 195
The *Moonlight* and *Kent* ashore at Marquette. The wreckage and logs on the beach are evidence of the terrible gauntlet that the life savers had to make their way through.

Marquette
Maritime Museum

FIGURE 196
Wrecking tugs at work
recovering the *Kent* from
the beach. Cleary is on the
left and Marquette pioneer
Peter White on the right.
The keepers were highly
respected members of the
local marine community,
and their opinions on
salvage operations and
methods were sought after.
*Marquette
Maritime Museum*

It has been said that the keeper as the coxswain had to know the moods of the wind and water better than he knew those of his own wife. In either instance an error in timing or lapse in judgement could mean disaster.

Service regulations approved three methods of landing through a surf. Before entering the broken water the boat's bow was turned into the waves and it was backed ashore. Just before each wave, several strokes were taken to provide enough forward motion to allow the inertia to successfully carry it over the wave. This was considered the safest method in a truly heavy surf.

The same technique could be used with the boat rowing bow-first to the beach but backing just before each wave. It could be modified by having the two stern rowers facing forward and back the boat at each wave.

The last method used a "drogue" or "drag." The boat was brought in bow first with the drogue towed astern. A drogue was a tapered canvas bag approximately two feet wide at the mouth and four and a half feet long. It was towed with the mouth ahead by a strong rope while a light tripping line was attached to the small end. The drogue quickly filled with water, offering resistance and holding the boat back preventing it from broaching. By pulling in the tripping line, the drogue reversed itself and ceased to act as a drag. Reversing the process allowed the drogue to again brake the

boat. It was recovered by letting go the heavy rope and hauling it aboard with the tripping line. The drogue allowed the boat to come in slower than the surf and the keeper to pick the right moment to beach.

Cleary elected not to use the drogue. Instead, he ran bow-in but had the crew back hard before each wave. His skill paid off as the boat slid safely onto the beach.

Using a volunteer, Nelson Coty, in place of the regular but injured crewman, Cleary quickly launched again. For a second time the surfboat battled through the raging surf and boiling wreckage. Thirty yards short of the *Kershaw* three powerful seas slammed into the boat in rapid succession. The first two were ridden out safely. But as the result of losing headway, the third caused her to broach and capsize. Righting itself, a huge comber knocked her over a second time. The long hours of boat drill for the crew now paid off handsomely. Although rolled twice in the midst of a roaring gale, it didn't faze them. Cleary's men kept their heads. They did their best to right the boat and keep going, but it wasn't to be. Surging waves drove the floating wreckage against it, damaging it beyond use. Eventually the life savers and boat were driven ashore. When they emerged from the boiling surf, two more life savers, Patrick Connors and Harry Gibbs, were injured and couldn't continue.

Cleary and those of his crew not hurt immediately returned to the station to get the big lifeboat. At this time the *Kershaw* showed signs of imminent break-up. The remaining crew aboard lowered the yawl in the lee of the stern and slid down a rope into it. Another rope secured the yawl to the steamer. Although the boat was protected from the worst of the storm, the crew still had to work desperately hard to keep it from swamping.

At 1 p.m. Cleary returned with the lifeboat. Supplementing his crew with local volunteers, Frank Colure, William Parker, Engineer Collins and Nelson Coty, he launched again for the wreck. The heavy lifeboat was more difficult to maneuver, but with its great strength, it just plowed through the crashing seas, shrugging them off without effect. The lifeboat safely reached the yawl and hauled the half dead sailors aboard.

Cleary toyed with the idea of rowing back to the station, a mere 2½ miles away, but the storm was still raging and his crew spent. They were too tired to even effectively row to the beach. He shipped oars and trailed his drogue. Considering the state of his crew and his untrained volunteers, using the drogue was the safest way to come ashore. He successfully landed without injury, thus completing one of the most difficult rescues ever made on the Great Lakes.

Commenting on the actions of the life savers, the *Marquette Mining Journal* stated, "...as plucky and skillful a piece of work on the part of all concerned as the shores of Lake Superior have ever seen, or as the gallant annals of the Life-Saving Service can boast." Cleary's feat was well documented as hundreds of towns people turned out to watch the crew at work. It is always easy after the event to speak of how rough the water was. In the case of the *Kershaw,* the facts recorded in the station journal speak clearly of the difficulty. Out of 10 possible descriptions of sea conditions, the tenth, or "very high," was marked for each six hour period of September 29. There was no worse description.

The *Kershaw* proved to be a total loss. The barges were later recovered and returned to service, but only after considerable effort.[15]

Chapter 23
The Whistle Blew Itself

The November 25, 1898, wreck of the steamer *St. Lawrence* illustrated many of the life saver's tools. Coston signals, surfboat, beach apparatus and resuscitation were all needed to bring the episode to a conclusion.

The *St. Lawrence,* a 1,437-ton vessel, was bound from Chicago to Prescott, Ontario, with a cargo of corn. She was manned by a crew of 15. The steamer was following the normal shipping course which placed Point Betsy on the starboard bow and then swung around to the east of the Manitou Islands, traveling between the islands and Sleeping Bear Point. Thick snow was falling that greatly complicated the captain's navigation. Gale force winds made for a decidedly rough trip. At 5:30 p.m. the *St. Lawrence* ran aground about two miles south of the Point Betsy Station. Although the waves were running high, the vessel was not in imminent danger. The captain began blowing his whistle which was plainly heard at the life saving station. Since they were not proper distress signals, however, it was thought they were coming from a car ferry due in to Frankfort. Keeper Miller believed the signals were too close to the beach and was worried. He sent a life saver out to warn the ferry off with a Coston signal.

Making his way down to the shore, the surfman didn't see the lights of the steamer until he was abreast of her. He estimated her about 350 yards offshore. After burning a Coston, he realized she was aground. Getting no reply, he burned a second signal. Finally the steamer responded with a series of whistle blasts. Quickly the life saver returned to the station and reported.

Keeper Miller acted quickly. One man was sent for a team. The others went to prepare the surfboat and wagon. Within half an hour the team arrived and the crew was on the way. The trip was difficult, over driftwood, logs, mud, soft sand and snow. Thick snow squalls frequently blinded the men as they trudged along on their mission of mercy. All the while the black night was pierced only by the weak yellow glow of their oil lamps. A total of 22 inches of snow would fall before morning. Forty-five minutes of hard trekking brought the life savers to the beach opposite the wreck.

As soon as possible the crew rapidly launched their surfboat. Between the darkness and swirling snow the life savers were unable to properly see the waves forming. While crossing the outer bar, an unseen breaker struck the boat, filling it with water. With his surfboat icing up, Keeper Miller returned to the beach. He sent the crew and team back to the station to get the beach cart.

Because of the difficult route, two trips were necessary to bring the full load of equipment. During the second trip, one of the surfman named Jeffs stopped to trim the wick of his lamp. When he started again, he was startled to see a apparent apparition rise from the beach and stagger toward him. It was no ghost, but a member of the steamer's crew. Barely able to stand and shaking with cold, the sailor related that he and four others had tried to come ashore in the yawl but had capsized. Pressing on, Jeffs discovered two more survivors huddling on the beach, including the mate. Arriving at the wreck site, he told the keeper of his find.

Since the *St. Lawrence* was in no immediate danger of breaking up, Keeper Miller decided to do all he could for the survivors on the beach. Emptying the beach cart of all gear, he used it as a rough wagon to bring the sailors to shelter at the station. With the life savers pulling on the drag lines, he and his crew headed back. On the way they discovered the missing two men. One was alive. The second, found lying at the water's edge, was inert and didn't respond to resuscitation efforts. When later closely examined by lantern, he had numerous bruises on his head, evidence of being struck by heavy objects in the surf.

The survivors said the ill-advised trip was directed by the mate, who declared that "he could land without getting his feet wet." The yawl barely left the steamer before she went over. Had the life savers not found the survivors when they did, they surely would have frozen to death on the lonely shore.

After assuring that the survivors were well cared for at the station, the life savers returned again to the wreck site. Using the Lyle gun, they neatly laid a shotline across the steamer. It was now approximately 3 a.m. Nothing happened. There was no response from the sailors aboard the wreck. The life savers fired another shotline across the steamer. Still nothing happened. Disappointed, they began to haul the second line ashore when the whistle suddenly began to blow.

Later the life savers learned that the sailors aboard the *St. Lawrence* were unaware of the life savers' efforts. When the sailors heard their own whistle blowing they were utterly startled since they knew that they weren't blowing it. Searching for the cause they discovered the shotline was across the whistle cord. Every time the life savers pulled, the whistle blew.

Realizing that rescue was at hand, the sailors hauled the shotline, whip and hawser aboard, but managed to foul them preventing a proper rigging of the breeches buoy. Undaunted, the life savers launched the surfboat. Instead of rowing, they used the whip to pull themselves out to the steamer hand over hand. Visibility was still nil and boat, men and lines iced up quickly. They reached the steamer at 4 a.m. It took two agonizing trips to rescue the remaining sailors.

The steamer's crew later commended the life savers highly, stating that the rescue was "simply one of the most heroic acts that any of them ever knew."[16]

FIGURE 197
This photo was taken the morning after the rescue of the crew of the *St. Lawrence*. Although there is no record of its use, an overturned lifecar is in the background.
Ted Richardson Collection

Chapter 24
"A Gold Medal Was Awarded"

Rescues were not always made with equipment. A case in point occurred on November 21, 1900, in Buffalo Harbor. In midafternoon a terrific 80-mile-per-hour southwest gale screamed across the harbor. The vicious wind broke two unnamed scows from their moorings at the south end of the breakwater and blew them toward the pounding surf. Aboard were several sailors.

When the lookout saw the problem, he quickly summoned the crew. Under the able leadership of Winslow W. Griesser, the station lifeboat slid down the ways and into the water. The tug *Mason* towed the boat to a position three-quarters of a mile to the windward of the scows and released it. Driven before the wind, Griesser brought the boat to a point just out from the breakers and dropped the anchor. Using it as a pivot he intended to swing the boat to the scows and recover the sailors. But in the hard bottom, the lifeboat anchor failed to grab! A succession of three heavy breakers struck the lifeboat. The last snapped the anchor hawser and threw the boat end over end. All of the crew except one was swept out of her. In the confusion of waves, one lifesaver made it back aboard. Before the boat finally washed ashore, it rolled at least three times.

Well trained and conditioned, Griesser and his men safely reached the shore a quarter of a mile away. There the keeper learned that all of the scow sailors were safe on the beach except for one who had been swept along the breakers and was holding on to one of several pilings about a third of a mile away. Flagging down a passing Lehigh Valley Railroad locomotive, the lifesavers climbed aboard and headed for the besieged sailor. The man was 500 feet offshore and clinging desperately to a wooden piling. Gale-whipped waves regularly swept over him. Clearly time was critical if he was to be saved.

The keeper considered his options only briefly; a surfboat could never get in among the pilings and there wasn't time anyway to return to the station. He told surfman Greenland to tie a line to his wrist and follow him. With a line also fast to his own wrist, Griesser and his companion plunged into the surf. Both were thrown back. Undaunted by the set back they again entered the wild water. Greenland was 150 feet out when he was hammered into a piling, knocking the air out of him. Unable to go on, he was pulled ashore by the line. Griesser continued alone. Slowly, stroke by stroke, he worked his way further and further out through the waves. Frequently he disappeared from view, buried by the billowing seas.

When he got close enough to the sailor, he threw him the line and shouted for him to tie it off around his waist and to jump into the water. Before the job was done a huge roller slammed into the pilings washing away the rope in a snarl. Disheartened but far from defeated, Griesser recovered the rope and, after 15 minutes, cleared the foul. When ready he signaled to his crew ashore and they hauled away, quickly bringing the sailor to safety. Griesser swam in alone and unaided only to collapse in the surfline. He was so exhausted that his crew had to carry him to dry land. The keeper did not escape unscathed. During the rescue a floating telegraph pole slammed into his back several times scraping him badly. In recognition of his heroism, Griesser received the gold medal.[17]

FIGURE 198
Winslow W. Griesser, the hero of Buffalo. His brother Daniel was the keeper at Marblehead.
Ted Richardson Collection

CAPT. W. W. GRIESSER.

Chapter 25
"This Deplorable Case"

The men of the Life-Saving Service had a justifiable reputation for "derring-do," for risking their lives willingly to save others. Unfortunately, there were blemishes on this reputation. One example occurred in Holland, Michigan, on November 21, 1906.

The entrance to the Holland harbor was through an 1,800-foot-long, 200-foot-wide channel running between Lake Michigan and Black Lake. Two piers, one on the north side and one on the south, marked the channel. Beyond each pier, a rock breakwater was being constructed. The first part of each extended 300 feet northwest and southwest respectively, then turned inward for 800 feet, finally stopping with the ends about 300 feet apart. At the time of the life savers' disgrace, only the outer end of the north breakwater was finished. The rest of that section had been filled only to about the surface. Nothing had been done on the inner 800-foot gap.

The weather on November 21 was rainy with periods of severe squalls. For most of the morning, work on the breakwater was suspended because of the foul conditions. When the weather cleared somewhere between noon and 1 p.m., five men, including a government inspector, took a gas launch out to the northern portion. They moored next to a work scow alongside the breakwater.

At 2:30 p.m. the wind shifted from the east to the south and began to blow a gale. One man later said it struck with "the force of a tornado." The men immediately left their work and ran for the launch, planning to get into the harbor as quickly as possible. The wind was violent enough that one of them was blown off the breakwater and into the water. After climbing back on the breakwater he was almost blown off again. Four of the men made it in to the launch. The fifth remained on the scow and held the lines waiting for the engine to start before shoving her clear. The balky motor failed to start, but confused by the situation, he pushed the launch clear. Attempting to jump into the boat, he missed and landed between it and the scow. With trouble he was hauled aboard.

At this point the scow's mooring lines broke and it began to bump along the cribwork. The powerless launch drifted along behind. The stern of the boat hit a partially submerged pile at the same time a large swell heaved the bow

up onto the scow, where it stayed. As a result, the boat began to ship a large amount of water over the stern. Fearing it would sink, the men jumped aboard the scow. Three of them took the opportunity to scramble back onto the breakwater. Two stayed back and pushed the launch off the scow. Fearing that both vessels would beat themselves to pieces against the rocks, one man on the scow jumped to the breakwater. The other hesitated and lost his chance when the scow drifted away leaving a gap too large to leap across. Alone in the boat, he thought he was surely lost and that those on the breakwater would soon be rescued by the life savers. The waves were hitting the breakwater with such force that spray was flying completely over the men, partially hiding them from shore. However, the scow with the launch following along drifted clear of the rocks and, after a harrowing ride, fetched up on the beach about a mile and a half north of the piers. Cold and wet, the lone worker survived.

When the squall hit, the life savers were rebuilding the station launchway. The lookout saw the men on the breakwater scramble for the launch and immediately called the keeper, Chauncey D. Pool, up to look. After a quick observation, Keeper Pool said, "I guess the fellows out there are having their troubles." Running from the tower, he called his crew into action. Since the launchway was out of commission, the surfboat was being kept at a commercial dock on Black Lake 200 yards away.

Because of the violence of the wind, a strong flood of water was running through the channel. Making way against it was tough, but by hugging the south side they had some protection. When the life savers reached the point where the pier turned southward, the full force of the current hit them and progress was nil. Spectators on the pier grabbed the painter and pulled the boat along until they reached the end of the south pier. There they cast off. But row as hard as they could, the life savers were not able to make any progress against the combined force of wind and sea. They returned to the station.

Keeper Pool next decided to use the Lyle gun. Since the top of the pier was rotten, he was unable to pull the beach cart to the end. Each item had to be manhandled out separately, by either life saver or citizen. The screaming wind was so strong, at times the men just had to stop work and hang on until the blast subsided. Eventually all the necessary equipment reached the small lighthouse at the end of the pier.

After aiming the gun far to the windward of the breakwater, Pool charged it with a 5-ounce cartridge and let fly. The No. 7 line landed in the water several yards short of the breakwater. The current grabbed the line with such force that when Pool stepped on the spool to stop it from going out, his weight had no effect. Three of his crew grabbed it, but the line continued to run through their hands. Only when they hurriedly threw a half turn around a stanchion did it stop briefly before it snapped. Keeper Pool abandoned additional efforts with the gun. Back at the station Pool discussed the situation with local citizens. Saugatuck, Benton Harbor and Grand Haven were telephoned in an effort to find a tug willing to come out and help with the rescue. None would leave a safe harbor. To keep watch on the situation, a patrol was maintained on both the north and south beaches.

At the meeting, the local citizens expressed their dissatisfaction with the life savers' efforts. They felt a more determined effort with the surfboat would have succeeded. A second shot with the Lyle gun was also needed. The crews' failure to accomplish anything was roundly and strongly condemned.

Nothing was done until 8 a.m. the next morning. By then the wind had shifted to the northwest creating a lee on the south side. In the relative calm, the surfboat was able to reach the breakwater without trouble. Instead of finding survivors, Pool and his crew found the bodies of three men. The fourth was missing. It was presumed it washed off during the high waves. The body was never recovered. Although there was little doubt that the men were quite dead, when they were brought to shore efforts were made to revive them.

The life savers could have gone out to the breakwater sooner, but the surfboat was damaged in the earlier attempt when it struck the pier while being pulled along by the civilians. No effort had been made to repair it that night, thus losing two hours or more in the morning. The lifeboat was unavailable since it was left in the boathouse while the launchway was under repair.

Because there was a loss of life, Service regulations required a thorough investigation. Lieutenant J.G. Ballanger, Revenue Marine, the Assistant Inspector of the Twelfth District, performed this duty. A total of 21 witnesses were interviewed and 250 pages of testimony taken. After reviewing the investigation, Secretary

Kimball reported to the Secretary of the Treasury, "I...have reached the conclusion that while it appears quite probable that none of them could have been saved, owning to the suddenness and fierceness of the tempest, the conduct of the life-saving crew was not characterized by the energetic, continuous and persistent endeavor that the attendant circumstances seemed to call for.

"The evidence does not entirely satisfy me that it was impossible for the crew at the trial made with the boat to get a little farther beyond the piers and thus enter the current sweeping northward and pass through the gap between the end of the pier and the breakwater. Whether, having gone through the gap, they could have proceeded under the lee of the breakwater to the imperiled men, is in my judgement, problematical, but the alternative of the boat being swept to the northern beach would have satisfied the onlookers and community. The station crew should at least have made a more prolonged and vigorous attempt to get beyond the entrance to the piers.

"Furthermore, it seems to me that after the first failure the crew should have made another effort with the boat, either repeating their former maneuver or attempting a launching from the beach above the north pier. More than one attempt should have been made with the breeches-buoy apparatus. It appears that but one shot was fired with the Lyle gun, using a No. 7 line ($^7/_{32}$ inch in diameter) and 5 ounces of powder, and that the projectile fell at a distance from the men variously estimated at from 2 to 8 yards.

A second trial with 6 ounces of powder – the prescribed maximum charge – would probably have thrown the line over the pier where the men were. If not, there was still the reserve line No. 4 ($^4/_{32}$ inch in diameter) which, in my judgement would have carried the distance. I am at a loss to understand why these attempts were not made. The answer given by the crew that even had a line reached the men they could not have been saved is not sufficient. It may be correct, but an opinion or a theory is not so convincing as a demonstration.

"The crew having made these two unsuccessful attempts (with the surfboat and the breeches-buoy apparatus) discontinued their efforts and retired to the station. In my judgement they should have continued to do something toward effecting a rescue until darkness compelled them to stop. Their cessation of activity under the circumstances I regard as unpardonable.

The keeper of course is to be held primarily responsible, but testimony shows that some talk was made by the crew in the boat after it had been towed out to the end of the south pier and the towline or painter, released.

"The nature of this conversation was not clearly brought out, but I think it may be inferred that it related to the practicability or wisdom of further efforts to reach the men. It is in evidence that at least one of the crew in conversation with outsiders made the assertion that he did not have to risk his life, and said other things which gave the hearers an unfavorable impression of his courage. His attempt in his testimony to explain his language does not appear to me to be satisfactory."

Kimball also directed that "...Keeper Pool and the surfman who thought his duty did not require him to risk his life were (be) dismissed, and instructions were issued that no member of the station crew who was on duty at the time of the disaster should be permitted again to enlist at the Holland station, where, obviously, their further employment was inadvisable."[18]

Chapter 26
"An Ice-Covered Boat, Its White Bow Bearing The Emblem Of The Life-Saving Service"

Life savers rescuing the crew of a big steel freighter was a rare occurrence. Most of their work involved schooners and wooden steamers. However, the rescue of the crew of the 451-foot, 4,422-ton *L.C. Waldo* on November 11, 1913, was the exception. The story is further compounded by the fact that not one but two life saving crews participated.

The *L.C. Waldo* was downbound on Lake Superior for Cleveland with ore from Two Harbors, Minnesota, when the great storm of 1913 overtook her. This infamous storm wrecked 17 vessels; 11 were sunk with all hands. An estimated 244 sailors lost their lives in the worst series of disasters ever to strike the Great Lakes maritime community. On Lake Superior the steel freighter *Leafield* disappeared near Angus Island in the western lake; the *Turret Chief* went ashore east of Copper Harbor; the barge *Allegheny* was blown on the beach west of Vermilion Point; the *Mary McLachlan* was on the rocks off Port Arthur and the big steel steamer *Henry B. Smith* "went missing" somewhere in mid-lake.

Battered by the hurricane-like storm, the *Waldo* slowly struggled on, working her way through the ravages of wind and wave as best she could. About midnight on the 7th, when she was west of Keweenaw Point (a rocky projection often called "Old Treacherous" by sailors), a series of tremendous seas boarded the steamer. The grasping waves swept off her pilothouse, seriously damaged her steering gear and knocked out her electric system. The greatest loss was the compass, which went overboard with the pilothouse.

Captain John Duddleson was also nearly killed when the pilothouse went, making a narrow escape to the severely damaged lower wheelhouse. Duddleson was nothing if not resourceful. Using a lifeboat compass set on a stool and illuminated by the flickering yellow glow of an oil lamp, he used the emergency steering apparatus to keep the *Waldo* on course. Unsure of his position in the howling gale and blinding snow, but believing that he was near Manitou Island, he hoped to make his way between Gull Rock and Keweenaw Point. Once clear, he would swing to starboard and shelter behind the hook of the Keweenaw.

For three or four hours the wounded steamer limped along, running before the 70-mile-per-hour storm. Waves boarded her stern and rushed over her spar deck to smash with pile-driver force into the lower wheelhouse. Eventually the powerful seas broke in the aft cabin, and the crew fled forward to the safety of the steel windlass house.

Below in the engine room the watch kept the fires burning. With the pitching and rolling of the steamer, just shoveling coal into the furnaces was a challenge. Nonetheless, the *Waldo*'s propeller continued to turn, giving the desperately beleaguered steamer a chance.

About 4 a.m. on Saturday, November 8, the steamer plowed bow first into Gull Rock. The *Waldo* soon cracked in two amidships cutting the crew, all of whom where now forward, off from the galley aft, as well as the warm clothing in their cabins. The steam pipes from the engine room also broke, leaving them without heat. The crew of 24, including two women, huddled in freezing despair, knowing that the end was near.

The ingenuity of Albert Lembke, the chief engineer, saved the *Waldo* crew's lives. Bringing the captain's bathtub to the windlass room, he had it turned upside down on the steel deck, leaving one end propped up. Using the emergency stock of fire buckets, he had the sailors kick out the bottoms and fit them together into a makeshift chimney from the tub's drain out a dead light. The tub became a rough stove. Cabin wood was used as firewood. Since there wasn't enough room for all of the crew to stay next to the bath tub simultaneously, the captain divided them into groups who took turns exercising for warmth, gathering wood and warming up.

Stranded on her rocky perch, the *Waldo* became thickly covered with ice, resembling a grotesque ice sculpture. Ice covered the doors, trapping the crew inside. Encased by the ice, freezing despite the makeshift stove and starving to death, the crew became increasingly convinced of the hopelessness of their situation. No one even knew they were there. Surely they would perish.

Unknown to the *Waldo* crew, they had been sighted. Late Saturday, through a break in the snow, the 407-foot steamer *George Stephenson* caught sight of the grounded *Waldo*. Badly battered by the storm, the *Stephenson* worked its way to the shelter of Bete Gris and anchored. Bete Gris was about 13 miles to the west of Gull Rock. To report the wreck, the mate of the *Stephenson* lowered the ship's lifeboat and rowed to shore. There he hiked through the teeth of a blizzard eight miles to Delaware where he telephoned the news to the lighthouse at Eagle Harbor. The life saving station there had just become operational the year before and no telephone line was installed yet. The lightkeeper summoned the life savers to his station by signal flag and at noon on the 9th passed on the message.

The Eagle Harbor Station had two motorized boats: an eight-horsepower surfboat and the 34-foot motor lifeboat *Success*. The lifeboat was best suited for the rescue, but it's motor was broken. The life savers had worked on it all morning, but were unable to repair it. The distance to the *Waldo* was 32 miles and the weather terrible. It would be a desperate run for the lifeboat but near suicidal for the surfboat. Nevertheless, at 2:30 p.m. keeper Charles A. Tucker manned the

Str. L. C. Waldo
Wrecked Nov. 8 - 11 - 1913
Manitou Island, Lake Superior.   Photo By A. F. Glaza.

small boat and headed for the wreck. The old life savers' motto said they had to go out. It didn't say anything about coming back.

They made it about eight miles before Tucker reluctantly concluded that conditions were too severe. In the 20-degree temperatures the surfboat had iced up and was almost unmanageable. The life savers were totally drenched as the result of boarding seas and flying spray and were quickly becoming ineffective. Tucker swung the helm around and returned to the station, arriving at 6:15 p.m. Frozen to their seats and stiff with ice-covered oil skins, the crew had to be helped out of the boat by family members.

Tucker immediately put his No. 1 surfman, Anthony F. Glaza, and surfman Thomas F. Bennett to work on the lifeboat engine. After working through the night, they came through, coaxing the reluctant engine to coughing life. At 3 a.m., Tucker launched the lifeboat.

The storm had moderated a bit, but the waves were still mountainous. It was a cold, tough

FIGURE 199
The *L.C. Waldo* aground on Gull Rock. The photo was taken by Anthony F. Glaza, the number 1 surfman at Eagle Harbor.
Jack Deo
Superior View Studio

FIGURE 200
Captain Charles A. Tucker of Eagle Harbor.
Michigan
Department of History

FIGURE 201
Anthony F. Glaza, pictured wearing a Coast Guard uniform and his gold life saving medal, had a long and distinguished career as a life saver. His hard work resulted in getting the lifeboat engine running.
Michigan
Department of History
Fort Wilkins Complex

FIGURE 202
Iced up surfmen during the
L.C. Waldo rescue.
*Michigan
Department of History*

run, the type legends are born from. Shouldering its way into the waves, the lifeboat churned its way toward Keweenaw Point. Spray froze on its decks and rails. The surfmen huddled out of the force of the worst of the wind and seas, but the cold was intense, chilling them to the bone. Relentlessly the lifeboat continued. At 7 a.m. they reached the iced-over steamer.

About noon on the 10th, word of the *Waldo*'s plight also reached the Portage Life-Saving Station and keeper Thomas H. McCormick. To be certain help was coming, the *Stephenson*'s mate telephoned both Eagle Harbor and Portage. The quickest route from the Portage Station to the *Waldo* was 60 miles, and the entire way the crew would be exposed to the full brunt of the storm. Running down the Portage Lake Ship Canal and then up the lee of the Keweenaw was longer by 20 miles, but offered the advantage of being under protection for the entire distance. McCormick decided on the longer route. He ran the lifeboat to the Lower Entry where Captain B. Nelson and the tug *Daniel Hebard* took it in tow for Gull Rock. Fourteen hours later, 3 a.m. on the 11th, the Portage crew arrived at the vicinity of Gull Rock, but instead of trying to find the steamer in the dark, they sheltered behind the Point until daylight. During the run up, although they were relatively protected, waves broke over the lifeboat continually. Although it was self-bailer, the outlet valve iced up and had to be constantly chopped open to allow the water to drain. A heavy layer of ice formed on the decks making it list badly and difficult to handle.

Even when towed, Service regulations re-

quired the lifeboat to be at least partially manned. Enough men were needed to be able to handle it if the line parted or had to be cast adrift. A crewman always had a hatchet handy, ready to cut the line quickly if needed. Except for the hatchet man, all others rode in the stern to keep the weight aft. This didn't make for a comfortable ride since the stern was usually wet from spray.

The *Annual Report* for 1914 recorded the drama of the lifeboat's arrival. "The imperiled company had caught no glimpse of a ship since a steamer passed them in the early hours of their misfortune, apparently leaving them to their fate. They had now ceased to hope that assistance would come to them. Their surprise may therefore be imagined, when looking out from their shelter, they beheld in the early morning light of the 11th a grotesque, ghostly shape top a wave, poise on its crest for a moment, then sink out of sight as the wave slipped from under it and went racing on. When the object again came into view it was nearer, and the mystery was explained, and with understanding the watchers felt the warming blood leap in their chilled veins. What they saw was an ice-covered boat, its white bow bearing the emblem of the Life-Saving Service."

When the Portage crew came within hailing distance of the *Waldo*, someone on board yelled to them to stand clear until they could chop themselves free. Every door on the *Waldo* had iced shut. While the Portage crew was waiting, the Eagle Harbor lifeboat arrived. It was as iced up as the Portage boat. (Later, back at the Eagle Harbor Station, it was discovered that the pounding of their run had opened the port side copper air chambers, and they had filled with water!)

The lake was still very rough. Waves were breaking high over the *Waldo*, and she offered very little lee. The water around her was shallow and littered with rocks. When the *Waldo* signalled that she was ready, the Portage boat carefully ran in and loaded 10 of the crew. With great agility some life savers boarded the steamer to help with the evacuation. Some sailors came down a rope ladder. Others jumped from the deck. Icy spray from the waves slamming on the weather side of the *Waldo* rained down on everyone. In response to the great swells, the lifeboat rose and fell with a violent motion. After the Portage boat pulled away, the Eagle Harbor boat came in and loaded the remaining 12 men and two women. They also rescued the ship's dog.

The survivors were nearly frozen and in very poor shape. Eagle Harbor surfman Glaza reported, "Some had towels wrapped around their heads, and some were wearing socks for mittens. The majority had neither. We put our mackinaws and caps on them until we could get them to the tug. The women cried for joy when we wrapped them up in warm blankets, and when we put them on the tug they offered a prayer of thanksgiving and asked the blessing of Heaven upon our captain and crew."

The *Hebard* was anchored in Keystone Bay, just a few miles to the west. There the survivors were warmed and fed. They had eaten virtually no food for 90 hours. The tug returned them to Houghton as rapidly as possible.

The Eagle Harbor boat had run more than 70 miles and the Portage boat 160. Every mile was under storm conditions. The rescue stands as a remarkable example of the life saver's seamanship, daring and just plain guts.

The Eagle Harbor crew was not finished with their work, however. On the run back to the station they discovered the wreck of the steel turret steamer *Turret Chief* ashore east of Copper Harbor. During the trip out they had missed it in the inky blackness. Only after landing and

assuring that the steamer's crew was safe did the life savers resume their trip. The weather was still bad and the boat was leaking continuously.[19]

As reward for their heroics, the entire Portage and Eagle Harbor crews received gold life saving medals.[20] To this author's research, this is the only instance in the history of the Service such a double award was made. Recipients from the Eagle Harbor crew included keeper Charles A. Tucker, surfmen Anthony F. Glaza, Thomas W. Bennett, Serge Anderson, John Beck, Charles Kumpula, Chester O. Tucker, George Halpainen and Henry Tadberg. From Portage they were keeper Thomas H. McCormick, surfmen John C. Alfsen, Fred G. Tollman, John McDonald, Paul Liedtke, Collin T. Westrope, David M. Small and Oscar Marshall (temporary).

Each medal was simply inscribed with the bearer's name and "for heroic conduct in saving life, November 8, 1913."

FIGURE 203
The steamer *Turret Chief* ashore on the Keweenaw. During their predawn run to the *L.C. Waldo,* the Eagle Harbor crew ran past the vessel without seeing it.
Lake Superior Marine Museum

FIGURE 204
The Eagle Harbor crew that performed the dramatic rescue.

Jack Deo Superior View Studio

Chapter 27
"Without Waiting For A Full Crew"

The life savers not only reacted to the effects of storm and navigational accident, but also to explosion and fire. On June 11, 1913, the 1,809-ton steamer *E.M. Peck* was moving up the Racine River with a cargo of coal when her starboard boiler exploded with an awe-inspiring roar. The accident happened a bare 300 yards east of the life saving station. Seven of her 18 crew were instantly killed. Luckily, when the boiler let go, many of the sailors were clear of the engine room. Two men, including the captain, were ashore, four were portside forward and five were on the stern.

The force of the explosion was terrific, propelling the boiler forward, glancing off the pilothouse and flying at nearly a right angle several hundred feet through the air finally landing on a coal dock! The detonation ripped out steel deck beams, destroyed the boiler house, main mast, funnel and deckhouse.

The keeper actually saw the explosion. A wrong whistle signal from the *Peck* to the bridge tender at the Main Street bridge had attracted his attention to the steamer moments before she blew. Without waiting for a full crew to assemble, the keeper, three of his men and the keeper of the light station quickly launched the Beebe-McLellan power surfboat and headed for the steamer.

Reaching the *Peck,* they hauled one of the crew out of the water. Seriously injured, he was immediately brought to shore for hospitalization. Finding no more survivors in the water, they boarded the smoking steamer and located four men and a woman on the stern. Apparently uninjured, they were also run ashore. Boarding the steamer again, they found an injured crewman in what was left of the deckhouse. He was also sent to the hospital.

During this time, the *Peck* had been drifting in the river current and finally fetched up against a dock. Searching throughout the shattered remains, the life savers discovered a body in the wreckage of the boiler room and another in the forward hold. Two more were later discovered under coal abaft of the engine room. Another was located in the river 12 days later.

The life savers responded rapidly and without regard to their own safety. For all they knew, the port boiler also could have exploded at any time.[21]

1. *Annual Report, U.S. Life-Saving Service, 1879,* pp. 94-95.

2. *Annual Report of the U.S. Life-Saving Service, 1879,* pp. 26-29.

3. *Annual Report, U.S. Life-Saving Service, 1880,* pp. 21-26

4. *Annual Report, U.S. Life-Saving Service, 1880,* p. 38.

5. Samuel Sullivan Cox, "The Life-Saving Service," *The North American Review,* Vol. 132, May 1881, p. 490.

6. *Detroit Free Press,* nd, 1915.

7. *Annual Report, U.S. Life-Saving Service, 1880,* pp. 89-91.

8. *Annual Report of the U.S. Life-Saving Service, 1881,* pp. 19-34.

9. Frederick Stonehouse, *Went Missing* (Au Train, MI, 1984), pp. 137-147.

10. *Annual Report, U.S. Life-Saving Service, 1883,* pp. 140-142.

11. *Annual Report, U.S. Life-Saving Service, 1887,* pp. 162 166.; *Journal of the Lighthouse Station at Marquette,* November-December 1886; *Mining Journal* (Marquette), November 20, 27, 1886; December 4, 11, 1886; May 28, 1887; July 2, 1887.

12. *Annual Report, U.S. Life-Saving Service, 1887,* pp. 44-47.

13. *Annual Report, U.S. Life-Saving Service, 1888,* pp. 143-144.

14. *Annual Report, U.S. Life-Saving Service, 1889,* pp. 23-27.

15. *Annual Report, U.S. Life-Saving Service, 1896,* pp. 88-89; *Journal of the Life-Saving Station at Marquette, Michigan,* September 29, 1895; *Marquette Mining Journal,* October 5, 12, 1895.

16. *Annual Report, U.S. Life-Saving Service, 1899,* pp. 23-25.

17. *Annual Report, U.S. Life-Saving Service, 1901,* pp. 41-42, 103-104.

18. *Annual Report, U.S. Life-Saving Service, 1907,* pp. 52-58.

19. *Annual Report, U.S. Life-Saving Service, 1914,* pp. 88-92; *Houghton Mining Gazette,* November 12, 1913; *Journal of the Eagle Harbor Life-Saving Station,* November 9-15, 1913; *Journal of the Portage Life-Saving Station,* November 9-15, 1913.

20. Permanent Record of Life Saving Medals, p. 147, RG 26, NARA.

21. *Annual Report, U.S. Life-Saving Service, 1913,* pp. 84-86.

Part IV

The End Of An Era

Chapter 28

The End Of An Era

By 1914 the Life-Saving Service had grown into a network of 271 stations covering the Atlantic and Pacific coasts, Gulf coast and Great Lakes. Single stations were at Louisville on the Mississippi and Nome, Alaska.

But the fundamental characteristics of their mission changed. Less and less were schooners and steamers driven on coastal sandbars or blown ashore. Previously this type of rescue composed the bulk of the life savers' work. More and more, the big steel freighters stayed clear of coastal hazards. When they got into trouble it was far offshore, beyond the scope of the life savers' operations.

To improve economy and efficiency, in 1913 the Treasury Department proposed to merge the Revenue-Cutter Service and Life-Saving Service. A bill to this end was introduced to Congress and after some delay passed by the Senate on March 12, 1914. The House passed it on January 20, 1915, by a vote of 212 to 79.[1]

Kimball, in his 1914 *Annual Report,* endorsed the concept of a combined Revenue-Cutter Service and Life-Saving Service stating, "As the work of the two services is similar, as far as relates to the saving of life and property from shipwrecks, and the personnel of the two bureaus are in constant cooperation in that line of endeavor, the joining of the two services as proposed, and the granting of equal benefits to the officers and employees of each alike, would seem to be a step in the interest of efficient and economical administration and deserving of the favorable consideration of Congress."[2]

As the Life-Saving Service sprang from the old Revenue-Marine, a harmonious relationship always existed between the two. The original June 10, 1872, act stipulated that life saving stations were to be erected "under the supervision of two captains of the Revenue-Service." The 1878 act required the Secretary of the

Treasury to detail Revenue-Marine officers as inspectors of the Service. In 1911 four captains and nine other officers were working for the life savers. Kimball was felt to be the reason for this unique relationship. At the time of the creation of the Life-Saving Service he was head of the Revenue-Marine. When he assumed the same role for the life savers, he brought old allegiances with him.[3]

The new organization, to be called the Coast Guard, was to be part of the Treasury Department during peacetime, but in time of war transfer to the Navy Department. The new Coast Guard was composed of approximately 1,800 officers and men from the Revenue-Cutter Service and approximately 2,200 from the Life-Saving Service.[4]

The life savers found themselves now part of a military organization far different from the civilian one they were used to. The district superintendents became commissioned officers, keepers warrant officers and surfmen enlisted men. The No. 1 man became a petty officer. All vacancies were filled by promotion from within. For the life savers the most important aspect of the consolidation was finally being eligible for pensions. Retirement benefits provided to the Revenue-Cutter Service in 1902 were given to all members of the new Coast Guard. After 30 years of service, a retirement at three-quarters pay was now possible.[5] Anything less than 30 years meant the man was ineligible. There is one example of a Duluth surfman dying one day short of the magic 30 and receiving nothing, leaving his family destitute.

In the eyes of the old time life savers, the retirement was the key to the new Coast Guard. Without a doubt many of them held on as long as they did strictly to be eligible for a pension. For example, it's hard to argue that Jerome Kiah, the district superintendent for lakes Huron and Superior when he retired at age 72, remained on duty so long for any other reason. Of 19 keepers in Kiah's district, two retired almost immediately and nine more had 30 years of service and were eligible.[6]

After assuring that the Coast Guard was off to a solid start, Kimball was retired as general superintendent at three-quarters pay. He was 78 years old and had held the office for 44 years. His contributions to life saving did not stop however. In May 1915, he was appointed as President of the Board of Life-Saving Appliances. It was a position he held for another five years.[7]

Although in several ways the new Coast Guard was a superior organization, the legislation did not remedy one of the most critical problems of the Life-Saving Service. Surfmen were still generally only employed for the navigation season. For the rest of the year they were forced to do what ever odd jobs could be found. It wasn't until World War I that the crews were finally placed on a year-round footing.[8]

For a time the new Coast Guard organization paralleled that of the old Life-Saving Service. The stations were divided into 13 districts. On the Great Lakes, the Tenth was composed of lakes Erie and Ontario; the Eleventh, lakes Huron and Superior; the Twelfth, Lake Michigan.

While the Coast Guard combined the duties of both Services, there was no effort to immediately combine the men. It largely functioned as two separate entities, combined at the top under a commandant. The old life savers continued to run the stations and the old Revenue-Cutter Service sailed the ships. Mr. Oliver M. Maxam, Kimball's assistant general superintendent for a decade, assumed the duties of the civilian chief of the operations division. He largely ran the life savers in the tradition of Kimball.

The record achieved by the old Life-Saving Service was enviable. Service-wide from 1871 to 1914, 28,121 vessels and 178,741 persons were assisted through service operations. Only 1,455 lost their lives in those areas under the watchful scope of Service operations.[9] On the Great Lakes for report years 1876 to 1914, 9,763 vessels and 55,639 persons were assisted. 275 persons were killed.

In an era of bloated government, fed incessantly by a pork-driven Congress, the old Life-Saving Service stood in stark contrast. By any measure, Kimball operated his agency on the leanest of budgets, always searching for ways to do more with less. Every effort was made to mend and repair instead of throw away and issue new. Condemned surfboats and lifeboats became supply boats. Old oars became signal flag staffs. Nothing was wasted.

The eventual merging of the Service with the Revenue-Marine to form the Coast Guard was in itself an effort to economize. Although it wasn't an action Kimball was initially an advocate of, when the benefits became clear, he heartily endorsed it. What Federal agency today would willingly merge with another simply on the grounds of efficiency and economy?

1. Robert Erwin Johnson, *Guardians of the Sea, History of the United States Coast Guard, 1915 to the Present* (Annapolis: Naval Institute Press, 1987), p. 32.
2. *Annual Report, U.S. Life-Saving Service, 1914.*
3. Smith and Powell, *The Coast Guard,* pp. 32-33.
4. Bennett, "The Life-Savers," p. 62.
5. Johnson, *Guardians of the Sea,* p. 33.
6. *Detroit Free Press,* nd, 1915.
7. Johnson, *Guardians of the Sea,* p. 33.
8. Johnson, *Guardians of the Sea,* p. 34.
9. Dennis C. Noble, *A Legacy, The U.S. Life-Saving Service* (Washington, D.C.: U.S. Coast Guard), p. 20.

Some Reflections Today

FIGURE 206
The Sleeping Bear Dunes National Lakeshore visitor center at Empire, Michigan, was built to convey the theme of an old life saving station.

Author's Collection

Despite their immense contribution to maritime safety as well as Great Lakes history, the old U.S. Life-Saving Service today is largely ignored, relegated to history's backwater. They are our forgotten heroes. By contrast, the public is enamored of lighthouses.

I find this remarkable. It took neither courage or bravery to run a lighthouse. That the light keepers may have had qualities of courage and bravery that went untested is a moot point. The primary requirement to man the light was reliability – to always be there assuring that the light shone brightly. The skills needed were generally mechanical, to fix and maintain the equipment.

By contrast it took courageous, brave and reliable men to lead a life saving station. And these qualities were tested every time the boats went out! I keep thinking of the example of the storm raging in full fury on the lake while the wickie sat comfortably in his warm house,

enjoying perhaps a good cigar and dram of rum and wondering aloud that "it must be hell afloat tonight." But the life saving keeper was afloat! In a frail surfboat he was leading his crew in a desperate battle to reach a foundering vessel miles offshore. The lives of the passengers and crew hung in the balance. Their only hope was the guts and tenacity of the "storm warriors." Every moment huge cresting seas threatened to dash the boat into pieces, make widows of their wives and orphans of their children. While mechanical skills were not a necessity for a keeper, the ability to handle a boat and make critical decisions under often ferocious conditions were vital to success and, in many instances, simple survival. In every area the life saving keepers stood head and shoulders above their lighthouse brethren.

Yet today its the lighthouses that are the recipients of the public interest. They are protected, preserved and seemingly listed on every conceivable register of historic buildings. Local historical societies and interested individuals restore them left and right. Many old lights have become museums. The Great Lakes "arts" community has also jumped on the light-house train. They are photographed and paint-ed in every condition, dawn, dusk, night, storms and high noon. Several manufacturers even market lighthouse miniatures. There are also postcards, calen-dars, stamps, video-tapes, paintings, prints, coffee cups, books, T-shirts, Christmas cards and caps. The lights are being loved to death.

With the rarest of exceptions nothing is done for the old life saving stations. When was the last time anyone sold a coffee cup commemo-rating a life saving station? If any of the old buildings remained they were bull dozed into oblivion. In many instances the Coast Guard led the way in the destruction of its own past. Closed stations were destroyed regardless of condition as if even their memory was to be blotted out. On the Great Lakes the only bright spots (forgive the pun) that shine like a beacon on a very dark night are the National Park Ser-vice reconstruction of the Sleeping Bear Point Station at Glen Haven and the Huron City Museum at Huron City, Michigan. It's very lit-tle when contrasted with the multitude of pam-pered lighthouses.

It is sad to stand on the site of an old station

FIGURE 207
The National Park Service has recreated the old Sleeping Bear Point station.
Author's Collection

FIGURE 208
The original 1876 station building at Vermilion, Lake Superior. Although several additions have been made to the building, the core of it remains an important historical structure. It is currently owned by Lake Superior State University and unfortunately no efforts to preserve it have been made.

Author's Collection

and find nothing but perhaps the remains of a concrete sidewalk. This is especially poignant when the station was co-located with a lighthouse and the light, although abandoned, still stands and is an active museum. When a guide

FIGURE 209
Only the old light remains at Crisp's Point. Any evidence of the life saving station is long gone, another example of the Service's lost past.
Author's Collection

explains that the old life saving station building, still perfectly good, was demolished years before, it is all the more distressing.

To a degree I understand the public fascination with lighthouses. After all they are still standing, while the life saving stations are generally not. Lights were substantial structures built of stone, brick and mortar. They were intended to withstand the ravages of time. Life saving stations were wood frame buildings with the associated higher maintenance costs and a shorter useful life. But to forget them and the men that manned them is unforgivable.

What I find most distressing is the neglect by the Coast Guard. "Forgetting" the Life-Saving Service is akin to forgetting their parents. After all, the Coast Guard was formed in 1915 by merging the life savers and the Revenue-Marine. The Lighthouse Service was only added in 1939. Current plans call for the Coast Guard to build 30 new buoy tenders by the year 2006. They will replace the World War II 180-foot *Balsam*-class tenders. The seagoing *Juniper* class will be named for famous old buoy tenders and the coastal *Ida Lewis* class

after famous lighthouse keepers.

A wonderful opportunity was missed to honor the "storm warriors."

Instead the wickies get the glory!

My personal theory is that under the Coast Guard the old life savers suffered from a sort of benign neglect. When the life savers and the Revenue-Marine merged, the Revenue-Marine was the glamorous older sister. It dated from 1790 in contrast to the life savers' 1871. Revenue-Cutters cruised far and wide across the world's oceans, fought pitched battles and defended America's interests and honor wherever needed. The life savers were just a bunch of scruffy men manning isolated beach stations. Despite Kimball's best attempts, they were still only second fiddle. In the new Coast Guard, the old Revenue-Marine still roamed the seas while the life savers continued to man their lonely little stations. As technology improved, the big cutters got fancier. Radios, electric depth finders and similar devices required increased crew sophistication and training. Coast Guard airplanes brought more glamour. The addition of the civilian Lighthouse Service in 1939 added a new and strong advocacy group. The simple surfmen were pushed to the bottom of the pecking order.

Up until the 1940s, men entering the Coast Guard had a choice of the cutter or life saving branch. There still was a clear division of activities. As the emphasis shifted to the glamorous cutters and aircraft and coastal shipwrecks became less frequent, the men who continued the old life saving tradition grew less and less visible. Stations closed and missions grew less frequent. As the result, the exploits of the old life saving service simply faded into history. Today, although the Coast Guard honors much of its past, it never seems to get around to the life savers.

We should remember that losing touch with our past is losing our history. We are in danger of losing our Great Lakes life saving history.

The Life Savers In Poem

THE LIFE SAVERS
To the Men in the Life-Saving Service

by Joe Lincoln

When the lord breathes his wrath upon the bosom of the waters,
    When the rollers are a-pounding on the shore,
When the mariner's a-thinking of his wife and sons and daughters,
    And the little home he'll, maybe see no more;
When the bars are white and yeasty and the shoals are all a-frothin',
    When the wild no'theaster's cuttin' like a knife,
Through the seethin' roar and screech he's patrolin' on the beach -
    The gov'ment's hired hand for the savin' life.

He's strugglin' with the gusts that strike and bruise him like a hammer,
    He's fightin' sand that stings like swarmin' bees,
He's list'nin' through the whirlwind and the thunder and the clamor,
    A list'nin' fer the signal from the seas,
He's breakin' ribs and muscles launchin' life boats in the surges,
    He's drippin' wet and chilled in every bone,
He's bringin' men from death back ter flesh and blood and breath,
    And he never stops to think about his own.

He's a-pullin' at an oar that is freezin' ter his fingers,
    He's a-clingin' in the riggin' of a wreck,
He knows destruction's nearer every minute that he lingers,
    But it don't appear to worry him a speck,
He's draggin' draggled corpses from the clutches of the combers -
    The kind of job a common chap 'ould shirk -
But he takes 'em from the waves and he fits 'em for the grave,
    And he thinks it's all included in his work.

He's a rigger, rower, swimmer, sailor, undertaker,
    And he's good at every one of 'em the same,
And he risks his life fer others in the quicksands and the breaker,
    And a thousand wives and mothers bless his name,
He's an angel dressed in oilskins, he's a saint in a "sou'wester,"
    He's as plucky as they make, or ever can,
He's a hero born and bred, but it hasn't swelled his head,
    And he's jest the U.S. Gov'ment's hired man.

Poems did not always speak of the "grand and glorious" aspects of the life saver's job. The following ditties were written or at least recorded by a surfman at the Manistee Station in 1904.

The Life-Saving Station
anonymous

How dear to my heart is the life saving station,
    Which fond recollections brings back to my view.

The patrol posts, the boatroom and that box of a lookout,
    Where often I' spent a long hour or two.

And fresh in my mind are the logs on the lake shore,
    Where often I've struggled with big Number One.

To find them, to saw them, to split up and dry them,
    And let them dry out in the wind and the sun.

And always on Tuesdays we take out the surfboat,
    And pull with a will 'bout two miles from the shore.

And then we pull back 'gainst a head wind and current,
    While we listen to Hanson's wild howl and his roar.

Oh it's fun and a pleasure at midnight to shiver,
    And think of the lookout that's up overhead.

And wish you were snug and warm under the kivver,
    The thing on the top of your own little bed.

If you want to have lots of fun and enjoyment,
    Come down for a while to this beautiful place.

For here you can take Father Time by the whiskers,
    And gage for a while at his angelic face.

All things come so easy and go in the same way,
    Oh, don't for Christ's sake your own dear back break.

In that lead-colored station,
That Government station,
That Life-Saving Station that stands by the lake.

Keepers could also be the target of a surfman's poetry.

Here's to old Hanson, the son of a bitch,
    May his ---- rot off with the seven year itch.

A little pink cookie up his --- we will stick,
    And make him walk backward clear up to Pine Crick.

Tis working for old Hanson,
    Isn't worth a damn.

Some day I'll join the navy,
    And work for Uncle Sam.

Civil Service Application

The following explanation from the 1898 *Annual Report* well describes the great difficulty encountered in translating essentially bureaucratic requirements into a functional capability.

"Were it practicable, the most accurate and satisfactory test would unquestionably be by actual trial in the surf. Such a test, however, would entail much expense upon both the candidates and the Government, and would be extremely dangerous. Numerous boards of examiners would have to be organized, one at least for each district, and in some districts two or three. A place of trial having been set, a majority of both board and candidates would have to travel great distances to reach it, and when assembled, in nine cases out of ten, they would be obliged to wait several days for a suitable surf. This obtained, boat-load after boat-load of candidates of all degrees of skill and experience, unaccustomed to work together, and used to different words of command for the same maneuver or action, would be called upon to exploit their proficiency. Loss of life would be the inevitable result. It is true there would be less hazard in giving oars to one or two candidates at a time in a boat, the remaining oars being taken by members of a life-saving crew, but this would prolong the examination beyond practicable limits, and would by no means insure the safety of life. In such a sea, and under such conditions as would afford the requisite test, a slight lack of dexterity or a misunderstanding of orders by a candidate might prove disastrous. Indeed, the danger alone attending a test of surfing skill by actual trial in the surf puts such a method entirely out of the question.

"Written examinations would not fulfill the purpose. General educational attainments, in testing which such examinations are usually employed, are of little account as qualifications for men whose principal duties are to battle with wave and storm for the lives of imperiled mariners and to patrol the beaches, keeping watch and ward for endangered vessels. A series of questions could easily be framed concerning the management of boats in different conditions of surf and weather, the manner of using wreck ordinance, the breeches-buoy apparatus, and other means practiced in the Service, but their application to competitive examinations would often prove to be only a sort of scholastic test in which the competitor who had best committed to memory the explicit 'Rules for the Management of Rowboats in the Surf,' the 'Beach Apparatus Drill' and the instructions and advice contained in the 'Regulations' and other manuals published by the Service, would pass the best examination, though he might have had less practical experience than any of his competitors, and perhaps, even none at all. Such a method examination would be as unsatisfactory in its results as the method of actual trial would be dangerous.

"In considering whether any practicable means of testing qualification in surfmanship by competitive examination could be devised, the idea of making experience the criterion suggested itself. Upon consultation, the Civil Service Commission approved of the suggestion, and steps were taken to reduce the proposition to a practical system of application. To adapt it to the different conditions and requirements of different localities and stations was a work demanding great care and judgment; and owing to the vast amount of additional labor thrown upon the Commission by the President's order, the pressure of the current business upon the office of the Life-Saving Service, it was not until the middle of January 1897, that the details of the plan were formulated.

"On the 14th of that month regulations governing admission to the grade of surfman, approved by the Commission and the Secretary of the Treasury, were promulgated. For the purpose of establishing eligible registers, the several life-saving districts were divided into convenient sections, number 32 in all. Forms of application were provided, which could be obtained of any of the officers of the Service, but an applicant was required to file his application with the keeper of the station nearest his residence, which he could do at any time. Provision was made for the establishment of an eligible register for each section semiannually, at the beginning of June and the beginning of December. If a lack of eligible for any section should render it necessary, a special examination could be ordered. An applicant was required to be a citizen of the United States, to be not under 18 nor over 45 years of age, not less then 5 feet 6 inches in height, not less then 132 or more than 190 pounds in weight, to reside not more than five miles inland from the ocean, bay or sound shore, or the shore of the Great Lakes (except applicants for the Louisville Station at the Falls of the Ohio River), and to be able to read and write the English language. Each applicant was required to furnish two vouchers under oath as to his experience as a surfman, sailor or boatman, from persons by whom or with whom he had been employed as such; also a certificate of his physical condition, executed by a medical officer of the Marine Hospital Service. The physical examination was to be made within five days preceding the filing of the application. Each station keeper, each district superintendent and the General Superintendent were required to note any misstatement in the application known to any of them, and to call attention to any disqualification which would affect the eligibility of the applicant for the position of surfman. No person was to be examined who had not had at least three years' experience as a surfman, sailor or boatman, unless a sufficient number of eligible with this amount of experience from whom to make certification for vacancies could not be obtained, in which case applicants of less than three years' experience might be examined.

"The elements to be considered in the examination were, first, physical condition; second, experience; third, age; and these elements were to have, respectively, a relative weight of 7 for physical condition; 2 for experience, and 1 for age, in an aggregate of 10. To determine the general average of a competitor the mark of each element was to be multiplied by the number indicating the relative weight of that element; the sum of the products divided by the sum of the relative weights, would produce the average percentage. A competitor furnishing a medical certificate showing him to be physically qualified in every respect for service as a surfman was to be marked 100 for physical condition. A proportionate deduction from 100 was to be made for any physical defect noted by the medical officer which in his opinion did not disqualify the competitor for the service. A competitor of five or more years' experience as a surfman was to be marked 100 for experience, a proportionate deduction from 100 being made for less then five years' experience. A competitor of five or more years' experience as a sailor or boatman was to be marked 40 for experience, a proportionate deduction from 40 being made for less than five years' experience. A competitor who had experience as a surfman and also separate experience as a sailor or boatman, or in all of these occupations, was to be given a mark calculated upon the experience in each occupation, the aggregate mark in any one or more of these occupations not to exceed 100. A competitor between the ages of 18 and 25 years was to be marked 100 for age. In the case of a competitor between the ages of 25 and 35, a deduction of 1 from 100 was to be made for each year or fraction thereof in excess of 25. In the case of a competitor between the age of 35 and 45 a deduction of 2 from 80 was to be made for each year or fraction thereof in excess of 35.

"The names of all competitors attaining an average percentage of 70 or over was to be entered in the order of their percentages upon the register of eligible, which was to be kept on file at the office of the Commission. A copy for each of the several sections in a life-saving district was to be furnished to the superintendent of that district. Whenever a vacancy should occur at a station the keeper was to make requisition upon the district superintendent for a certification of eligible, the superintendent was to certify the names of the three eligible standing highest on the register for the section in which the vacancy existed, and from this certification the keeper was to make his selection, certifying, in compliance with section 10 of the act of May 4, 1882, that the choice was made with reference to fitness only and without reference to political or party affiliations. The person selected was then to enter into a contract with the Government to serve as surfman under certain terms and conditions therein stipulated.

"A relative weight of 7 for physical condition in an aggregate of 10 may seem an undue preponderance, but it must be remembered that physical strength and endurance are of prime importance, and it will also be noted that all competitors are required to be virtually sound, a person physically disqualified being rejected at once, and his qualifications in other respects not considered at all. All competitors, therefore, being at the outset nearly upon an equality respecting physical condition, the relative standing of the candidates in the final result would depend very largely upon the element of experience. However, in December 1897, the relative weights were change to 6 for physical condition and 3 for experience, thus causing the relative standing of candidates to turn almost entirely upon the point of experience.

"The test to which applicants for the grade of surfman should be subjected having been decided upon, and there being a number of vacancies in the stations of the three lake districts, which would go into commission at the opening of navigation in the spring of 1897, between the 1st and 15th of April, notice of a special examination to take place in March was announced. A larger number of applications than was anticipated were filed, and on March 23 eligible lists for the three districts sufficient for supplying all the vacant places were forwarded to the superintendents. The regular June examination yielded eligible lists for all the districts so that at the commencement of the active season on the seacoast on August 1, 1897, admission to the grade of surfman (original admission to the Service) was under the government of the civil-service rules throughout the Service.

"The next step was to provide a system of promotion from the grade of surfman to the grade of station keeper that should be in conformity with the rules. With some misgivings it was determined to try the method of written examination. When a vacancy in the grade of keeper occurred at a station all the surfmen of that station and of the two nearest stations, twenty-one men, were invited to compete. The examination was held at the station in which the vacancy existed, and all the candidates were examined at the same time and under the same conditions. The questions were entirely practical, and were designed solely to test the qualifications indispensable in a keeper. Three examinations of this kind were held. The results of the first two were satisfactory, but the third developed the difficulties apprehended and feared from the beginning. The three who passed highest, from whom, under the rules, selection was to be made, were by no means the three best qualified for the position, but were the three who has best studied and remembered, or could best tell what they remembered of the regulations of the Service and the various drills and instructions which had been published for the guidance and information of the crews. The man who, according to the assertion of both of the district officers and in the opinion of the neighboring community, could best handle the steering oar in a bad time at sea, who possessed the clearest judgment and the best faculty for governing men, stood tenth on the list and did not even attain the minimum standard of 70.

"Considering these facts and the further fact that other essential qualities, such as courage and coolness under trying and exciting circumstances, could not thus be tested, it became necessary to resort to some other method selection.

"Formerly a keeper was appointed upon the nomination of the district superintendent, accompanied by a statement that the selection was made solely with reference to fitness and without reference to political or party affiliations, the nomination being supported by the recommendation of the General Superintendent. The appointment was not necessarily by promotion, and until within a few years it was not uncommon to appoint as the keeper of a new station a person from the vicinity who had not previously been in the Service. The plan which was now adopted and which is still in practice is as follows:

"Whenever a vacancy exists the district superintendent and the resident assistant inspector, if there be one, make a joint recommendation to the General Superintendent of some member of a crew in the district whom they deem best fitted for the vacant position, setting forth explicitly the reasons for their selection. The recommendation is accompanied by a certificate from these officers stating that the person recommended is, in their judgment, the best qualified man available in the district, and that the nomination is made solely with reference to his fitness for the position and without reference to his political or party affiliations. The recommendation is also accompanied by a certificate, executed by a medical officer of the Marine Hospital Service, showing the exact physical condition of the nominee as ascertained at an examination made not more than ten days previously. Unless the General Superintendent has some objection, which he must state in writing, he recommends for appointment the person selected by the district officers. If the General Superintendent objects to the selection, and the Secretary of the Treasury approves of the objection, the district officers are called upon to submit another selection.

"If the district officers cannot agree upon a name for submission, each must submit a separate recommendation, conforming to the requirements above set forth, also stating the reasons for his preference over the choice of the other officer. In such case the General Superintendent may recommend either of the persons proposed, or if he deems it for the interest of the Service, may himself select for nomination any surfman in the district, accompanying his recommendation to the Secretary with his certificate similar to that above required from the district officers, and also with the required certificate of medical examination. Where there is no resident assistant inspector, the district superintendent alone makes the recommendation required of the district officers, accompanied by the certificates above indicated.

"The examination in the above method consists of the physical examination by a medical officer of the Marine Hospital Service and an examination of the past record of the candidate by the district officers and the General Superintendent."[1]

---

1. *Annual Report, U.S. Life-Saving Service, 1898*, pp. 45-60.

Bibliography

BOOKS

Baarslag, Karl. *Coast Guard to the Rescue.* New York: Farran and Rinehart, 1937.

Coston, Martha. *A Signal Success: The Work and Travels of Mrs. Martha J. Coston, An Autobiography.* Philadelphia: J.B. Lippincott, 1886.

Barnett, J.P. *The Lifesaving Guns of David Lyle.* South Bend, IN: South Bend Replicas, 1976.

Bennett, Commander Robert F., U.S.C.G. *Surfboats, Rockets and Carronades.* Washington: Government Printing Office, 1977.

Canfield, Edward J., D.O. and Allan, Thomas A., Ph.D. *Life on a Lonely Shore, a History of the Vermilion Point Life-Saving Station.* Sault Ste. Marie, MI: Lake Superior State University Press, 1991.

Dobbins, David Porter. *The Dobbins Life-Boat.* Buffalo: David Porter Dobbins, 1886.

Emery, Edwin. *History of Sanford, Maine.* Fall River, MA: Privately Printed, 1901.

Francis, Joseph. *Metallic Life-Boat Corporation.* New York: William C. Bryant, 1883.

Johnson, Robert Erwin. *Guardians of the Sea, the History of the United States Coast Guard 1915 to the Present.* Annapolis, MD: Naval Institute Press, 1987.

Kaplan, H.R. and Hunt, J.F. *This is the Coast Guard.* Cambridge MD: Cornell Maritime Press, 1972.

Kimball, Sumner I. *Organization and Methods of the United States Life-Saving Service.* Washington: U.S. Government Printing Office, 1912.

Law, Rev. W.H. *Deeds of Valor by Heroes and Heroines of the Great Lakes Water World.* Detroit: Pohl Printing, 1911.

Law, Rev. W.H. *Heroes of the Great Lakes, With an Account of the Recent Disasters.* Detroit: Pohl Printing, 1906.

Law, Rev. W.H. *The Life-Savers in the Great Lakes, Incidents and Experiences Among the Life Savers in Lake Huron and Superior (known as District 11).* Detroit: Winn and Hammond, 1902.

Mansfield, J.B. *History of the Great Lakes.* Chicago: J.H. Beers and Co., 1899.

Markstrum, John A. *Les Cheneaux Islands.* Detroit: John A. Markstrum, 1973.

Middleton, E.W. *Lifeboats of the World.* New York: Arco Publishing, 1978.

Mills, James C. *Our Inland Seas.* Chicago: A.C. McClurg, 1940.

Nalty, Bernard C., Noble, Dennis L. and Strobridge, Truman R. editors. *Wrecks, Rescuers and Investigations, Selected Documents of the United States Coast Guard and Its Predecessors.* Wilmington: Scholary Research, 1978.

Noble, Dennis L. *A Legacy, the U.S. Life-Saving Service.* Washington: U.S. Coast Guard, n.d.

Noble, Dennis L. *Great Lakes, A Brief History of the United States Coast Guard Operations.* Washington: Commandants Bulletin Bicentennial Series, 1976.

Noble, Dennis L., compiler. *Historical Register, U.S. Revenue Cutter Service, 1790-1914.* Washington: U.S. Coast Guard, 1990.

Noble, Dennis L. *United States Life-Saving Service Annotated Bibliography.* Washington: U.S. Coast Guard, 1975.

O'Brien, T. Michael. *Guardians of the Eighth Sea, A History of the U.S. Coast Guard on the Great Lakes.* 1976.

O'Connor, William D. *Heroes of the Storm.* Boston: Houghton Mifflin and Co., 1904.

Pittman, Philip McM. *The Les Cheneaux Chronicles, Anatomy of a Community.* Charlevoix, MI: Peach Mountain Press, 1984.

Pond, James L. *History of Life-Saving Appliances and Military and Naval Constructions, Invented and Manufactured by Joseph Francis, With Sketches and Incidents of His Business Life in the United States and France.* New York: E.D. Slater, 1885.

Portrait and Biographical Album of Huron County. Chicago: Chapman Brothers, 1884.

Powell, Hickman. *What the Citizen Should Know About the Coast Guard.* New York: W.W. Norton, 1941.

Prescott, R.E. *Volume V, Historical Tales of the Huron Shore Region and Rhymes.* Alcona County Herald, 1939.

Sandman, Pete. *Frankfort's Royal Frontenac Hotel.* Frankfort, MI: Harbor Lights Motel and Condominiums, 1990.

Scully, Vincent J. Jr. *The Shingle Style and the Stick Style.* New Haven: Yale University Press, 1971.

Shepard, Birse. *Lore of the Wreckers.* Boston: Beacon Press, 1961.

Smith, Darrell Havenor and Powell, Fred Wilbur. *The Coast Guard: Its History, Activities and Organization.* Washington: The Brookings Institution, 1929.

Stonehouse, Frederick. *Lake Superior's Shipwreck Coast.* Au Train, MI: Avery Studios, 1985.

Stonehouse, Frederick. *Marquette Shipwrecks.* Au Train, MI: Avery Studios, 1977.

Thorton, Neil. *Around the Bay.* Tawas City, MI: Printers Devil Press, 1991.

Stories of the Great Lakes, Retold From St. Nicholas. New York: The Century Co., 1909.

Weeks, George. *Sleeping Bear Dunes, Yesterday and Today.* Franklin, MI: Altwerger and Mandel, 1990.

Wilkerson, William D. *Nineteenth Century Coast Lifeboats in the Collections of the Mariners Museum.* Newport News, VA: Mariners Museum, 1992.

Woolford, Arthur M. *Charting the Inland Seas: a History of the U.S. Lake Survey.* Detroit: U.S. Army Corps of Engineers, 1991.

U.S. Life-Saving Service. *Annual Report of the United States Life-Saving Service.* Washington: U.S. Government Printing Office, 1876 - 1914.

PERIODICALS

Abbott, Jacob. "Some Accounts of Francis's Lifeboats and Lifecar." *Harper's Monthly Magazine,* No. 14, (July 1851), pp. 165-181.

Bennett, Robert F. "The Life-Savers: For Those In Peril on the Sea." *Proceedings, United States Naval Institute,* (March 1976).

Bibb, A.B. "The Life-Saving Service on the Great Lakes." *Frank Leslie's Popular Monthly,* Vol. XIII (April 1882), pp.386-98.

Black Diamond Monthly, Vol. VII, No. 1 (January 1903).

Brotherton, R.A. "The Wreck of the *Moonlight* and *Kent*." *Inland Seas,* Vol. 4, No. 2 (Summer 1948), pp. 124-126.

Carpenter, F.G. "Uncle Sam's Life Savers." *Popular Science Monthly,* Vol. 44 (January 1894), p. 346.

Clark, E.P. "Life Saving Service." *Nation,* Vol. 69 (September 1899), p. 182.

Claudy, C.H. "Fighters of the Sea." *Yachting,* (February 1908), pp. 84-88.

Cox, Samuel Sullivan. "The Life-Saving Service." *North American Review,* Vol. 132, (May 1881), pp. 482-490.

Crawford, Remsen. "Uncle Sams Life-Saving Service." *Van Norden Magazine,* (December 1907), pp. 112-130.

Dancy, Thomas B. "Twin Strandings at Ludington." *Inland Seas,* Vol. 3, No. 2 (April 1947), pp. 59-65.

Davis, Rebecca Harding. "Life Saving Stations." *Lippincott's Magazine,* Vol. XVII (March 1876), pp. 301-310.

Doughty, Francis Albert. "Life at a Life-Saving Station." *Catholic World,* Vol. 65, (July 1897), pp. 514-527.

Glaza, A.F., CBM, USCG. "Great Lakes Hazards." *The U.S. Coast Guard Magazine,* Vol. 5, No. 1 (November 1931), pp. 12-15.

Hager, George J. "The United States Life-Saving Service, It's Origin, Progress and Present Condition." *Frank Leslie's Popular Monthly,* Vol. V, No. 2, pp. 165-181.

Harbaugh, Charles A. "The United States Life-Saving Service." *The Aetna,* Vol. XLIV, No. 2 (February 1911), pp. 31-43.

Hewitt, Arthur. "The Coast Patrol." *Outlook,* Vol. 79 (March 4, 1905), pp. 531-542.

"How Mariners May Cooperate With the Life-Saving Service." *United Service, A Monthly Review of Military and Naval Affairs,* Vol. IV, (April 1881), pp. 461-466.

"Human Side of the Service." *Outlook,* Vol. 96 (December 24, 1910), pp. 885-886.

Imlay, Miles, RADM, USCG (ret). "The Story of the Lifecar." *Alumni Association Bulletin,* Vol. XX, No. 3-4 (July-August 1958), pp. 52-62.

Johnson, Theodore. "The Life-Saving Service of the Great Lakes." *Magazine of Western History,* Vol. IV (June 1886), p. 226.

Kloster, John. "Always Ready." *Anchor News,* (September-October 1981), pp. 100-105.

Lamb, M.J. "The American Life-Saving Service." *Harpers New Monthly Magazine,* Vol. CCCLXXXI (February 1882), pp. 357-373.

Law, W.H. "A Hero of the Great Lakes." *The Sailors Magazine,* (March 1901), pp. 2-4.

"Life-Saving Service." *American Architectural and Building News,* Vol. XVI, No. 455 (September 1884), p.124.

"Life-Saving Service." *Nation,* Vol. 69, No. 1784 (September 7, 1899), pp. 182-183.

Lonsdale, Adrian L. "Rescue in '86." *Inland Seas,* Vol. 28, No. 2 (Summer 1972), pp. 96-101.

McLellan, Captain C.H. USRCS. "The Evolution of the Lifeboat." *Marine Engineering,* (January 1906), pp. 7-11.

Merryman, Captain J.H. "The United States Life-Saving Service." *Harpers Magazine,* 1882, pp. 4-44.

Miller, Al. "Lake Superior Sentinel, the Life and Times of Captain Albert Ocha." *Nor'Easter,* Vol. 17, No. 1 (January-February 1992), pp. 1-9.

Miller, Al. "Lake Superior Sentinel, the Life and Times of Captain Albert Ocha." *Inland Seas,* Vol. 49, No. 2 (Summer 1993), pp. 93-108.

Monti, Minne Sweet. "Beached in a Storm." *Inland Seas,* Vol. 1, No. 3, (July 1943), pp. 46-49.

Noble, Dennis L. "Disaster, Heroism and Controversy in Chicago Harbor." *Coast Guard Engineer's Digest,* Vol. XXIV (April-June 1974), pp. 58-62.

Noble, Dennis L. "Incident In 94." *Telescope,* Vol. XXIV (January-February 1975), pp. 14-16.

Noble, Dennis L. "Man the Surfboat." *Inland Seas,* Vol. 31, No. 3 (Fall 1975), pp. 14-16.

Noble, Dennis L. "The Old Life Saving Station at Michigan City, Indiana: 1899-1914." *Indiana History Bulletin,* Vol. 51 (October 1974), pp. 136-43.

Noble, Dennis L. "They Are All Gone." *U.S. Naval Institute Proceedings,* Vol. 102, (March 1976), pp. 92-94.

Noble, Dennis L. "Vessel Ashore." *Shipmates,* Vol. III, No. 5, (Fall 1975), pp. 36-40.

O'Conner, W.D. "United States Life Saving Service." *Popular Science Monthly,* Vol. 15 (June 1879), p. 182-196.

O'Conner, W.D. "United States Life Saving Service." *Appleton's Annual Cyclopedia of the Year 1878.* 1878.

O'Neill, Frank L. "Some Jobs Well Done." *The U.S. Coast Guard Magazine,* Vol. 5, No. 1 (November 1931), pp. 6-11.

Piper, Horace L. "The Life-Saving Service." *The Technical World,* (September 1904), pp. 1-9.

Piper, Horace L. "U.S. Life Saving System." *Journal of the Franklin Institute.* Vol. 133 (January 1892), pp. 1-22.

Rankin, Earnest H. "Captain Henry J. Cleary, Life Saver Showman." *Inland Seas,* Vol. 33, No. 2 (Summer 1977), pp. 128-141.

Rouse, Edith Maude. "Captain Dobbins and His Lifeboat." *Inland Seas,* (Spring 1959), pp. 47-49.

"Services of Life-Saving Crews on the Great Lakes." *Inland Seas,* Vol. 49, No. 2 (Summer 1993), pp. 119-137.

Spears, John R. "Heroes of the Surf." *The Junior Munsey,* (November 1900), pp. 259-264.

Staniland, C.S. "Lifeboats and Lifeboatmen." *English Illustrated Magazine,* No. 29, (February 1886), pp. 333-342.

Strobridge, Truman R. "Captain Daniel Dobbins, U.S. Revenue Service – One Man History Has Forgotten." *Coast Guard Engineers Digest,* No. 178 (January-March 1973).

Stuart, William M. "In Service Since 1790." *The U.S. Coast Guard Magazine,* Vol. 6, No. 2 (December 1932), pp. 37-41.

"The Life-Saving Service and the Revenue Marine." *Republic,* Vol. 5, (August 1875), pp. 81-86.

"United States Life-Saving Service." *Marine Review,* Vol. XXIX, No. 10 (March 10, 1904), pp. 49-51.

Weber, Charlotte. "Heroes of the Surf." *Outlook,* (March 7, 1903), pp. 548-554.

Wolcott, Merlin D. "Heroism at Marblehead." *Inland Seas,* Vol. 16, No. 4 (Winter 1960), p. 269-274.

Wolcott, Merlin D. "Great Lakes Lifesaving Service." *Inland Seas,* Vol. 18, No. 1 (Spring 1962), pp. 14-21.

Wolcott, Merlin D. "Marblehead Lifesaving Station." *Inland Seas,* Vol. 24, No. 4 (Winter 1969), pp. 295-300.

Wolff, Julius F. Jr. "A Lake Superior Life-Saver Reminisces." *Inland Seas,* Vol. 24, No. 2. (Summer 1968) pp. 108-117.

Wolff, Julius F. Jr. "One Hundred Years of Rescues." *Inland Seas,* Vol. 31, No. 4 (Winter 1975), p. 255 and Vol. 32, No. 1 (Spring 1976), p. 32.

PUBLIC DOCUMENTS AND COLLECTIONS

Canal Park Marine Museum. Duluth, MN.

Grand Haven Public Library. Grand Haven, MI.

Great Lakes Historical Society. Vermilion, OH.

Institute For Great Lakes Research. Perrysburg, OH.

Manistee County Museum. Manistee, MI.

Manitowoc Maritime Museum. Manitowoc, WI.

Marquette County Historical Society. Marquette, MI.

Marquette Maritime Museum. Marquette, MI.

Michigan Maritime Museum. South Haven, MI.

Michigan State Archives. Lansing, MI.

Northwestern University Archives. Evanston, IL

Register of the U.S. Life-Saving Service, July 1, 1914, Washington: Government Printing Office.

Revised Regulations For the Government of the Life-Saving Service and the Laws Upon Which They are Based. Washington: Government Printing Office, 1884.

Rose Hawley Museum. Ludington, MI

Sleeping Bear Dunes National Lakeshore. Empire, MI

U.S. Life-Saving Service Records (Coast Guard). Record Group 26, National Archives and Record Administration (Washington, DC).

SERIALS

Detroit Free Press.

Daily Mining Journal.

Duluth Evening Herald.

Duluth News-Tribune.

Grand Haven Daily Tribune.

Grand Marais Herald.

Manistee Daily News.

Marquette Chronicle.

Marquette Mining Journal.

Milwaukee Journal.

Port Huron Daily Times

Port Huron Times

Port Huron Tribune

Seattle Post-Intelligence.

South Haven Messenger.

UNPUBLISHED MATERIAL

King, Rilla M. (Whitten). "The Years at Hammond Bay." Presque Ile Lighthouse Museum, n.d.

York, Wick. "The Architecture of the United States Life-Saving Service." Boston, 1981 (photocopy).

Johnson, Gardner E. "My Early Years, 1869-1889." Ted C. Richardson Collection (photocopy).

Index

Other publications of Lake Superior Port Cities Inc.

Julius F. Wolff Jr.'s Lake Superior Shipwrecks
    Hardcover: ISBN 0-942235-02-9
    Softcover: ISBN 0-942235-01-0

Shipwrecks of Lake Superior by James R. Marshall
    Softcover: ISBN 0-942235-00-2

Shipwreck of the Mesquite by Frederick Stonehouse
    Softcover: ISBN 0-942235-10-x

The Superior Way, Second Edition by Bonnie Dahl
    Spiralbound: ISBN 0-942235-14-2

Michigan Gold, Mining in the Upper Peninsula by Daniel Fountain
    Softcover: ISBN 0-942235-15-0

Lake Superior Magazine (Bimonthly)

Lake Superior Travel Guide (Annual)

Lake Superior Wall Calendar (Annual)

Lake Superior Wall Map

For a catalog of the entire Lake Superior Port Cities collection of books and merchandise, write or call:

Lake Superior Port Cities Inc.
P.O. Box 16417
Duluth, Minnesota 55816-0417
USA

218-722-5002
800-635-0544
FAX 218-722-4096